The S.O. Combat Manual

Volume I

Fourth Edition

By

James P. Coghill

© Copyright 2018

"Every mother of a son in America should be scared to death that something like this can be done so easily."
(Mother of a Duke Lacrosse player. CBS 60 Minutes)

Dedication

I rejoice in the awakening of the Buddha's and also in the spiritual levels of their sons.

With folded hands I beseech the Buddha's of all directions to shine the lamp of Dharma for all bewildered in the gloom of misery.

With folded hands I beseech all the Buddha's who wish to pass away, to please remain for countless eons and not to leave the world in darkness.

My foes will become nothing. My friends will become nothing. I too will become nothing. Likewise, ALL, will become nothing.

Just like a dream experience, whatever things I enjoy will become a memory. Whatever is passed will not be seen again.

I alone will liberate those not liberated. I alone will release those not released. I alone will relieve those unrelieved. And set living beings in Nirvana!

The Buddha's neither wash away ill deeds with water, nor remove beings sufferings with their hands, nor transfers their realizations to others. Beings are released through the teachings of the truth. The final reality.

Thus by the virtue that has collected through all that I have done, may the pain of every living creature be completely cleared away.

Preface

What you are about to read is the culmination of 10 years of experience and research in the American Injustice System. It comes from direct experience of being branded a sex offender or S.O. and beating the charge. Beating it is the hardest thing I have ever had to do. It is my intention to share this experience with you so you may be better prepared if and when it happens to you. The thing to remember is that every day in this country it is happening to somebody somewhere and you are not immune. No one is.

This author does not care if you're guilty or innocent. This author does not care what you did or didn't do. The only thing this author cares about is that you are insured a fair trial and I don't see how without this manual you're going to get one. That's why this manual is written. What you need to recognize immediately if you're already headed for trial is that the trial is not about making a judgment based on the facts. It's about putting you through an ordeal of such drama and far-reaching repercussions that your confession is obtained and you take a plea bargain. It's a game and your life is the ball, nothing more. That's justice in America.

It may be treated as a game, but the game is still governed by rules. These rules are the criminal statutes, rules of evidence, rules of court, rules of criminal procedure, ethics rules and case law that you must learn till you can quote them without this book and quote them when they apply. If you can do this you stand a better chance of keeping everyone honest and getting a fair trial.

There is no doubt advice in this book is going to piss off a lot of people for various reasons and it doesn't take a genius to figure out in advance who they are and what they represent. That's just tough. If you are an American, you stand by a fair and just legal system. Therefore, if you oppose this book you need to re-evaluate your political philosophy and affiliations accordingly.

Table of Contents

Chapter 1 The Playing Field

I call this book a combat manual. If you're about to be charged, have been charged or engage in risky behavior make no mistake, you are at war with those who would seek to make you spend the rest of your life in prison. Life in prison! Now that sounds a bit extreme. In most states you can get multiple charges from one offense and the sentences can be "stacked" or run consecutively, making for what amounts to a life sentence. This applies to almost all offenses, not just those involving minors. Here is a list of offenses in the vernacular that will get you branded a sex offender, you may be surprised:

01. Peeping Tom
02. Flashing
03. Public urination/defecation
04. Mooning
05. Streaking
06. Pimping
07. Prostitution
08. Illegal pornography (non-child)
09. Rape of an adult
10. Sex with children
11. Bestiality
12. Necrophilia
13. Child pornography
14. Sado masochism
15. Groping

Some of these acts seem appropriate by their title alone until you consider that wearing a bathrobe late at night as you take Fido out for a dump and your bathrobe falls open for a moment as you bend down to scoop Fido's poop, can land you with a charge of public indecency, get you labeled as a sex offender and in some cases you may be forced to register as a sex offender for the rest of your life. I have personal experience with a man who had exactly this happen to him. He told his wife that if they were going to make him register for life or go to prison he never would have taken a plea bargain. Now my friend has a public indecency

offense on his record. Forever branded a pervert at all future job applications where they do a ten-year background check. It's definitely not a career move. In my friend's case a neighbor unintentionally saw his brief moment of public exposure and then she called the cops. Now maybe the neighbor thought all that what happened is a scolding from the police, but that's not how it works. The cops are expected to generate revenue with each call. Consequently when you call the cops on someone, that someone is going to jail. No question about it. Something to think about the next time you consider making that call.

Because my experience originates from the state of Arizona and Arizona has the stiffest sex offender laws in the nation, all of the statutes, rules of evidence, rules of court, rules of criminal procedure etc. presented in this book will be from that state. This doesn't mean however that these laws are unique to Arizona. In most cases you will find similar regulations in your state. The indexing system may be different but generally speaking the rules are the same. State Bar regulations are determined by the American Bar Association, the State Supreme Court and are generally speaking identical from state to state. If you file a complaint with your State Bar association they will not consider your complaint if it is a matter being decided on appeal or references a violation of statute. Statutory violations of law are decided by the courts only. It is therefore a waste of time and effort to pursue this direction. The only jurisdiction they have are over their own ethics rules. The only avenues of discipline they can exert are disbarment, which means they can no longer work as a lawyer in that state. It doesn't stop them from taking the bar exam in another state, but that's a tough one to pull off for anybody after spending years at work away from law school. They can also sanction and fine an attorney which means they can't try cases for a period of time usually one month to a year. The bar can also insist on mandatory ethics training at the attorneys expense. The training would relate to the area of ethics the attorney violated. In 10 years I encountered only one disbarment and one censure and it didn't work for me. So realize it may be a waste of time to pursue this. In addition the attorney accused by you will have a copy of your complaint faxed to him to respond to. Something to consider if handwriting is an issue in your trial and they never got a sample from you. Your complaint goes into the attorneys file along with the bar's judgment for three years. The State Bar will seldom side in your

favor. The State Bar is an employee union, not a policing organization, they only get involved in the things they have to.

Also seldom productive is requesting a state grand jury (S.G.J.). The purpose of a state grand jury is to investigate corruption of government officials. To request one you must petition in the attorney general of your state. If you're Attorney General is himself a corrupt official you aren't getting anywhere with that either. I know, I tried.

Writing your Governor or the press will be as productive as panning for gold in your own shower. Don't waste your time. It is more important that you learn the law. Learn how the criminal injustice system works. If you stand with the law and on the law eventually your cause will be heard in a court that is far from the local influence of corruption and your claims will be recognized.

Many of those accused suffer from life histories of debilitating abuse that has left them feeling incapable of learning and completely helpless. The first thing you must do is to throw out the idea that you can't learn the law. Once in prison you are left with only two options. To fight and ignore everything that says I can't or to give up and settle in for a long stay. Most people opt out for the latter because it is easier. You should remember the Brooklyn Bridge was built by someone who didn't have a high school diploma or engineering degree. What's stopping you from getting where you want to go? The answer to that question could be the most important thing to happen to you in your life.

Never assume your attorney knows the law so well that you can sit back and let him do all the work on your case. Some public defenders are not as bad as they are made out to be and some paid attorneys may have never tried a case before a jury and always urged their clients to take a plea bargain. I'll get more into this later. The point is you should be researching the law and case law as much as you think your attorney is. In the event you discover your attorney is a dud, then you can take over temporarily until they appoint you a new one. Doing the homework on your own will put you in a better position for appeal as well.

To do your legal research you will need the Georgetown Law Journal (G.L.J.), the annotated Revised Statutes for the criminal code of your state, Blacks Law Dictionary, annotated Rules of Court, annotated Rules of Criminal Procedure, annotated Rules of Evidence and if you are on the outside access to Westlaw's database of case law on the Internet. Some superior courts will provide up to 10 free case laws a day via e-mail. Annotated books provide case law relevant to the issues concerning a rule or a statute. Westlaw on the Internet can be your one-stop place for all of these materials.

Chapter 2 What To Do When the Police Come To Call

Most accusations and subsequent prosecutions arise from a spouse, girlfriend or roommate. If an accusation has been directed at you personally, your safest course of action is the immediately leave and have no further communication with that person and I do mean NO COMMUNICATION. The reason for this advice is that most states permit the recording of personal or telephone communications as long as one party knows the conversation is being recorded. Consequently a favorite tactic of the police is to record any personal or phone conversations in the hope that the conversation will give you the opportunity to insert your foot in your mouth and give them something to a Grand Jury to have you arrested. When a telephone is used for this purpose the police refer to it as a confrontation call. When the police do this any evidence obtained is completely admissible in court and will be used against you even though you may never have been read your Miranda Rights. The safest course of action is to cease all personal communication, hire an attorney and communicate only through them. Sex offenses come in two varieties. Contact crimes and noncontact crimes. What you do when the police come to call depends on which category of charge you are or will be accused of. Don't believe for a second that because you're being charged with a noncontact crime you're going to get off lightly. Prosecutors today are exceptionally adept at creating multiple charges from a single offense. Too bad they aren't equally adept at writing a valid indictment. More on that later.

Contact Crimes

Contact crimes always involve two or more people. When the police arrive they will try to question you about the event. You need to act like a prisoner of war at this point. Just as a prisoner of war under the Geneva Convention is required to give his name, rank and serial number, likewise you should only give your name, age and address. If asked any questions about who you know or the crime itself, invoke your Miranda right to have an attorney present at questioning on your own. When asked if you know the victim the correct response is, "at this time I invoke my Miranda right to have an attorney present at questioning. Am I under arrest?" If they say no, immediately lock the door to your house and leave. Remain absent for approximately eight hours after which time you may return. When you return you

may find your house or apartment has been searched by the police. There may be crime scene tape across your door. If crime scene tape bars your entry, leave the area immediately and spend the night with a friend. Crime scene tape indicates the search is still in progress and they just went home for the evening. Walking across crime scene tape can get you a charge all on its own. The next morning you need to find out if a warrant for your arrest has been issued. If it has, turn yourself in. That's right-turn yourself in. The reason for this is that your treatment by the police will be courteous if you do, compared to what you will experience if you make them come after you. In addition the fact that you turn yourself in goes miles with the jury. Before turning yourself in, if you have the money to afford an attorney or already have one, inform your attorney that you're turning yourself in and to be prepared to get you out on bail. Bail is considerably less for those who turn themselves, because obviously they are not a flight risk. The starting fee for an attorney for a sex charge is $51,000. It is important not to pay your attorney the full amount up front. An attorney who works hard is a hungry attorney. Attorneys have only one food item in their diet. It's money. Consequently it is a very wise step to use a trust fund to pay your attorney. This means that he can't get the money until his job is finished, but he can look at the balance and gloat over its contents as frequently as he wants. If at some future point he needs some cash you can authorize a release a specific amount. It is important to get rid of anything you have of value, such as a house or other property. You are going to trial and if you lose you won't need it anyway and if you win you can always get it back after you sue the state for wrongful imprisonment and malicious prosecution.

At this time it is important to gather all your telephone numbers and addresses before you turn yourself in. You need to put them in an address book or on a piece of paper. Include everyone and everything you can think of. These will become your lifeline to freedom. It is important to remember that your cell phone will be confiscated upon arrival in jail and you won't be allowed access to the phone numbers in it past this point. Therefore, be prepared going in. The only phone calls you will be allowed to make are collect calls and you will not be able to make calls to a cell phone. Some of your friends will need to set up their phones to receive collect calls or they won't be able to help you. As you're being booked it is a wise move to request protective custody at that time. This will put you in a

segregated area assigned for sex offenders rather than be put into general population.

Until a warrant has been issued for your arrest you should use every free moment to prepare for what is to come. Do not think for a moment this will pass away. Detectives today do not detect crimes, they invent them. They will selectively examine testimony to see how it can be used to support the initial complaint. Forget about DNA saving your ass. That only happens on television and in the movies. The prosecutor doesn't need it and it's so much easier for him if the crime has no DNA to compare with, because there's less evidence to refute. If there are alibi witnesses or alibi evidence you need to use this time to gather that information because in all likelihood you'll be fighting your case from the inside of a county jail. Gather names addresses and phone numbers of all alibi witnesses. If you question them on your own, record it. If there is alibi evidence you need to obtain it now rather than wait for your attorney to do it for you later because he might not do it. I know a person who had exactly this happen to him and he got 19 years. Don't be stupid.

A frequent tactic by the police is to ask you if you would take a polygraph examination. **Don't!** The fact the police are doing this is a prime indicator of a lack of evidence to try you, so they are on a fishing expedition for more evidence and they are hoping that you are stupid enough to give it to them. This technique is used to get well-meaning cooperative citizens to participate in their own arrest. Unfortunately this is how most innocent people are brought to trial. Don't be naive! These people are not your friends and they aren't going to stop or go away till they get you any way they can. Even the illegal ways. You are not going to help yourself by being cooperative; you're only going to help them put you a way.

Another trick they use is to come back at you weeks or months later or maybe even when the complaint is filed with the police and ask you if you would be willing to talk to detectives about this matter. The correct response is the one I gave you a moment ago. This is another fishing expedition. Even if you have not been mirandized whatever you tell them will be used to discredit any defense you mount in trial any way they can make it fit. This is one of the tricks they used on

me. Don't think that because you are not Mirandized they can't use what you say against you. They can and will.

The selective use of testimony and evidence to support the theory of the prosecutor uses the same kind of reasoning that Perceval Lowell used to support the idea there was civilized life on Mars. He saw the canals on Mars through his telescope, he saw them change shape along with what appeared to be changing seasons. Canals on Mars means water. Water and canals are used on earth for crop irrigation therefore there must be civilized life on Mars. Science always tests a hypothesis to make sure they are right and this is where the similarities between scientists, prosecutors and detectives end. Prosecutors and detectives don't look for evidence that proves them wrong, they look for evidence that proves them right and ignore everything else. This is what is called junk science. Consequently if prosecutors and detectives were involved in space exploration today we would all believe there was a highly advanced agricultural civilization on Mars. This is the kind of mentality that you'll have to fight against in court.

Noncontact Crimes

Noncontact crimes come in two varieties. Those with only eye witnesses and those with evidence. Those with only eye witnesses as evidence are, again in the vernacular:

1. Peeping Tom
2. Flashing
3. Public urination/defecation
4. Mooning
5. Streaking

The crimes above, generally speaking, leave no evidence behind.

Noncontact crimes with evidence include:
1. Illegal pornography (non-child)
2. Child pornography

Noncontact, no evidence crimes present a problem for prosecutors because the only evidence is the witness and because you have a constitutional right to confront your accuser in a court of law and seldom is the accuser willing to testify in court, there is very little a prosecutor can do except to try to terrorize you into a confession. In reality the prosecutor does not want to take these cases to trial because of the expense and the fact that in most cases there is only one witness who usually doesn't want to testify. If this is your charge and the conditions just described fit your case stick to your guns, demand a jury trial and in most cases the state will drop the charges because they don't want to waste the money on a trial of this kind. However if your case has multiple witnesses, that creates another issue and increases the chances that one of those witnesses will come forward in a court trial.

Noncontact crimes with evidence include two types. The evidence exists as photographs or images and video clips on a computer. The cases involving photographs do not have a record of viewing that the computer cases do. Although proving that photographs were viewed doesn't seem to be an issue to the prosecutor in those cases I know about involving photos. Naturally photos most likely have fingerprints on them which is suggestive of viewing, but not conclusive proof. I am aware of one case where fingerprints on photos did not match the accused. That fact didn't stop the jury from giving him 121 years. In computers, proving that contraband files were viewed is not a problem. The computer keeps a record of every file it works with. The fact that none of the contraband files in my case were viewed didn't stop a jury from sending me to prison for 155 years. I bring these points out not to highlight the futility of fighting the charge, but to illustrate how evil your enemy is and how hard you will have to work to beat him. Hard, but not impossible.

If there's evidence in your case you can use the time after you told the police they can't enter your residence to destroy it. Photos burn, hard drives can be demagnetized and CD's can be totally destroyed after a few seconds in a microwave oven. If during this time the police come to pick you up, don't be stupid, don't run, don't resist arrest at all. The cops already don't like you for the charge you have, don't give them a reason to use force or you could wind up dead or in a hospital. Your battle is with the courts now, not the police. Remember also

there are time limits to everything. For certain crimes there is a seven-year time limit to bring charges, for others there is no statute of limitations. Know the time limits that affect your case. There are also speedy trial rights that may vary among the states. Don't allow them to prosecute you after these limits expire.

Chapter 3 Pretrial

Now things start to get difficult. The game is afoot and the war begins in earnest. Everything now becomes a test of your endurance, strength of mind and willpower. You will never experience a more powerful test of your character in civilian life. It definitely equates to being a P.O.W. Being told you have a terminal disease doesn't come close to this. With a terminal disease you can count on the pain going away at some point. Prison however is the gift that keeps on giving, where nothing is certain except that you will be behind bars tomorrow somewhere.

What happens to you during the pretrial phase and what you can do to assist in fighting your own case is going to be determined primarily by where you are living during the pretrial phase. If you are able to stay at home then you have all the resources of the outside world at your fingertips. If you are incarcerated in a jail that's a different story. If you are incarcerated in a jail during the pretrial phase whether or not you have access to the jail law library will be determined by whether or not you are representing yourself. If you are representing yourself than you have whatever access to the jail wall library you are allowed. If you are not representing yourself you have only the resources of your own attorney and will not be permitted to go to the jail law library. If you're incarcerated during the pretrial phase it is important that you use this time to socialize with the other inmates. You're probably thinking that I'm nuts for even suggesting this but it's true. There are a lot of people out there who are making false accusations against people for sexual molestation and they are using court ordered restitution to augment their income. Consequently it is not uncommon for two inmates to get together and discuss their case only to find that they have the same accuser for two or more separate incidents. I know of one person who found when he was incarcerated in the county jail, five other inmates who all had the same accuser he had. There's only one word for this and it's called FRAUD! If you don't get out there and socialize you may be missing something important to you. Being incarcerated prior to trial is a handicap and you are not going to win if you don't attempt to turn every handicap into an advantage through your own actions.

There's something else going on of a similar nature that I need to relate to everyone. You will find people in the post-trial phase making a tidy profit too and I

will have to relate a personal story in order to show you how it's done. When I was in prison I was a member of a legal club and when it became obvious to me that I was going to be released I promise all its members that I would do whatever I could to help them with their battle in the courts. To this day this fight continues. When I decided that it was in my best interests as well as bears to go back to college and get a bachelor of science in paralegal studies I was given the opportunity to have access to LEXIS-NEXIS which is a legal research database of case law and just about everything else you could think of that you might need as an attorney. One of the things that I immediately saw a need for was an index of reversed sex offender cases which you can download from the so combat manual online. So I decided to produce just such an index. When I did this I discovered that there were numerous lawsuits in the ninth circuit involving insurance companies. I thought this was extremely odd because I knew there was no way that you could obtain an insurance policy against sexual assault. So what reason would insurance company have to even be involved in a subject like this? Below are some examples of what I found.

Allstate Ins. Co. v. Izzo, CV 90-4073 (ADS), UNITED STATES DISTRICT COURT FOR THE EASTERN DISTRICT OF NEW YORK, 1993 U.S. Dist. LEXIS 16421, November 13, 1993, Decided
Where civil actions alleged that minors were subjected to sexual abuse, rape, and sodomy by one of the insureds, the acts were intentional conduct for which the insurer, under a homeowner's policy, did not have to indemnify or defend the insureds.

Western Protectors Ins. Co. v. Shaffer, CASE NO. C08-5316BHS, UNITED STATES DISTRICT COURT FOR THE WESTERN DISTRICT OF WASHINGTON, 624 F. Supp. 2d 1292; 2009 U.S. Dist. LEXIS 1731, January 9, 2009, Decided, January 9, 2009, Filed,
Reconsideration denied by Western Protectors Ins. Co. v. Shaffer, 2009 U.S. Dist. LEXIS 4916 (W.D. Wash., Jan. 23, 2009)
An insurer was entitled to summary judgment in its declaratory judgment action that it was not entitled to defend its insureds against charges of sexual abuse of minors in an underlying state court action; however, it was not entitled to summary judgment on its duty to defend its insureds against charges of invasion of privacy.

Prudential Prop. & Cas. Ins. Co. v. Emmert, No. 96APE01-76 (REGULAR CALENDAR), COURT OF APPEALS OF OHIO, TENTH APPELLATE DISTRICT, FRANKLIN COUNTY, 1996 Ohio App. LEXIS 2757, June 27, 1996, Rendered , THE LEXIS PAGINATION OF THIS DOCUMENT IS SUBJECT TO CHANGE PENDING RELEASE OF THE FINAL PUBLISHED VERSION. Where a homeowner's insurance policy excluded coverage for bodily injury from intentional acts and sexual acts, the insurer was entitled to summary judgment in its declaratory judgment action to determine coverage for intentional, sexual acts.

Now it should be noted that the above referenced cases came up in a search for criminal cases in citation mode on LEXIS NEXIS where 50 cases at a time are displayed. Thus making these insurance cases representative of 6% of all the cases listed. It should also be noted that these are only the cases that went to trial. Cases that settle out of court will not show up in a case law search.

It wasn't until about a year later when I was speaking with the parent of another incarcerated sex offender that I discovered the reason why. It would appear that it is common knowledge to some, that all you have to do is falsely accuse someone of sexual assault, be willing to testify in trial against them and sue your insurance company and you too can have a, "Fuck Palace", (that's what the false accuser calls his home), a Mitsubishi Eclipse, and a Cadillac Escalade just like the ones pictured below.

Pretrial is the time to interview witnesses, gather evidence for your defense, research case law and plan a strategy for your defense. Interviewing witnesses is a key event and it is here you'll learn what the witnesses are going to say on the witness stand. When it comes to the detectives you should assume that they are not going to tell you everything. They didn't in my trial. They will always try to spring something they never mentioned during pretrial interviews if the trial is going badly. Another factor to consider in regard to pretrial interviews is whether or not they are deposed. In my home state of Illinois, in criminal trials, all of the witnesses are deposed. This means that during the pretrial interviews the witnesses make statements under oath with a court reporter present. In Arizona however they do not. What's the difference? The difference is that when actual depositions are taken during the pretrial stage the statements made by the witnesses are under oath and a witness is capable of perjuring themselves as a result of the statements they make at the pretrial interview of witnesses if their statements don't match. It's a very effective way of catching a witness in a lie and serves as a very good deterrent against lying during the pretrial questioning of witnesses. In short it makes the testimony of witnesses during the pretrial stage much more reliable. In Arizona they can say anything they want during pretrial and nothing will happen to them, which can result in the defense being led astray by pretrial testimony. It is important for you to attend these pretrial interviews with your attorney. At this stage, nobody, especially your attorney, knows anything about what happened beyond the general story except you. You are there to assist your attorney with the

questioning of witnesses. It is part of the attorney/client relationship and can't be interfered with by anyone. But the prosecutor will try to. They will try to take you out of the meeting, especially if the meeting occurs in the county attorney's office. They did it to me. If possible have the meeting take place anywhere except the county attorney's office. The reason is that this office is regarded by them as their own little kingdom and they feel they can do anything they want in it. If they refuse your participation don't get upset. You object to their action, you bring it up on the record in a status conference, you record the date and time and who threw you out of the meeting and move on. If you don't object to this in court you can't list it as an argument on appeal. This is how the process works. If you believe a wrong has been done to you, record all the information about the event you can. Then you object to it in court. If the court denies your argument the responsibility for the denial is then blood on the judge's hands. If it is a serious matter you can always go over the judge by filing a special action along with an order to show cause. Both of these are fancy names for a type of motion. They are written a little differently than an ordinary motion and examples are given in the book.

During the pretrial stage it is important to do a check on the prosecutor's bond and oath of office as well as the judges bond and oath of office. If the state government has no record of the judges or the prosecutor's bond and oath of office, then both of them, or either of them, is holding office illegally and the court has no jurisdiction to proceed until the matter is corrected. It's also important for you to do research on your victim. Many of these victims have reported numerous instances of sexual abuse against a great many number of people. They have developed it into a profession and are using court-appointed restitution to augment their income or to obtain welfare. I am personally aware of several people, who when they were placed in jail, found other inmates who supposedly molested the same person in different crimes.

As you progress along the trial process your number one objective is to preserve every possible claim you can for appeal by objecting in court to the perceived wrong done to you. This is where things get a little tricky because you ideally should have your attorney do this for you. If your attorney is a dud and sits there like a bump on a log give him a quick kick in the shins underneath table. I'm serious. Just a little kick under the table and then tell him what he should do. If he

doesn't, you have a problem. If this happens, raise your hand and wait for the judge to recognize you. Then ask the judge to order your attorney to provide you with effective assistance counsel after you explain the perceived wrong and that your attorney is refusing to take action on the matter. This automatically places a complaint by you of an incidence of ineffective assistance on the record which can be used by you on appeal. You should not do this for something small and insignificant. Only for something major.

If in your trial something huge happens (huge is bigger than major) you have the right under the Arizona rules of court rule 81 to address the court directly, thus sidestepping your attorney on a particular issue. The best time to do this is if your attorney fails to pursue something in your trial involving a specific violation of state law, rule of court or evidence, or a violation that is as plain as the nose on your face. Never mind that you might piss somebody off, this is your life on the line, which seems to be a fact everyone but you doesn't understand. By the time they drive home for dinner you'll be a fading memory so don't worry about it.

Pretrial is the time for filing motions. Generally you can file motions up to 20 days before the scheduled date of trial. As continuances are granted the 20 days are automatically adjusted to the new trial date. It is vitally important that you learn how to write motions. An example is included in the download file. It's not difficult to do and any violation of state law, rule of court or evidence, or a violation that is as plain as the nose on your face. Never mind that you might piss somebody off, this is your life on the line, which seems to be a fact everyone but you doesn't understand. By the time they drive home for dinner you'll be a fading memory so don't worry about it.

Pretrial is the time for filing motions. Generally you can file motions up to 20 days before the scheduled date of trial. As continuances are granted the 20 days are automatically adjusted to the new trial date. It is vitally important that you learn how to write motions. An example is included in the download file. It's not difficult to do and any documents submitted to the court by you will not be held to the same standard as an attorney. You need to make it clear to your attorney that you demand to be present at all court proceedings, that you want copies of every document he files and that if he refuses to file a motion you tell him to without a

sound legal explanation you will file a motion on your own. That's why you need to learn to write motions.

Although the details of every case are different they are still composed of similar parts or issues. Consequently a motion written for one case will apply to another once it is adjusted for the details in the other case. If you know a motion that worked for somebody else then there is no need to re-invent the wheel, use that motion as a model for your own case and adjust it to fit the details of your case. No need to worry about legalese and the case law research that supports the motion will already have been done for you. When you submit a motion you'll need to send to the clerk of the court the appropriate number of copies. In Superior Court you send 4 copies, appellate court you send 6, state Supreme Court you send 8, for U.S. District Court and the Ninth Circuit Court of Appeals you send 10 copies. In your state this may be different so you need to check in the revised statutes of your state for the number of copies you'll need to send. As you can see the expense of copies can add up quickly. In the system you're either indigent and get free copies or if you have $12 or more on your account you'll have to pay for them with your own money. Be sure somebody on the outside can help you and knows about this.

Asking for an attorney before questioning should eliminate the good cop bad cop interrogation routine so loved by movies and television. You should know that once you ask for an attorney all questioning by the police is supposed to stop until your appointed attorney arrives and/or they decide to arrest you. If that doesn't happen remain calm and keep your mouth shut. During interrogation they may tell you that the child involved was put through what is called a safe child interview and that he/she admitted that you're guilty, that they have it on videotape and will use it in trial. The police often use tactics like this to break a person to confess just to get the madness over with if for no other reason. Of course you and most of the public are ignorant of the law and the police use it is to their advantage in custodial interrogations. That's why this book was written. Another trick they use in interrogation is that they have the victim on videotape and they don't even need to call her or him as a witness. They're just going to play the tape in court. Not true! The confrontation clause of the sixth amendment to the United States Constitution secures the right of the accused to confront his or her accusers in an open court of

law. The age of the accuser makes no difference to this right. Make no mistake about it, your accuser will be in the courtroom or there will be no trial. And about that videotape? Videotape interviews have been successfully attacked in court because it allows the victim to testify twice which adds more weight and reinforcement of the victim's testimony over others in the trial.

The detectives in these cases are mostly scurrilous individuals who will tell you anything to get you to confess. They will tell you they have DNA evidence when none exists, fingerprint evidence when none exists. They will lie about computer forensics reports that haven't been done yet. Remain calm pay attention to nothing they tell you and maintain your innocence. This is not the time to think about plea bargains or going to trial. This is the time for damage control. This is the time to preserve your position and cut your losses by keeping your mouth shut. The prosecutor may even offer you a sweet deal in exchange for your confession. You should know that only the prosecutor can offer deals, not the cops.

During pretrial, since your initial plea is not guilty, you'll begin to receive discovery that you were not aware of before. Discovery is evidence found and/or testimony obtained in your case. Had you cracked and confessed before this stage of the game you would never know what this discovery is and the prosecutor would never have had to produce it. Discovery is submitted in increments as it is acquired. There is initial discovery which contains all the police reports from the victim or the victim's parents in contact crimes, along with any forensic evidence obtained. In noncontact crimes the initial disclosure may include a fingerprint report, but even this much evidence would be unusual at this time. This is where the prosecutors and police make their biggest mistakes. In their rush to throw someone in prison they file an information or go to a grand jury against someone before the forensics has been completed. They do this because most prosecutors know that few cases go to trial and with the ones that do, they can get a guilty verdict more times than not, because juries are so stupid and are prone to verdicts based on emotion, sympathy and horror. All the prosecutor wants is a body in prison, he doesn't care who it is as long as it's not his own. The trial is not about finding the truth, it's all about convicting YOU!

The initial disclosure is going to show you what they've done and what they haven't. Don't think for a moment that all of their forensic work has been completed. This is especially important with computer cases because in nearly all of them the computer forensics has not been done yet and you've already been charged and arrested. In my case it took six months to get the computer forensics report after I was arrested because it had been done yet. The evidence that has not been evaluated can save your butt, and by giving up and giving in, without having this information, you are insuring that you will NEVER have it. As well as making the work of the police and the prosecutor so much easier. Make them work for a living, don't submit to them. By giving up you only allow them to start working early on the next guy behind you, which is another thing to consider. Prosecutors know that the public is so terrorized from news reports about sex offenders and that a jury will convict with hardly any evidence at all. As a result most people are so afraid of a possible life sentence they will say anything to avoid it, even if it is untrue. The work of a prosecutor is easy and the public is so willing to oblige them. By demanding a jury trial you're making it less likely for them to prosecute the case coming up behind yours due to the expense and the time it takes to conduct trial. It cost the state $240,000 to conduct trial. If everyone accused demanded a trial the state does not have the money or the resources to handle it. This would force the state to pick only cases they were sure about winning and drop all the bogus cases they now enjoy so much. In addition if everyone wanted a trial there would be a massive backlog of forensic work to be done before trial could commence. Again not enough resources or money to handle it. By waiting for full disclosure you are not losing a thing and not allowing a conviction on your record when the state all along never had sufficient evidence to convict you. At least if your ship is sunk, you'll know it's sunk and know the reasons why. You will have made the state do the homework they should have done before coming after you. In my case the computer forensics report exonerated me because there was no evidence of viewing or downloading. Had the state done its homework before arresting me it would have seen that and never charged me. Had I given up early I never would have known that. There are ways to deal with a guilty verdict that I had to use that I will discuss in the post-trial chapter concerning appeals.

During the pretrial phase there will be some evidence the state does not want to process because if they did, that evidence could exclude you as a guilty party and point to someone else. Such was the case in my trial. Such evidence is referred to as Brady Material. Brady Material refers to a case where the prosecutor accused Mr. Brady of a crime and then refused to hand over evidence that it had at trial that exonerated him. Mr. Brady found out about it and brought it up successfully on appeal. Now his name is forever attached to this type of evidence. If this kind of evidence is the only evidence the state has to support their claim that a crime was committed the state has no choice but to drop the charges. The judge can also dismiss the case on his own, with or without prejudice. With prejudice means your constitutional rights were violated, the state prejudiced you and as a result you can't be tried again. Without prejudice means the state can try you again.

Most sex offender cases involve some kind of informant. Many times the informant is also guilty of committing a crime just in reporting the event. Often the prosecutor will choose not to charge them and charge you instead. This is called selective prosecution and it is a crime. This type of misconduct can get you a new trial if you have proof that this happened. Then there is the situation where the prosecutor offers immunity to the person in exchange for his testimony against you in trial. This also is a crime and testimony acquired in this manner is inadmissible because it is obtained under coercion and duress and is therefore tainted. With every trial involving an informant a motion should be filed demanding the prosecutor disclose if the witness was offered immunity in exchange for his or her testimony.

Once you have reviewed all of the evidence and testimony that is to be used against you, have formulated your defense strategy, then it is time to determine if there is sufficient evidence to convict you. If you feel there is not enough evidence to convict you it is important to file a motion for an omnibus hearing to determine the sufficiency of evidence to be used at trial. Many times the judge is a better jury than a jury. Judges hear trials just like yours day in and day out to the point they're bored to tears, but if you've got an approach to the evidence that is unique, when the evidence points to someone else and not you, there's a great chance the judge will listen to what you have to say. It is also important to size up the judge

beforehand because not all judges are open minded. In such an evidentiary hearing the whole trial can come to an end right there.

Another type of document you can present to the court is called an Amicus Curiae Brief. There are certain people who are qualified to submit an Amicus brief. People with expert knowledge of a particular field of study relevant to your case or any person with direct knowledge of the evidence of your case can submit an Amicus brief. Amicus Curiae is Latin for a "friend of the court". As a friend of the court, in the interest of justice, a brief is submitted by an expert on your behalf. For an example of an Amicus brief see the download file, there is a brief submitted in a New Jersey case that got a man freed. An Amicus brief from other states can be referenced in any motion, but they don't carry the same weight as those submitted in your own home state. An Amicus brief submitted in similar cases in your state can be used like case law in your own case even though it wasn't written for you.

There is one last document to be covered called an affidavit. An affidavit is a written statement from an expert or a person of interest in your case made under the penalty of perjury. It is a written statement that is the equivalent of testimony given on the witness stand. If you use one, the prosecutor will no doubt be opposed to it and try to stop its admittance into trial. The usual complaint is that an affidavit does not allow the opposing party to cross-examine the witness, similar to complaints about videotaped interviews. Sometimes you can get them admitted and sometimes you can't, but you never know till you try.

Careful planning and the proper use of motions in the pretrial phase can stop a trial before it begins. It is the most important part of any trial and one where information that can save your life is lost forever if not done right. Don't rely on your attorney to do this work for you. He may not. If that happens, you'll know what to do.

Just prior to trial you'll need to evaluate your position and ask yourself, "Can I win?" If the answer is I think I can or yes, I would press on with pride. If not, take a plea bargain, which by now should have gotten a lot better than the first offer. My position for those who are innocent is to never take a plea bargain. If you take a plea bargain here's what you lose:

The chance that the prosecutor will make a mistake in trial so severe you get a mistrial, your verdict overturned or reversed on appeal.

That the judge will do the same as above.

The right for a direct appeal (rule 31).

I also do not recommend taking a bench trial, because if you have a bench trial there is no jury. Therefore you lose the ability to file a Rule 31 Direct Appeal. When that happens you lose the chance of an independent review and that cooler more level headed judges not connected with your trial will review your case.

Prosecutors today are so sloppy, so careless in regard to rules of court and ethics they couldn't try a fair trial to save their lives. You lose out on all of this by taking a plea. Overturning or vacating a plea bargain is next to impossible, because it is a voluntary admission of guilt, that once is made can rarely be unmade. It is easier to get rid of cancer than it is to get rid of a plea bargain.

Each state has its own judicial system, with each judicial system having its own set of rules and regulations, so it is impossible to give regulations which will apply to all of them; however, a general thread of structuring flows thru them all. The United States is divided into 10 judicial districts.

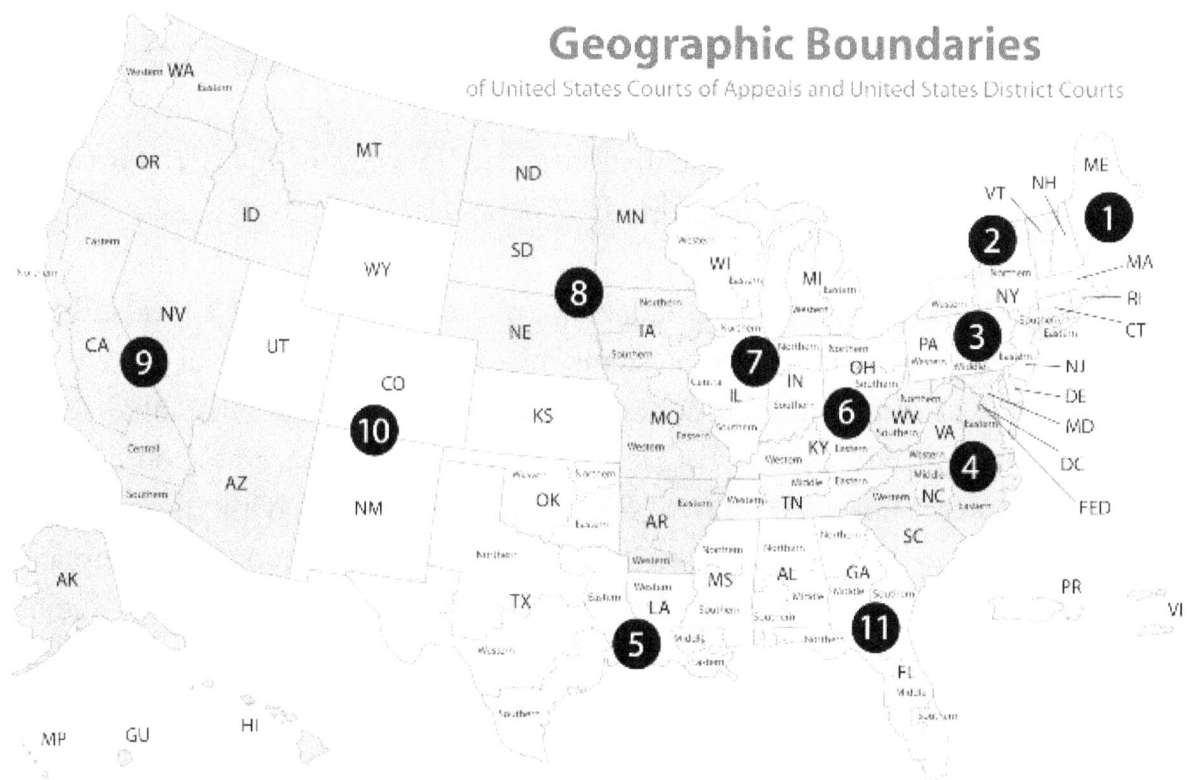

Geographic Boundaries
of United States Courts of Appeals and United States District Courts

You will notice that the 9th Circuit covers the largest geographical area and the largest number of states. That might have worked in the days of the wild west when few people lived in this area, but today the opposite is true. Because of this you can easily experience five or six years before you pass through the Federal courts. It's absolutely ridiculous! Most state systems have two initial courts consisting of a district court and, probate court. District courts hear misdemeanor cases and preliminary evidence in felony cases which includes arrest and search warrants. Most district courts hear only civil cases where the amount in dispute is under $10,000.

The majority of probate court matters involve juvenile cases but spills over into parental abuse, child neglect, and custody cases. Probate court does not handle cases which arise out of a divorce or paternity action. This court also addresses problems of children and mental incompetents and appoints guardians if needed. In addition to juvenile matters a probate court also handles wills and distribution of property for the deceased. Since we are dealing with state courts here, the age of a "juvenile" will vary according to that state's laws. Stepping up the rung to the next

ladder of appeal, one runs into the circuit courts. Circuit courts handle all cases which include felony prosecutions, injunctions, mandamus from a higher court, divorce, paternity actions, and civil matters which involve amounts over $10,000. Remember, misdemeanor cases usually start their journey in district court while felony cases commence in circuit court.

From this rung of the judicial ladder we move to the court of appeals, then to the state supreme court. Most state systems mirror the federal judicial system with the exception that state courts only address state matters. If a substantial federal issue is involved, it will usually be kicked from the state Supreme Court level to the United States Supreme Court. Since we are dealing with diverse states, exceptions exist, to all of the above. It is incumbent upon anyone contemplating petitioning these courts to check your state's structure to be sure which judicial ladder you will be climbing. Don't forget to secure addresses and phone numbers for all clerks of the courts along the way as this is where you will be mailing your pleadings. Some states have police courts and local magistrates/justice of the peace courts. These courts are the lowest rung of the judicial ladder, and any case heard is usually reviewed de novo by a higher state court. De novo (see Legal Latin in the Ancillary Index) simply means to hear anew, so all decisions handed down by these courts are ignored and heard 'over again.

Take your best shot at the state levels, but prepare your case as if you were going to be in federal court from square one. Factually, in most legal pleadings prepared at the state level, the majority of law utilized is federal. Lawyers aren't ignorant; they understand Teddy Roosevelt's rationale of "carrying a big stick." That guy with the black robe up there behind the bench might not care what another local or state judge has to say, but if you beat him over the head with a United States Supreme Court ruling, he'll snap to attention instantly.... if not sooner! By including at a minimum, one federal case law for every argument you present you are performing what is known as the "Federalization" of your appeal. While federal case law is not dictum for state courts it does however serve as a guide for the courts to follow if they so choose. In addition to this it informs the lower courts that there is federal case law on your claim and that once you reach a federal court of appeals you will obtain relief there. It sends a message to the lower

courts that you will eventually receive relief on the claim so why waste everyone's time and just go along with it.

INTERACTION OF STATE AND FEDERAL COURTS

In most instances you will find that the state and federal courts act as separate systems with the exception being when the U.S. Supreme Court reviews a federal question decided in a state court. From this point onward the overview becomes a bit more complicated due (again!) to the fact that we are dealing with 50 separate sovereigns and a federal system which attempts to maintain some semblance of continuity. We will first examine instances of state courts hearing federal issues, then shift over to federal courts hearing state issues. As a rule of thumb federal constitutional claims can be litigated in state courts, and, while most courts will hear civil rights claims brought Linder § 1983, some will not. It should also be noted that in Heck v. Humphrey SCOTUS ruled that you cannot file a § 1983 in regard to any matter that may have a tendency to overturn your conviction. You must overturn your conviction first. Further complicating this already insoluble mish-mash of near incomprehensible state laws is the fact that some states will allow a federal constitutional claim to proceed without invoking § 1983. The wisdom of this move is questionable as your rights under §1983 are well settled while what you might secure for "rights" by proceeding under a state statute could be ambiguous at best. Your best course of action is to always check your state's jurisdictional statutes before proceeding.

A dilemma here must be resolved before proceeding to your next course of action, and that is whether to proceed in a state or federal court. Both have their advantages and disadvantages; below listed you will find a few of the factors you should consider before making that decision:

One of the first actions should be a call to both the federal and state clerks of Courts to determine how backed up they are with over 20 million cases Currently being litigated, they will be backed up. And while you're conversing with the clerk of court, try to get a "feel" for the type of case you're litigating. Most clerks will know which judges are sympathetic to which types of cases.

1) Don't be afraid to ask questions or pick their brains; it is your carcass they are going to be chewing on if you chose the incorrect court or judge. Most judges have an established "track record" that will steer you in the right direction. If the clerk can't assist you (or doesn't want to hang their own carcass out in the wind), then spend a few hours sifting thru the law books for nuggets .of information. Most cites are written in an easy-to-read format that anyone can understand.

2) Which is your stronger claim: state or federal? Be honest with yourself and don't fudge on this issue. If you have a federal claim that is not that strong oil the law the chances are more than even the federal court will hold that you have only a state claim and relegate your action to a state court for review. Your loss here is clear; you could spend literally years wasting your time in the federal court while a state court could have issued a final decision. Always remember that in a state civil action suit the doctrine of "collateral estoppel" and "res judicata" (see "Commonly Used Legal Words" in the Ancillary Index for a full explanation of these terms) prevent you from re-litigating your suit in federal court.

3) Are you mixing up your issues? A good percentage of cases filed in the courts contain both federal and state issues which are complex in nature. You might have a valid constitutional complaint, but it will be buried, mixed up, and glossed over by numerous state issues. Don't be afraid to let the state take a shot at resolving it first. States are usually qualified to resolve the issues presented, and this course of action will provide you with two avenues of attack (state and federal) instead of one (federal). There is always the chance you can secure the relief sought at the state court level. Another factor to take into consideration is the "discovery" permitted in your state. One advantage of the federal courts is their liberal discovery rules. Before making a final decision whether to go state or federal, you should review your state's discovery rules."

4) Last but not least is the party you are going to be slapping with a suit. This is a critical point because if you don't sue the guilty party or the guilty party in an incorrect manner, you face an immediate dismissal of your action. In federal court you can sue individual officials (including prison officials), and, under some circumstances, you can also litigate against cities and counties. You cannot sue a state, but some states provide a legal vehicle where you can sue the state, city, or

county under a theory titled RESPONDENT SUPERIOR. Some restrictions apply: 1) you may not have the right to a jury trial; 2) you may find that punitive damages may not be available; and 3) you may have to pursue your action in the court of claims. If you're looking for naked revenge, the federal courts may be more to your liking; but if you're looking for some compensation (see "Types of Relief" in the Ancillary Index), then pursue your quest in the state courts.

ADMINISTRATIVE AGENCIES

It is impossible to go thru a discourse on courts without rendering the administrative agencies their tribute. Factually, there is more agency "code" in the Internal Revenue Service (federal) than in most states' entire statutes. Clearly, a basic understanding of the administrative agencies is mandatory if you are to get a better overall view of the system.

All government in the United States, both federal and state, is segmented into three branches: legislative, executive, and judicial. In theory administrative agencies come under the control of the executive branch which means they have either a governor or President at their head. But that is only in theory; in reality way are separate entities and represent the purest form of bureaucracy. They are more than vaguely reminiscent of the hydra monster in ancient Greek mythology in that for every rule or regulation deleted two more appear. Fact! Administrative agencies come into existence thru the legislative creation of a statute which authorizes their existence. Depending on how the statute is worded, it will define what the powers of that agency are, what its jurisdiction is, and for what those powers are to be used. All agencies may be sued and forced to comply with the statutes which originally brought them into existence. Federal agencies are litigated in federal court while state agencies are sued in state courts.

As a part of their administrative functions, administrative agencies are required to formulate and promulgate rules and regulations governing their activities and the activities of the individuals they are regulating. Therein lies the catch almost all agencies formulate these internal rules and regulations pretty much on their own with only a cursory wink from their controlling authority, i.e. the

President or governor. The final result is predictable in that they become the multi-headed monster which does nothing but grow and grow.

The Administrative Procedures Act (APA) establishes the procedures for enacting rules with the federal APA being found at 5 U.S.C. §§551 et seq. Federal procedures are also published in a separate book titled the Code of Federal Regulations (CFR) which is very informative and can be obtained by writing the Library of Congress in Washington, D.C. Regulations can also be secured by writing the agency direct or from ancillary publications which contain said regulations. Many states have their own Administrative Code but whether you can obtain them depends on who publishes them. Again, we are dealing with 50 separate entities which means you will have to slog thru this or that inquiry in the hopes of securing a copy of your state's Administrative Code.

All prisons, be they federal or state, are administrative agencies, but there is a loophole here in that most local jails are technically exempt from the Administrative Procedures Act because most are an agency of a county or city and not the state. Most agencies are required to follow the rules applicable to their agency. The court's current mind set appears to reinforce the trend of making these agencies follow their own rules with numerous court orders and directives being issued, directing these agencies to follow their own rules and regulations.

When you have a basic understanding of what the states and administrative agencies have to offer, you are ready to dig into that upper three per cent of the law which is federal in origin.

Once there, it is a stroll down the boulevard. Basically there are there are five (5) sections of books one must rummage around in. All have a specific purpose and are easily identifiable. We'll start with the least important and work up the ladder from there Congress and General Provisions are under the first five titles. All United, States Code is also "Sheped" by Shepard's so, if you're looking for another way to attack your charges, it might prove fruitful to check the most recent release of the Sheps. There is always the possibility the prosecutor was too busy to do so and wasn't aware that he or she charged you under the incorrect statute.

STEP 3 - THE DISTRICT COURTS

This is the first tier, or step, in the federal courts system of "justice." It consists of one federal judge sitting on his bench and uttering a "Memorandum Decision." Don't let the big name scare you. A Memorandum Decision may be placed in the Federal Supplement for any reason, or, sometimes, for no reason at all. Usually a decision is placed there due to unique circumstances which exist in a specific case, or, some quirk in the law which the judges' decision might have a bearing on. Always bear in mind that it is no more than one judge sitting in one particular court and that decision has no precedent beyond that judge in that court. His ruling is very seldom applicable to another case unless you happen to be standing in front of that very same judge with the same set of circumstances surrounding your case. Possible, but surely not probable.

A basic overview is necessary at this point as the "filing system" for this and the following two levels are identical. Take a common cite -Benny v. Pipes, 799 F2d 789 (9th Cir. 1986)" Benny v. Pipes" are the litigants. In this case Benny is bringing a grievance against Pipes. The "799 F2d 789" is even easier ... 799 means this particular case is found in book number 799 of the Federal Reporter, 2nd Series, and that number is prominently engraved on the binding of the book. Page 789 is where the case itself is located in book 799. Super easy. Benny was heard in the 9th Circuit and the decision rendered in 1986 which are the numbers inside the punctuation marks.

All memorandum cases at the district level are published in the Federal Supplement which presently comprises a little over 730 volumes. If you lose at this level, your next step will surely be your most meaningful: the Appellate Courts.

STEP 4 - THE APPEALS COURTS

This is the biggie. Why? For a number of important reasons every case heard in the district court has an automatic right of first appeal to one of the twelve Federal Judicial Circuits. Jurisdiction is conferred on the appellate courts thru 28 U.S.C. §1291-1294 with final decisions from the district courts being heard by the designated appellate court for that region.

Other areas of law are also covered by the appellate courts. 1) granting of leave to file an appeal to a non-final lower court order (interlocutory appeal); and 2) issuing orders regarding a denial or grant from an injunction. Some actions by the district courts cannot be appealed until final disposition, i.e.; 1) decisions on discovery issues; and 2) orders granting or denying class actions. Usually between 12 and 18 judges regularly sit on the appellate courts with temporary appointments from the district courts as needed to fill in vacancies. Three judges will comprise a panel which hears cases from the district courts with decisions from one three judge panel binding on other three judge panels from the same circuit. On occasion, when the law of the circuit is being challenged or the United States Supreme Court has ordered it so, all judges will sit "en banc" a fancy French term meaning "The court with all the qualified judges sitting in a case." Both the district and appellate courts are bound by decisions by the United States Supreme Court. The Federal Rules of Appellate Procedure govern all decisions rendered by the appellate courts.

If you're found guilty or have an issue on appeal you're going to end up in one of these courts. Even more important is the fact that in most cases this is your last shot at securing meaningful relief. Your chances of the United States Supreme Court granting you "certiorari" are approximately one out of 150. A slim shot for sure so take your best shot at the appellate level. Another important fact to remember is that if you've been represented by either a court appointed attorney or a public defender at the local level you're entitled, as a matter of right, to a meaningful appeal in the appellate circuit.

With the exception of the cases "non-published," almost every case making it to this level receives the royal treatment, i.e.: it appears in the Federal Reporter. Opinions coming out of your circuit are the ones to research carefully as they will be the ones you'll base your pleadings on, and the more "circuit" law you have in them, the closer the appellate court will pay attention to it: fact. Assuming you've made it to this level, and you are now ready to do battle; let's take a closer look at what is going on.

Upon arrival at this level your case is given an appellate "docket number", then assigned to a panel of three judges who will eventually decide the issues you've raised on your appeal. Be sure to raise every available issue because any issue not raised here is deemed moot. Although you can utilize a "Motion to Vacate" under Title 18, 2255 to attack your sentence after appeal you must remember this legal vehicle is channeled back to your original judge. Not the way to go since you're in the appeals court because that very same judge originally denied you the relief you sought. Focus on the appeals courts and you'll come out ahead in the end.

Depending on the complexity of your appeal and the overloading, the appellate court is experiencing when your appeal is docketed, it will take between 2 to 24 months for a decision to be rendered sometimes longer. The time it takes an appeal to be returned by the court appears to have no bearing on whether your appeal is affirmed or denied, but it does on the length of the decision rendered. The longer and more rambling the decision, the longer it takes to get it to the appellant.

All cases published at the appellate level are done so in the Federal Reporter 2nd Series" which presently consists of over 900 books. They use the same filing system as the other volumes referenced, so you should have no 'opportunities' finding your cites. This one set of books is, in all likelihood, the most used in any law library.

If an adverse decision is handed down, a timely "Suggestion for hearing en banc" may be submitted to the full court suggesting they incorrectly applied the circuit law. Be specific and to the point. Cite the case law you feel they have erred on and make every effort to stay within the circuit's prior rulings. If an "en banc" hearing is granted, all judges of that circuit will hear your case. When this happens, the circuit is usually preparing to make a major shift in its position. As in the United States Supreme Court, you're bucking the odds. Depending on which circuit you're in, your chances are approximately 1 in 150. If you're handed an adverse decision by the full court. you have one more avenue of relief: the United States Supreme Court.

STEP 5 - THE SUPREME COURT

Any decisions handed down by the United States Supreme Court are the law of the land. Jurisdiction of the Supreme Court is defined by Article III of the Constitution and by 28 U.S.C. §1251-1258. Actions in the Supreme Court are regulated in accord with the Rules of the United States Supreme Court and are published in both the USCA [United States Code Annotated]. Needless to say, the Supreme Court is not bound by any other court's rulings. Usually, but not always, our highest court will adhere to its prior rulings. This practice is known as the rule of "stare decisis".

In reality there are two legal vehicles with which you can petition the Supreme Court; appeal and certiorari.

When you appeal a case in which a state statute is being challenged as violating the federal Constitution, it is termed an "appeal". You are entitled to present a constitutional question to the United States Supreme Court even though your state's highest court will not hear the case. However, in order to present this question to the United States Supreme Court, you must first apply for review in your state. Review of state court decisions is mandated under 28 U.S.C. §1257, and in order for the Supreme Court to hear a state court decision, it must present some question of federal law. The Supreme Court is obligated to hear this type of appeal but can also dismiss it on grounds that the question involved is "insubstantial."

"Certiorari" is the other legal vehicle provided for a review by the United States Supreme Court. Technically it is termed a "Petition for a Writ of Certiorari." When you petition the Supreme Court to review your case thru certiorari, they have total discretion as to whether it will be heard. Review from lower federal court decisions is granted via 28 U.S.C. §1254.

There is a third option, but it has been exercised only 5 times in 200 years and that is in a case of original jurisdiction. Issuance of these writs are extremely rare and only on issues of extreme importance.

However, don't get your hopes up as it seems our highest court is only interested in hearing major cases these days, and the twenty thousand pounds of marijuana found in your basement which you claim to know nothing about would not merit a raised eyebrow in this legal forum. Yes, they will, from time to time, address a minor issue, but only if it is a case they are looking to change the law. With everything running to the conservative extreme these days, the granting of "cert" by the Supreme Court could be the kiss of death to any relief you seek. How extreme is extreme consider this in 1988 the Supreme Court heard 27 cases out of the 9th Circuit, our most liberal circuit, AND REVERSED 26 OF THE 27! Not the court to roll your dice in, my friend.

The Supreme Court is covered by several publications, but the most prominent is a set of books published by The Lawyers Co-Operative Publishing Company and styled as the United States Supreme Court Reports Lawyers Edition 2nd - LEd2d for short. There are currently 113 volumes in publication with the last nine being of the soft cover variety. For some reason the Supreme Court consumes an extended period of time before its cases are published, which means you will be waiting up to three years before a hardback edition is published. This should present no "opportunities" for the enterprising individual as the advance sheets are usually published by the aforesaid Lawyers Co-Op within three to six weeks of issuance. They follow the same format as the previously described editions, so you should be able to find your way thru them without difficulty.

In theory there exists two higher levels of relief. You could always petition the World Court in Hague, Netherlands, but when the United States received an adverse decision regarding Nicaragua it refused to accept the ruling and has since declined to recognize this body. You form your own conclusions.

Finally, and we do mean FINALLY(!), you can have any decision by the Supreme Court overruled by statute or constitutional amendment, but this involves an effort far beyond the means of any individual presently known to exist on this planet.

Chapter 4 Trial

When you finally get to trial, all of your motions will be decided if they weren't decided before trial began. If you did good work things may not go beyond this point. If this is not what happens your next step is jury selection. Due to some recent developments in court cases out of Maricopa County that revealed collusion between Phoenix detectives and Superior Court reporters to alter court transcripts to sabotage a person's appeal I highly recommend that you purchase a digital pocket voice recorder and record the proceedings yourself. This way if a discrepancy appears you will have your own electronic recording of what was said. They only cost about $35. That's real cheap insurance compared to life in prison. I also strongly advise that you request the proceedings be audio recorded at a minimum, but preferably videotaped for the same reason. It's not automatic. You have to ask for it and if you don't you will forever give that up.

Jury selection is also called in legalese voir dire and if it is happening to you is very dire indeed. Jury selection is pretty self-explanatory. You try to take the best jurors for your side while a prosecutor is going to pick the best for his side. The process begins with a packed courtroom. In my case jurors had to stand there were so many.

The first question asked the group is about the amount of time the trial will cover and if anyone has a scheduling problem. With each question jurors are eliminated. The next question concerns the nature of the charges and does anyone feel they couldn't be fair and impartial because of the charges in this trial. I have a real problem with telling this to a jury. Sure, those who can't remain fair and impartial because of some events in their life are going to bow out, but in alerting the jury to the nature of the offense I believe it sets the accused up to have a stealth or rogue juror. Voir dire relies on potential jurors being honest about their impartiality, but by alerting them to the nature of the offense you're inviting anyone who is biased the chance to become a juror and get revenge or satisfaction by convicting the accused and all they have to do is a lie about their impartiality. I would rather deal with one or two jurors that have a bias and have to wrestle with it because they got sucked into the trial, than invite the entire jury to attack me.

In jury selection each side gets what are called preemptory strikes. You get to remove some jurors that the prosecutor wants and the prosecutor gets to remove the same number of yours. From the defense point of view you don't want cops, friends of cops or the court. I wouldn't want someone who watches Bill O'Riley, Montell Williams or Opra on television. In addition I would not want teachers, counselors, psychologists, psychiatrists or emergency room nurses and doctors. And I definitely wouldn't want someone who works at CPS. Jury selection goes by way to quickly and you should do your best to slow the process down so nothing slips by. In my case a friend of a sheriff got on my jury and I never knew it until I reviewed my court transcripts.

After jury selection opening statements are given. The opening statements have few regulations. They do not have to contain facts like closing statements do. In the trial the prosecution goes first on everything from opening statements to the calling of witnesses. It is best as the witnesses for the state testify, that you make notes of all the inaccuracies and lies made by the state's witnesses. Then give your notes to your attorney for cross-examination of the witness. By doing it this way, little will get missed by your attorney and the cross-examination will be more effective. The state always calls its witnesses first and it can seem at this time to be a bit overwhelming or that you are destined to lose. You must remind yourself that the jury hasn't heard your side of the story yet and that things can change quickly.

It is not advisable to request a Rule 11 which is a ruling from the court that you are mentally incapable assisting in your defense. What will happen if you do this and succeed is that you will be placed in the care of a psychiatrist at the Arizona State Hospital (ASH) which is a mental institution. The purpose of the psychiatrist is to provide treatment to you either through medication, psychoanalysis or some other medieval treatment until you are declared fit to stand trial, at which time the proceedings against you begin anew. ASH is not a place anyone wants to be and it will only delay the inevitable and make your life worse than it already is. In addition this maneuver could result in civil commitment after you have already serve your sentence, which means you will never see the light of freedom again.

After the state rests its case your attorney should request a rule 20 motion. Rule 20 determines if the state has presented enough evidence for conviction. Rule 20 is decided by the judge and from my experience is seldom given. Don't get upset if you don't get a rule 20 because you're next at bat.

Sometimes the prosecutor will believe that a piece of evidence is related to the religious beliefs of the accused. This happened in my trial. This is very thin ice for a prosecutor to be standing on because one instance of overzealousness or a slip of the tongue and a mistrial can be declared on the spot if you have a good attorney who knows the rules of court. Unfortunately I didn't. A mistrial is where the prosecutor and sometimes the judge commit an error that violates the law to the extent that your rights have been violated and the jury is now tainted because of it. Judges and prosecutor's hate mistrials. Judges don't like them because it's a bad mark on them that they either caused or allowed it to happen. Prosecutor's hate mistrials because they have to start over from jury selection or drop the charges. Trials are not cheap just see the look on their faces in traffic court when you tell them you want to go to trial with the photos you took of the skid marks on the road if you don't believe me.

In trial you should take the position that although the prosecutor may have gained the upper hand temporarily by violating the law to gain your conviction, he's actually done you a favor. Don't worry if they violate the law to get you, as long as you object to it, your claim is preserved for appeal. If your attorney fails to object to something you have a right to object yourself. It doesn't matter if you don't express yourself like a lawyer, the law doesn't require you to. In addition to that, every person in that courtroom has a responsibility to make certain you understand what is going on in that courtroom. If they deny your objection they have to explain it till you understand why. No legalese, just a plain language commonsense explanation. Make them honest men and women, because they sure aren't going to be on their own. I'm quite certain that lawyers have no hearts in their bodies. I think law school removes them somehow.

If the verdict is guilty don't be stupid and resist your incarceration. There's no escape, except to win on appeal and retrial. This is what you must do and you will do it.

Chapter 5 Post Trial

I would have loved to have not taken you here, but the truth is once charges are placed against you there are only two outcomes. You take a plea bargain or you go to trial. There is no plan C. In all the cases I have studied and the people I have met there are only two people I know of who won their case on the first trial. They are Steve Karban and Tonya Craft. Just because you lost the trial doesn't mean the war is over, it's just shifting to another phase and in this process there will be many of them. When a prosecutor enters your life it's like being bitten by a Gila monster. The only way to release its jaws once it bites down on you is to cut its head off. The minute the verdict is in and you have been carted away, the judge will ask your attorney if he wants to interview the jury. You have a right to this interview, don't give it up. This interview allows your attorney to ask the jurors what part of the trial convinced them of your guilt. The answer to this question can help you immensely in trial number two. Other important questions to the jury can point out the weak spots of the presentation and areas you might try to avoid the next time around or approach differently. This is vital information that is too important to just give up. I had no idea my attorney gave this opportunity away until I read my transcripts a year later. Now that you know this walking in you can demand this from your attorney before you get there and your attorney can provide you with transcripts of what was said.

Another thing that can be done I didn't find out about till my legal research was underway is that your attorney immediately after the verdict can file a motion to vacate (remove the verdict) under rule 24.2. Other states will have a similar law. Certain conditions must be present to apply for it and you aren't always going to get it. If you get it you are out on appeal until the court of appeals makes a ruling on your appeal, at which time your appeal is considered perfected. Under the right conditions, with a good trial attorney, you can go through this entire trial including appeal without spending more than a few days behind bars. Thus giving you more time for research.

If your attorney fails to do this you'll be sent to the county jail to await sentencing. Ordinarily sentencing will occur in two weeks' time. However a reduction of sentence can be had if your attorney petitions court for a psychosexual

evaluation by a state psychologist. It worked for me and added only two weeks to the entire process. The reasoning behind this is that the psychosexual evaluation can make the judge feel more comfortable about giving a shorter sentence.

Approximately two weeks after sentencing you'll be sent to a classification center. In Arizona it is known as Alhambra. I've never been to a scarier looking place. It used to be a mental institution until a new facility was built and the buildings were given over to the department of corrections. During your stay there you will be placed with general population. Your best option is to lie convincingly about your crime and lay low. Do not ask for protective custody there. Protective custody does not exist there in the same sense as it does at the jail. Asking for protective custody in prison is asking to be placed on a DIC 67 list. By asking for protective custody you will increase your time in Alhambra by up to a month. Definitely not something you want to do. I know, because it happened to me. DIC 67 is for gang members who are not to be housed with rival gang members or for a person who is not to be housed with other individuals, generally speaking for informants. I can just about guarantee you it's not going to help you at all.

By the time you arrive on the sex offender yard your application for rule 31 or rule 32 will have been filed by you or your trial attorney, along with an application for indigency. Indigency means you don't have the money to hire an attorney so the state must provide one. If you had a paid trial attorney an indigency hearing must take place.

A rule 32 is an application for post-conviction relief. Although the writ of habeas corpus is still on the law books, if you file one it will get converted into a rule 32 and you will remain in prison till the rule 32 is decided. The writ of habeas corpus can't be removed from the law books because it is a right guaranteed by the U.S. Constitution. To sidestep the Constitution they supersede the writ of habeas corpus with rule 32 and leave habeas corpus as a powerless, hollow shell because it can't be removed from law without writing a new U.S. Constitution. Some people might argue this point, but until you have had to file one you don't know what you are talking about. A rule 32 can shorten your sentence by getting you resentenced where sentencing errors exist. It can get you a new trial where there was a major error in trial, new evidence that didn't show up at the first trial, or when there has

been a major court ruling or change in the law that directly affects your trial. In some cases a rule 32 can be converted into a rule 31 which is a direct appeal. Generally speaking this happens when a rule 32 has been decided improperly. All rule 32's are decided by the trial judge you had in trial and the trial judge is not likely to admit that he made a mistake. Therefore he is not likely to rule in favor of your rule 32. When this happens you can file a rule 31 with the court of appeals contesting the judge's decision. In a rule 31 you can't raise the claim of ineffective assistance of counsel. Ineffective assistance of counsel is a claim that your trial attorney's performance failed to meet criteria set for effectiveness. This is the most frequent claim on rule 32's. The point to remember with retrials is that it does you no good to go through a retrial without a significant change in strategy and or evidence. A rule 31 deals only with testimony and evidence presented to the jury. It deals primarily with errors made by the court or wrongs done by the prosecutor. New evidence cannot be presented in a rule 31. A rule 31 at its best can get you released. Usually you get a reversal with a remand for new trial.

In my case I created a short list of things the prosecutor did that I felt were wrong and prejudiced the jury against me. One of the items on my list was the introduction of the presence of adult pornography and testimony. I claimed this introduction should not have been allowed and prejudiced the jury against me. In my rule 31 appeal I had an excellent public defender. The first day we talked on the phone he asked me what I thought might claims were. He took almost every suggestion I had and worked them into the appeal. You need an attorney like this who is willing to work with your ideas. But before this, you have to have ideas and that means that you have to think like a lawyer and a court combined. The appellate court unanimously (all three judges) agreed I was right about the adult pornography issue and granted me a reversal with a remand for retrial. Remember, all arguments or claims must be supported by case law wherever possible. You don't have to include the entire case law, just citations of the relevant parts.

During the post-trial phase you'll also undergo a pre-sentencing interview with a probation officer. The presentencing report contains recommendations to the court for your terms of release. All of the presentence reports I've read including mine are a scandalous distortion of the facts or outright lies. What most probation officers don't tell you when they begin the pre-sentencing interview is that you

have a right to have an attorney present at this interview. I highly recommended you do this and that you ask him to appear with a tape recorder. You also have the right to remain silent during all of this, which is probably the best thing you could possibly do. The adult probation officer's job is to lie and they're pretty good at. After all they can't have adult probation saying you're a nice person can they?

During the time between conviction and sentencing the judge is supposed to review the letters sent by people on your behalf begging for mercy on you. The more letters you get sent the better. However, in reality these letters will never amount to more than the band on the Titanic did. Letters on your behalf from friends, employers and relatives become a part of your case file and can be looked at later as well. They should be sent the minute action is taken against you and a docket number is assigned to you.

At sentencing immediate family members get to speak on your behalf to plead for mercy from court and to speak their mind. Things said by your family become part of the record, but because they don't occur in front of the jury, they too become like the band on the Titanic. Sentencing, especially for sex crimes at least in Arizona, has become the most convoluted, confusing subject in the entire code of laws. For example just selecting a case at random I find three sentencing statutes selected for one count and the sentence imposed for each statute is different. The question is which one applies? Most attorneys can't figure it out. If you pick one sentencing statute and read it, you'll be referred to another sentencing statute you aren't even charged with, which then refers you to another statute you were charged with, which then refers you to another statute. The purpose of this is pure deception and sleight of hand. If I am to believe this is the only way the law could be written, then I'm being asked to believe that it was impossible for our lawmakers to attach one sentencing statute to one kind of crime which is utterly absurd.

Sentencing involving aggravating factors requires the jury to hear those aggravating factors and vote on them. (see case law on Aprendhi) the situation is that sentencing takes place about two weeks after the trial.

Long after the jury has been released. The state doesn't want to call them back because of the expense, as well as the irritation factor. So they just aggravate your sentence without a jury. No big deal right? I mean it's not like the convict is going to know it's against the law. Right? Well you do now!

Chapter 6 Prison

When you arrive in prison you will be faced with two options, to fight your conviction or settle in and get used to it. For heroes, fighters and the strong-willed there is only one choice. To fight! To accomplish this task you need to hook up with an unofficial legal club on the yard. In almost every yard you'll find small groups of people gathering together to discuss law. It is in these groups that you will obtain a tremendous amount of moral support as well as sound legal advice. While some might disagree, I would personally take three legal eagles from a prison yard than some paid attorneys. The more sources of yard than some paid attorneys. The more sources of information you have the better. Be a good student with them. Just like it was a school, you listen to who's speaking and then ask questions. In a couple years you'll be doing the talking. To encourage the free exchange of information always pass on to others the latest word along with whatever knowledge you have acquired so that others will be encouraged to do the same for you.

You need to start collecting case law citations like baseball cards and put them in a case law citation book. In the beginning you need to collect only the case law relevant to your case. Later you may wish to copy other people's case law books and add them to your own.

When you arrive at the prison you'll discover there is no legal library like there was at the jail. At least there aren't in Arizona prisons. The Arizona department of corrections interpreted the wording of law to say that keeping a fully functioning legal library could be eliminated if inmates had access to a paralegal. So they got rid of the legal libraries and hired paralegals. The only problem is that they hired one paralegal to handle four units, so access becomes a problem. This would be bad enough if it wasn't for some other issues that developed with the paralegals. Arizona department of corrections set criteria for the position of paralegal. They had to have a college degree and a certificate from an accredited paralegal school. Just as the power of the state habeas corpus was nullified by Rule 32, so too was the federal habeas corpus emasculated by the antiterrorism and effective death penalty act. Here is a copy of what it says.

The anti-terrorism and effective death penalty act of 1996, pub. L. No. 104-132, 110 stat. 1214, (also known as AEDPA) is an act of congress signed into law on April 24, 1996 to "deter terrorism, provide justice for victims, provide for an effective death penalty, and for other purposes." it was passed with broad bipartisan support by congress (91-8-1 in the united states senate, 293-133-7 in the house of representatives) following the Oklahoma city bombing and signed into law by president Bill Clinton.

The AEDPA had a tremendous impact on the law of habeas corpus in the United States. One provision of the AEDPA limits the power of federal judges to grant relief unless the state court's adjudication of the claim resulted in a decision that was contrary to, or involved an unreasonable application of clearly established federal law as determined by the supreme court of the united states; or based on an unreasonable determination of the facts in light of the evidence presented in the state court proceeding.

While critics have charged that this limitation effectively forecloses the power of federal courts to remedy unjust convictions, federal judges have found ways to grant relief to prisoners in habeas cases despite the limitation. One of AEDPA'S most controversial changes is the requirement that any constitutional right invoked to vacate a state court conviction rooted in a mistake of law by the state court must have "resulted in a decision that was contrary to, or involved an unreasonable application of, clearly established federal law, as determined by the supreme court of the united states." thus, a U.S. court of appeals must ignore its own precedents and affirm a state court decision contrary to its precedents, if the U.S. supreme court has never squarely addressed a particular issue of federal law.

Other provisions of the AEDPA created entirely new statutory law. For example, before AEDPA the judicially created abuse of the writ doctrine restricted the presentation of new claims through subsequent habeas petitions. The AEDPA replaced this doctrine with an absolute bar on second or successive petitions. Petitioners who attempted to bring claims in federal habeas proceedings that have already been decided in a previous habeas petition would find those claims barred. Petitioners who had already filed a federal habeas petition were required to first secure authorization from the appropriate federal court of appeals. Furthermore,

AEDPA took away from the Supreme Court the power to review a court of appeal's denial of that permission, thus placing final authority for the filing of second petitions in the hands of the federal courts of appeals.

In addition to the modifications that pertain to all habeas cases, AEDPA enacted special review provisions for capital cases from states that enacted quality controls for the performance of counsel in the state courts in the post-conviction phase in state court. States that enacted these quality controls would see strict time limitations enforced against their death-row inmates in federal habeas proceedings coupled with extremely deferential review to the determinations of their courts regarding issues of federal law. As of yet, only Arizona has qualified for these additional provisions, yet it has not been able to take advantage of them because it has not followed its own quality control procedures. More states may qualify for these additional provisions in the future because in 2005 congress took the power to determine whether a state had qualified away from the federal courts and gave it to the attorney general.

Soon after it was enacted, AEDPA endured a critical test in the Supreme Court. The basis of the challenge was that the provisions limiting the ability of persons to file successive habeas petitions violated article I, section 9, clause 2 of the U.S. constitution, the suspension clause. The Supreme Court held unanimously in Felker v.Turpin, 518 U.S. 651 (1997), that these limitations did not unconstitutionally suspend the writ.

In 2005, the ninth circuit indicated that it was willing to consider a challenge to the constitutionality of AEDPA on separation of powers grounds under city of Boerne v.Flores and Marbury v.Madison, but has since decided that the issue was foreclosed by circuit precedent.

The AEDPA allows for the filing of one federal habeas corpus per crime and you have one year from the exhaustion of state remedies to file. The legal libraries were removed before the AEDPA became law. The paralegals never informed inmates of the change. Consequently inmates filing on their own, had no idea they had only one chance or that there were time limits to filing. This meant the quantity of federal habeas filings never changed and as a result they have been

denied by the truckload. Ultimately this raised a question about what the paralegals were actually doing, which led to the investigation of the paralegal's that revealed some underhanded business with regard to their qualifications. The paralegals were found to not possess a college degree and/or a certificate from an accredited paralegal school. One of them had actually tried cases in the Superior Court of Safford, Arizona as a defense attorney, using a Phoenix attorneys' state bar number. All of this is as illegal is hell. I myself requested paralegal Ullaberry to provide mean a copy of <u>State v.Pool</u>. I included the full case law citation number. She reported back to me that she was unable to find it. Gee, I wonder why? Could it be she doesn't know how to find it because she's really not a paralegal? The paralegal and the library Nazi of Meadows unit work as a team to hinder inmate's access to courts by, reading the documents they intend to put before the court, removing pages and exhibits from those proceedings, and declaring that DOC regulations prohibit the copying of them. As a result of their efforts I've had to call my attorney to demand my exhibits be copied and have had to resort to my father to get some materials copied because the library Nazi of Meadows unit wouldn't copy them. Keep in mind it made no difference to her that I was paying for the copies out of my own money, or that they were part of a legal document, or covered legal issues. It also didn't matter that hundreds of complaints have been filed against the library Nazi of Meadows unit. She seems to have immunity from a higher source in the administration which wreaks of conspiracy. I will have an entire chapter devoted to the library Nazi of meadows unit in my upcoming book, "Letters From Prison". The purpose of all this is to inform you of what and who you can count on for help. The added stigma of being an S.O. allows the Arizona Department of Corrections to create special conditions for us that don't exist for GP inmates, all with the intention of slowing our legal work down or interfering with our access to courts.

One of the first groups of people you'll be exposed to is the sovereignty people. These folks believe that maritime law and that being recognized as sovereign citizens will get you out of prison. This position is flawed because it was the law that put you in prison and only the law can get you out. I'm not denying that some of the points of the sovereignty people are valid. It's just that in two years not one of them I know has gotten out and in the same amount of time I have. It seems that with these folks there is always the next document that will free them.

Don't waste your time and effort on this when it can be better used to attack your case by using their own law against them.

Many people when they arrive in prison and have had their faith in the judicial system destroyed decide to do it on their own. I know one man who did this and only received partial results. He now has an attorney working for him. When his attorney first took over his case he showed her a document he had drafted with the intention of overturning his conviction. The courts denied review of it. When his attorney read the document she was so impressed with it she filed at as her own, with no changes, except for her name, bar number and address at the top of the document. The court granted him review. The point of the story is that I have read the many inmate created document from inmates representing themselves, that had very clear arguments, supported by valid case law, only to get turned down by the courts. It always made me wonder if it wasn't due to the fact that an attorney didn't write them. This incident tends to support that conclusion and you would be wise to find an attorney willing to work with your ideas and research. It worked for me and my friend. It will work for you too. If you decide to do your own appeal it is very important that you include a statement affirming that you are not guilty. Steve Karban's rule 31 appeal was done by an attorney who failed to include a statement like this and his appeal was shot down for the lack of it.

There will be a few people get together so they can talk law, share information and plan strategy. You need to get to know all of these people as well as you can. If a family member can do case law research on the internet for you, offer that up to a couple people as a way to break the ice. Internet assistance is a highly prized commodity in prison and it is something Arizona prisoners are forbidden by law in Arizona. Forget that nearly all business both government and private is conducted on the net today, Arizona doesn't care. The thing that really pisses me off the most is that the library Nazi of Meadows unit once refused to make copies of something I had and told me to print them up from the internet. She's either very stupid or very cruel. I haven't figured out which.

Without getting into advice about how to survive prison life which is a work yet to come, I have covered all the topics about fighting your case from prison. The

prison chapter is very short for a reason. There's not much that happens there and there's nothing you can do about it. Prison is a waiting room and everybody leaves one way or another. Which I think is the most important thing to remember. Although the department of corrections has become quite adept at throwing obstacles on the path to release, the resourcefulness of the inmates is a tribute to their ingenuity and indomitable desire to be free. It leaves me in awe.

Up until this point you have been keeping a record of everything that took place before trial, including names, dates and places. Now you're going to add to that document, a complete transcript analysis. The first thing that you have to do is obtain a copy of your trial transcripts. The law says that you are entitled to one free copy. However that one free copy is going to go to your appellate attorney. If you want one for yourself you're going to have to pay for it. Unfortunately that's just the way things are. When you receive your trial transcripts you need to break out a notepad and pen and begin reading your transcripts from the beginning. When you encounter a statement of fact by a witness you write down the day of trial, the page number and line the statement occurs on. Then you continue reading. As is often the case you will find later on in the witness's testimony that they contradict their earlier statement. When this happens you write down the contradictory statement with the word perjury at the end and then cross-reference the location of the two statements with each other. By doing it this way the two statements become linked so that when they are encountered they can be reference in two directions, both forward and backward. You should also reference the violations of state statutes that occurred during trial. This is how a professional attorney does a trial analysis. By doing this in advance of your second trial you are insuring that any attorney who comes after this document is completed will be able to read it and get up to speed with the issues of your case as quickly as possible. Because this document is composed of your pretrial and post-trial notes, along with your trial analysis I have referred to this document as a, "Frankenstein Document." A document put together from a bunch of dead parts and brought back to life. Just as creating Frankenstein, the dead were brought back to life, creating a Frankenstein Document will bring you back to life.

Another thing that is very important is to obtain a copy of your record on appeal (ROA). Most attorneys don't spend a lot of time talking to their clients. Consequently this leaves many clients to believe their attorneys aren't doing anything for them. Once you get a copy of your record on appeal you'll discover that your attorney submitted many documents that you were never even told about. You may discover documents that you never knew existed. You may discover that there were records that were sealed by the court that you never knew about. One thing is for certain, the index of records on appeal is the most important document you can get hold of from your trial, other than the trial transcripts themselves. You'll see your case in a whole new light. I cannot advise strongly enough to get a copy of the record on appeal.

After your trial is over there will be many trial events that transpired that you believe are wrong or unfair. You may discover through your legal research that there are violations of state law in regard to these issues. If such is the case, you need to make these arguments part of your appeal, so the prosecutor will not be able to do them to you a second time. If you are unable to win the first time around, you want to use the appeal process to restrict the prosecutor's ability to attack you in the second trial, or the third trial, or the fourth trial etc. Until eventually the prosecutor has no more avenues left to proceed against you. This is how you win in today's judicial system. Who determines when the fat lady sings? **You do!**

While you are waiting for your appeal one of the things that you will have to wait for is the production of the court transcripts. Depending on the caseload of the court reporters this can take no more than a few days or it can take a year or more. If it appears to the Court of Appeals that the court reporters are dragging their feet, the Court of Appeals will begin to find the court reporter's $50 a day until the transcripts have been completed. This money comes out of their bond so it doesn't really affect them that much. Several things to remember while you are waiting for the transcripts to be produced is that while you have a right to a speedy trial you do not have a right to a speedy appeal. In addition to this, as the appellant, technically you have the responsibility to provide the Court of Appeals with a record, although there is not much you can do when the transcripts are late except asked the court to tell the court reporter to get the transcript delivered. It is the appellant's

responsibility to ensure that the record on appeal is complete and the Court of Appeals presumes any missing documents support the Superior Court's decision. See: State v. Rivera, 168 Ariz.102, 103, 811 P.2d 354, 355 (App. 1990). Don't even think about filing a motion for dismissal before the Court of Appeals. What you have to realize is that the appeal is an action that is brought about by you and not the state. Therefore the Court of Appeals would be all too happy to dismiss your case before them and leave you sitting exactly where you are because it would reduce their workload. When the action is brought by you a motion for dismissal is a statement that says, "I'm happy with the verdict that I got and I don't want to proceed with any further action." I personally had to wait a year before the court reporters finally produced the court transcripts of the last day of trial and there was nothing that I could do about it. When it finally arrived and I read it I discovered why it took so long to get it. The court transcripts had been **redacted**, leaving out a statement by my accuser that clearly indicated he had been told what to testify to and references by the prosecutor that compared me to Bill Clinton, Senator Larry Craig and Bernie Madoff which was illegal and a tactic the prosecutor always used when he felt the possibility of losing a case. I tried to go back to the recording but I was told by the court reporter that because I hadn't requested at the beginning of trail that the proceedings be recorded I was **forever barred** from gaining access to them and they were only to be used by the court reporters. A very important thing to ask for at the beginning of trial. The reason why it's so important is that you can't prove something wrong happened if you can't point to it in the transcripts.

And finally a word about how much study and work is going to be required to beat this. If you are not spending every waking moment researching your case, then there's a problem with your motivation. You are only going to get out of it what you put into it. You need to eat, sleep and breathe the law. I personally know of people who put in 16 hours a day working on their case. I was one of them.

I can't throw everything I've learned in two years of study about the law into this book, which is not my intention. I'm trying to provide an overview of the most common mistakes, the ones I made and one's others made. I also want you to know when someone's lying to you and the common tactics a lot of people fall for. The

reference books I've mentioned previously will provide you with the details along with the statutes and case law in this book.

WRITING A PLEADING

Before beginning this rather technical discourse on the formulation of legal pleadings one point should be made clear. Pleading guilty is out! Never plead guilty unless the evidence against you is overwhelming. It is a legal fact that 94% of the people charged get 'sifted out' of the system before a jury verdict is rendered. Individuals make deals, plead out, agree to testify, cop a plea, or throw themselves on the mercy of the court to avoid the chance of being found guilty, always to their detriment, as when they short circuit the system by pleading out they effectively isolate themselves from that multitude of rights, privileges and constitutional protections the law provides. Unless you are caught "Dead Bang", always fight your case. You might be found guilty but you'll have the appellate court system working for you and odds are you'll end up doing substantially less time than the individual who plead out. With that thought in mind let's get our feet wet. Examples of the following types of documents can be found in your state revised statutes and some of them are in the download section.

Defining a legal document/pleading/brief/motion is an inexact science at best. A better definition would be to place it under the heading of art. Let's commence with the basics and that is the types of documents you will, in all likelihood, be working with:

1) Complaint or Petition
A pleading by which the plaintiff or petitioner sets out the cause of action and invokes the jurisdiction of the court.

2) Brief
A concise and brief statement of authorities addressing the issues and questions involved as they appear from the pleadings. Briefs may oppose or support a point of view and may be presented at any time of the judicial process.

3) Motion

An application made to the court or judge for the purpose of obtaining an order or rule directing something to be done in favor of the applicant.

4) Habeas Corpus

Meaning, literally, "To produce the body." A writ of ancient origin utilized to liberate those who may be imprisoned without sufficient cause and to deliver them from unlawful custody, or, to obtain proper custody of persons illegally detained from the control of those who are entitled to their custody.

5) Judgment or Order

A document prepared by the applicant which, if signed by the court or judge, directs the parties involved to perform a specific action.

6) Affidavit

Any voluntary ex parte statement reduced to writing in which someone swears to certain facts. These are usually notarized but in some courts, including federal court, they can be sworn to under penalty of perjury. See 28 U.S.C.A.§ 1746.

Before dissecting all of the above it is critical that one has a basic understanding of some terms utilized by the courts.

Jurisdiction

Confers upon a specific court the power to hear the subject matter of a particular legal matter. Simply put; the power to hear, determine and adjudicate. There are two types of jurisdiction;

1) Exclusive Jurisdiction

Occurs when a matter can be legally heard in only one court; and

2) Concurrent Jurisdiction

When the matter can be heard in more than one court. At times this term (jurisdiction) also refers to the power or authority of administrative or executive agencies. When you are formulating your complaint you must invoke the jurisdiction of the court by citing the relevant statutes.

Venue

Is not to be confused with jurisdiction since jurisdiction may not be conferred by consent or waiver, whereas the venue of an action may be changed by the consent of the litigating parties. Venue is simply the county or district where the cause is to be tried. A geographical location if you prefer.

Plaintiff or Petitioner

This is the person or party(s) seeking relief from the court. A person who brings a suit, action, bill or complaint. A complaint is filed by a plaintiff, while a petition (usually habeas corpus) is filed by a petitioner. A petition may also be a formal request in writing, directed to one in a position of authority, or to a body such as a municipal counsel. This type of petition is usually signed by a number of persons.

Defendant or Respondent

The person against whom an action or proceeding is brought. Identify the defendant/respondent by both proper name and the title of the office they hold. If there is a relationship between the defendants/respondents specify exactly what that relationship is. Remember, the court doesn't know you from Adam so you've got to lay it all out in clear, concise terms. Usually, but not always, a defendant refers to a criminal action while a respondent is 'responding' to a civil action.

COMPLAINTS AND PETITIONS

Don't panic at the thought of formulating and filing a complaint. When all the smoke blows away all you're really doing is writing a letter to the court. Be brief, to the point, follow some basic rules and always (ALWAYS!) be honest with the court. Format is important but content is CRITICAL! A splendid example of the above is <u>BOAG V MacDougall</u>, 454 US 364, 70 LEd2d 551, 102 S.Ct. 700 (1982) in which BOAG was incarcerated in punitive segregation without access to even the basic necessities such as paper. He scribbled an appeal on toilet paper to the United States Supreme Court certiorari was granted and relief was issued from the inhumane conditions he was being held under.

A caption containing the court's name and circuit is placed prominently at the top and center. Directly under this heading place the parties involved on the left

margin with a space directly opposite for the case number which will be assigned by the clerk of the court.

There is an advantage to the breaking up of allegations or facts it requires the other side to respond in detail which is to your advantage. The facts they admit too will not have to be proved in court. The more detailed your complaint is the more they will have to admit or deny. Moreover, if your opponent fails to respond to your claims by not denying or admitting them they are deemed to have been admitted by the court. It's a no lose situation.

Another item not to be overlooked is the exhaustion of administrative remedies. This is especially true if you are suing either a state or government agency as in order to present your claim you'll almost surely have to demonstrate that you've exhausted your administrative remedies. Once you have fought your way thru the labyrinth of administrative appeals you'll be eligible to file with the court system. Like everything else, there is an exception to this rule and that is if you're filing a civil rights complaint against the state system in federal courts under 42 U.S.C. §1983 you are not required to exhaust your administrative remedies, but, you should demonstrate that you have exhausted your administrative remedies in state court.

Moving back to the main argument again there are a multitude of ways to attack your opponents argument but when all the smoke blows away they break down to one or more of the categories listed below:

1) DIRECT AUTHORITY
You demonstrate how a case citation, statute or other authority directly supports your position.

2) ANALOGOUS AUTHORITY
You demonstrate how a case citation, statute or other authority applies to a case or situation which is comparable to the one your presenting. Your argument here would be that since the other case is so similar to yours that the law which applies to it should apply to your case.

3) DISTINGUISHING AUTHORITY

If your attempting to make a legal point and are having a hard time finding supporting case law you can use adverse cases then "distinguish" your case by showing how you situation is opposite from the one cited or how it could not apply to your case. Distinguishing authority is the reverse of Analogous Authority. If an adverse point of law is thrown at you the last action you want to take is no action as both the state and federal systems will deny you relief on that issue if you do not address it in your brief (see Appeals).

4) LEGISLATIVE INTENT

If there is no case law supporting your stance you can rely on a constitutional provision, statute, administrative provision or court rule and argue that the drafters of that rule intended to include your situation. Your argument should show that the language, spirit and purpose or the rule support your position.

5) MISCARRIAGE of JUSTICE

This type of attack is independent of case law, either supportive or adverse, and instead rests on basic fairness. You must show how, if the court renders an adverse decision, it will work an unfair hardship on you or your client. It is basically a moral question so don't get 'greasy' with the court when you initially present it; a little sympathy from the court will not hurt your position.

6) UNDESERVED REWARD

You can demonstrate to the court how, if it grants relief to the opposing party, they will receive an undeserved reward or windfall. This point of attack is especially apropos in liability cases where someone is asking an outrageous amount for a minor injury.

7) FORKED TONGUE

If you're lost on an issue or not sure how the court is going to rule you can aver that you should win no matter how the court rules on the issue. If the court rejects the issue it will automatically accept another. This can get a little 'tricky' but the results are worth the effort. By making one argument on one side of an issue and another argument on the other side it becomes a no lose situation.

8) ABSURDITY

Show how, if the court renders an adverse decision in your case, the results will be illogical, absurd or ridiculous. This type of attack can be used more often than not but requires an issue that is borderline.

9) GENERAL PRACTICE or PUBLIC POLICY

You can argue that the court should rule in your favor for the public benefit. A showing of adverse public opinion or reaction if it doesn't rule in your favor or the good which will result from your rule is always a good move on your part. There is always some individual or group in the media crusading for this or that cause; work your point of view in with this blossoming media stampede and ride the crest of public opinion to victory.

10) UNSUPPORTED POSITIONS

In this attack you have a relatively weak position, but, so does your opponent. There is no authority supporting your position or your opponents. If you elect this form of attack you can also zero in on ancillary issues such as the record does not support your opponent's position and that his argument is fatally flawed.

To add a touch of class you can close with a line which reads "AFFIANT FURTHER SAYETH NAUGHT." Sign the complaint, place your name, address and phone number (if applicable), and date it. Finally you should have it notarized or add a "Statement Under Penalty of Perjury" which comes under 28 U.S.C.A. §1746.

BRIEFS

During World War II Winston Churchill had a cardinal rule which was broken only one time any paperwork placed in front of him was to be double spaced and not over a half page in length. He firmly believed that if you can't get your point across in 2 hundred or so words something was wrong. Factually, the sole time this 'rule' was broken was when he was presented with a report on the atom bomb. That very same ra66nal still holds true for legal "briefs" in that the key word here is BRIEF. If you want to lose someone's attention present them with a lengthy, dry reading document and watch the frown form on their previously smiling faces Although a brief can be of any length they are sometimes limited by court rules; such as briefs

to the federal appellate courts (55 pages). Yes, you can petition the court to file a longer 'brief' but you will be defeating your original purpose of keeping this critical pleading "brief."

Always check with the court your filing in to see if there are any special requirements before filing a brief with that court. This is one of the few instances when the federal court system loses it continuity as each district and appellate court have their own 'pet peeves' and court rules. It is up to the individual filing the brief to check on and comply with said rules. Another idiosyncrasy of the federal courts is the requirement for a "Statement of the Case" which delineates the procedural history of the action.

As said before, all you're really doing is writing a sophisticated letter to the court, but, keep it as simple and legible as possible. A sage action here would be to pass along your brief to someone who is not familiar with your case, then, after she or he has read your brief, question them regarding its content. If they can't understand what your trying to say the courts aren't going to have much more luck with it. Keep your language simple and easy to read. If you don't know the exact meaning of a word don't use it; you'll avoid an embarrassing mistake and look better in the eyes of the court. When writing your brief never infer that the judge is biased, unfair or lazy even if they are.

Heaving insults at the judiciary will secure you nothing but trouble and take the focus of the court off the relief you seek. Use neutral terms and never accuse anyone of misconduct unless you've got the facts in a safe deposit box and are prepared to "go to the wall" with them or present them to the States Attorney's office. If the court makes an adverse decision take it to the appellate court with the aversion that "the lower courts conclusions are unsupported by either the record or the facts of the case" then proceed to dissect the lower court's opinion with facts: not allegations. Never let your emotions take control of your writing or computer keyboard. Ever!

If the court directs you to file your brief before your opponent you may face a thorny proposition and that is deciding whether to respond to an argument you think your opponent may address in his brief. There is an 'opportunity' here you

don't want to focus your oppositions attention on an issue they may not address, however, if your dead bang sure they are going to hammer it, you should hit it first, hard and at the earliest opportunity. Writing a brief is never easy but with practice, patience and old fashioned stick to-it-tiveness the pieces will fall in place.

When writing Briefs and Motions a convention has been developed to help you write them in a standardized way. It's called the F.I.R.A.C. method and here is how it works. When briefing a case, your goal is to reduce the information from the case into a format that will provide you with a helpful reference in class and for review. Most importantly, by "briefing" a case, you will grasp the problem the court faced (the issue); the relevant law the court used to solve it (the rule); how the court applied the rule to the facts (the application or "analysis"); and the outcome (the conclusion). You will then be ready to not only discuss the case, but to compare and contrast it to other cases involving a similar issue.

Before attempting to "brief" a case, read the case at least once. Follow the "FIRAC" method in briefing cases:

Facts

Write a brief summary of the facts as the court found them to be. Eliminate facts that are not relevant to the court's analysis. For example, a business's street address is probably not relevant to the court's decision of the issue of whether the business that sold a defective product is liable for the resulting injuries to the plaintiff. However, suppose a customer who was assaulted as she left its store is suing the business. The customer claims that her injuries were the reasonably foreseeable result of the business's failure to provide security patrols. If the business is located in an upscale neighborhood, then perhaps it could argue that its failure to provide security patrols is reasonable. If the business is located in a crime-ridden area, then perhaps the customer is right. Instead of including the street address in the case brief, you may want to simply describe the type of neighborhood in which it is located. (Note: the time of day would be another relevant factor in this case, among others).

Procedural History

The procedural history should be included with the fact section and contains the relevant historical information about the case as it was tried.

Issue

What is the question presented to the court? Sometimes, only one issue may be discussed, but often there will be more. Issues are what you are asking the court to decide and is usually presented in the form of a question.

Rules

Determine what the relevant rules of law are that the court uses to make its decision. These rules will be identified by you and discussed by the court. There may be more than one relevant rule of law to a case and rules are not just statutes, but case law as well.

Application/Analysis

This may be the most important portion of the brief because this is the section where you explain how the rules relate to the facts and the issues, which leads to the outcome you are looking for. The court will have examined the facts in light of the rule, and probably considered all "sides" and arguments presented to it. How courts apply the rule to the facts and analyze the case must be understood in order to properly predict outcomes in future cases involving the same issue. What does the court consider to be a relevant fact given the rule of law? How does the court interpret the rule? Resist the temptation to merely repeat what the court said in analyzing the facts: what does it mean to you? Summarize the court's rationale in your own words. If you encounter a word that you do not know, use a dictionary to find its meaning.

Conclusion

What was the final outcome of the case? In one or two sentences, state what should be the court's ultimate finding and why. Note: "Case briefing" is a skill that you will develop. Practice will help you develop this skill.

MOTIONS

Simply put a "Motion" is a request submitted to the court moving them to perform a favorable action on your part. A motion can be for a court order, the return of property, an extension in time to file a pleading, change of address, or one of a numberless housekeeping items the courts are continually dealing with. If you get caught up in litigation this legal vehicle will surely become familiar to you; and quickly. Never hesitate to formulate a motion. State what you want, what the law is and make sure the court can grant it. You should also check to see if there is a local court rule governing motions. If there is have the clerk of court send you a copy of the rules for future reference. As with every court in this country you must send a copy of the motion to all parties of the litigation. Don't forget to add a Certificate of Service and have it notarized if required by the court.

A motion is actually a miniature lawsuit in that it uses the same format: a header, style, case number, a title plainly stating what the motion is about, an argument, closing and certificate of mailing. The only difference is that it is usually a few pages in length versus scores of pages for a suit. If the other side files a motion, or response to one of your motions, you have the option of filing and in another motion in opposition to their motion. Basically, you are legally arguing with the opposing party which, can, at times, turn into a literal volley of motions. The same rules apply to motions as to all other legal pleadings; keep it to the short, to the point and address only the issues raised.

HABEAS CORPUS

You file a writ of habeas corpus to either obtain immediate relief from confinement or speedily resolve issues concerning the length of a sentence. It is the one writ which really 'works.' By that we mean the court will usually render a decision in a matter of days or weeks versus months and years for other litigation.

If you're fighting your conviction, confinement, length of sentence, the sentence itself, attempting to shorten your sentence, contesting a good time loss, addressing your parole eligibility date, or seeking release you are REQUIRED to utilize this writ. If you're a state prisoner there are a couple cadets; you must first

exhaust your state remedies and, when you file your writ with the federal courts, there must be a federal question involved. Filing a writ of habeas corpus is governed under 28 U.S.C. §2241 et seq. with state prisoners specifically coming under 28 U.S.C. §2254. Treatment by state prison officials and challenges to their conditions of confinement should be brought under § 1983 and not via a writ of habeas corpus.

It has long been written in concrete that a federal court action cannot be used as a substitute for a state court appeal. Federal court have long been suspicious of prisoners filing habeas actions which are based on facts from their state conviction because they have this thought running around in the back of their minds that state prisoners are attempting to use a federal vehicle to bypass normal state appeal procedures. Attempt this avenue of relief without first exhausting your state remedies and you will find out exactly how hard that federal 'concrete' really is. Exhaust your state remedies first then have a go at it if you must.

If you're a federal prisoner you will also have to exhaust your administrative remedies before proceeding into court. If you think your federal conviction was in violation of the statutes, unlawfully obtained, or imposed in an unlawful manner you must first appeal and raise all the issues you feel relief can be granted on. Not only is a direct appeal your best shot at obtaining relief, but with the conservative trend of all the courts, it is becoming increasingly difficult to obtain post-conviction thru the habeas corpus vehicle. If you elect to proceed with a writ of habeas corpus after appeal you will be restricted to issues of jurisdiction or errors of a fundamental nature which were almost surely raised and addressed by the appellate court. The 'bright spot' here, if there is one, is if your challenging the way your sentence is being carried, sentence computation, parole procedures, or the loss of good time thru disciplinary actions you've got a good chance of securing relief via a writ of habeas corpus. Remember that a writ of habeas corpus must be filed in the district where the prisoner is currently being held. There is also a provision under the Bureau of Prisons Program Statements (5100.1) which prohibits the moving of an inmate from the institution till the habeas issue has been resolved, but that rule only exists if the prison staff are made aware that you have filed a habeas action. This is usually accomplished via the United States Marshals within 7 days as that is how long it takes to serve a summons on the warden. If you're not

happy with this set up you can send the warden a certified letter notifying him that you have filed a habeas corpus action and would invoke the provisions of Program Statement 5100.1.

There is another advantage of a habeas action and that is the courts cast a somewhat more lenient eye on habeas actions which is accompanied by a matching liberal authority to appoint counsel. If you're a prisoner filing a civil suit you will be extremely lucky to secure an attorney, try this with a habeas action of a meritorious nature and the odds are almost exactly opposite in your favor.

JUDGMENTS & ORDERS

Something that may seem a little strange is the court rarely writes their own judgements and orders. That is usually done by the prevailing attorney on the issue. When you type or write out a proposed judgment or order that is exactly what it is "PROPOSED" until it is signed:

PROPOSED
A judgment or order does not take on any official meaning until someone with the proper authority puts their "John Hancock" on it. If the order is of a minor, very minor, nature it is possible that a clerk of court will sign it, but, this is the exception not the rule. Anytime you file a legal pleading with the court asking for relief you may submit an order with it which rewards you with the relief you seek. When an order is issued, either orally or in writing, you can bet it will require someone, somewhere to do something or authorize someone, somewhere to do something.

Judgments are a specialized type of order in that they put forth in writing the final resolution of the case as determined by the court. When you have the opportunity to write your own order, do so, as that is the only way you can be sure of the proper relief being granted. Some judges will not sign judgments for any number of reasons but this should not stop you from placing it on his desk for finalization whether he signs it or not as that way he will know what relief your seeking and (hopefully) have a format to go by. Both judgments and orders follow the normal formatting of legal forms as outlined previously in this Of course with

the sole exception being that when you commence writing the section which contains the relief you seek you must start the first paragraph with "IT IS ORDERED then follow up further paragraphs with "IT IS FURTHER ORDERED In addition to leaving a spot for the judges signature also leave one for the clerk of court to affirm the judges signature.

AFFIDAVITS

The person making the statement or affidavit is technically known as the affiant or deponent. If you give an affidavit to anyone for anything you should be aware of a few facts i.e. 1) you should only make statements which you can swear to in a court of law or have personally observed; 2) if you did not personally observe it you can still place this into the affidavit but add that it is on your "information and belief;" and 3) making false statements will subject you to criminal prosecution for false swearing, perjury, fraud and possible contempt of court. If you're going to use affidavits to prove some critical point in your suit get as many individuals as possible to give you an affidavit. Where the court might give only passing credence to one or two affidavits they will stand up and pay attention if buried with 10 or 20. Make your point with all the legal force possible.

Chapter 7 Appeal / Retrial

The appeal process is pretty much a waiting game on your part. Hopefully you've completed your transcript analysis before your appellate attorney has filed his brief. If such is the case then you're in a good position to be in. I wasn't that fortunate and my attorney's brief was submitted long before my transcript analysis was completed. Consequently there were quite a few arguments that could have been included that got missed, but it didn't matter because I had most of the good arguments in my head when my attorney called on the first day to ask me what I thought my issues were. If I hadn't had that much together in my mind when he called I would have been in a far worse situation than I was. This is what I think happens to a lot of people when they reach this point. They don't know how to think like an attorney and as a result they are unable to recognize a valid argument to use on appeal. All they know is that they're angry and because of that anger they are inclined to use those events that angered them most. Unfortunately the events in trial that angered them most aren't always the ones that make the best arguments on appeal. This is where I think a lot of people go wrong in the appeal process, especially those individuals who decide to file their appeal on their own. This is also why it is best to have a jailhouse attorney review your transcripts. Having your case examined by someone who isn't so personally involved, who has some knowledge of the law, will allow you to see where your most valid claims for appeal are. I personally took advantage of this and recommend it highly.

After you win on appeal, things become very confused. Inmates will be coming at you out of the woodwork that you have never knew before, all wanting to give you their advice. 99.9 percent of it will be crap. One of the biggest areas of confusion concerns the retrial itself. There are those who will tell you that you can't be retried after a reversal with a remand for new trial. There are those who will tell you that you can't be retried after a reversal with a remand for new trial without new evidence. Both of these positions are 100 percent wrong. The reason why this confusion exists is because so many people never get to this position. Consequently there's nobody who has any direct and accurate knowledge about it. The truth is that when you file your rule 31 direct appeal you are in effect waving your double jeopardy rights. You are in effect saying, ", If the Court of Appeals will review my case and if they find cause to grant a retrial I give up my

constitutional right to not be tried a second time." That's how things really work. This is why after appeal with a reversal and remand for new trial the only way to stop the second trial is through a claim of prosecutorial misconduct and in order to make that work you must have objected to the actions of the prosecutor in the first trial.

Proving prosecutorial misconduct is a very difficult situation. There are some interesting technicalities that are not readily known in regard to prosecutorial misconduct. For example, if the prosecutor commits an action that could be construed as prosecutorial misconduct, if your attorney fails to object to the prosecutor's actions, there is no foul. Your attorney has in effect given license to the prosecutor's actions. In addition to this, if the judge takes no action against the prosecutor by telling him to stop doing what he's doing, there is no foul. If both your attorney in the judge fails to object to the prosecutor's actions then you have no legal recourse at a later date. You are just screwed. Even if the prosecutor were to violate a statute in your trial, as long as the judge and your attorney remain silent about it, there's nothing you can do about it at a later date. You even lose your ability to use it as an argument on appeal. Now to those who have an inner sensibility of fairness this is going to seem outrageous. However the truth is, this is the way the game is played and these are the rules that decide the fate of men's lives in this country. If this isn't right, then only WE can do something about it and we have a moral responsibility to our fellow men to change it.

Chapter 8 Parole / Probation

Parole and probation are really quite similar, as far as the restrictions placed upon you are concerned. Parole is a term of monitoring attached to your release from prison and probation is a term of monitoring attached to your sentence.

When people take a plea bargain, in almost every case, lifetime probation is part of the deal. People have no clue what the impact of lifetime probation is actually going to be on their lives. Do you own a house and plan to live in it when you are released? Is it within 1000 feet of a school? If it is you can forget about living there forever. There are a few trials that set up grandfathering for properties if you owned the house before being convicted, but you will have to fight in court to take advantage of it. You might as well sell the house for all the good it's going to do for you. Do you like using computers, digital cameras, regular cameras and Polaroid cameras? You'll never see one again until you get off probation, or for the rest of your life, depending on your circumstances. Even if computers and cameras are not a factor in your crime. Do you like beer? Forget it; you'll be drug tested for everything once a month and sometimes more. Do you like Playboy magazine? Forget it; you can't even have a swimsuit calendar in your garage. It is believed by therapists and probation officers alike that these things sexually objectify women, which encourages deviant behavior. Forget the fact that the human form is considered beautiful by most normal human beings. Forget the great art of history because any depiction of the naked female form is considered deviant or encouraging deviancy. These are just the biggies and it gets far worse than this. On parole there is a specific area set by artificial lines on a map you are not supposed to cross, even if you're unconscious and being taken to the hospital in an ambulance to a hospital across county lines because it's better equipped to treat your injuries. There are no extenuating circumstances. It's just too damn bad you didn't die in prison. That's the way the state looks at. People don't think of these things and that's how they get sent back to prison with additional charges. Every one of these incidents I've seen with my own eyes.

A recent development in Arizona law is a change that prevents people from rejecting probation and going back to prison to kill their number. Here's how it works. Suppose for whatever reason you just can't put up with the bullshit of

lifetime probation. It used to be that you could go back to court and receive a fixed prison sentence and return to finish the time the state says you have to do instead of lifetime probation. This would then kill your prison ID. number and upon release you would then have no further obligation to the state. Now you can't do that. What happens now if you reject probation and return to prison is that you will not receive a fixed sentence instead of lifetime probation and all you have done is bought yourself more prison time, because upon release you will be staring at the same lifetime probation you had when you walked in.

One of the things that really boils my blood are these talking heads on television who tell their viewers that the recidivism rate for sex offenders is astronomical, yet they offer no proof of their claims. The recidivism rate for S.O.'s is around 5.3%, far lower than any form of crime. Here is the proof and it comes from the National Criminal Justice Reference Service operated by the U.S. Department of Justice Bureau of Justice Statistics. This report presents, for the first time, data on the re-arrest, reconviction, and re-imprisonment of 9,691 male sex offenders, including 4,295 child molesters, who were tracked for 3 years after their release from prisons in 15 States in 1994.

The 9,691 are two-thirds of all the male sex offenders released from prisons in the United States in 1994. The study represents the largest follow-up ever conducted of convicted sex offenders following discharge from prison and provides the most comprehensive assessment of their behavior after release. Highlights include the following: Within 3 years following their release, 5.3 percent of sex offenders (men who had committed rape or sexual assault) were rearrested for another sex crime; on average the 9,691 sex offenders served 3 1/2 years of their 8-year sentence; compared to non-sex offenders released from State prisons, released sex offenders were four times more likely to be rearrested for a sex crime; the 9,691 released sex offenders included 4,295 men who were in prison for child molesting. "Recidivism of Sex Offenders Released From Prison in 1994 by Patrick A. Langan Ph.D.; Erica L. Schmitt; Mathew R. Durose, November 2003." (http://www.ncjrs.gov/App/publications/abstract.aspx?ID=198281) Retrieved 04/17/2011 So there you go. Now compare the above with these recidivism statistics for other crimes, again from the U.S. Bureau of Justice Statistics:

•Of the 272,111 persons released from prisons in 15 States in 1994, an estimated 67.5% were rearrested for a felony or serious misdemeanor within 3 years, 46.9% were reconvicted, and 25.4% re-sentenced to prison for a new crime.

•The 272,111 offenders discharged in 1994 accounted for nearly 4,877,000 arrest charges over their recorded careers.

•Within 3 years of release, 2.5% of released rapists were rearrested for another rape, and 1.2% of those who had served time for homicide were arrested for a new homicide.

•Sex offenders were less likely than non-sex offenders to be rearrested for any offense - 43 percent of sex offenders versus 68 percent for non-sex offenders.

Tell me people, do the statistics justify the paranoia?

One other favorite tactic probation officers use is the five-year plan. You get out and are as good as can be. You organize your life till it's a well-oiled machine. You're always early for everything. You're a model of perfection for five straight years. Then your probation officer searches your house and violates you for the most minute infraction. They recommend your full or remaining sentence be imposed, claiming you are incorrigible and a threat to the public and after five long years of exemplary behavior you are sent to prison and that plea bargain becomes piece of paper that only got you five years of freedom and what you hoped to avoid by taking a plea bargain in the first place has now come to pass. That's why if you do accept a plea agreement it should be a "BINDING PLEA AGREEMENT" which can't be revoked for any reason except a re-offense and new charges. But people don't know such a thing exists and never ask for it. We're not talking about small time sentences here. We're talking about long time sentences and long time periods of probation and how they use the two of them to suck the last ounce of life out of you. Although it is completely illegal, I know of people who are incarcerated and as a result of probation violations coupled with their original sentence, have actually spent more time in prison as a result of taking a plea bargain and they would have, had they simply gone to trial. This is the major

reason not to take a plea bargain. It only delays the inevitable and if that's what's going to happen to you anyway, you might as well fight because you've got nothing to lose and everything to gain. The five-year plan has become so successful at filling the prisons there is actually a bill to eliminate this power from probation officers unless there was a commission of a new crime.

When I first arrived on probation I told my probation officer in my surveillance officer embedded to expect probation to last much longer than five years. They asked me why and I told them that every person that I had interviewed who told me they were there for a probation revocation had only lasted five years under probation. There were one or two people that I ran into where the revocation occurred at four years, or six years, but they were few in number. My probation officers assured me that this was not the case. However at five years and several months I have had all of probation that I was going to take. There were increasing restrictions that essentially turned regular probation into intensive probation. Such as producing a weekly movement schedule and reporting every instance during the course of a month where my eyes beheld the presence of a child, including places, dates and times. That was what they considered to be human contact. I realized at the time that what they were doing was tightening a noose around my neck and the next thing I would feel would be a firm jerk. I realized I was going to be taken down anyway regardless of what I did and that this whole thing was a Trick Bag.

So I rejected probation went back to prison for 2 1/2 years and when I did I contracted scabies three times. At the time for back pain I was prescribed gabapentin and naproxin, both drugs hit your kidneys pretty hard. One day I get called into the health unit to be read results of a urine test where I was told that I was +3 for protein and +2 for occult blood. In brief my kidneys were damaged. Also the presence of white blood cells was indicated which meant that I had an infection and it also meant that the damage to my kidneys was more severe than suspected because white blood cells are larger than red blood cells and should not be passing with my urine. Later I did an Internet search and discovered there is a causal link between scabies infestations and kidney disease. Today I'm +5 for protein and +4 for occult blood in my urine and my glumerol filtration rate is 31%. Obviously something serious happened to my health in prison. Lab tests don't lie.

People used to tell me that parole was easier than probation. I did not find this to be true. I was immediately told that I could not take a job without their permission and that I couldn't cross county lines. I never intended to succeed at parole. I considered it just as intrusive as probation and that is in fact how it turned out to be. My objective was to get this over with as quickly as possible. Had I decided to remain in prison it would've added another seven months to my sentence, extending my release date by a total of 14 months. My intention was a quick hop out followed by a quick hop back in for seven months. So I really didn't care what happened. But I certainly wasn't going to pass up any opportunities that came my way and if I could turn it into an act of defiance then so much the better.

One Monday morning I received a phone call from a helicopter training company. Before I had returned to prison it was my hope that I might be able to get some helicopter training in exchange for doing maintenance on their aircraft. I am an airframe and powerplant mechanic with 18 years working on large jets for the airlines. They were calling to see if I would be interested in an interview. I was quite surprised that this little company had kept my resume for 2 1/2 years till a position had opened up. Thinking that I might have an opportunity to learn to fly a helicopter I immediately drove to the airport. A job offer was made which I took and was scheduled to work the following Wednesday. On my way out the door to go home from the interview I contacted my parole officer informed him that I had a job offer working on helicopters. I gave him the name of the company and its phone number and told him that I was waiting for his approval which I did not expect would take longer than a day. It turns out that Wednesday was too soon for him.

While I was working that Wednesday we were informed that a GPS had been picked up at the airport in Eloi Arizona. My supervisor asked me if I wanted to ride along and I told him that I would. What he didn't know was that I had a GPS device strapped to my ankle at the time. He told me that he would give me an hour of helicopter instruction time on my logbook while we went to get the GPS. So I flew the helicopter from Falcon Field in Mesa to Eloi and crossed a county line in the process. We landed on the ramp, picked up the GPS and got back into the helicopter to fly away. We only spent about 30 minutes on the ground before flying back to Falcon Field. When I arrived at the hangar my phone was ringing

and I was told that I didn't have permission to work in that I had just crossed the county line and had to report to my parole officer's boss at 9 AM in the morning.

It doesn't take much brain power knowing the circumstances to imagine what was said in that office that morning. When they proceeded to lecture me about crossing county lines I took tremendous delight in saying, "Well I flew the helicopter!" When I said that my parole officer's boss's head spun around like Linda Blair in the Exorcist. I think he'll be able to complete his entire career without ever hearing that again. Then he proceeded to lecture me about how I was found guilty of 15 counts of sexual exploitation of a minor. At which point I shouted at him, "NO! I WASN'T!" Then he told me that he was tired of my attitude, at which point I told him, "I'm sick to death of you being so misinformed." That I had only been found guilty of one count. It was then that he told me that he didn't believe that I ever intended to abide by the conditions of parole and snapped his fingers. To which a man and a turtle suit appeared and placed me in handcuffs and I was carted off to Alhambra after only 16 days on parole.

There are two types of probation. Regular probation and intensive probation or (IPS). On regular probation you do your drug testing, community service, and see your probation officer once a month. On IPS you have to submit a movement schedule. Any deviation from that schedule must be reported. A deviation can be anything more than one minute. I know of a man who had his IPS revoked for being five minutes late for putting gas in his truck. People on IPS also have to submit to more home inspections. Home invasions is a more accurate word. On IPS it can be once a month, on regular probation it could be every couple months. On all probations a surveillance officer will be following your every move and will stop you from time to time to give you a breathalyzer to make sure you're not drinking.

Probation officers for sex offenders will enter your place of employment notify your employer and fellow employees that you are a sex offender, just to make sure they know in the event you didn't tell them. They will appear at your job just to create a general nuisance of themselves, hoping to get you fired. If you get a girlfriend they will demand her name and phone number, so they can call her and tell her you are as sex offender. Go to church? They'll call them too. I'm not

making this stuff up. Every probationer I've met had one or more of these things happen to them and were sent back to prison, where I met them and heard their story. There is a group of sex offenders in California who were forced into homelessness and destitution as a result of the conditions they were forced to deal with outside prison. They united together to file a class action lawsuit against the state of California because of it.

Being a sex offender is a lot like taking a long journey in a strange land that you used to call home. The strange land is the country you grew up in but never really knew anything about. Once you are branded a sex offender, the America you used to know ceases to exist. You are given the option of certain roads to travel and that's all you've got. You can fight your case or take a plea. If you fight your case and lose you pretty well know what that road ahead is going to be like, but even that road has some surprises and most of them are unpleasant. Take a plea, and you start down a road you know nothing about because nobody will tell you in advance and you've never been there before. That's why this chapter was written.

So is there something you can do about it? Every sex offender gets lifetime probation, so sooner or later every sex offender experiences life on probation. Recently in the courts lifetime probation has been attacked successfully as cruel and unusual punishment. The basis of this argument is that even murderers don't get lifetime probation and that it is in effect double punishment. It is important to remember that although sex has been going on as long as humans have been in existence, the current methods of the application of these laws has only been around a short while. Consequently it takes some time to amend the application of the law to something a little more just. We are in exactly this adjustment period. What you need to know is that after two to three years on probation with no violations you can request a downgrade in your probation status or your removal from probation altogether. The only problem with this is that it takes a lawyer to do it and they don't work for free. Consequently many sex offenders don't do this and wind up back in prison. This is another reason why you need to study the law because there is nothing to stop you from doing this yourself. The other problem is that most people assume lifetime probation is for life and never learn it can be fought in court so they never try.

I know this guy that is physically handicapped with Limb-Girdle Muscular Dystrophy (LGMD), and is 56 years old, and confined to a wheelchair. He faces the problem on probation that most S.O.'s don't, and that is, he basically has three handicaps; (1) first, is of course the physical handicap, which makes it hard to find an apartment due to the fact that he has to function in it and most apartments that are in his price range are not wheelchair friendly, (2) second is, that he has the financial handicap of only getting $637.00 a month on SSI, which severely limits the type of apartment that he can afford, and (3) is of course the 'SOCIAL HANDICAP' of being an S.O. and barred from 90% (or more) of the possible apartment complexes to rent from, because the cities here in Arizona have made apartment complexes 'CRIME FREE ZONES' meaning that they are not allowed to rent to anyone with a felony, especially an S.O. felon. He has been living in a homeless shelter for the past 6 months due to the fact that he could find no place to live, and finally he found a place to live which is a very small studio apartment and his rent is $475.00 a month that does include utilities. That only leaves $162.00 dollars to buy things that he needs to survive. Could you live on this under this condition?

The probation officers don't care, and don't even try to help him in his plight, simply because they would rather put him back in prison to help the state obtain more federal funds for their prison and injustice system budgets. It makes no difference that he already spent nearly 15 years in prison, they'd just as soon as send him back for another 7 years, which would end his sentence entirely (killing your number). Of the two, probation is far harder to complete than parole, because you have two different types of criteria to meet and different types of thinking between the prison arm and the court's arm.

To make things worse for this guy, he was innocent and has spent nearly every waking hour while incarcerated studying the law and the facts of his case applying what he learned. He is very well versed in the law and writes pleadings as good as or even better than some lawyers, but because he represents himself, it is nearly impossible for him to get any play from the courts. One reason could be, that he writes very blunt pleadings calling the judge[s] criminals of the master kind and clearly demonstrating how they blatantly violate their own 'public records' law (i.e., here in Arizona is A.R.S. § 13-2407) and also the state employee's statute on

'making and giving a false certificate' (i.e., A.R.S. § 38-423). He rubs their nose in it knowing full well that no prosecuting attorney will ever file criminal charges against their fellow brother[s]-of-the-bar, especially judges whom they have to go in front of every day. He merely does it to make a record for future events. Every lawyer (both defense and prosecutor), as well as judges make false statements in [ALL] pleadings and court orders, and of course, these pleadings and orders are public records. However, they will never be prosecuted because they won't prosecute their own. I'm encouraging my friend to write a detailed book on this subject and he will if he can stay out of the clutches of the state long enough to do so. He filed a criminal complaint with the courts and prosecutor's office against 36 lawyers and judges, but they would not prosecute. They did not say that he was incorrect in his accusations against these lawyers and judges, merely that he could not be the one to file a criminal complaint. My friend Robert Hoke who is the subject of this story committed suicide when probation tried to send me back to prison for probation revocation proceedings and I miss him very much. You see, only a person who has been through this understands what you have endured at the hands of the government.

Anyway, back to probation and parole. If at all possible, if you take a plea bargain (a horrible term, because there is usually no bargain in it, it is just one sided to benefit the prosecution), try very hard to not take any probation in the deal, if necessary, take a longer time in prison rather than probation, as probation of any kind is just a trick bag to get you back in prison.

So now you know what you are really fighting for. You are fighting to get your life back and get Uncle Sam out of your business, by proving your innocence in court, or even if your guilty, to fight them when they lack the evidence to convict you. Don't be a sap and roll over for them! If you don't think that's worth fighting for then enjoy your LONG stay in prison, because my friend, that's all you've got left. Is it even possible to win? Oh yes! It most assuredly is possible, but as anyone who's done it will tell you, it's not easy.

Chapter 9 Registration

Registration for sex offenders is unique. No other crime compels you to register yourself with the police. Local regulations vary from state to state so with business or personal travel you can find yourself in trouble without knowing it. The general rule of thumb is that if you spend more than 72 hours in a place outside your registered area, you must register with the police. If you change your residence, even if it is across the street, or to another apartment in the same complex, you must notify your probation officer and register within 72 hours. If you move on a Friday morning and wait until Monday morning you'll have violated the terms of your release. The fact that the police station was closed on the weekend will make no difference. I've seen this happen.

When you register, it is the same process as being booked into the jail. You are photographed and fingerprinted and your new address is recorded. You don't just walk in and say, "Hey man I've moved." and they type in your new address and off you go. Now prison has been extended to the outside world. For you the whole world is a prison and there is no escape. The fact that so many endure all this without going insane boggles my mind. Probation violations and registration violations will get you put back into prison quickly. Probation can be eliminated after a few years. Registration cannot.

When you're first brought into prison your crime is classified as a level one, two or three sex offender. The various levels determine the conditions of your release. This varies from state to state and changes every year, which itself makes compliance difficult, because they aren't going to inform you of the changes. They'll just wait to violate you and send you back to prison. These rules change so much, so often, even though I would like to talk about them there is little I can say today without being wrong tomorrow. Changes occur in regard to GPS monitoring (ankle bracelet), the jobs you can have, where you can live etc. That's about all I can say without venturing off into shifting sands. For example one year ago, level one sex offenders weren't required to submit to GPS monitoring. Now all sex offenders do. Given time it will change again with popular opinion, which is really what this is all about. This isn't about safety or control, this punishment by popular opinion and the proof is in the fact that the law changes so frequently and in

accordance with popular opinion as opposed to any scientific study or rational basis.

In regard to registration if you're a level two or three sex offender fliers are mailed to your neighbors, which guarantees you'll be moving soon at the least, or windup dead on your front lawn as a result of someone's retaliation and hatred. There is a 23-year-old man who frequently comes into the Pima county jail, because he has been severely beaten, sometimes almost to the point of death by his friendly neighbors. This situation is rapidly escalating to the point that there is pressure to change the registration policies, because so many S.O.'s are being killed because of the notification sent to neighbors. No other form of crime requires lifetime probation and lifetime registration or registration in any shape or form. The fact that the public is so paranoid about living next to a sex offender is very hard for me to understand because it's so illogical. The public would rather have stringent controls placed on sex offenders, but not on people that might kill them. The housing restrictions that are applied to sex offenders indicate the public would rather live next to someone who might kill them, than someone who might have sex with them. This position doesn't seem to make a lot of sense to me because you can always come back from rape, but you can't come back from dead!

Here is a list of requirements for a sex offender registrant. These statutes do not provide for termination of the registration requirement, except for registrants who committed offenses as juveniles. See A.R.S. § 13-3821(F) - (H). 7 Thus, once imposed, sex offender registration is a lifelong obligation. See Fisher v. Kaufman, 201 Ariz. 500, 502 P 8, 38 P.3d 38, 40 (App. 2001); State v. Lammie, 164 Ariz. 377, 382-83, 793 P.2d 134, 139-40 (App. 1990). The duration of the registration requirement makes this statutory consequence much more severe than a comparatively short probation period. See United States v. Nachtigal, 507 U.S. 1, 5, 113 S. Ct. 1072, 122 L. Ed. 2d 374 (1993) (holding that the Sixth Amendment does not require a jury trial when the potential penalty is five years of [***15] probation).

At the time of registration, the offender must provide, in addition to any other information required by the director of the Department of Public Safety, all

names by which he is known, his mailing address, his physical residence, fingerprints, photograph, any "required online identifiers,"

For the rest of his life, a sex offender must notify law enforcement within seventy-two hours of any move or change of name. Id. § 13-3822(A)-(B). A move requires notification to sheriffs in both the original county and the destination county; each must be informed in writing, and the latter must also be informed in person. Id. An offender who studies or works at an institution of postsecondary education must initially notify the county sheriff of that jurisdiction and keep him informed of any changes in enrollment or employment status. Id. § 13-3821(N). A transient offender must register with the local sheriff every ninety days. Id. § 13-3822(A). If an offender changes a required online identifier, he must notify the sheriff within seventy-two hours and before using the identifier. Id. § 13-3822(C). An offender who fails to register is guilty of a class 6 felony, and a registrant who does not keep his information updated is guilty of a class 4 felony. Id. § 13-3824. [***17] Those offenses carry, respectively, one-year and two-and-one-half-year presumptive prison sentences for first-time offenders. Id. § 13-701(C) (2001).

Widespread publicity accompanies sex offender registration. For a level two or three offender, the offender's name, address, age, current photograph, conviction, and risk [**543] [*292] assessment level appear on the sex offender website. Id. § 13-3827(A)-(B). Id. § 13-3826(E)(1)(a). For level one offenders, law enforcement may notify the people with whom the offender resides. Id. § 13-3826(E)(1)(b). For offenders who are students [***18] or employees of postsecondary education institutions, law enforcement must notify the administration of the institution and, in some instances, the campus community. Id. § 13-3825(G). The Department of Public Safety may also communicate with businesses and organizations that offer electronic communication services about whether an offender's online identifier is being used on their systems. Id. § 13-3827(E). The statutory requirements of warnings to various communities about the identities and presence of sex offenders confirm that the legislature views sex offenses as serious crimes. Cf. Noble, 171 Ariz. at 177, 829 P.2d at 1223 (noting potential stigmatic effect of widespread access to sex offender registration information).

Technically registration is unconstitutional. Article 2 § 13 of the AZ. Constitution states, "No law shall be enacted granting to any citizen, class of citizens, or corporation other than municipal, privileges or immunities which, upon the same terms, shall not equally belong to all citizens or corporations." This idea was the premise for the elimination of the Jim Crow laws of the south and the Civil Rights movement of the 60's. All citizens (convicted or otherwise) are entitled to equal protection under the law which means that the government cannot use the law to create a class of people such as negro's or SO's. As lawyers say, "The law is not a respecter of person's." Which means it doesn't matter if you are the President of the United States or an SO they are both equal in the eyes of the law. The are some Constitutional Rights you lose as a convict and some you never do and equal protection under the law is not one of them. If government wants to register SO's they can't use the law to create a class of people and force restrictions on their liberty unless they force all convicts to register without regard to the offense. Most state constitutions have similar statements. The problem is that no one with the resources has stepped up to the plate to challenge these laws. This is partly due to the fact that they are so new. I bring this up with the hope that someone challenges the constitutionality of these laws soon. The reason why is that creating a class of people, no matter who they are, or what they've done, is no different than forcing people to wear yellow arm bands, with the word JUDEN on them. Lifetime probation and registration makes American government no different than Nazi Germany and here's the proof:

"Those who would sacrifice their liberty for a little temporary security deserve neither liberty or security."
(Benjamin Franklin)

"You need only reflect that one of the best ways to get yourself a reputation as a dangerous citizen these days is to go about repeating the very phrases which our founding fathers used in the struggle for independence."
(Charles Austin Beard)

That last one is a clear indicator that as a nation we have lost the values we used to treasure and lost our liberty because of it! I hope what I just wrote offends the hell out of people. It's about time this offended the hell out of somebody!

Another trick the state does in regard to registration is arrest people on registration sweeps for violation of registration policies when those policies didn't exist at the time their crimes were committed and they were therefore not required to register. That didn't stop the state from throwing a man I knew in prison. It took him two a half years to fight his way out.

Chapter 10 S. O. T. P.

S. O. T. P. stands for sex offender treatment program. Most people are required to attend one by court order, either through a plea agreement or terms of release. You are required to pay for this abuse from your own money, which is a nice way of insuring that you get a job. Fall behind in your payments and you will be violated and sent back to prison. The term violated his starting to take on a new meaning at this point. Isn't it?

If you are unfortunate enough to be required to attend an S. O. T. P. program do a good background check of the instructor's credentials. In one case regarding an S.O.T.P. instructor out of Tucson, a check of the instructor's educational and training credentials revealed his background had been falsified. If you find something like this, turn them in to the court and the press and stop attending.

S. O. T. P is currently being attacked in the courts. The instructor is required by law to report everything he or she hears to the courts. Which then makes the participant in the program a witness against himself which is a violation of your Fifth Amendment rights. (See S. O. T. P. case law).

In prison inmates may be required to take an S. O. T. P. class. However in most cases it will not apply to any S.O.T.P. requirements outside of prison so why take it? Originally these programs were taught by trained professionals, then they were attacked because the instructors were informing the courts about their students and reporting their findings back to the courts. Now these programs are run by inmates who follow guidelines for the program on their own. If you're placed in one of these programs be very careful what you say. Tell them only what they want to hear if they are operated by a professional. If your right to appeal remains in effect, you have no business participating in one of these programs and should refuse to attend.

The use of lie detectors is widely accepted and used sometimes as evidence against you even though polygraph evidence is inadmissible in a court of law. It may be inadmissible in trial, but a different set of rules exists at hearings for probation and it will be allowed.

The use of a plethysmograph (erection detector) is waning although you can still run into their use once awhile. The use of this machine and the results it produces has been heavily attacked in the courts as being invalid. Check case law if you wind up with your member in a wringer. Makes me wonder why there isn't a moisture detector for female sex offenders. The male bias is profoundly evident here.

The following is a list of items you will be required to provide the therapist in a sex offender treatment program after you have served your sentence. You will instantly recognize how intrusive this program is by the information you are required to provide them. Please note that failure to tell them what they want to hear becomes an issue of noncompliance they can bring before the court to send you back to prison. **The statement that this information cannot be used against you in a court of law is a lie!** A.R.S. 13-4066(a) specifically states that information permissible under A.R.E. 404(b and c) can be used against you in a court of law and we all know that unless the door to such evidence is completely prohibited this exception will be abused by the state. The interesting thing to note here is that rule 404 is what governs the admissibility of all evidence in Arizona courts. A.R.S. 13-4066(a) was created to provide the illusion that you are protected when in fact you are not. In addition there is nothing to protect you from information you reveal in S.O.T.P. being used to bring out of state charges, or federal charges against you at a later time. The following was obtained from an actual S.O.T.P. program.

Information You Should Know About Your Upcoming
Sexual History Polygraph Examination

Although denial and secrecy obviously served you at one point, no form of secrecy is tolerated in treatment. Despite how it may feel, disclosure results in treatment progress, acceptance by the group and therapist, reduced pressure from probation/parole staff, and personal relief to have purged yourself of the secrets.

By the time you take the sexual history polygraph examination, you already have been given every reasonable opportunity to disclose all the relevant matters in treatment. The examination may take 2-3 hours or more. During the pretest

interview, you will have another opportunity to disclosure any information that has not been disclosed in treatment. You and the examiner will create examination questions together and discuss the ability to pass these questions truthfully before you are tested. Your honesty and diligence are mandatory for your success. The examination questions will be repeated several times during the test If your results show deception, the examiner may confront you with the problem and you will be given the opportunity to further disclose any information which may relate to your failure on any given question. Your probation officer and therapist are subsequently advised of the test results via the telephone and/or in writing. The written report will include the relevant test questions, all information disclosed during the examination and the polygraph examiner's conclusions regarding your truthfulness or deception.

Test results showing deception will be presented to the group by the therapist and you will be confronted in group. Probation staff will also address the issues with you, and confer with the therapist and examiner about the results. If you disclose further information, a follow-up polygraph examination may be conducted to determine if you are now telling the truth to the issues in question. If you show deception on an examination, you will be asked to retake that exam at the discretion of probation and treatment personnel. Decisions to expel you from treatment due to polygraph results are made by the therapist in consultation with probation staff. Failure to successfully complete a polygraph examination is not an option. However, providing information that you believe could potentially carry ramifications is often necessary to successfully complete a polygraph examination. These admissions are not to be used in a court of law against you in any way, but are utilized for ongoing meaningful and effective treatment. However, failure to successfully complete a polygraph examination will be deemed non-compliance at the discretion of treatment and probation staff and could result in severe consequences including incarceration.

Probation is a privilege and not a right, therefore, the trial court's discretion is broad in establishing the conditions of probation. The courts do not view the polygraph as a violation of personal rights, but as an agreement by you in accepting probation in lieu of a penitentiary sentence. Because you have accepted this condition as part of your probation, a refusal to be polygraphed or "taking the

fifth" is seen as non-compliance and consideration is given to returning the offender to the sentencing court.

After you have completed the sexual history disclosure packet and all victim forms, you will be required to pass the sexual history polygraph, indicating you have fully disclosed all sexual information and have not purposely withheld anything. Complete honesty is crucial to successfully complete your treatment. The polygraph examination will be taken at the discretion of probation and treatment staff. Your therapist will provide you with the sexual history disclosure packet. It is required that you bring the completed sexual history disclosure packet with you at the time of your polygraph examination.

If you are currently experiencing serious health issues and/or under the direct care of a physician, please inform your polygraph examiner at the time you schedule your appointment. Also, if you are taking prescription medications please bring a list of those medications to your scheduled appointment.

It is your responsibility to pay for your examination unless you quality for funding. It is suggested that you set aside money from the beginning of your treatment if necessary to pay for your polygraph examination. Please contact your probation officer for any questions regarding your eligibility for funding. If you have any questions regarding your polygraph examination, you are allowed to contact the assigned polygraph examiner regarding those questions.

Remember: "The truth may not lead you to where you thought you were going, but, it will always lead you somewhere better."

FULL DISCLOSURE SEXUAL HISTORY Packet – Instructions

1. Complete pages 4 through 19 first. DO NOT attempt to complete page 3 (Table of Contents/Summary Information),until after completing pages 4 through 19.

- Sign and date all pages when they are completed.
- Do not leave any pages blank.

- For any behaviors that do not apply, you must clearly indicate that in writing, on the page.
- You may list approximate ages if exact ages are not known (do not leave any ages blank).
- List all sexual contacts/behaviors up to and including the date you are completing the form.
- Attempt to list sexual contacts/behaviors in chronological order.

2. Complete one Sexual Contact/Victim Form (Attachment) for each identified person in pages 4 through 19.

- Make additional copies of individual pages or the Sexual Contact/Victim Form (Attachment) as necessary.

Do not leave any item blank. Answer YES or NO to every item.

Code the bottom of each Sexual Contact/Victim Form, indicating on which section A through P the person is listed.

3. Complete the Table of Contents/Summary (page 3) for Part 1 after you have completed pages 4 through 19.

- Provide all of the summary information required for each item (from. Worksheets A through P) on page 3.
- Do not leave any item blank, (including attached Sexual Contact/Victim Forms), all sexual contacts/behaviors should be totaled at the bottom of the Table of Contents/Summary (page3).

4. Complete Part 2 (page 20) regarding other sexual behaviors.

- Attach a written summary description of your involvement in any of the behaviors listed on page 20.
- Additional pages should be hand-numbered as 20-X where X is the item number on page 20. For example, page 20-1 would pertain to item 1 on page 20 (deviant fantasies), while page 20-18 would pertain to item 18 on page 20 (sexual infidelity).

5. If you need further assistance or have questions, contact your therapist, supervising officer or other treatment group members as instructed.

6. Review your written disclosure with your treatment group and supervision and treatment team members, pursuant to the guidelines provided by your community supervision team and treatment group, prior to your polygraph examination date.

7. Provide your treatment provider and supervising officer with copies of your completed sexual history disclosure packet as requested.

8. Keep a copy of your sexual history disclosure packet for your own records.

9. Bring a copy of your completed sexual history disclosure packet to your polygraph examination - If you cannot do so for whatever reason you are responsible for making alternative arrangements. If you are currently incarcerated, your supervising officer or therapist will provide necessary arrangements.

10. Direct all technical questions about the polygraph test to the polygraph examiner. Soliciting information about the polygraph from friends, books or other media is unlikely to improve your test results and tends to be correlated with cynicism, resistance, unresolved test results and failure to progress in treatment.

11. Any attempt to falsify or alter your polygraph examination results will be regarded as non-compliance and a deliberate attempt to interfere with the process intended to assure and promote safety in the community and your progress in treatment. Such behavior will become the basis for sanctions in treatment and supervision.

Here is another aspect of the S.O.T. P. you will have to participate in. To be honest I can't see how this is supposed to help you. The following was obtained from an actual S.O.T.P. program.

SAMPLE ASSAULT SCRIPT - First molest of 10 y.o. niece at age 18.

Phase One *involves sitting still in one place and thinking about one's current life, what is dissatisfying, what I need emotionally and/or sexually to feel better and then thinking about where and how I can get it. When one thinks of who and how to meet the need, the mood shifts 180 degrees from frustrated, hopeless or just bored to excited and hopeful. That motivates fantasies, planning and finally optimism that one can actually execute a plan that will meet those frustrated needs. Adrenalin starts kicking in.*

Just another shitty day; so hot and crowded. It was bad enough before Janet and her 8 kids moved in, but now there's no relief. Suffocating and they never leave. Then she makes it worse by acting like nothing I do is ever good enough for her. She's just like Mom and Dad. Doesn't matter that I get all A's and B's, do all my chores. Hell, some of her kids are as old as me and they don't do any chores! And when I say anything to Mom and Dad, they just say "Janine needs your help Joseph because she can't get her kids to help." Bull Shit!

I'm sick of being unappreciated. Even with all these people in the house, I'm always lonely. I miss feeling wild, free and excited like I did as a kid before they all moved in. If I'm gonna put up with all these people and all this extra work, I at least need to feel appreciated and special to someone. I glance over at my hunting knife and think "I could just end it all."

I miss my stepsister Elizabeth. We made each other feel special while we stayed virgins. I can't and won't get close with any of the girls at school. They don't even care about their virginity being special and not something to just get rid of as soon as possible to be more "popular." They think the only thing special about a man is how much money he can spend on them or how popular he is and how many girls he's had sex with. Some of the girls may still be virgins, but I need to know for sure and I don't want to take the time to find out. With all my classes and all my chores, I don't have time to find out.

So who do I know that makes me feel special and I'm sure is still a virgin? Well, Celest's only 10 but she's sweet, forgiving, attentive. She appreciates me and

thigh, stopping only briefly to massage her pussy lips and keep them wet. She shivers with excitement and squealing against my erection making it start to throb. I'm not sure how long I can take her teasing me like this. The warmth of her hot little pussy lips pressing against me is about to make me explode.

I slide both my hands under her skirt, squeezing her ass and pulling her firmly against me. Rhythmically, I move her up and down my shaft as I again start kissing her neck. She sorta kisses me back but she is too excited. She says "That feels kinda funny Uncle Tony?" I smile and move both my hands up to her face. This time I slip just the tip of my tongue into her mouth and move it slowly around her teeth and tip of her tongue. Then I gently suck her tongue into my mouth. Her eyes grow wide but she makes no attempt to break free or anything. Still I better slow down a little., don't want to scare her. I assure her she is an excellent kisser. The sweet taste of her saliva is still fresh in my mouth. Her warm and slightly moist pussy lips are still pressed against my erection. Her smile and wide eyes again assure me she is curious, excited and ready for more. I slide my a hands up lifting her loose top quickly over her head. She reacts like she's cold so I wrap the blanket over us. I lean her back against my legs and kiss gently down her neck onto her hard little nipples. She is very still now and ready to let me do whatever I want with her aroused little body. I slip both hands under her skirt to her waist, this time sliding my fingers inside the waist of her panties and back down bring her panties with them. The bare skin of her ass is now resting in my hands and against my thighs. I lift her just enough to slide my finger forward between her tight little pussy lips. She jerks and shivers with excitement. "Was that her first orgasm?" I wonder. I move just the tip of my finger in and out of her increasingly wet little pussy a few more times, then slip my hand away and pull her tight against my erection one more time. I give her nipples each one more good suck then return to gently sucking her tongue. I squeeze her hot bare little ass with both hands and move her wet little pussy rhythmically against me. It all feels so perfect. The warmth and wetness of her pussy lips moving up and down my clothed erection, the firmness of her bare ass in my hands. The perkiness of those sweet little nipples, the warm sweet taste of her tongue in my mouth. I feel the spasms in my crotch as I explode into my shorts. I can feel the heat of my cum against my body. I think for a moment how much sweeter it will be when I can let Celeste feel me

explode inside of her tight little pussy. But that will have to wait. I don't want to rush or scare her. This has to be mostly about her pleasure.

I slip my hands from under her skirt, pulling her panties up as I do. I help her slip her shirt back over her head and give her a hug and smile once it's in place. I remind her that she's my special girl and that keeping this secret is part of what makes it so special. I tell her it wouldn't be special and worse we probably couldn't be together any more if anyone else finds out. Celeste tells me she wants to go take a shower, so I jump up, unlock and open the door for her. As she heads into her room, I sit back on my bed and feel the darkness start closing in again. I take the hunting knife from my nightstand and slide it across my palm drawing a bright red line of blood. Just then Celeste comes out of her room wrapped in a towel. She sees me looking sad, looks a little concerned and says "I love you Uncle Tony," then heads into the bathroom. She gives me my one good reason to keep living.

If you find this diatribe as revolting as I do and don't want to participate in something like this, then you must fight your charges in court and never surrender. When I first read this I thought it was smut. When I was handed this document by a friend I couldn't read more than half of it before I got sick to my stomach and asked my friend, "How does fantasizing about this help anyone who has a problem with it?" For example if you have an over-eating disorder, you're not going to solve it by eating more food. Somehow the logic of this escapes those who are running these programs.

Another thing you will have to deal with during S.O.T.P. is undergoing numerous polygraphs. Most people operate under the misconception that a polygraph is inadmissible in a court of law. This statement is simply untrue. The truth is that polygraph cannot be used in a criminal trial against you, but polygraph evidence is admissible in a court of law that is conducting a hearing against you. Typically these hearings are used to revoke a person's probation and sends them back to prison, which makes the polygraph and essential tool which is used in the five-year plan. The difference between a criminal trial and a hearing has to do with the degree your constitutional rights come into play. In a criminal trial all of your constitutional rights are in effect, in a hearing such as a probation revocation hearing they do not because you would not be the focus of the hearing if you had

not already been found guilty. In the United States when you're found guilty of a crime you enter into a condition which is referred to in legal parlance as a disabled status. Because of this disabled status some of your constitutional rights are lost. This gives adult probation and the state the ability to use polygraph evidence against you.

The polygraph is a crude tool that hasn't been improved upon since the day it was invented. This fact alone is a key indicator that the device is based upon junk science. If the polygraph had been based upon real science, then as scientific knowledge progressed a continual improvement of the devices would have occurred. With the polygraph this is not the case. To read more about polygraphs and their use please go to the download page and download the file containing the document, "the lie behind the lie detector".

One of the carrots that is dangled before you is the policy that you can request the court to terminate S.O.T.P. if you pass a specific offense polygraph. If you truly believe in your heart that you can pass this type of polygraphic examination then go for it. But before you make that fateful final decision please read what is contained below to learn just exactly what it is they're going to ask you for a specific offense polygraph. You should know in advance what you are getting yourself into and now you will.

SEX HISTORY POLYGRAPH QUESTIONNAIRE
AGREEMENT OF UNDERSTANDING

DEFENDANT:_____

CAUSE NUMBER:_____

The above listed defendant understands that the purpose of the sex history polygraph process is for treatment purposes and is meant to give him/her the greatest chance for success in treatment. The above listed defendant further agrees that he/she has fully completed the sex history questionnaire and has fully disclosed all information to the best of their ability. The above listed defendant of violence that they have been completely honest in the information provided and have not made any attempts to conceal or fabricate information, or mislead the treatment team with any of the information provided. It is further understood that the goal is to be completely open and honest in the sex history polygraph process. THIS GOAL WILL NOT BE ACHIEVED UNTIL THE POLYGRAPH RESULTS ARE NO DECEPTION INDICATED (TRUTHFUL RESULTS) as determined by the polygraph examiner. The above listed defendant further understands that they may be required to undergo polygraph testing, at their own expense, until this goal is achieved and/or as directed by the probation team.

_____   _____
Signed   Date

The treatment provider and probation officer have reviewed the sex history questionnaire as provided by the above listed defendant. It is agreed that all questions appear to have been adequately answered and that it is appropriate to proceed to polygraph testing for sexual history.

_____   _____
Treatment Provider   Date

_____   _____
Adult Probation Officer   Date

Sexual History Disclosure Packet-Instructions

1. Complete pages 4 through 25 first. Complete table of contents/summary (page 3) after completing pages 4 through 25.
   - Write your name and date of birth at the top of every page.
   - Sign and date all pages when they are completed.
   - Do not leave any blank.
   - For any behaviors that do not apply, it is clearly indicate that by writing (N/A) on the page.
   - You may list the approximate ages if exact pages are not known (do not leave any age is blank).
   - Lists all sexual contacts/behaviors up to and including the date you are completing this form.
   - Attempts to list all sexual contacts/behaviors in chronological order.
2. Complete one sexual contact form (attachment) for each identified person on pages 4 through 25.
   - Make additional copies of individual pages or the sexual contact form (attachment) as necessary.
   - Do not leave any item blank. Answer yes or no to every item.
   - Code at the bottom of each sexual contact form, indicating on which of pages 4 through five the person is listed.
3. Complete the part 1 Table Of Contents/Summary Page (page 3) only after completing pages 4 through 25.
   - Provide all of the summary information requested for each person (from worksheets made through the) on page 3
   - Do not leave any item blank (including attached Sexual Contact Forms). All sexual contacts/behavior should be totaled at the bottom of the Table Of Contents/Summary page (page
4. Complete part two (page 26) regarding other sexual behaviors.
   - Attach a written summary description of your involvement in any of the behaviors listed on page 26 (other behaviors).
   - Additional pages should be hand numbered as 26-X where X. is the item number on page 26. For example page 26-1 would pertain to item 1 on page 26 (deviant fantasies), while page 26-22 would pertain to item 22 on page 26 (sexual infidelity).
5. If you need further assistance or have questions, contact your therapist, probation team, or other treatment group members as instructed.
6. Review your written disclosure with your treatment group and supervision/treatment team members, pursuant to the guidelines provided by your community supervision team and treatment group, prior to your polygraph examination date.
7. Provide your treatment provider and supervising officer with copies of your completed sexual history disclosure packet.
8. Keep a copy of your sexual history disclosure packet for your own records.
9. Bring a copy of your sexual history disclosure packet to your polygraph examination-your examiner may not need to read it but you may want to refer to it (it's better to have it and not need it than she needed and not have it.)
10. Direct all technical questions about the polygraph test to the polygraph examiner. Soliciting information about polygraphs from friends, books or other media is unlikely to improve your test results and chanced to be correlated with cynicism, resistance, unresolved test results and failure to progress in treatment.
11. Any attempt to falsify or alter your polygraph examination results may be regarded as noncompliant and deliver it attempt to interfere with a process intended to assure and promote safety in the community and your progress in treatment. Such behavior may become the basis for sanctions in treatment and supervision.

Sexual History Part 1 - Sexual Contacts
Table of Contents and Summary

				#Persons	#Times	Last time	Page
A.	After age 18 sexual contact with anyone under age 15	Yes	No				
B.	Sexual contact with relatives or family members	Yes	No				
C.	Forest or violent sexual contact (prevent escape or resistance)	Yes	No				
D.	Sexual contact with helpless or incapacitated persons	Yes	No				
E.	Prior to age 18 sexual contact with anyone 4 or more years younger	Yes	No				
F.	After age 20 for sexual contact with anyone age 15 or 16 or 10 or more years younger	Yes	No				
G.	Sexual contact with anyone under age 18 while in a position of trust	Yes	No				
H.	Coercive (nonviolent) sexual contact	Yes	No				
I.	Frotage (sexual rubbing against unsuspecting persons)	Yes	No				
J.	History of computer solicitation (solicitation via any electronic device)	Yes	No				
K.	Voyeurism (peeping)	Yes	No				
L.	Exhibitionism (public nudity)	Yes	No				
M.	Prostitution (solicitation or pandering)	Yes	No				
N.	Public masturbation (masturbation in public places)	Yes	No				
O.	The use of another's undergarments / clothing / property for sexual behavior	Yes	No				
P.	History of stalking	Yes	No				
Q.	Child pornography (use/production/distribution)	Yes	No				
R.	Sexual contact with animals	Yes	No				
S.	Institutional sexual contact (out of home pleasure)	Yes	No				
T.	Obscene phone calls	Yes	No				
U.	Arson and sexually motivated fire setting behaviors	Yes	No				
V.	Domestic Violence	Yes	No				

Summary

Your age at the time of your first identified offense   Male_____+ Female_____Total_____

Number of adult victims as adult   Male_____+ Female_____Total_____

Number of underage victims as an adult   Male_____+ Female_____Total_____

Number of victims as a juvenile   Male_____+ Female_____Total_____

Total   Male_____+ Female_____Total_____

(The total number of identified victims should equal the total number of completed sexual contact forms.)

_____   _____

Signed   Date

Name:_____   DOB:_____

A.

Sexual Contact With Anyone Under Age 15. After You Turn To Age 18

Include all persons with whom you engaged in any form of rubbing or touching (including attempts) of a person's sexual organs (i.e. breast/chest area, buttocks, vaginal area, penis) either over or under clothing, if it was for the purpose of sexual arousal, sexual gratification or stimulation, or "sexual curiosity, "along with all persons whom you caused or allowed to rub or touch your private parts, either over or under clothing, for the purpose of sexual arousal, sexual gratification, or stimulation or sexual curiosity. Also include persons with whom you engaged in any sexual petting (i.e. sexual hugging and kissing) behaviors.

Complete a separate sexual contact form (attachment) for each listed contact.

Person's name or identifier	Relationship to you	Person's gender (F./M.)	Persons age at time	Your age at time	Max # sexual contacts	Last sexual contact M/Y	Type of sexual contact

_____   _____
Signed   Date

Name:_____   DOB:_____

B.

Sexual Contact With Relatives or Family Members

In sexual contact (including attempts) was all persons related by blood, marriage (excluding spouse or someone in a spousal role) or adoption (e.g. mother, father, sister, brother, aunt, uncool, grandparents, grandchildren, cousins, nieces, nephews, stepchildren, in-laws). Include all relatives with whom you engaged in any sex play games (e.g. mommy-daddy, house, doctor, show-me, spin the bottle, truth or dare, etc.) or sexuality education lessons.

Complete a separate sexual contact form (attachment) for each listed contact.

Person's name or identifier	Relationship to you	Person's gender (F./M.)	Persons age at time	Your age at time	Max # sexual contacts	Last sexual contact M/Y	Type of sexual contact

_____   _____

Signed   Date

Name:_____   DOB:_____

C.

Forced (Violent) Sexual Contacts

Sexual contact (including attempts) with any person (including spouses or partners) whom you physically hit or struck, physically restrained using your body strength or any object, or threatened to harm through the use of weapons including implied or improvised weapons, threatening gestures, or verbal threats of harm, including threats of harm towards the persons relatives or family members (including pets), in order to prevent the person from resisting or escaping.

Complete a separate sexual contact form (attachment) for each listed contact.

Person's name or identifier	Relationship to you	Person's gender (F./M.)	Persons age at time	Your age at time	Max # sexual contacts	Last sexual contact M/Y	Type of force (Violence)

_____   _____

Signed   Date

Name:_____   DOB:_____

D.

Sexual Contact With Sleeping, Incapacitated, Or Helpless Persons

Include all sexual contacts (including attempts) involving persons when they were (or appeared) asleep, severely intoxicated, drugged/sedated, unconscious, mentally or physically incapacitated, or persons that you intoxicated, drugged or sedated with the purpose of sexual contact. Also include sexual peeping or acts of voyeurism against persons who were (or appear to be) asleep or incapacitated.

Complete a separate sexual contact form (attachment) for each listed contact.

Person's name or identifier	Relationship to you	Person's gender (F./M.)	Persons age at time	Your age at time	Max # opportunities sexual contacts	First opportunities sexual contact (M/Y)	Last opportunities sexual contact M/Y	Describe method of access

_____   _____

Signed   Date

Name:_____ DOB:_____

E.

Sexual Contact With Anyone Four Or More Years Younger Then You, While You Are Under Age 18

Include all persons with whom you engaged in any form of rubbing or touching (including attempts) of a person's sexual organs (i.e. breasts/chest area, buttocks, vaginal area, penis), either over or under clothing, it was for the purpose of sexual arousal, sexual gratification or stimulation, or sexual curiosity, along with all persons whom you caused or allowed to rub or touch your private parts, either over or under clothing for the purpose of sexual arousal, sexual gratification or stimulation, or sexual curiosity. Also include persons with whom you engaged in any sexual petting (i.e. sexual hugging and kissing) behaviors. Including all younger children with whom you engaged in any sex play games (e.g. mommy-Patty, house, doctor, show-me, spin the bottle, truth or dare, etc.) or sexuality education lessons.

Complete a separate sexual contact form (attachment) for each listed contact.

Person's name or identifier	Relationship to you	Person's gender (F./M.)	Persons age at time	Your age at time	Max # sexual contacts	First sexual contact (M/Y)	Last sexual contact M/Y	Type of sexual contact

_____   _____

Signed   Date

Name:_____   DOB:_____

F.

Sexual contact with anyone age 15 or 16, or 10 years or more years younger, since the age of 24

Include all persons with whom you engaged in any form of rubbing or touching (including attempts) of a person's sexual organs (i.e. breasts/chest area, buttocks, vaginal area, penis), either over or under clothing, it was for the purpose of sexual arousal, sexual gratification or stimulation, or sexual curiosity, along with all persons whom you caused or allowed to rub or touch your private parts, either over or under clothing for the purpose of sexual arousal, sexual gratification or stimulation, or sexual curiosity. Also include persons with whom you engaged in any sexual petting (i.e. sexual hugging and kissing) behaviors.

Complete a separate sexual contact form (attachment) for each listed contact.

Person's name or identifier	Relationship to you	Person's gender (F./M.)	Persons age at time	Your age at time	Max # sexual contacts	First sexual contact (M/Y)	Last sexual contact M/Y	Type of sexual contact

_____   _____
Signed   Date

111

Name:_____   DOB:_____

G.

Sexual Contact With Anyone Under The Age Of 18, With Whom You Had Any Type Of Position Of Trust (I.E. Babysitter, Teacher, Coach, Older Relative, Foster Parent, Etc.)

Include all persons with whom you engaged in any form of rubbing or touching (including attempts) of a person's sexual organs (i.e. breasts/chest area, buttocks, vaginal area, penis), either over or under clothing, it was for the purpose of sexual arousal, sexual gratification or stimulation, or sexual curiosity, along with all persons whom you caused or allowed to rub or touch your private parts, either over or under clothing for the purpose of sexual arousal, sexual gratification or stimulation, or sexual curiosity. Also include persons with whom you engaged in any sexual petting (i.e. sexual hugging and kissing) behaviors.

Complete a separate sexual contact form (attachment) for each listed contact.

Person's name or identifier	Relationship to you	Person's gender (F./M.)	Persons age at time	Your age at time	Max # sexual contacts	First sexual contact (M/Y)	Last sexual contact M/Y	Type of sexual contact

_____   _____

Signed   **Date**

Name:_____ DOB:_____

H.

Coerced (nonviolent) sexual contacts

Sexual contact (including attempts) with any persons (including spouses or parents) whose compliance you obtained through any nonviolent form of coercion (i.e. bribery, manipulation, money, drugs, loss of relationship) despite the persons expressed or implied reluctance.

Complete a separate sexual contact form (attachment) for each listed contact.

Person's name or identifier	Relationship to you	Person's gender (F./M.)	Persons age at time	Your age at time	Max # sexual contacts	First sexual contact (M/Y)	Last sexual contact M/Y	Type of coercion (nonviolence)

_____   _____

Signed   Date

Name:_____   DOB:_____

I.

Frottage Or Opportunistic Sexual Rubbing, Bumping Or Touching Against Strangers Or Unsuspecting (Non-Incapacitated) Persons

Include sexual touching (including attempts) of others private parts or by using any your private parts to touch them during any play, horseplay, wrestling or athletic activities, or unsuspecting persons in public places (e.g. school, work, stores, gym, crowds, etc.).

Complete a separate sexual contact form (attachment) for each listed contact.

Person's name or identifier	Relationship to you	Person's gender (F./M.)	Persons age at time	Your age at time	Max # sexual contacts	First sexual contact (M/Y)	Last sexual contact M/Y	Describe method of access

_____   _____

Signed   Date

Name:_____   DOB:_____

J.

Solicitation Via Computer Or Electronic Devices

Include all sexual contacts/interactions and attempted sexual contacts/interactions via computer, cell phone or electronic devices, including e-mails, texting, chat rooms, cyber sex, live WebCams, pictures, electronic bulletin board systems, Internet relay chat, DCC chat channels, private bulletin boards, other youth groups. List age or approximate ages of the victims at the time of contact include law enforcement agents who posed as persons willing to engage in any of the above sexual contacts, even though the actual contact may have been prevented.

I.   Describe how you attempted to seek sexual contacts/interactions on the computer or electronic devices (including frequency, sites, search keywords, search engines and time frames):

_____

_____

_____

_____

_____

_____

Complete a separate sexual contact form (attachment) for each listed contact.

Person's name or identifier	Person's gender (F./M.)	Persons age at time	Your age at time	Where did you meet or attempted meet	Number of face to face contacts	Number of sexual contacts	Type of sexual contacts

_____   _____

Signed   Date

Name:_____   DOB:_____

K.

Voyeurism Or Sexual Peeping

Include all sexual behaviors (including attempts) involving peeping or more years of, including all attempts to look into someone's home, bedroom or bathroom without the person's knowledge or permission, in an attempt to view someone naked, undressing/dressing, or engaging in sexual acts. Include all voyeurism attempts involving using or creating a whole opening to view others for sexual arousal, including all attempts to use any optical devices (i.e. cameras cell phones with cameras, mirrors, binoculars, or telescope) to view others for sexual purposes.

Complete a separate sexual contact form (attachment) for each listed contact.

Person's name or identifier	Relationship to you	Person's gender (F./M.)	Persons age at time	Your age at time	Max # sexual contacts	First incident (M/Y)	Last incident M/Y	Brief description (where, method, devices used, etc.)

_____   _____

Signed   Date

116

Name:_____ DOB:_____

L.

Exhibitionism Or Indecent Exposure

Include all incidents in which you actually or intentionally exposed (including attempts) your bare private parts to unsuspecting persons in public places. Include incidents where you wore loose or baggy clothing that allowed your sexual organs to become exposed to others. Also include moving, streaking or flashing behavior, and public urination while in view of others.

Complete a separate sexual contact form (attachment) for each listed contact.

Person's name or identifier	Relationship to you	Person's gender (F./M.)	Persons age at time	Your age at time	Max # incidents	First incident (M/Y)	Last incident M/Y	Brief description (where, how, etc.)

_____   _____

Signed   Date

Name:_____   DOB:_____

M.

Prostitution

Include all sexual contacts (including attempts) in which you paid for sex, or where you performed sexual acts for money, property or

Complete a separate sexual contact form (attachment) for each listed contact.

Person's name or identifier	Relationship to you	Person's gender (F./M.)	Persons age at time	Your age at time	Max # sexual contacts	First sexual contact (M/Y)	Last sexual contact M/Y	Brief description (form of payment, your role in transactions, etc.)

_____   _____

Signed   Date

Name:_____   DOB:_____

N.

Public Masturbation

List all incidents of masturbation (including attempts) in public places (i.e., outside your residence, bedroom, or bathroom) in which you could view others or could possibly be observed by others while masturbating, including public restrooms, workplace/school settings, parks or other community locations, vehicles, and others homes.

Complete a separate sexual contact form (attachment) for each listed contact.

Location of property (city/state)	Owner of property	Relationship to you	Dates of incident (M/Y)	Your age at time	Number of masturbation incidents at location	Brief description (

_____   _____

Signed   Date

Name:_____   DOB:_____

Use Or Theft Of Underwear, Undergarments, Or Personal Property For Masturbation Or Sexual Arousal

Including taking or keeping undergarments (including other trophies or personal property) from sexual partners, relatives, friends, victims, or strangers for masturbation or sexual arousal. Include all incidents in which you tried on or wore another person's underwear or undergarments without their knowledge or permission. Also include all incidents in which you returned someone's underwear or undergarments after using them for masturbation or sexual arousal.

Complete a separate sexual contact form (attachment) for each listed contact.

Name or identifier of property owner	Relationship to you	Person's age and sex	Description of property	Your age at time	Max # incidents	First incident (M/Y)	Last incident M/Y	Brief description (how and where property obtained, how property used, frequency of use, current location of property)

_____   _____

Signed   Date

Name:_____   DOB:_____

P.

Stalking Behaviors

Include all behaviors involving following someone without their wares for permission. Include all incidents of following someone to their home, workplace or vehicle, or following others around a store, I'll, parking lot, campus, or community. Include all other efforts to monitor or observe the person's behavior without their knowledge.

Complete a separate sexual contact form (attachment) for each listed contact.

Person's name or identifier	Relationship to you	Person's gender (F./M.)	Persons age at time	Your age at time	Max # incidents	First incident (M/Y)	Last incident M/Y	Brief description (where, method, devices used, type of contact etc.)

_____   _____

Signed   Date

Name:_____ DOB:_____

Q.

Child Pornography

Include all activities related to viewing, possessing, using, producing, or distributing of nude or sexualized images of minors (persons under age 18).

Complete a separate sexual contact form (attachment) for each listed contact.

Person's name or identifier	Relationship to you	Person's gender (F./M.)	Persons age at time	Your age at time	Max # incidents	First incident (M/Y)	Last incident M/Y	Description of materials (where, what, how, your participation, type, etc.) and how those materials were used

_____   _____

Signed   Date

Name:_____ DOB:_____

R.

Sexual Contact With Animals

Include all sexual behaviors (including attempts) involving domesticated, farm/ranch, or wild animals, whether living or deceased, and whether whole or dismembered. Include all sexual contact with pets, whether your own or belonging to others.

Complete a separate sexual contact form (attachment) for each listed contact.

Type of animal	Owner of animal	Your age at time	Max # of contacts	First sexual contact M/Y	Last Sexual contact M/Y	Brief description

_____   _____

Signed   Date

Name:_____   DOB:_____

S.

Institutional Sexual Contact

Include all sexual contact (including attempts) with persons and institutions including jail, prison, at detention facilities, group or foster homes, treatment centers, medical or psychiatric hospitals, nursing homes, or any out of home placement.

Complete a separate sexual contact form (attachment) for each listed contact.

Person's name or identifier	Relationship to you	Person's gender (F./M.)	Persons age at time	Your age at time	Max # sexual contacts	First sexual contact (M/Y)	Last sexual contact M/Y	Type of sexual contact

_____   _____

Signed   Date

Name:_____ DOB:_____

T.

History Of Obscene Phone Calls

Include your age, or proximate age, and the description of your behaviors at the time.

Complete a separate sexual contact form (attachment) for each listed contact.

Person's name or identifier	Relationship to you	Person's gender (F./M.)	Persons age at time	Your age at time	Max # obscene phone calls	First obscene phone calls (M/Y)	Last obscene phone calls M/Y	Description of obscene phone calls

_____   _____

Signed   Date

Name:_____ DOB:_____

U.

Arson Or Fire Setting Behaviors

Include all behaviors involving fire setting for destructive or sexual purposes.

Complete a separate sexual contact form (attachment) for each listed contact.

Description of property burned (occupied or unoccupied)	Owners of property	Relationship to you	Location of property (city/state)	Your age at time	Date of fire setting incident M/Y	Brief description (method, devices used, length of time remained on the scene,)

_____   _____

Signed   Date

Name:_____   DOB:_____

V.

Domestic Violence

Include your age, or proximate age, and the description of your behaviors at the time.

Complete a separate sexual contact form (attachment) for each listed contact.

Person's name or identifier	Relationship to you	Person's gender (F./M.)	Persons age at time	Your age at time	Max # incidents	First incident (M/Y)	Last incident M/Y	Description (words used, threats made, physical items used, property damage etc.)

_____   _____

Signed   Date

127

Name:_____   DOB:_____

Sexual History Part 2 – Other Behaviors

Answer each item. Attach a separate page(s) to describe all "YES" responses.

				Frequency	Last time
1	Experience Dream Fantasies	Yes	No		
2	Masturbated to Deviant Fantasies	Yes	No		
3	Cruising Behaviors	Yes	No		
4	Made Photos or Videos of Yourself or Others for Sexual Purposes	Yes	No		
5	Abused Animals	Yes	No		
6	Arousal to Offending Memories	Yes	No		
7	Abuse or Assault of a Spouse or Partner	Yes	No		
8	Participation in Cults or Hate Groups	Yes	No		
9	Alcohol Usage	Yes	No		
10	Illegal Drug Usage	Yes	No		
11	Provided Alcohol/Drugs to Minors	Yes	No		
12	Contact with Victim After Release	Yes	No		
13	Violated Release/Supervision Rules	Yes	No		
14	Necrophilia (Sexual Contact with Dead Animals or People)	Yes	No		
15	Self-Mutilation (Cutting or Other Self Abuse Behavior)	Yes	No		
16	Use of Feces for Sexual Purposes	Yes	No		
17	Use of Urine for Sexual Purposes	Yes	No		
18	Use of Inanimate Objects for Sexual Arousal or Masturbation	Yes	No		
19	Nudity in Public Places	Yes	No		
20	Sexual Contact in Public Places	Yes	No		
21	Consensual Sexual Contacts (Nonabusive and Not Unlawful)	Yes	No		
22	Sexual Infidelity	Yes	No		
23	Anonymous or Casual Sexual Contact (Persons Known Less Than 24 Hours)	Yes	No		
24	Sexual Contact with Same-Sex Partners (As a Juvenile and Adult)	Yes	No		
25	Group Sex Activities	Yes	No		
26	Consensual Bondage Activities	Yes	No		
27	Sexual Sadism (Arousal to Another's Pain or Humiliation)	Yes	No		
28	Sexual Masochism (Arousal to Your Own Pain or Humiliation)	Yes	No		
29	Anal Sex Activities	Yes	No		
30	Sexual Victimization (Were You Ever Sexually Assaulted or Sexually Abused)	Yes	No		
31	Pornography Use	Yes	No		
32	Violent Pornography	Yes	No		
33	Photography Production, Distribution (Made Nude Images of Self or Others)	Yes	No		
34	Masturbating to Nonpornographic Sexually Stimulating Images	Yes	No		
35	Computer Sex Behaviors (Cybersex/Sax Chat Via Computer or Electronic Device)	Yes	No		
36	Telephone Sex Behavior S (Phone Sex Lines, Obscene Phone Calls)	Yes	No		
37	Used a personal or dating service (telephone, computer or electronic device)	Yes	No		
38	Visited or Frequented Topless Bars, Strip Clubs	Yes	No		
39	Visited Frequented Adult Bookstores or Novelty Shops	Yes	No		
40	Visited or Frequented Erotic Massage Parlors, Erotic Massage Services)	Yes	No		
41	Transexualism (Wanting to Be a Member of the Opposite Sex)	Yes	No		
42	Transvestitism (Dressing As a Member of the Opposite Sex)	Yes	No		

_____   _____

Signed   Date

Name:_____ DOB:_____

Sexual Contact Form

Complete one form for each separate person identified in part one (worksheets A through V)

Persons Name/Identifier_____Relationship_____

Gender Male/Female   Persons Age(s) At Time of Contact _____Persons Age(s) At Time of Contact _____

	Type Of Contact Behavior (Circle Words That Apply)			Most Possible Times
1	Rubbed/touched persons breasts/chest area over clothing	Yes	No	
2	Rubbed/touched persons bear/chest area	Yes	No	
3	Rubbed/touched persons bare vagina/penis over clothing	Yes	No	
4	Rubbed/touched persons bare vagina/penis	Yes	No	
5	Rubbed penis/vagina against persons clothes vagina / penis / breasts / buttocks	Yes	No	
6	Rubbed penis/vagina against persons bare vagina / penis / breasts / buttocks	Yes	No	
7	Put tongue in persons mouth (i.e. French kissing)	Yes	No	
8	Placed mouth/tongue on persons clothes vagina/penis	Yes	No	
9	Placed mouth/tongue on persons bare vagina/penis area	Yes	No	
10	Put mouth/tongue on persons anus even slightly	Yes	No	
11	Put a finger inside person's vagina even slightly	Yes	No	
12	Put finger inside person's anus even slightly	Yes	No	
13	Put penis inside person's anus even slightly	Yes	No	
14	Put penis inside person's vagina even slightly	Yes	No	
15	Put penis against/inside person's anus even slightly	Yes	No	
16	Put object inside person's vagina/anus	Yes	No	
17	Masturbated in presence of person	Yes	No	
18	Ejaculated in presence of person	Yes	No	
19	Masturbated using someone's clothing/photos/property	Yes	No	
20	Ejaculated in or on persons anus/vagina/body/mouth	Yes	No	
21	Made/possessed nude or partially nude photos/videos of persons	Yes	No	
22	Person rubbed my penis/vagina over clothing	Yes	No	
23	Person touched/rubbed my bare penis/vagina	Yes	No	
24	Person placed mouth/tongue on my bare penis	Yes	No	
25	Person placed penis against/in my anus/vagina	Yes	No	
26	Person put finger in my anus/vagina/penis even slightly	Yes	No	

List other sexual behaviors with this person (not included above)_____

First contact_____last contact_____total sexual contacts_____frequency_____

Where did these contacts occur?_____

How did you gain this person's compliance?_____

Describe any use of physical force (restraint, strike) against person_____

Describe any threats to harm this person or family (weapons, gestures etc.)_____

Describe any type of physical pain you caused this person._____

Did you caused this person to be sexual with others? If so when? _____

Who also was present at the time of these contacts? _____

Do you consider this person a victim?   Yes   no

Worksheet coding (circle which part 1 pages apply) A B C D E F G H I J K L M N O P Q R S T U V

_____   _____

Signed   Date

Chapter 11 New Trial

Now that I've completed the process of a new trial there are some things that I need to say to eliminate any concerns you may have about enduring a new trial. As the date for my new trial approached I was of the opinion that all that would result from the trial would be a repeat performance of the first one. Once the trial had begun I realized that my fears were unfounded and here's the reason why. Even if you have no new evidence to present at trial it's still a new trial because you have a new jury. You have a completely different set of minds to decide your fate. A new jury always means a new trial. I had never thought of it this way because I assumed that the prosecutor was going to run rampant in the courtroom the second time just like he did in the first trial and that the judge was going to let him. I believed that as long as you had these two clowns running the show there was no choice but to obtain the same outcome as the first trial. Breathe easy and be assured that a new trial really is a new trial.

The first trial is always what is known as trial by ambush and the reason for this is that even though you are aware of what discovery the prosecutor is going to present, that's still not enough information for you to figure out his strategy before you go to trial. You won't find that out until it is way too late to do anything about it. In my first trial my attorney didn't present one motion in limine or a single case law to the court. The most crucial documents a defense attorney can present the court are motions in limine. The reason for this is that motions in limine restrict what the prosecutor is capable of saying or doing during the trial. The problem is that in the first trial you have no idea what kind of dirty tricks he's going to pull, so there is very little that you can present in the way of motions in limine to reign him in. In the second trial this condition is not true. In the second trial the prosecutor is stuck with his storyline and it will either prove correct or become a boat anchor around his neck. It is your job and the job of your attorney to make sure that it's the latter and not the former and the way you do it is through motions in limine. Motions in limine are argued before trial begins so that everyone has agreed upon how the game is going to be played. Once there is agreement between you and the prosecutor and the court in regard to these motions and the prosecutor decides to ignore them because he isn't doing so well, this gives you a legal basis to object to

the actions of the prosecutor or ask for a mistrial. In addition it gives you an outstanding claim on appeal if you happen to lose.

Just as in the first trial the witnesses who will testify will undergo pretrial questioning a second time. Just like in the first trial is important for you to be there and there are numerous strategic reasons why. The biggest reason is because there you are, sitting 3 feet across a table from the person who is trying to send you to the big house for life. For some people it's difficult to lie about a person sitting in front of you, knowing what the potential outcome is going to be. Some people just don't have the stomach for it and will recant their testimony on the spot. If this happens there may not be a second trial. Both your attorneys and the prosecutor will be present at these interviews and in some states it will be deposed testimony under oath. If the one and only witness against you recants his testimony in front of the prosecutor on a sworn deposition, it's game over and the prosecutor will have no choice but to drop the charges against you with prejudice. Unfortunately in Arizona witnesses in a criminal trial are seldom deposed under oath which means the witness can say anything he wants during the interview and then completely changed his story at trial without encountering a charge of perjury. This condition does not permit the gathering of valid and accurate testimony in my opinion and it shouldn't be too difficult to understand why.

In the pretrial phase of your second trial your attorney should conduct a more thorough examination of the forensic evidence that will be used against you than was accomplished in the first trial. It is vitally important that you do this because nobody knows at this point what may reveal itself with a deeper investigation than what took place for the first trial. My extremely conscientious attorneys for my second trial did this for me without even having to be asked. Because we conducted a more thorough investigation the second time around we discovered that the hard drives that were seized from my motorhome had 312 files that had been unforensicallly accessed by the detective in my case, one month after they had been seized and 11 months before the computer forensics had actually been done. This is what is known as spoliation of evidence. Spoliated evidence is inadmissible in a court of law, however in our case we wanted to present this fact to the jury so we filed no motion in limine to preclude the hard drive evidence. In addition to this there was other evidence concerning my accusers use of his e-mail

address during periods of time when he testified at the first trial that he was not present in my motorhome. Had the hard drive evidence been precluded we would not have been able to present these facts to the jury.

To testify or not to testify, that is the question. Having undergone two trials it has become apparent to me that if you are going to testify it is vitally important that you testify at the first trial and not at the second one. The reasons why this is so is due primarily to the fact that even though you may have notes to guide you in your second testimony, it is very difficult, even for an honest person, to testify a second time without making small errors or deviations from your testimony in the first trial. In the second trial if you testify a second time the prosecutor is going to jump all over you in regard to these minor errors or deviations in order to impeach your testimony. If you don't testify a second time you don't have to worry about this. In addition to this is the strategic condition you create concerning what you testified to in the first trial. The prosecutor needs to present the statements you made at the first trial in order to refute them and he is not going to be able to do this without revealing to the jury that this is the second trial, if you don't testify a second time. Revealing to a jury that this is the second trial is never a prize winning strategy for a prosecutor because it informs the jury that something went wrong with the first trial and that this is the reason why a second trial is being conducted. This information can have a profound effect on the jury in the arena of reasonable doubt.

As I stated in the chapter about first trials it is vitally important that you make your own audio recording of the trial. Don't count on the state to record the trial for you. Both of the trials I attended in Pima County were not recorded. The equipment is available in some of their courtrooms but not all of them. The reason for this is because there is evidence to support the conclusion that the record of many trials in the state of Arizona is altered. If you do discover a discrepancy between the written transcripts and your recording, if your recording is crisp and clear, leaving no ambiguity there is probably a 60 / 40 chance that the judge will admit your recording as evidence and agree with what you have discovered. It is important to remember that if you don't have a recording of the trial then there is no chance for you to object to what is contained in the record regardless of the fact that you made the recording. Before you begin recording it is always preferable to

ask permission first and if you are denied there are ways of handling this problem and getting a recording anyway without getting yourself in trouble. For example if the judge refuses to permit you to record the trial, give the recorder to a family member, have them turn it on before entering the courtroom and stick it in their shirt pocket. They should also sit as close to the front of the courtroom as possible. In this scenario you asked the judge for permission to record and the judge refused to give you permission, but the judge didn't refuse your family member and as long as the fact your brother, sister or friend doesn't get discovered there is no problem. If an issue presents itself with regard to the transcripts don't worry about raising it on appeal. The judge refused to give you permission, he didn't refuse your brother, sister or friend. Without obtaining permission however it is not likely the recording will be admitted as if the proceedings had been recorded by the court, but at least you will know there is a problem with the record and won't be spending a huge chunk of your life wondering if you have a faulty memory about what was said or what happened in trial.

Chapter 12 Case Law

Every legal decision sets a precedent for all similar matters that come after it. Quite often, and more lately than in the past, a law is written with an element of vagueness about it. Does the law apply or not apply? When the court makes a determination in regard to the question, that decision can be used when a similar situation comes up again, as long as somebody knows about it and cites the prior case in court. That's how case law works.

Case law is created by the higher courts, the Court of Appeals and the state Supreme Court, as well as federal court and federal Court of Appeals. When a decision is made in regard to an issue it is seldom changed. There are more changes to a state's statutes than there are to case law. Because of this a case law citation book is a highly valued commodity that never goes out of date. The best commercially available case law citation book is the Georgetown Law Journal (G.L.J.). Out of all the case law books out there, it provides the most bang for the buck. You can't live without it and it's so reasonably priced at $10 in the year 2008.

The federal courts are divided into judicial districts, which encompass more than one state. Case law from a particular judicial district is valid as law with that district right down to the superior courts and is referred to by attorney's as having dicta. Case law from outside your judicial district does not carry the weight of law, but it can be used for guidance in a ruling. There are some people who believe that using case law from judicial districts outside their own or from federal courts is ineffective. This is simply not true. Federal courts always supersede state courts. Check for case law about a subject within your judicial district first, but if you can't find one you can use case law from another district usually without any problems.

To begin case law research you pick an event you feel was wrong in your trial and not in your favor. You then read case law in the area it pertains to such as due process etc. looking for something that fits your issue. When you find one you use it. Simple as that.

You do not need a huge book full of case law to fight your case. You do not need a ton of case law to back up an argument. In every case a small notebook is

all that need to defend yourself on your second trial. It is best to have your cite book with you on your second trial because the areas the prosecutor violated once, he will be likely to violate again. Having the statutes and case law with you can stop him dead in his tracks. Even better is to have your Frankenstein Document with you as well for obvious reasons. These two documents give you a spear and a shield with which to fight again. A small number of good case law's, used well is better than a large number of good case law's used poorly.

As you examine case law you discover that two or more case laws can be combined to back up a larger issue than raised by the two smaller case laws. For example, you can cite the violation of a state law in your trial and then use Lambright v.Lewis to establish a violation of due process which is guaranteed to get you a new trial. However it is not a good idea to combine two claims into one argument. Doing so can result in a valid argument being denied because it includes an invalid claim with a valid one. Because they are both part of the same argument and not addressed as separate issues the entire argument will be denied. The courts of course, will not educate you on your mistake. The law works like locks and keys. Without the right key the lock won't open. Many times a key will go into the lock, but the key won't turn. Drafting motions and other court documents operates exactly the same way. In many cases you may have the right idea, but because you didn't express something in the document that needed to be addressed no success was obtained. This is why it is best to use motions that have worked for others, rather than venture off creating your own documents. Once you become a member of a legal club, you should have access to documents that have worked for people in the past and be allowed to copy them.

How to Read a Case Law Citation

Knowing how to read and write case citations is an important skill for everyone studying criminal justice. The figure below and the comments that follow may help with your understanding of the basic elements. Those of you going on to law school will become aware of greater complexity than is shown here. But this level of understanding is sufficient for most of us.

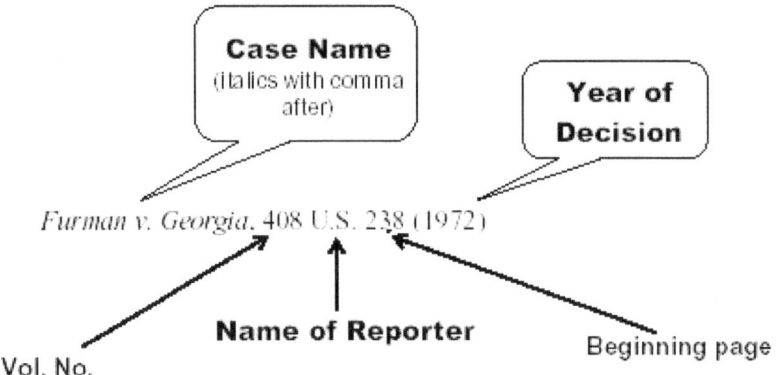

Above are the parts of a standard case citation. The citation tells us that a case called Furman versus Georgia was decided in 1972 and can be found in Volume 408 of the United States Reports, starting on page 238. Some Variations 1. When using a direct quote from the case, it is important to provide the specific page on which that quote is found. In that case, the citation would have the page added as follows:

Furman v. Georgia, 408 U.S. 238, 240 (1972)
OR
Furman v. Georgia, 408 U.S. at 240 (1972)

- Because federal appeals courts (circuit courts) are found in one of twelve different districts, the specific district is typically added as follows: *Cooper v. Pate*, 382 F.2d 443 (7th Cir. 1967)
- Ninety-four federal district courts are spread throughout the country (there is at least one in every state and the more populated states have as many as four). The specific district should be identified: *Howard v. United States*, 864 F.Supp. 1019 (D. Colo. 1994) Case Name

There are typically two names for a case. Usually, the first name identifies who is bringing the court action and the second name is the person against whom action is being brought. In a criminal law case action is almost always brought by the state (e.g., People or State) against a person (e.g., Joe) as in *People v. Joe* or *State v. Joe*. Cases are cited by an italicized case name as shown above, but the

problem is that you can't italicize handwriting well, so it is permitted to underline the case name instead.

However, the "defendant" may not always stay the same. In the Furman v. Georgia case, Furman was originally the defendant in a murder case being prosecuted in Georgia. However, Furman appealed his conviction and in doing so he became the person taking action against the state.

Year

This is the year in which the decision was delivered by the court. It may not be (and in appellate cases, probably isn't) the year in which the case was heard. Name of Reporter A "reporter" is a multi-volume publication where court decisions are found. The full name and abbreviations for the reporters you are most likely to encounter as undergraduates are:

Full Name	Official Abbreviation	Type of Case Reported
United States Reports	U.S.	U.S. Supreme Court
Supreme Court Reporter	S.Ct.	U.S. Supreme Court
Federal Reporter (First through third series)	F., F.2d, and F.3d	Federal Appeals Courts
Federal Supplement (First and second series)	F.Supp, F.Supp2	Important decisions from Federal District Courts

Volume Number and Beginning Page

Without knowing what volume of the reporter to look in, and what page the case starts on, it would be very difficult to track the case down. Not impossible, however, as you can use the table of cases in digests like West's *United States Supreme Court Digest* or, for very recent cases, *U.S. Law Week*. Similar digests exist for other federal and state cases. The information for this handout was gleaned from several sources. Especially useful were, *Legal Research: How to Find & Understand the Law*, by Elias and Levinkind, and from Ferdico's *Criminal Procedure for the Criminal Justice Professional.*

A STRING CITATION is one that contains multiple case law citations that each say essentially the same thing. See example below:

US v. Cooks, 52 F.3d 101 (5th Cir. 1995)
Giglia v. US, 405 US 150, 31 L.Ed.2d 104, 92 S.Ct. 763 (1972)
Napue v. Illinois, 360 US 264, 2 LEM 1217, 79 S.Ct. 1173 (1959)
Where the government fails to disclose evidence of any understanding or agreement as to future prosecution of a key government witness, due process may require reversal of the conviction ... also ... the government has a duty to disclose such understandings for they directly affect the credibility of the witness. This duty of disclosure is even more important where the witness provides the key testimony against the accused. When writing a string citation the most recent decision is listed first.

When creating a string citation the order of the cases in the string go from the highest court to the lowest following this example:

US Supreme Court
Circuit Court of Appeals
Federal District Court
State Supreme Court
State Appellate Court
State Superior Court
International Courts

NOTICE: All case law citations in this book conform to the Blue Book Citation Format.

On the next page you will find an index of all the case law requests made by the Legal Club since my release in 2007. You will never find a more motivated group of people when it comes to case law research and they have been of tremendous benefit to me in my trials and they can help you too. The incredible thing about the SO Combat Manual is how it has become a tool for the inmates and the outmates to help people in trouble all across America. When you are on the inside one thing that becomes apparent is that as far as the rest of the world is

concerned you might as well be dead. The SO Combat Manual proves that this is not true!

AMMENDMENTS TO THE CONSTITUTION OF THE UNITED STATES

AMENDMENT 1

Congress shall make no law respecting an establishment of religion, or prohibiting the free exercise thereof; or abridging the freedom of speech, or of the press; or the right of the people peaceably to assemble, and to petition the Government for a redress of grievances.

AMENDMENT 2

A well-regulated militia, being necessary to the security of a free state, the right of the people to keep and bear arms, shall not be infringed.

AMENDMENT 3

No soldier shall, in time of peace be quartered in any house, without the consent of the owner, nor in time or war, but in a manner to be prescribed by law.

AMENDMENT 4

The right of the people to be secure in their persons, houses, papers, and effects, against unreasonable searches and seizures, shall not be violated, and no warrants shall issue, but upon probable cause, supported by oath or affirmation and particularly describing the place to be searched, and the persons or things to be seized.

AMENDMENT 5

No person shall be held to answer for a capital, or otherwise infamous crime, unless on a presentment or indictment of a Grand Jury, except in cases arising in the land or naval forces, or in the militia, when in actual service in time of war or public danger; nor shall any person be subject for the same offence to be twice put jeopardy of life or limb; nor shall be compelled in any criminal case to be a witness against himself, nor be deprived of life, liberty, or property, without due process of law; nor shall private property be taken for public use, without just compensation.

AMENDMENT 6

In all criminal prosecutions, the accused shall enjoy the right to a speedy and public trial, by an impartial jury of the State and district wherein the crime shall

have been committed, which district shall have been previously ascertained by law, and to be informed of the nature and cause of the accusation; to be confronted with the witnesses against him; to have compulsory process for obtaining witnesses in his favor, and to have the assistance of counsel for his defense.

AMENDMENT 7

In suits at common law, where the value in controversy shall exceed twenty dollars, the right of trial by jury shall be preserved, and no fact tried by a jury shall be otherwise reexamined in any court of the United States, than according to the rules of common law.

AMENDMENT 8

Excessive bail shall not be required, nor excessive fines imposed, nor cruel and unusual punishments inflicted.

AMENDMENT 9

The enumeration in the Constitution, or certain rights, shall not be construed to deny or disparage others retained by the people.

AMENDMENT 10

The powers not delegated to the United States by the Constitution, nor prohibited by it to the States, are reserved to the states respectively, or to the people.

AMENDMENT 11

The Judicial power of the United States shall not be construed to extend to any suit in law or equity. commenced or prosecuted against one of the United States by Citizens of another State, or by Citizens or Subjects of any Foreign State.

AMENDMENT 13
Section 1

Neither slavery nor involuntary servitude, except as a punishment for crime whereof the party shall have been duly convicted, shall exist within the United States, or any place subject to their jurisdiction.

Section 2

Congress shall have power to enforce this article by appropriate legislation.

AMENDMENT 14

All persons born or naturalized in the United States, and subject to the jurisdiction thereof, are citizens of the United States and of the State wherein they reside. No State shall make or enforce any law which shall abridge the privileges or immunities of citizens of the United States; nor shall any State deprive any person of life, liberty, or property, without due process of law; nor deny to any person within its jurisdiction the equal protection of the laws.

Abreviations

Abreviations
A.R.S. = Arizona Revised Statutes
A.R.C. = Arizona Rules of Court
F.R.C. = Federal Rules of Court
A.R.Cr.P. = Arizona Rules of Criminal Procedure
F.R.Cr.P. = Federal Rules of Criminal Procedure
A.R.C.P. = Arizona Rules of Civil Procedure
F.R.Cr.P. = Federal Rules of Civil Procedure
A.R.E. = Arizona Rules of Evidence
F.R.E. = Federal Rules of Evidence
G.L.J. = Georgetown Law Journal
C.J.S. = Corpus Jurus Secundum
E.R. = Ethics Rule (State Bar)

Ex Parte Wilson, 114 US 417, 426 (1885)
Defendant has the right to insist that he shall not be put upon his trial except on the accusation of the grand jury.

US v. Gordan, 172 F.3d 753 (10th Cir. 1999)
Due process and ineffective assistance of counsel claims raised in motion to vacate or not addressed on direct appeal, and therefore were not procedurally barred.

US v. Griffin, 765 F.2d 677 (7th Cir. 1985)
Kaufman v. US, 394 US 217, 22 L.Ed.2d 227, 89 S.Ct. 1068 (1969)
Failure to bring issue on direct appeal bars raising that issue in a §2255 motion unless good cause for not raising that matter on direct appeal is demonstrated.

State v. O'Grady, 312 US 329, 61 S.Ct. 572, 85 L.Ed. 859, 1941 US Lexis 921
Petitioner pled guilty to simple burglary but was sentenced to burglary with explosives.

42 USC §1983

Church of Scientology v. US Dept. of Justice, (1979) 612 F.2d 417, 425
For reference; the word "person" in legal terminology is perceived as a general word which normally includes in its scope a variety of entities other than human beings.

Hafer v. Melo, (1991, US) 116 L.Ed.2d 301,112 S.Ct. 358, 91 CDOS 8883, 91 daily journal DAR 13658, 57 BNA FEP CAS 241, 6 BNA IER CAS 1487, 57 CCH EPD ¶ 4109
State officials sued under 42 USC § 1983 for damages in their personal capacities are subject to personal liability since they fit within statutory term "person".

US v. Miles, 207 F.3d 988 (7th Cir. 2000)
US v. Goodson, 165 F.3d 610 (8th Cir. 1999)
Thompson v. Calderon, 109 F.3d 1358 (9th Cir. 1996)
US v. Hanna, 55 F.3d 1456 (9th Cir. 1995)
US v. Blais, 98 F.3d 647 (1st Cir. 1996)
US v. Wong, 78 F.3d 73 (2nd Cir. 1996)
US v. Clarke, 988 F.2d 1459 (6th Cir. 1993)
The same laws that allow you to sue a judge also covers a prosecutor, with the exception that they are covered by only "qualified immunity" which means you can sue them for monetary damages in both their official and individual capacities. Did the prosecuting attorney withhold exculpatory testimony? Did the prosecuting attorney use knowingly perjured testimony? Did the prosecuting attorney abuse the judicial process? Note: You have to prove a bad faith motive to have a case.

Will v. Michigan Dept. of State Police, (1989, US) 105 L.Ed.2d 45, 109 S.Ct. 2304, 49 BNA FEP CAS 1664, 50 CCH EPD ¶ 39067
A state is not a person within meaning of 42 USC § 1983 which provides a person acting under color of state law in violating another's federal constitutional rights is liable to injured party.

Access to the Courts

Abdul-akbar v. Watson, 4 F.3d 195 (3rd Cir. 1993)
Standard in applying prisoners constitutional right of access to the courts is whether legal resources available to prisoner will enable him to identify legal issues that he desires to present to relevant authorities, including courts, and to make communications with and presentations to those authorities understood.

Allen v. City and County of Honolulu, 39 F.3d, 936 (9th Cir. 1994)
A prisoner cannot be forced to choose between the law library and recreation.

Allen v. Sakai, 40 F.3d 1001 (9th Cir. 1994)
Inmate was not required to show that denial by prison officials of photocopying services and use of pen actually prejudiced his right to access to the courts in order to defeat summary judgment on official's claim of qualified immunity; it was enough that he alleged conduct on part of officials that, if true, violated clearly established constitutional rights.

Alston v. Debruyn, 13 F.3d 1036 (7th Cir. 1994)
Inmate's fundamental constitutional right to access to the courts is not diminished when he is held in segregation.

Bear v. Kautzky, 305 F.3d 802, 804 (8th Cir. 2002)
Right of access claim stated because prisoner regulation restricted inmate to inmate legal communication.

Benjamin v. Fraser, 264 F.3d 175, 184 (2nd Cir. 2001)
Regulations that unjustifiably obstruct availability of professional representation or other aspects of the right of access to the court are invalid.

Bieregu v. Reno, 59 F.3d 1445 (3rd Cir. 1995)
First Amendment right to petition is birthplace for the right of court access.

<u>Bound v. Smith</u>, (1977) 430 US 817, 52 L.Ed.2d 72, 97 S.Ct. 1491

Fundamental constitutional right of access to courts requires state prison authorities to assist inmate in preparation and filing of the meaningful legal papers by providing prisoners with adequate law libraries or adequate assistance from persons trained in law; it is irrelevant that expenditure of funds for appointment of counsel in some state post-trial conviction proceedings for prisoners whose claims survive initial review by courts may be authorized by state, and creation of adversary inmate grievance commission does not answer constitutional requirement for legal assistance to prisoner. Prisoners have fundamental constitutional right to adequate effective and meaningful access to courts to challenge violations of constitutional rights.

<u>Bribiesca v. Galaza</u>, 215 F.3d 1015, 1020 (9th Cir. 2000)

Incarcerated criminal defendant who chose to represent self has constitutional right to access law books or other tools to assist in preparing defense.

<u>Casey v. Lewis</u>, 43 F.3d 1261 (9th Cir. 1994)

State is required to provide legal assistance for inmates deemed security risks and denied access to prison's law library. To assure compliance with inmates' constitutional right to access to courts, injunction properly required that prisoners be allowed at least three 20minute phone calls per week to their attorneys. Order requiring that Arizona Department of Corrections (ADOC) law libraries remain open for at least 50 hours each week was reasonable to accommodate inmates' constitutional right to access to courts.

Importance of prisoners' fundamental right to meaningful access to courts cannot be overstated; since it is the right upon which all other rights depend.

The right to legal assistance, especially in the context of the constitutional right to the writ of habeas corpus, means that absence of other adequate assistance, as through a functioning public defender system, a state may not deny prisoners legal assistance of another inmate.

Cepulonis v. Fair, 732 F.2d 1 (1st Cir. 1984)
The district court did not abuse it's discretion in ordering a satellite law library established in the segregation unit.

Ching v. Lewis, (1990, CA9 Ariz.) 895 F.2d 608 Arbitrary policy of denying prisoners contact visits with attorney prohibits effective attorney client communication and unnecessarily abridges prisoners right to meaningful access to court in violation of 14th amendment.

Demallory v. Cullen, 855 F.2d 442 (7th Cir. 1988)
Bounds v. Smith, 430 US 817, 52 L.Ed.2d 72, 97 S.Ct. 1491 (1977)
Ex Parte Hall, 312 US 546, 85 L.Ed.2d 1034, 61 S.Ct. 540 (1941)
Prisoners have a fundamental right to adequate, effective, and meaningful access to court to challenge violations of their Constitutional rights.

Farmer v. Brennan, 1114 S.Ct. (1970)
Estelle, 429 US at 105, 97 S.Ct. at 2 91-92
Arizona prison officials violated prison inmate's rights to access to courts by failure to provide sufficient number of trained legal assistants and by maintaining inadequate law library.

Ganey v. Garrison, 813 F.2d 650 (4th Cir. 1987)
Prisoner who received favorable verdict in §1983 suit against warden for denial of adequate access to prison's law library was "prevailing party" entitled to award of attorney fees.

Garcia v. Miller, (1982, CA7 Ill.) 688 F.2d 480,cert. denied, (US) 74 L.Ed.2d 1000, 103 S.Ct. 976
Prisoners have due process right to access to courts which requires prison authorities to assist inmate in preparation and filing of meaningful legal papers by providing prisoners with a reasonable access to adequate law libraries or adequate assistance from persons trained in law.

Gluth v. Kangas, 951 F.2d 1504 (9th Cir. 1991) It is the states burden to provide inmates with meaningful access to the law library and to demonstrate that its chosen method was adequate.

Housley v. Dodson, 41 F.3d 597 (10th Cir. 1994)
Pembroke v. Wood County Texas, 981 F.2d 225 (5th Cir. 1993)
Inmate's allegations that he was denied all access to any legal resources during his six month confinement in county jail was sufficient to state claim against jail officials based on denial of right of access to courts.

In Re Workers' Compensation Refund, 46 F.3d 813 First amendment right of court access cannot be impaired either directly or indirectly.

John v. Adams, 969 F.2d 228 (6th Cir. 1992)
Incarcerated juveniles have a constitutional right of access to the courts.

Johnson v. Avery, 393 US 483, 21 L.Ed.2d 718, 89 S.Ct. 747 (1969)
Like others, prisoners have a constitutional right to petition the government for redress of their grievances, which includes a reasonable right of access to the courts. Prisoners right of access to courts may not be denied or obstructed. Prison must make available certain minimal legal materials.

Knop v. Johnson, 977 F.2d 996, 1006 (6th Cir. 1992)
Meaningful access denied because state failed to provide competent paralegals to assist inmates; paralegals defined as intelligent layperson who can right coherent English and has had a modicum of exposure to legal research and prisoners rights law.

Lewis v. Casey, 518 US 343,349 (1996)
Prisoner must demonstrate actual injury resulting from a denial of access to courts in order to allege a constitutional violation. Constitutional violation shown only when failure to provide legal assistance or library causes actual injury to prisoners contemplated or existing litigation.

Morello v. James, 810 F.2d 344 (2nd Cir. 1987)

Wright v. Newsome, 795 F.2d 964 (11th Cir. 1986)

2.1 Allegation that prison officials seized inmate's pleadings and law book and destroyed other legal papers clearly stated claim of denial of access to courts.

2.2. Allegation that officer had taken inmates pro se brief adequately stated claim for denial of access to the courts.

Nestle Ice Cream Co. Vs. N.I.R.B., 46 F.3d 578 (6th Cir. 1995)

Right to petition for redress of grievances includes right of access to courts.

Payne v. Superior Court of Los Angeles County, (1976) 17 Cal 3d 908, 132 Cal Rptr. 405, 553 P.2d 565

Indigent prisoner seeking to defend civil suit due process right of access to courts, where he would almost inevitably suffer default judgment is unable to afford counsel to appear as his surrogate.

Strickler v. Waters, 989 F2d 1375 (4th Cir. 1993)

Connet v. Sakai, 994 F2d 1408 (9th Cir. 1993)

Petrick v. Maynard, 11 F.3d 991 (10th Cir. 1993)

Prisoner's constitutional right of access to the courts requires prison authorities to assist inmates in preparation and filing of meaningful legal papers by providing prisoners with adequate law library or adequate assistance from persons trained in the law. Affirmative obligations are imposed on states to assure all inmates access to the courts and assistance in preparing and filing of legal papers.

Ruark v. Sqlano, 928 F2d 947 (10th Cir. 1991)

Prisoner's constitutional right to access to legal resources is not conditioned on showing of need. When correctional employee failed to answer prisoners request for access to resources a valid claim for denial of access to legal materials was stated.

Sands v. Lewis, 886 F.2d 1166 (9th Cir. 1989)

Prisoner claiming inadequate law library or legal assistance need not show actual injury resulting from denial of access to courts.

Shabazz v. Askins, 14 F.3d 533 (10th Cir. 1994)

Goff v. Burton, 7 F.3d 734 (8th Cir. 1993)

Prison officials may not retaliate against or harass inmate because of inmate's exercise of his right of access to the courts.

Terry v. Rees, 985 F.2d 283 (6th Cir. 1993)

Criminal trials are fundamentally unfair if state proceeds against indigent defendant without making certain that he or she has access to law materials integral to building a defense.

Tucker v. Randall, 948 172d 388 (7th Cir. 1991)

Unreasonable restrictions on prisoners telephone access may violate 1st and 14th Amendments.

Williams v. Leeke, (1978, CA4 SC) 584, 1336, cert. denied, 442 US 911, 61 L.Ed.2d 276, 99 S.Ct. 2825

Inmate is entitled to reasonable access to courts and such access is not provided inmate serving substantial sentence of confinement if, without other legal assistance, inmate had access only to law library which was so restrictive as to be un-meaningful.

Aid And Abet

US v. Beutenmuller, 29 F.3d 973 (5th Cir. 1994)
To convict defendant of aiding and abetting, government must prove that defendant intentionally associated with criminal venture and sought by his action to make venture succeed. To prove aiding and abetting, government must demonstrate beyond reasonable doubt that each element of offense that defendant is accused of aiding and abetting was committed by some other person.

US v. Davis, 61 F.3d 291 (5th Cir. 1995) To sustain conviction of aiding and abetting offense, government must show that defendant associated with criminal venture, participated in venture, and sought by action to make venture succeed.

US v. Garcia, 45 F.3d 196 (7th Cir. 1995) Crime of aiding and abetting requires knowledge of illegal activity that is being aiding and abetted, desire to help activity succeed and some act of helping.

US v. Murray, 988 F.2d 518 (5th Cir. 1993)
US v. Gonzales, 999 F.2d 1326 (9th Cir. 1993)
To aid and abet another to commit crime, it is necessary that defendant is some sort associate himself with venture that he participates in it as something that he wishes to bring about and that he seeks by his action to make it succeed.

US v. Hadley, 918 F.2d 848 (9th Cir. 1990) To constitute "attempt" there must be more than mere preparation to commit crime; there must be some appreciable fragment of crime in progress.

US v. James, 998 F.2d 74 (2nd Cir. 1993)
Aider and abettor, unlike accessory after the fact, is punishable as a principle.

US v. Jaramillo, 42 F.3d 920 (5th Cir. 1995)
Mere presence and association are not alone enough to sustain a conviction for aiding and abetting.

US v. Lyon, 949 F.2d 240 (8th Cir. 1991)

To prove aiding and abetting government must show that each defendant associated himself with unlawful venture, participated in it as something he wished to bring about, and sought by his actions to make it succeed.

US v. Langston, 970 F.2d 692 (10th Cir. 1992)

As a prerequisite to aiding and abetting, government is required to prove that someone has committed the underlying substantive offense.

US v. Salamanca, 990 F.2d 629 (D.C. Cir. 1993)
US v. Rodriguez Alvarado, 985 F.2d 15 (1st Cir. 1993)
US v. Head, 927 F.2d 1361 (6th Cir. 1991)

Mere presence at scene of crime and guilty knowledge of crime are not enough to convict defendant of aiding and abetting.

US v. Walser, 3 F.3d 380 (11th Cir. 1993)

Aiding and abetting statute applies to all federal criminal statutes and prohibits one from causing another to do any act that would be illegal if one did it personally.

US v. Williamson, 53 F.3d 1500 (10th Cir. 1995)

Mere presence at scene of drug transaction, without more, is insufficient to support conviction for aiding and abetting.

Appeal

<u>Abney v. US</u>, 431 US 651, 658 - 59 (1977)

Denial of motion to dismiss indictment on double jeopardy grounds immediately appealable because collateral issue and delay irreparably harm's defendants right not to be tried for same offense.

<u>Aldrich & Steinberger v. Martin</u>, 172 Ariz. 445, 447 - 48, 337 P.2d 1180, 1182 - 83 (App. 1992)

<u>In Re Estates of Spear</u>, 173 Ariz. 565, 567, 845 P.2d 491, 493 (App. 1992)

For example, on the appropriate occasions our Supreme Court has considered issues briefed neither in the trial nor in the Court of Appeals, e.g. <u>Barrio v. San Manuel Div. Hosp. for Magma Copper Co.</u>, 143 Ariz. 101, 104, 692 P.2d 280, 283 (1984), an example we have followed in reaching un-briefed but dispositive issues which require no additional facts.

<u>Benigni v. City Of Hemet</u>, 879 F.2d 473 (9th Cir. 1989)

Credibility of witnesses and weight of evidence are issues for jury and are generally not subject to appellate review.

<u>Bettner v. Sadoff & Rudoy Industries</u>, 728 F.2d 820 (7th Cir. 1984)

Generally, party who is awarded attorney's fees for winning in district court will be awarded fees for defending victory in court of appeals.

<u>Brookhart v. Janis</u>, 384 US 1, 4 (1966)

For waiver to be effective it must be clearly established that there was an intentional relinquishment or abandonment of a known right.

<u>Brown,___ Ariz. at ___ ¶ 12</u>, 99 P.3d at 18

In a case in which multiple aggravating facts are alleged the jury must find these facts.

Chartered PLC v. Price Waterhouse, 190 Ariz. 6, 39, 945 P.2d 317, 350 (App. 1996)

The courts often declined to apply waiver when the issue is of constitutional importance, is of general statewide importance, or will dispose of the appeal.

Hamling v. US, 418 US 87, 41 L.Ed.2d 590, 94 S.Ct. 2887 (1974)

Glasser v. US, 315 US 60, 86 L.Ed 680, 62 S.Ct. 457 (1942)

When reviewing the sufficiency of the evidence to support a guilty verdict the evidence, and all reasonable inferences, is viewed in the light most favorable to the government.

Houston v. Lack, 487 US 266, 101 L.Ed.2d 245, 108 S.Ct. 2379 (1988)

Pro se prisoner's notice of appeal held filed, for purposes of time limit under Rule 4(a)(1) of Federal Rules of Appellate Procedure, at moment of delivery to prison authorities for mailing to the court.

Jimenez v. Sears Roebuck Co., 183 Ariz. 399, 406 n.9 904 P.2d 861, 868 n.9 (1995)

Constitutional issues advanced in neither trial nor Court of Appeals were reached. The issue presented in this case is an important one of constitutional dimension. We therefore decline to apply waiver. Even if the error were waived, we can review for fundamental error.

Johnson v. Zerbst, 304 US for 58, 464 (1938)

What is at issue is a defendant's right to a jury trial on sentencing factors. The record reveals no proper waiver of that right. Accordingly defendant cannot be said to have waived it. A.R.Cr.P. Rule 18.1

North Carolina v. Pearce, 395 US 711, 23 L.Ed.2d 656, 89 S.Ct. 2072 (1969)

A prosecutor is "without right to put a price on appeal. A defendant's exercise of a right of appeal must be free and unfettered." 395 US 724.

Note: The Supreme Court has held that denials of three types of motions are immediately appealable under collateral order doctrine: Pre-trial motions to dismiss an indictment based on double jeopardy clause, Pre-trial motion to dismiss an indictment based on speech and debate clause, and Motion to reduce excessive bail.

Owens v. New York City Housing Authority, 934 F.2d 405 (2nd Cir. 1991)
On appeal, all doubts in factual record must be resolved in favor of party opposing motion for summary judgment.

People of Territory Of Guam v. Bqrja, 983 F.2d 914 (9th Cir. 1992)
US v. Sasser, 971 F.2d 470 (10th Cir. 1992)
Governments right to appeal is narrow, and government may not appeal in criminal case in the absence of express statutory authority.

Ring, 204 Ariz. at 561, ¶ 82, 65 P.3d at 942
No reversible error occurs when the evidence overwhelmingly establishes the factor the defendant stipulated to the facts constituting the aggravating circumstances, or the fact is implicit in the jury's verdict of guilt. Id at ¶ 86.

Romero v. Tansy, 46 F.3d 1024 (10th Cir. 1995)
Johnson v. Dugger, 911 F.2d 440 (11th Cir. 1990)
Defendant's right to effective assistance of counsel applies not just at trial but also on direct appeal.

Satcher v. Honda Motor Co. Ltd., 984 F.2d 135 (5th Cir. 1993)
Davis v. Locke, 936 F2d 1208 (11th Cir. 1991)
Notices of appeal are generally to be read liberally.

Snyder v. Sumner, 960 F.2d 1448 (9th Cir. 1992) Issue may be heard for first time on appeal when plain error has occurred and injustice might otherwise result

State v. Alvarez, 205 Ariz. 110, 112 n.1, 67 P.3d 706, 708 n.1 (App. 2003)

State v. Johnson, 103 Ariz. 358, 360, 903 P.3d 1116, 1118 (App. 1995)

Sentencing enhancement elevates the entire range of permissible punishment while aggravation and mitigation raises or lowers a sentence within that range.

State v. Bor Boa, 102 P.3d 183, 190 (Wash. App. 204)

Because the error was not waived, we proceed to consider whether it was harmless. Failure to submit an aggravating factor to the jury is subject to review for harmless error.

State v. Burton, 144 Ariz. 248, 697 P.2d 331 (1985)

Where a sufficient specific motion in Limine is made and ruled upon on the merits, the objection raised in debt motion is preserved for appeal without the need for specific objection at trial. A.R.C.P. Rule 7.2

State v. Chaney, 141 Ariz. 295, 302, 686 P.2d 1265, 1272 (1984)

To establish actual prejudice, the defendant must show that, "the jurors have formed preconceived notions concerning the defendant skills and that they cannot put those notions aside.

State v. Davolt, 84 P.3d 456 (Ariz. 2004) ¶ 49.

In the absence of presumed prejudice, the defendant must demonstrate that the pre-trial publicity was actually prejudicial and likely deprived him of a fair trial.

State v. Gendron, 168 Ariz. 153, 154, 812 P.2d 66, 67 (1991)

Blakely error is reversible on appeal as fundamental error.

State v. Hardwick, 183 Ariz. 649, 656 - 57, 905 P.2d 1384, 391 - 92 (App. 1995)

The failure to submit an aggravating factor to the jury may be harmless when no reasonable jury could find that the state fails to prove the factor beyond a reasonable doubt.

State Ariz. v. John Carl Munninger, Court of Appeals Division I Cause No. 2002-091835

Sentence vacated and remanded under Blakely. ¶9 we need not apply waiver even when a party has fails to preserve an issue. The practice of not addressing issues for the first time on appeal is merely a rule of procedure and does not confirm our jurisdiction. The appellate court has discretion whether to apply waiver standard.

State v. King, 1998 Ariz. LEXIS 60
Inmate's request for review was timely where he had filed a proper request for an extension and urged several meritorious grounds, so the court of appeals' dismissal was vacated as improper.

State v. Oaks, No. 2 CA - CR 2002-0386, 2004 WL to 2955944, at 5, 12 (Ariz. App. Jan. 14 2005)
State v. Resendis - Felix, Ariz.___, ___,¶ 6,100 P.3d 457, 459 (App. 2004)
The application of the fundamental error doctrine comports with a long line of Ariz. cases that regard an illegal sentence, including a sentence that results from improper consideration of a fact to increase the sentence, as fundamental error.

State v. Paxson, 203 Ariz. 38, 42 ¶ 19, 49 P.3d 310, 324 (App. 2002)
Appellate court reviews question of law De Novo.

State v. Prince, 14 to Ariz. 256, 258, 689 P.2d 515, 517 (1984)
Whether defendants sentence was invalid under Blakely was not waived. Note: we express no opinion as to whether a defendant who has waived his right to a jury trial generally need specifically waive his right to a jury trial on sentencing factors. A defendant who has not waived his right to a jury, however has not waived the issue. As far as we can determine, all courts that have considered this question agree that a defendant who exercised his rights to a jury trial on his guilt, and who has not expressly waived his right to a jury trial of sentencing factors, has not waived his Blakely challenge because he has not waived a jury.

State v. Ring, 204 Ariz. 534, 552 ¶ 44, 65 P.3d 915, 933 (2003)
Sentencing error is harmless only if we can say with certainty that the same sentence would have been obtained if the error had not occurred.

State v. Smith, 184 Ariz. 456, 910P.2d (1996)
The appellate court's decision of whether to accept review from the denial of a P.C.R. is discretionary and also subject to review for an abuse of discretion.

State v. Smith, 197 Ariz. 333, 338, ¶ 16, 4 P.3d 388, 393 (App. 1999)
Before there can be a waiver, the record must show a knowing waiver by defendant.

State v. Thues, 203 Ariz. 339, 340 ¶ 4, 54 P.3d 437, 441 (App. 2002)
State v. Cox, 261 Ariz. 464, 468, ¶13, 37 P.3d 437, 441 (App. 2002)
Sentencing process was fundamentally flawed" due to consideration of incorrect sentencing range, even though lengths of sentence did not exceed statutory minimum. This includes the similar error of failing to submit to a jury a sentencing enhancement allegation.

State v. Wiley, 199 Ariz. 242, 16 P.3d 803 (App. 2002)
An appellate court will not disturb the trial court's ruling on a petition for post - conviction relief absent an abuse of discretion.

Tapiau v. Tansy, 926 F.2d 1554 (10th Cir. 1991)
Evitts v. Lucey, 469 US 387, 83 L.Ed.2d 821, 105 S.Ct. 830 (1985)
Effective assistance of counsel on first appeal is a right held guaranteed by due process clause of Fourteenth Amendment.

US v. Ameline, 02-303 26 (9th Cir. 2005)
Purcell v. Bank of Atlantic Financial Corp., 85 F.3d 1508, 1513 (11th Cir. 1996)
Noting that a dissenting Supreme Court opinion is not binding precedent and "does not tell us how a majority of the court would decide."

US v. Argentine, 814 F2d 783 (1st Cir. 1987)
When it is determined on appeal that error at trial compromised defendant's constitutional rights, defendant need not demonstrate actual prejudice; reasonable possibility of injury attributable to error warrants reversal.

US v. Benjamin, 30 F.3d 196 (1st Cir. 1994)
Absent exceptional circumstances, contentions not argued below would not be addressed for first time on appeal.

US v. Brentley, 961 F.2d 425 (3rd Cir. 1992)
Indigent defendant is entitled to free trial transcript on appeal; however, alternative method, such as videotape, may be satisfactory equivalent.

US v. Bushert, 997 F.2d 1343 (11th Cir. 1993)
There is no constitutional right to appeal; right to appeal is purely statutory.

US v. Colon - Munoz, 192 F.3d 210 (1st Cir. 1999)
Where an equal or nearly equal theory of guilt and a theory of innocence is supported by the evidence the Court of Appeals must reverse a conviction.

US v. Davis, 974 F.2d 182 (D.C. Cir. 1992)
For an appellate court to overturn a conviction under the "plain error" standard parties must meet 3 requirements:
Error must be plain (i.e. so obvious that judge should have recognized it on his own); Error must affect substantial rights of the parties; and the error must be one that seriously affects fairness, integrity, or public reputation of judicial proceedings.

US v. Davis, 55 F.3d 517 (10th Cir. 1995)
In general, passage of two years creates presumption of inordinate delay on appeal.

US v. Duggan, 936 F.2d 181 (5th Cir. 1991)
Manzoli v. C.I.R., 904 F.2d 101 (1st Cir. 1990)
Argument not presented in trial court cannot be raised for first time on appeal.

US v. Mendoza - Burciaga, 981 F.2d 192 (5th Cir. 1992)
In reviewing sufficiency of evidence to support conviction, court of appeals asks whether rational trier of fact could find that evidence established guilt beyond a reasonable doubt.

US v. Mitchelle's Lounge, 39 F.3d 684 (7th Cir. 1994)
Time period for appeal begins to run on day order appealed from is granted.

US v. Neal, 27 F.3d 1035 (5th Cir. 1994)
US v. Cashwell, 950 F.2d 699 (11th Cir. 1992)
Griffin v. Illinois, 351 US 12, 100 L.Ed 891, 76 S.Ct. 585 (1956)
Criminal defendant has right to record on appeal which includes complete transcript of proceedings at trial.

US v. Pellerito, 878 F.2d 1535 (1st Cir. 1989)
Need for competency survives trial and extends through sentencing phrase of criminal proceeding.

US v. Rodriguez, 15 F.3d 408 (5th Cir. 1994)
Although reply brief is not mandatory under Federal Rules of Appellate Procedure, it is best vehicle for narrowing true issues (and is especially important and called for when new point or issue is raised).

US v. Sitton, 968 F.2d 947 (9th Cir. 1992)
Defendant was entitled to raise claim on appeal where he made offer of proof at trial.

Wheeler v. City of Pleasant Grove, 746 F2d 1437 (11th Cir. 1984)
Arizona v. California, 460 US 605, 75 L.Ed.2d 318, 103 S.Ct. 1382 (1983)
On remand, district court is not free to deviate from court of appeals mandate, and, to determine scope of mandate, it is appropriate, and indeed often necessary, to look to court of appeals opinion. Supreme Court termed this the "An Amorphous Concept."

Wright v. Deyton, 757 F.2d 1253 (11th Cir. 1985) Willis v. Newsome, 747 F.2d 605 (11th Cir. 1984)
Harris Truck Lines v. Cherry Meat Packers, 371 US 215, 9 L.Ed.2d 261, 83 S.Ct. 283(1962)
Courts will permit an appellant to maintain an otherwise untimely appeal in unique circumstances (see Harris for "Unique Circumstances"). The Rules of Appellate

Procedure "Were not adopted to set traps and pitfalls by way of technicalities for unwary litigants." <u>Willis</u> at 607.

<u>Woods v. Thieret</u>, 903 F.2d 1080 (7th Cir. 1990)
<u>US v. Eatinger</u>, 902 F.2d 1383 (9th Cir. 1990)
Pro se petitioner's arguments must be liberally construed on appeal.

Arrest

Adams v. Metiva, 31 F.3d 375 (6th Cir. 1994)

Simmons v. Pryor, 25 F.3d 650 (7th Cir. 1994)

In order to prevail in unlawful arrest action, plaintiff must show lack of probable cause.

Arrington v. McDonald, 808 F.2d 466 (6th Cir. 1986)

Police officers who took individual into custody solely to ascertain her identity were not entitled to immunity. Officers knew it was illegal to make arrest solely for that purpose.

Estate Of Starks v. Enyart, 5 F.3d 230 (7th Cir. 1993) Chew v. Gates, 27 F.3d 1432 (9th Cir. 1994)

Harrell v. Decantur County, Ga., 22 F.3d 1570 (11th Cir. 1994)

Use of force to effect arrest is subject to Fourth Amendment's prohibition on unreasonable seizures.

Fontenot v. Cormier, 56 F.3d 669 (5th Cir. 1995)

Felony suspect cannot defeat lawful arrest begun in public place by escaping into private place.

Gainor v. Rogers, 973 F.2d 1379 (8th Cir. 1992)

First Amendment protects arrestee's right to verbally challenge police officer's actions in asking him for identification.

Groman v. Township Of Manalapan, 47 F.3d 628 (3rd Cir. 1995)

Where police lack probable cause to make arrest, arrestee has claim under §1983 for false imprisonment based on detention pursuant to that arrest.

Ludwig v. Anderson, 54 F.3d 465 (8th Cir. 1995)

Apprehension by deadly force is "seizure" subject to Fourth Amendment.

Maltby v. Winston, 36 F.3d 548 (7th Cir. 1994)
Any evidence that came to light after arrest is not relevant to inquiry into probably cause for arrest.

Ruehman v. Sheahan, 34 F.3d 525 (7th Cir.1994)
Arrest without probable cause is illegal no matter what officers believed.

Scott v. Henrich, 994 F.2d 1338 (9th Cir. 1992)
Under Fourth Amendment police may use only such force as is objectively reasonable under circumstance.

US v. Arias - Villanveva, 998 F.2d 1491 (9th Cir. 1993)
Morgan v. Woessner, 997 F.2d 1244 (9th Cir. 1993)
Government may stop and question any individual for any reason as long as person to whom questions are put remains free to disregard questions and walk away.

US v. Dixon, 51 F.3d 1376 (8th Cir. 1995)
Seizures under Fourth Amendment fall into two categories, investigative stops and arrests; there is no bright line demarcation between the two.

US v. Gooch, 6 F.3d 673 (9th Cir. 1993)
On Motion to Suppress, government has heavy burden of showing that exigent circumstances made warrantless arrest imperative.

US v. Hogan, 38 F.3d 1148 (10th Cir. 1994)
Protective sweep should last no longer than is necessary to dispel reasonable suspicion of danger and, in any event, no longer than it takes to complete the arrest and depart the premises.

US v. Johnson, 910 F.2d 1506 (7th Cir. 1990)
US v. Mendenhall, 446 US 544, 64 L.Ed.2d 497, 100 S.Ct. 1870 (1980)
US v. Brignoni - Ponce, 422 US 873, 45 L.Ed.2d 607, 95 S.Ct. 2574 (1975)
Beck v. Ohio, 379 US 89, 13 L.Ed.2d 142, 85 S.Ct. 223 (1964)
Three categories for police/citizen encounters in relation to the Fourth Amendment are an arrest, for which Fourth Amendment requires that police have probable

cause to believe that a person has committed or is committing a crime, investigatory stop, which is limited to a brief, nonintrusive detention and which is a Fourth Amendment seizure but for which the officer need only have specific and articulable facts giving rise to reasonable suspicion that a person has committed or is committing a crime, and situations involving no restraint on the citizens liberty, as when an officer seeks that citizen's voluntary cooperation through non-coercive questioning.

US v. Johnson, 22 F.3d 674 (6th Cir. 1994)
Absent exigent circumstances, police may not enter a person's home or lodging to effect a warrantless arrest or seizure.

US v. Lambert, 46 F.3d 1064 (10th Cir. 1995)
When law enforcement officials retain individual's driver's license in the course of questioning him, that individual, as a general rule, will not reasonably feel free to terminate encounter.

US v. Mesa, 62 F.3d 159 (6th Cir. 1995)
A hunch is not a "reasonable suspicion."

US v. Roch, 5 F.3d 894 (5th Cir. 1993)
US v. Arzaga, 9 F.3d 91 (10th Cir. 1993)
1. Reasonable suspicion for investigative detention must be formed before seizure occurs. 2. Even investigatory stop is improper unless it is based on reasonable suspicion that criminal activity is afoot.

US v. Shephard, 21 F.3d 933 (9th Cir, 1994)
Evidence in federal prosecution must be suppressed if product of illegal arrest under state law.

US v. Span, 970 F.2d 573 (9th Cir. 1992)
Federal officer who uses excessive force is not acting in good faith and may be resisted.

US v. Tehrami, 49 F.3d 54 (2nd Cir. 1995)
Length of detention may be so excessive as to convert it into arrest.

US v. Wadley, 59 F.3d 510 (5th Cir. 1995)
Warrantless arrest must be based on probable cause.

US v. Wanless, 882 F.2d 1459 (9th Cir. 1989)
Troopers did not have probable cause to arrest passenger for giving false information, and resulting search of his person.

US v. Weaver, 8 F.3d 1240 (7th Cir. 1993)
Arrest must be supported by probable cause.

A.R.S. 13-405

Sexual conduct with a minor; classification; definition.

A. A person commits sexual conduct with a minor by intentionally or knowingly engaging in sexual intercourse or oral sexual contact with any person who is under eighteen years of age.

B. Sexual conduct with a minor who is under fifteen years of age is a class 2 felony and is punishable pursuant to section 13-705. Sexual conduct with a minor who is at least fifteen years of age is a class 6 felony. Sexual conduct with a minor who is at least fifteen years of age is a class 2 felony if the person is the minor's parent, stepparent, adoptive parent, legal guardian, foster parent or the minor's teacher or clergyman or priest and the convicted person is not eligible for suspension of sentence, probation, pardon or release from confinement on any basis except as specifically authorized by section 31-233, subsection A or B until the sentence imposed has been served or commuted.

C. For the purposes of this section, "teacher" means a certificated teacher as defined in section 15-501 or any other person who directly provides academic instruction to pupils in any school district, charter school, accommodation school, the Arizona state schools for the deaf and the blind or a private school in this state.

A.R.S. 13-604.01

Dangerous crimes against children; sentences; definitions .
Note: This statute is now defunct and rewritten as A.R.S. 13-705 to include attempted charges.

In re Nickolas T., 223 Ariz. 403
At the age of 11, the juvenile was charged by delinquency petition with nine county of different sexual acts with a minor. He was adjudicated delinquent after entering into a plea agreement with the State, admitting that he committed sexual assault in exchange for the dismissal of the remaining charges. The juvenile was placed on probation, ordered to obtain in-patient treatment, and required to register as a sex offender. Two years later, the juvenile court released the juvenile from probation, conducted hearings, and granted the juvenile's motion requesting that the registration requirement be terminated. On review, the court held that, under Ariz. Rev. Stat. § 13-3821(G), the juvenile court was vested with the discretion to terminate the juvenile's registration requirement where the offense was committed by a juvenile under the age of 18 and where the juvenile delinquent after entering into a plea agreement with the State, admitting that he committed sexual assault in exchange for the dismissal of the remaining charges. The juvenile was placed on probation, ordered to obtain in-patient treatment, and required to register as a sex offender. Two years later, the juvenile court released the juvenile from probation, conducted hearings, and granted the juvenile's motion requesting that the registration requirement be terminated. On review, the court held that, under Ariz. Rev. Stat. § 13-3821(G), the juvenile court was vested with the discretion to terminate the juvenile's registration requirement where the offense was committed by a juvenile under the age of 18 and where the juvenile successfully completed probation. The juvenile court had the statutory authority to require the juvenile to register as a sex offender and the authority to terminate that requirement when it found that the juvenile had been sufficiently rehabilitated.

State v. Gonzalez, 216 Ariz. 11, 162 P.3d 650
Defendant petitioned for post-conviction relief from conviction for attempted second-degree sexual conduct with a minor under 15 years of age and contributing to the delinquency of a minor, as affirmed on direct appeal. The Superior Court,

Pima County, No. CR-20031557,Christopher C. Browning, J., denied petition. Defendant filed petition for review. The Court of Appeals, Howard, P.J., held that statute under which defendant was sentenced did not apply to his conviction. Petition for review granted and remanded for resentencing.

State v. Ortega, 220 Ariz. 320

Defendant argued that the charges in counts four and five, molestation of a child and sexual conduct with a minor under the age of 15, arose from a single act, and his convictions on both charges constituted a double jeopardy violation. It was necessary for the court to compare the elements of sexual conduct with a minor under 15 with the elements of molestation. Defendant could not commit sexual conduct with a minor under 15 without also committing molestation of a child. Because molestation was a lesser included offense of sexual conduct with a minor under 15, the court concluded that defendant's conviction of both the greater and the lesser offenses violated double jeopardy. Therefore, defendant's conviction on count four, molestation of a child, had to be vacated. Regarding defendant's contention the prosecutor exerted improper influence over a victim's testimony, rendering it unreliable, the court concluded that the prosecutor was entitled to introduce the victim's prior statements to refresh the victim's memory or for impeachment purposes. Therefore, there was no error or misconduct in the prosecutor's detailed questions concerning the victim's previous statements.

State v. Peek, Arizona Supreme Court No. CR-07-0412-PR, SUPREME COURT OF ARIZONA, 219 Ariz. 182; 195 P.3d 641; 2008 Ariz. LEXIS 200; 543 Ariz. Adv. Rep. 3, November 3, 2008, Decided, November 2, 2007, Filed

Trial court erred in imposing lifetime probation following defendant's conviction of attempted child molestation, which occurred between 1994 and 1996, because Ariz. Rev. Stat. § 13-902(E) (Supp. 1993) did not allow lifetime probation for second-degree offenses constituting Dangerous Crimes Against Children, including attempted child molestation.

State v. Ponsart, 233 P.3d 631

The appellate court noted that defendant was exposed to the prison term here only after the trial court had determined, following a contested hearing, that defendant had violated the terms and conditions of his probation--events that were not

consequences of his plea agreement. Because the legislature had not indicated whether it intended the phrase "pursuant to a plea agreement" to refer to more general or direct causal consequences of a plea, the appellate court could not agree with the state that the plain language of Ariz. Rev. Stat. § 13-4033(B) necessarily characterized defendant's sentence as one "entered pursuant to a plea agreement." The sentence defendant challenged could not have been raised in the original proceedings because no such sentence had yet been imposed. The trial court did not err in considering other aggravating factors or in imposing an aggravated sentence. The finding of emotional harm was reasonably supported by the victim's impact statement.

State v. Shrum, 220 Ariz. 115 Defendant argued that his second PCR petition was not precluded under Ariz. R. Crim. P. 32.2(b). The Supreme Court noted that under Ariz. R. Crim. P. 32.1(g), a defendant was not expected to anticipate significant future changes of the law in his of-right PCR proceeding or direct appeal. Nor should PCR rules encourage defendants to raise a litany of claims clearly foreclosed by existing law in the faint hope that an appellate court would embrace one of those theories. The Supreme Court noted that a prior case did not purport to overrule any prior opinion; it was merely the first appellate opinion interpreting Ariz. Rev. Stat. § 13-604.01. After this case, the law remained precisely the same. For purposes of Rule 32.1(g), a change in the law could not be established by the subjective opinions of counsel. The prior case was not a Rule 32.1(g) "significant change in the law."

State v. Thomas, Arizona Supreme Court No. CR-08-0051-PR, SUPREME COURT OF ARIZONA, 219 Ariz. 127; 194 P.3d 394; 2008 Ariz. LEXIS 201, October 30, 2008, Decided
Trial court did not err in enhancing defendant's sentences for drug convictions because an aggravated assault conviction was properly considered a "historical prior felony conviction" under Ariz. Rev. Stat. § 13-604.W.3(a)(i), even though it was committed after the drug offenses, because defendant was convicted of assault first.

A.R.S. 13-705 Dangerous crimes against children; sentences; definitions

A. A person who is at least eighteen years of age and who is convicted of a dangerous crime against children in the first degree involving sexual assault of a minor who is twelve years of age or younger or sexual conduct with a minor who is twelve years of age or younger shall be sentenced to life imprisonment and is not eligible for suspension of sentence, probation, pardon or release from confinement on any basis except as specifically authorized by section 31-233, subsection A or B until the person has served thirty-five years or the sentence is commuted. This subsection does not apply to masturbatory contact.

B. Except as otherwise provided in this section, a person who is at least eighteen years of age or who has been tried as an adult and who is convicted of a dangerous crime against children in the first degree involving attempted first degree murder of a minor who is under twelve years of age, second degree murder of a minor who is under twelve years of age, sexual assault of a minor who is under twelve years of age, sexual conduct with a minor who is under twelve years of age or manufacturing methamphetamine under circumstances that cause physical injury to a minor who is under twelve years of age may be sentenced to life imprisonment and is not eligible for suspension of sentence, probation, pardon or release from confinement on any basis except as specifically authorized by section 31-233, subsection A or B until the person has served thirty-five years or the sentence is commuted. If a life sentence is not imposed pursuant to this subsection, the person shall be sentenced to a term of imprisonment as follows: Minimum Presumptive Maximum 13 years 20 years 27 years.

C. Except as otherwise provided in this section, a person who is at least eighteen years of age or who has been tried as an adult and who is convicted of a dangerous crime against children in the first degree involving attempted first degree murder of a minor who is twelve, thirteen or fourteen years of age, second degree murder of a minor who is twelve, thirteen or fourteen years of age, sexual assault of a minor who is twelve, thirteen or fourteen years of age, taking a child for the purpose of prostitution, child prostitution, sexual conduct with a minor who is twelve, thirteen or fourteen years of age, continuous sexual abuse of a child, sex trafficking of a minor who is under fifteen years of age or manufacturing methamphetamine under circumstances that cause physical injury to a minor who

is twelve, thirteen or fourteen years of age or involving or using minors in drug offenses shall be sentenced to a term of imprisonment as follows: Minimum Presumptive Maximum 13 years 20 years 27 years   A person who has been previously convicted of one predicate felony shall be sentenced to a term of imprisonment as follows: Minimum Presumptive Maximum 23 years 30 years 37 years

D. Except as otherwise provided in this section, a person who is at least eighteen years of age or who has been tried as an adult and who is convicted of a dangerous crime against children in the first degree involving aggravated assault, molestation of a child, commercial sexual exploitation of a minor, sexual exploitation of a minor, aggravated luring a minor for sexual exploitation, child abuse or kidnapping shall be sentenced to a term of imprisonment as follows: Minimum Presumptive Maximum 10 years 17 years 24 years A person who has been previously convicted of one predicate felony shall be sentenced to a term of imprisonment as follows: Minimum Presumptive Maximum 21 years 28 years 35 years   E. Except as otherwise provided in this section, if a person is at least eighteen years of age or has been tried as an adult and is convicted of a dangerous crime against children involving luring a minor for sexual exploitation or unlawful age misrepresentation and is sentenced to a term of imprisonment, the term of imprisonment is as follows and the person is not eligible for release from confinement on any basis except as specifically authorized by section 31-233, subsection A or B until the sentence imposed by the court has been served, the person is eligible for release pursuant to section 41-1604.07 or the sentence is commuted: Minimum Presumptive Maximum 5 years 10 years 15 years   A person who has been previously convicted of one predicate felony shall be sentenced to a term of imprisonment as follows and the person is not eligible for suspension of sentence, probation, pardon or release from confinement on any basis except as specifically authorized by section 31-233, subsection A or B until the sentence imposed by the court has been served, the person is eligible for release pursuant to section 41-1604.07 or the sentence is commuted:

Minimum	Presumptive	Maximum
8 years	15 years	22 years

F. Except as otherwise provided in this section, if a person is at least eighteen years of age or has been tried as an adult and is convicted of a dangerous crime against children involving sexual abuse or bestiality under section 13-1411, subsection A, paragraph 2 and is sentenced to a term of imprisonment, the term of imprisonment is as follows and the person is not eligible for release from confinement on any basis except as specifically authorized by section 31-233, subsection A or B until the sentence imposed by the court has been served, the person is eligible for release pursuant to section 41-1604.07 or the sentence is commuted: Minimum Presumptive Maximum 2.5 years 5 years 7.5 years.

A person who has been previously convicted of one predicate felony shall be sentenced to a term of imprisonment as follows and the person is not eligible for suspension of sentence, probation, pardon or release from confinement on any basis except as specifically authorized by section 31-233, subsection A or B until the sentence imposed by the court has been served, the person is eligible for release pursuant to section 41-1604.07 or the sentence is commuted:

Minimum	Presumptive	Maximum
8 years	15 years	22 years

G. The presumptive sentences prescribed in subsections B, C and D of this section or subsections E and F of this section if the person has previously been convicted of a predicate felony may be increased or decreased pursuant to section 13-701, subsections C, D and E.

H. Except as provided in subsection F of this section, a person who is sentenced for a dangerous crime against children in the first degree pursuant to this section is not eligible for suspension of sentence, probation, pardon or release from confinement on any basis except as specifically authorized by section 31-233, subsection A or B until the sentence imposed by the court has been served or commuted.

I. A person who is convicted of any dangerous crime against children in the first degree pursuant to subsection C or D of this section and who has been previously convicted of two or more predicate felonies shall be sentenced to life imprisonment and is not eligible for suspension of sentence, probation, pardon or release from

confinement on any basis except as specifically authorized by section 31-233, subsection A or B until the person has served not fewer than thirty-five years or the sentence is commuted.

J. Notwithstanding chapter 10 of this title, a person who is at least eighteen years of age or who has been tried as an adult and who is convicted of a dangerous crime against children in the second degree pursuant to subsection B, C or D of this section is guilty of a class 3 felony and if the person is sentenced to a term of imprisonment, the term of imprisonment is as follows and the person is not eligible for release from confinement on any basis except as specifically authorized by section 31-233, subsection A or B until the person has served the sentence imposed by the court, the person is eligible for release pursuant to section 41-1604.07 or the sentence is commuted: Minimum Presumptive Maximum 5 years 10 years 15 years.

K. A person who is convicted of any dangerous crime against children in the second degree and who has been previously convicted of one or more predicate felonies is not eligible for suspension of sentence, probation, pardon or release from confinement on any basis except as specifically authorized by section 31-233, subsection A or B until the sentence imposed by the court has been served, the person is eligible for release pursuant to section 41-1604.07 or the sentence is commuted.

L. Section 13-704, subsection J and section 13-707, subsection B apply to the determination of prior convictions.

M. The sentence imposed on a person by the court for a dangerous crime against children under subsection D of this section involving child molestation or sexual abuse pursuant to subsection F of this section may be served concurrently with other sentences if the offense involved only one victim. The sentence imposed on a person for any other dangerous crime against children in the first or second degree shall be consecutive to any other sentence imposed on the person at any time, including child molestation and sexual abuse of the same victim.

N. In this section, for purposes of punishment an unborn child shall be treated like a minor who is under twelve years of age.

O. A dangerous crime against children is in the first degree if it is a completed offense and is in the second degree if it is a preparatory offense, except attempted first degree murder is a dangerous crime against children in the first degree. P. For the purposes of this section:

1. "Dangerous crime against children" means any of the following that is committed against a minor who is under fifteen years of age:

(a) Second degree murder.

(b) Aggravated assault resulting in serious physical injury or involving the discharge, use or threatening exhibition of a deadly weapon or dangerous instrument.

(c) Sexual assault.

(d) Molestation of a child.

(e) Sexual conduct with a minor.

(f) Commercial sexual exploitation of a minor.

(g) Sexual exploitation of a minor.

(h) Child abuse as prescribed in section 13-3623, subsection A, paragraph 1.

(i) Kidnapping.

(j) Sexual abuse.

(k) Taking a child for the purpose of prostitution as prescribed in section 13-3206.

(l) Child prostitution as prescribed in section 13-3212.

(m) Involving or using minors in drug offenses.

(n) Continuous sexual abuse of a child.

(o) Attempted first degree murder.

(p) Sex trafficking.

(q) Manufacturing methamphetamine under circumstances that cause physical injury to a minor.

(r) Bestiality as prescribed in section 13-1411, subsection A, paragraph 2.

(s) Luring a minor for sexual exploitation.

(t) Aggravated luring a minor for sexual exploitation.

(u) Unlawful age misrepresentation.

2. "Predicate felony" means any felony involving child abuse pursuant to section 13-3623, subsection A, paragraph 1, a sexual offense, conduct involving the intentional or knowing infliction of serious physical injury or the discharge, use or threatening exhibition of a deadly weapon or dangerous instrument, or a dangerous crime against children in the first or second degree.

A.R.S. 13-1001

Attempt; classifications

A. A person commits attempt if, acting with the kind of culpability otherwise required for commission of an offense, such person:

1. Intentionally engages in conduct which would constitute an offense if the attendant circumstances were as such person believes them to be; or

2. Intentionally does or omits to do anything which, under the circumstances as such person believes them to be, is any step in a course of conduct planned to culminate in commission of an offense; or

3. Engages in conduct intended to aid another to commit an offense, although the offense is not committed or attempted by the other person, provided his conduct would establish his complicity under chapter 3 if the offense were committed or attempted by the other person.

B. It is no defense that it was impossible for the person to aid the other party's commission of the offense, provided such person could have done so had the circumstances been as he believed them to be.

C. Attempt is a:
   1. Class 2 felony if the offense attempted is a class 1 felony.
   2. Class 3 felony if the offense attempted is a class 2 felony.
   3. Class 4 felony if the offense attempted is a class 3 felony.
   4. Class 5 felony if the offense attempted is a class 4 felony.
   5. Class 6 felony if the offense attempted is a class 5 felony.
   6. Class 1 misdemeanor if the offense attempted is a class 6 felony.
   7. Class 2 misdemeanor if the offense attempted is a class 1 misdemeanor.
   8. Class 3 misdemeanor if the offense attempted is a class 2 misdemeanor.
   9. Petty offense if the offense attempted is a class 3 misdemeanor or petty offense.

State v. Villarreal, 136 Ariz. 485, 666 P. 2d 1094 (1993)

The question of what constitutes "any step in a course of conduct planned to culminate in commission of an offense." Is for the trier of fact.

State v. Sanchez, 174 Ariz. 44, 846P. 2d 857 (1993)

"Offense" in this section (13-1001) refers to a substantive rather than to a preparatory offense.

State v. May, 137 Ariz. 183, 669 P. 2d 616 (1983)

The crime of attempt requires proof of a specific intent by the defendant to commit the substantial crime.

Note: Do not be misled by the title of the statute. It is only a title and does not necessarily depict the context of the statute. 13-1001 can be related to 13-109 (B) (7) and 13-110.

Sexual abuse; classification

A. A person commits sexual abuse by intentionally or knowingly engaging in sexual contact with any person who is fifteen or more years of age without consent of that person or with any person who is under fifteen years of age if the sexual contact involves only the female breast.

B. Sexual abuse is a class 5 felony unless the victim is under fifteen years of age in which case sexual abuse is a class 3 felony punishable pursuant to section 13-705.

A.R.S. 13-1406

Sexual assault; classification; increased punishment

A. A person commits sexual assault by intentionally or knowingly engaging in sexual intercourse or oral sexual contact with any person without consent of such person.

B. Sexual assault is a class 2 felony, and the person convicted shall be sentenced pursuant to this section and the person is not eligible for suspension of sentence, probation, pardon or release from confinement on any basis except as specifically authorized by section 31-233, subsection A or B until the sentence imposed by the court has been served or commuted. If the victim is under fifteen years of age, sexual assault is punishable pursuant to section 13-705. The presumptive term may be aggravated or mitigated within the range under this section pursuant to section 13-701, subsections C, D and E. If the sexual assault involved the intentional or knowing administration of flunitrazepam, gamma hydroxy butyrate or ketamine hydrochloride without the victim's knowledge, the presumptive, minimum and maximum sentence for the offense shall be increased by three years. The additional sentence imposed pursuant to this subsection is in addition to any enhanced sentence that may be applicable. The term for a first offense is as follows:

Minimum	Presumptive	Maximum
5.25 years	7 years	14 years

The term for a defendant who has one historical prior felony conviction is as follows: Minimum Presumptive Maximum 7 years 10.5 years 21 years

The term for a defendant who has two or more historical prior felony convictions is as follows:

Minimum	Presumptive	Maximum
14 years	15.75 years	28 years

C. The sentence imposed on a person for a sexual assault shall be consecutive to any other sexual assault sentence imposed on the person at any time.

D. Notwithstanding section 13-703, section 13-704, section 13-705, section 13-706, subsection A and section 13-708, subsection D, if the sexual assault involved the intentional or knowing infliction of serious physical injury, the person may be sentenced to life imprisonment and is not eligible for suspension of sentence, probation, pardon or release from confinement on any basis except as specifically authorized by section 31-233, subsection A or B until at least twenty-five years have been served or the sentence is commuted. If the person was at least eighteen years of age and the victim was twelve years of age or younger, the person shall be sentenced pursuant to section 13-705.

A.R.S. 13-1407

Defenses

A. It is a defense to a prosecution pursuant to sections 13-1404 and 13-1405 involving a minor if the act was done in furtherance of lawful medical practice.

B. It is a defense to a prosecution pursuant to sections 13-1404 and 13-1405 in which the victim's lack of consent is based on incapacity to consent because the victim was fifteen, sixteen or seventeen years of age if at the time the defendant engaged in the conduct constituting the offense the defendant did not know and could not reasonably have known the age of the victim.

C. It is a defense to a prosecution pursuant to section 13-1402, 13-1404, 13-1405 or 13-1406 if the act was done by a duly licensed physician or registered nurse or a person acting under the physician's or nurse's direction, or any other person who renders emergency care at the scene of an emergency occurrence, the act consisted of administering a recognized and lawful form of treatment that was reasonably adapted to promoting the physical or mental health of the patient and the treatment was administered in an emergency when the duly licensed physician or registered nurse or a person acting under the physician's or nurse's direction, or any other person rendering emergency care at the scene of an emergency occurrence, reasonably believed that no one competent to consent could be consulted and that a reasonable person, wishing to safeguard the welfare of the patient, would consent.

D. It is a defense to a prosecution pursuant to section 13-1404 or 13-1405 that the person was the spouse of the other person at the time of commission of the act. It is not a defense to a prosecution pursuant to section 13-1406 that the defendant was the spouse of the victim at the time of commission of the act.

E. It is a defense to a prosecution pursuant to section 13-1404 or 13-1410 that the defendant was not motivated by a sexual interest. It is a defense to a prosecution pursuant to section 13-1404 involving a victim under fifteen years of age that the defendant was not motivated by a sexual interest.

F. It is a defense to a prosecution pursuant to sections 13-1405 and 13-3560 if the victim is fifteen, sixteen or seventeen years of age, the defendant is under nineteen years of age or attending high school and is no more than twenty-four months older than the victim and the conduct is consensual.

A.R.S. 13-1410

Molestation of a child; classification

A. A person commits molestation of a child by intentionally or knowingly engaging in or causing a person to engage in sexual contact, except sexual contact with the female breast, with a child who is under fifteen years of age.

B. Molestation of a child is a class 2 felony that is punishable pursuant to section 13-705.

In Re Maricopa County, Action No. Jv. -121430, 172 Ariz. 604, 838 P.2d 1365 (1992)
The intent necessary to commit the crime of molestation is only that the actor being motivated by "sexual interest."

A.R.S. 13-1413

Capacity of minor sexual assault victim to consent to medical examination
Notwithstanding any other provision of the law, when it is not possible to contact the parents or legal guardian within the short time span in which the examination should be conducted a minor twelve years of age or older alleged to be the victim of a violation of section 13-1406 may give consent to hospital, medical and surgical examination, diagnosis and care in connection with such violation. Such consent shall not be subject to incapacity because of the victim's age. The consent of the parent, parents or legal guardian of such minor shall not be necessary to authorize such hospital, medical and surgical examination, diagnosis and care, and such parent, parents or legal guardian shall not be liable for payment for any services rendered pursuant to this section.

A.R.S. 13-1416

Admissibility of minor's statement; notice

A. Except as otherwise provided in title 8, a statement made by a minor who is under the age of ten years describing any sexual offense or physical abuse performed with, on or witnessed by the minor, which is not otherwise admissible by statute or court rule, is admissible in evidence in any criminal or civil proceeding if both of the following are true:

1. The court finds, in an in camera hearing, that the time, content and circumstances of the statement provide sufficient indicia of reliability.

2. Either of the following is true: (a) The minor testifies at the proceedings. (b) The minor is unavailable as a witness, provided that if the minor is unavailable as a witness, the statement may be admitted only if there is corroborative evidence of the statement.

B. A statement shall not be admitted under this section unless the proponent of the statement makes known to the adverse party his intention to offer the statement and the particulars of the statement sufficiently in advance of the proceedings to provide the adverse party with a fair opportunity to prepare to meet the statement.

A.R.S. 13-1417

Continuous sexual abuse of a child; classification

A. A person who over a period of three months or more in duration engages in three or more acts in violation of section 13-1405, 13-1406 or 13-1410 with a child who is under fourteen years of age is guilty of continuous sexual abuse of a child.

B. Continuous sexual abuse of a child is a class 2 felony and is punishable pursuant to section 13-705.

C. To convict a person of continuous sexual abuse of a child, the trier of fact shall unanimously agree that the requisite number of acts occurred. The trier of fact does not need to agree on which acts constitute the requisite number.

D. Any other felony sexual offense involving the victim shall not be charged in the same proceeding with a charge under this section unless the other charged felony sexual offense occurred outside the time period charged under this section or the other felony sexual offense is charged in the alternative. A defendant may be charged with only one count under this section unless more than one victim is involved. If more than one victim is involved, a separate count may be charged for each victim.

A.R.S. 13-1423

Violent sexual assault; natural life sentence

A. A person is guilty of violent sexual assault if in the course of committing an offense under section 13-1404, 13-1405, 13-1406 or 13-1410 the offense involved the discharge, use or threatening exhibition of a deadly weapon or dangerous instrument or involved the intentional or knowing infliction of serious physical injury and the person has a historical prior felony conviction for a sexual offense under this chapter or any offense committed outside this state that if committed in this state would constitute a sexual offense under this chapter.

B. Notwithstanding section 13-703, section 13-704, section 13-705, section 13-706, subsection A and section 13-708, subsection D, a person who is guilty of a violent sexual assault shall be sentenced to life imprisonment and the court shall order that the person not be released on any basis for the remainder of the person's natural life.

A.R.S. 13-3551

Definitions

In this chapter, unless the context otherwise requires:

1. "Communication service provider" has the same meaning prescribed in section 13-3001.

2. "Computer" has the same meaning prescribed in section 13-2301, subsection E.

3. "Computer system" has the same meaning prescribed in section 13-2301, subsection E.

4. "Exploitive exhibition" means the actual or simulated exhibition of the genitals or pubic or rectal areas of any person for the purpose of sexual stimulation of the viewer.

5. "Minor" means a person or persons who were under eighteen years of age at the time a visual depiction was created, adapted or modified.

6. "Network" has the same meaning prescribed in section 13-2301, subsection E.

7. "Producing" means financing, directing, manufacturing, issuing, publishing or advertising for pecuniary gain.

8. "Remote computing service" has the same meaning prescribed in section 13-3001.

9. "Sexual conduct" means actual or simulated: (a) Sexual intercourse, including genital-genital, oral-genital, anal-genital or oral-anal, whether between persons of the same or opposite sex. (b) Penetration of the vagina or rectum by any object except when done as part of a recognized medical procedure. (c) Sexual bestiality. (d) Masturbation, for the purpose of sexual stimulation of the viewer. (e) Sadomasochistic abuse for the purpose of sexual stimulation of the viewer. (f) Defecation or urination for the purpose of sexual stimulation of the viewer.

10. "Simulated" means any depicting of the genitals or rectal areas that gives the appearance of sexual conduct or incipient sexual conduct.

11. "Visual depiction" includes each visual image that is contained in an undeveloped film, videotape or photograph or data stored in any form and that is capable of conversion into a visual image.

A.R.S. 13-3552

Commercial sexual exploitation of a minor; classification

A. A person commits commercial sexual exploitation of a minor by knowingly:

1. Using, employing, persuading, enticing, inducing or coercing a minor to engage in or assist others to engage in exploitive exhibition or other sexual conduct for the purpose of producing any visual depiction or live act depicting such conduct.

2. Using, employing, persuading, enticing, inducing or coercing a minor to expose the genitals or anus or the areola or nipple of the female breast for financial or commercial gain.

3. Permitting a minor under the person's custody or control to engage in or assist others to engage in exploitive exhibition or other sexual conduct for the purpose of producing any visual depiction or live act depicting such conduct.

4. Transporting or financing the transportation of any minor through or across this state with the intent that the minor engage in prostitution, exploitive exhibition or other sexual conduct for the purpose of producing a visual depiction or live act depicting such conduct.

B. Commercial sexual exploitation of a minor is a class 2 felony and if the minor is under fifteen years of age it is punishable pursuant to section 13-705.

A.R.S. 13-3553

Sexual exploitation of a minor; evidence; classification

A. A person commits sexual exploitation of a minor by knowingly:

1. Recording, filming, photographing, developing or duplicating any visual depiction in which a minor is engaged in exploitive exhibition or other sexual conduct.

2. Distributing, transporting, exhibiting, receiving, selling, purchasing, electronically transmitting, possessing or exchanging any visual depiction in which a minor is engaged in exploitive exhibition or other sexual conduct.

B. If any visual depiction of sexual exploitation of a minor is admitted into evidence, the court shall seal that evidence at the conclusion of any grand jury proceeding, hearing or trial.

C. Sexual exploitation of a minor is a class 2 felony and if the minor is under fifteen years of age it is punishable pursuant to section 13-705.

State v. Kirby Stone, CR2001-017210
Maricopa Superior Court upheld defendant's motion that ARS 13-3553 was overbroad because of the definition of child pornography being "any visual depiction." This definition would include baby in a bath tub family photos, fine art, painting, drawings and computer generated images. Therefore ARS 13-3553 as worded is a violation of 1st Amendment rights. The same wording existed in the Federal child pornography laws until Ashcroft v. Free Speech Coalition forced the removal of "any visual depiction" from the language of the law and replaced it with something else.

ARS 13-3553 does not have exceptions or exemptions built into the statute so as to prevent law enforcement and justice system personnel from violating the same law. With no exceptions or exemptions present it causes the law to be arbitrarily and discriminately enforced. See the following:
Bland v. California D.O.C.
Grayned v. City of Rockford, supra, page 39

Contains a three-prong test for vagueness and over breadth. Fourteen states have put exceptions or exemptions into their sexual exploitation statutes. They are: CA, CO, IL, IN, IA, GA, MA, MI, MN, ND, OH, OK, OR and WY.

A.R.S. 13-3554

Luring a minor for sexual exploitation; classification

A. A person commits luring a minor for sexual exploitation by offering or soliciting sexual conduct with another person knowing or having reason to know that the other person is a minor.

B. It is not a defense to a prosecution for a violation of this section that the other person is not a minor.

C. Luring a minor for sexual exploitation is a class 3 felony, and if the minor is under fifteen years of age it is punishable pursuant to section 13-705.

Boynton v. Anderson, 205 Ariz. 45
Where crime of luring a minor for sexual exploitation was not listed as punishable as a "dangerous crime against children," appellate court held that the legislature did not intend the crime to be considered a "dangerous crime against children."

Mejak v. Granville, Arizona Supreme Court No. Cv. -05-0299-PR , SUPREME COURT OF Arizona, 212 Ariz. 555; 136 P.3d 874; 2006 Ariz. LEXIS 62; 478 Ariz. Adv. Rep. 27, May 24, 2006, Filed
Ariz. Rev. Stat. § 13-3554 was interpreted to require that the person lured by a defendant be a minor or a peace officer posing as a minor given the statutory language. Since the person that lured defendant was an adult television reporter, rather than a minor or peace officer posing as a minor, the indictment was insufficient to charge him.

A.R.S. 13-3557

Equipment; forfeiture

On the conviction of a person for a violation of section 13-3552, 13-3553, 13-3554 or 13-3560, the court shall order that any photographic equipment, computer system or instrument of communication that is owned or used exclusively by the person and that was used in the commission of the offense be forfeited and sold, destroyed or otherwise properly disposed.

A.R.S. 13-3559

Reporting suspected visual depictions of sexual exploitation of a minor; immunity. A. Any communications service provider, remote computing service, system administrator, computer repair technician or other person who discovers suspected visual depictions of sexual exploitation of a minor on a computer, computer system or network or any other storage medium may report that discovery to law enforcement officer.

B. A person who on discovery in good faith reports the discovery of suspected visual depictions of sexual exploitation of a minor is immune from civil liability.

C. It is an affirmative defense to a prosecution of ARS 13-3553 that on discovery a person in good faith reports the discovery of unsolicited suspected visual depictions involving the sexual exploitation of a minor.

Aggravated luring a minor for sexual exploitation; classification; definitions

A. A person commits aggravated luring a minor for sexual exploitation if the person does both of the following:

> 1. Knowing the character and content of the depiction, uses an electronic communication device to transmit at least one visual depiction of material that is harmful to minors for the purpose of initiating or engaging in communication with a recipient who the person knows or has reason to know is a minor.

> 2. By means of the communication, offers or solicits sexual conduct with the minor. The offer or solicitation may occur before, contemporaneously with, after or as an integrated part of the transmission of the visual depiction.

B. It is not a defense to a prosecution for a violation of this section that the other person is not a minor or that the other person is a peace officer posing as a minor.

C. Aggravated luring a minor for sexual exploitation is a class 2 felony, and if the minor is under fifteen years of age it is punishable pursuant to section 13-705, subsection D.

D. The defense prescribed in section 13-1407, subsection F applies to a prosecution pursuant to this section. E. For the purposes of this section:

1. "Electronic communication device" means any electronic device that is capable of transmitting visual depictions and includes any of the following:

> (a) A computer, computer system or network as defined in section 13-2301.
> (b) A cellular or wireless telephone as defined in section 13-4801.

2. "Harmful to minors" has the same meaning prescribed in section 13-3501.

A.R.S. 13-3821

Persons required to register; procedure; identification card; assessment; definitions
A. A person who has been convicted of a violation or attempted violation of any of the following offenses or who has been convicted of an offense committed in another jurisdiction that if committed in this state would be a violation or attempted violation of any of the following offenses or an offense that was in effect before September 1, 1978 and that, if committed on or after September 1, 1978, has the same elements of an offense listed in this section or who is required to register by the convicting jurisdiction, within ten days after the conviction or within ten days after entering and remaining in any county of this state, shall register with the sheriff of that county:

1. Unlawful imprisonment pursuant to section 13-1303 if the victim is under eighteen years of age and the unlawful imprisonment was not committed by the child's parent.
2. Kidnapping pursuant to section 13-1304 if the victim is under eighteen years of age and the kidnapping was not committed by the child's parent.
3. Sexual abuse pursuant to section 13-1404 if the victim is under eighteen years of age.
4. Sexual conduct with a minor pursuant to section 13-1405.
5. Sexual assault pursuant to section 13-1406.
6. Sexual assault of a spouse if the offense was committed before August 12, 2005.
7. Molestation of a child pursuant to section 13-1410.   8. Continuous sexual abuse of a child pursuant to section 13-1417.
9. Taking a child for the purpose of prostitution pursuant to section 13-3206.
10. Child prostitution pursuant to section 13-3212.
11. Commercial sexual exploitation of a minor pursuant to section 13-3552.
12. Sexual exploitation of a minor pursuant to section 13-3553.
13. Luring a minor for sexual exploitation pursuant to section 13-3554.
14. Sex trafficking of a minor pursuant to section 13-1307.
15. A second or subsequent violation of indecent exposure to a person under fifteen years of age pursuant to section 13-1402.

16. A second or subsequent violation of public sexual indecency to a minor under the age of fifteen years pursuant to section 13-1403, subsection B.

17. A third or subsequent violation of indecent exposure pursuant to section 13-1402.

14. Sex trafficking of a minor pursuant to section 13-1307.

15. A second or subsequent violation of indecent exposure to a person under fifteen years of age pursuant to section 13-1402.

16. A second or subsequent violation of public sexual indecency to a minor under the age of fifteen years pursuant to section 13-1403, subsection B.

17. A third or subsequent violation of indecent exposure pursuant to section 13-1402.

18. A third or subsequent violation of public sexual indecency pursuant to section 13-1403.

19. A violation of section 13-3822 or 13-3824.

20. Unlawful age misrepresentation.

21. Aggravated luring a minor for sexual exploitation pursuant to section 13-3560.

B. Before the person is released from confinement the state department of corrections in conjunction with the department of public safety and each county sheriff shall complete the registration of any person who was convicted of a violation of any offense listed under subsection A of this section. Within three days after the person's release from confinement, the state department of corrections shall forward the registered person's records to the department of public safety and to the sheriff of the county in which the registered person intends to reside. Registration pursuant to this subsection shall be consistent with subsection E of this section.

C. Notwithstanding subsection A of this section, the judge who sentences a defendant for any violation of chapter 14 or 35.1 of this title or for an offense for which there was a finding of sexual motivation pursuant to section 13-118 may require the person who committed the offense to register pursuant to this section.

D. The court may require a person who has been adjudicated delinquent for an act that would constitute an offense specified in subsection A or C of this section to

register pursuant to this section. Any duty to register under this subsection shall terminate when the person reaches twenty-five years of age.   E. A person who has been convicted of or adjudicated delinquent and who is required to register in the convicting state for an act that would constitute an offense specified in subsection A or C of this section and who is not a resident of this state shall be required to register pursuant to this section if the person is either:

1. Employed full-time or part-time in this state, with or without compensation, for more than fourteen consecutive days or for an aggregate period of more than thirty days in a calendar year.

2. Enrolled as a full-time or part-time student in any school in this state for more than fourteen consecutive days or for an aggregate period of more than thirty days in a calendar year. For the purposes of this paragraph, "school" means an educational institution of any description, public or private, wherever located in this state.

F. Any duty to register under subsection D or E of this section for a juvenile adjudication terminates when the person reaches twenty-five years of age.

G. The court may order the termination of any duty to register under this section on successful completion of probation if the person was under eighteen years of age when the offense for which the person was convicted was committed.

H. The court may order the suspension or termination of any duty to register under this section after a hearing held pursuant to section 13-923.

I. At the time of registering, the person shall sign or affix an electronic fingerprint to a statement giving such information as required by the director of the department of public safety, including all names by which the person is known, any required online identifier and the name of any website or internet communication service where the identifier is being used. The sheriff shall fingerprint and photograph the person and within three days thereafter shall send copies of the statement, fingerprints and photographs to the department of public safety and the chief of police, if any, of the place where the person resides. The information that is required by this subsection shall include the physical location of

the person's residence and the person's address. If the person has a place of residence that is different from the person's address, the person shall provide the person's address, the physical location of the person's residence and the name of the owner of the residence if the residence is privately owned and not offered for rent or lease. If the person receives mail at a post office box, the person shall provide the location and number of the post office box. If the person does not have an address or a permanent place of residence, the person shall provide a description and physical location of any temporary residence and shall register as a transient not less than every ninety days with the sheriff in whose jurisdiction the transient is physically present.

J. On the person's initial registration and every year after the person's initial registration, the person shall confirm any required online identifier and the name of any website or internet communication service where the identifier is being used and the person shall obtain a new non-operating identification license or a driver license from the motor vehicle division in the department of transportation and shall carry a valid non-operating identification license or a driver license. Notwithstanding sections 28-3165 and 28-3171, the license is valid for one year from the date of issuance, and the person shall submit to the department of transportation proof of the person's address and place of residence. The motor vehicle division shall annually update the person's address and photograph and shall make a copy of the photograph available to the department of public safety or to any law enforcement agency. The motor vehicle division shall provide to the department of public safety daily address updates for persons required to register pursuant to this section.

K. Except as provided in subsection E or L of this section, the clerk of the superior court in the county in which a person has been convicted of a violation of any offense listed under subsection A of this section or has been ordered to register pursuant to subsection C or D of this section shall notify the sheriff in that county of the conviction within ten days after entry of the judgment.

L. Within ten days after entry of judgment, a court not of record shall notify the arresting law enforcement agency of an offender's conviction of a violation of section 13-1402. Within ten days after receiving this information, the law

enforcement agency shall determine if the offender is required to register pursuant to this section. If the law enforcement agency determines that the offender is required to register, the law enforcement agency shall provide the information required by section 13-3825 to the department of public safety and shall make community notification as required by law.

M. A person who is required to register pursuant to this section because of a conviction for the unlawful imprisonment of a minor or the kidnapping of a minor is required to register, absent additional or subsequent convictions, for a period of ten years from the date that the person is released from prison, jail, probation, community supervision or parole and the person has fulfilled all restitution obligations. Notwithstanding this subsection, a person who has a prior conviction for an offense for which registration is required pursuant to this section is required to register for life.

N. A person who is required to register pursuant to this section and who is a student at a public or private institution of postsecondary education or who is employed, with or without compensation, at a public or private institution of postsecondary education or who carries on a vocation at a public or private institution of postsecondary education shall notify the county sheriff having jurisdiction of the institution of postsecondary education. The person who is required to register pursuant to this section shall also notify the sheriff of each change in enrollment or employment status at the institution.

O. At the time of registering, the sheriff shall secure a sufficient sample of blood or other bodily substances for deoxyribonucleic acid testing and extraction from a person who has been convicted of an offense committed in another jurisdiction that if committed in this state would be a violation or attempted violation of any of the offenses listed in subsection A of this section or an offense that was in effect before September 1, 1978 and that, if committed on or after September 1, 1978, has the same elements of an offense listed in subsection A of this section or who is required to register by the convicting jurisdiction. The sheriff shall transmit the sample to the department of public safety.

P. Any person who is required to register under subsection A of this section shall register the person's required online identifier and the name of any website or internet communication service where the identifier is being used or is intended to be used with the sheriff from and after December 31, 2007, regardless of whether the person was required to register an identifier at the time of the person's initial registration under this section.

Q. On conviction of any offense for which a person is required to register pursuant to this section, in addition to any other penalty prescribed by law, the court shall order the person to pay an additional assessment of two hundred fifty dollars. This assessment is not subject to any surcharge. The court shall transmit the monies received pursuant to this section to the county treasurer. The county treasurer shall transmit the monies received to the state treasurer. The state treasurer shall deposit the monies received in the sex offender monitoring fund established by section 13-3828. Notwithstanding any other law, the court shall not waive the assessment imposed pursuant to this section.

R. For the purposes of this section:
1. "Address" means the location at which the person receives mail.
2. "Required online identifier" means any electronic e-mail address information or instant message, chat, social networking or other similar internet communication name, but does not include a social security number, date of birth or pin number.
3. "Residence" means the person's dwelling place, whether permanent or temporary.

A.R.S. 22-341

Motion for new trial or arrest of judgment

A. At any time before judgment, defendant may move for a new trial, or in arrest of judgment.

B. A new trial may be granted in the following cases:

1. When the trial has been had in the absence of defendant, unless he voluntarily absents himself with full knowledge that a trial is being had.

2. When the jury has received any evidence out of court.

3. When the jury has separated without leave of court, after having retired to deliberate on the verdict, or when it has been guilty of any misconduct tending to prevent a fair and due consideration of the action.

4. When the verdict has been decided by lot, or by any means other than a fair expression of opinion on the part of all the jurors.

5. When there has been an error in the decision of the court on a question of law arising during the trial.

6. When the verdict is contrary to law or evidence.

7. When new evidence is discovered material to defendant, and which he could not, with reasonable diligence, have discovered and produced at the trial. When a motion for a new trial is made upon the ground of discovery of new evidence, defendant shall produce at the hearing affidavits of the witnesses by whom such newly discovered evidence is expected to be given.

C. The motion in arrest of judgment may be founded on any substantial defect in the complaint.

D. The effect of an arrest of judgment is to place defendant in the same situation in which he was before the trial was had.

Assault

Caldeorn-Ortiz v. Laboy-Alvarado, 300 F3d. 60 (1st CIR. 2002)
An inmate may sue a correctional facility under the 8th amendment for failure to provide adequate protection of inmates from attack by other inmates.

Canter v. Jones, 293 F3d 981 (7th CIR. 2002) Prison officials have a duty to protect prisoners from violence at the hands of other inmates.

Farmer v. Brennan, 511 U.S. 825, 114 S.Ct. 1970
Prisoner who was transsexual brought Bivens suit against prison officials, claiming that officials showed "deliberate indifference" by placing prisoner in general prison population, thus failing to keep him from harm allegedly inflicted by other inmates. The United States District Court for the Western District of Wisconsin, Shabaz, J., entered judgment for officials and appeal was taken. The Court of Appeals, Seventh Circuit, 11 F.3d 668, affirmed. Certiorari was granted. The Supreme Court, Justice Souter, held that: (1) prison officials may be held liable under Eighth Amendment for denying humane conditions of confinement only if they know that inmates face substantial risk of serious harm and disregard that risk by failing to take reasonable measures to abate it, and (2) remand would be required to determine whether prison officials would have liability, under above standards, for not preventing harm allegedly occurring in present case. Vacated and remanded.

Redman v. County of San Diego, No. 87-6139, UNITED STATES COURT OF APPEALS FOR THE NINTH CIRCUIT, 942 F.2d 1435; 1991 U.S. App. LEXIS 20028; 91 Cal. Daily Op. Service 6848; 91 Daily Journal DAR 10416, October 11, 1990, Argued En Banc and Submitted, San Francisco, California , August 26, 1991, Filed. Affirmed in Part, Reversed in Part.
Pre-trial detainee's right to personal security under the Fourteenth Amendment was violated by a county, jail officials, and employees, who acted with "deliberate indifference" or a knowing willingness to inflict harm.

State v. Diaz, 221 Ariz. 209

Convictions were reversed and remanded pursuant to fundamental error review, because the transcript showed only eleven jurors determined defendant's guilt, and there was an absence of other facts supporting the inferences that twelve jurors actually participated in the determination of defendant's guilt.

State v. Hutchison, 2009 Ariz. App. LEXIS 799

Where the victim testified that he was afraid when defendant pointed a gun to his head, there was ample evidence for the jury to believe that the victim was in reasonable apprehension of imminent harm. The trial court did not err when it denied defendant's Ariz. R. Crim. P. 20 motion for judgment of acquittal on the aggravated assault charge.

State v. Klokic, 219 Ariz. 241 In trial for aggravated assault, trial court erred in denying defendant's request to require the State to elect which particular act it was charging because defendant allegedly pointed a handgun on two separate occasions, which were not part of the same transaction.

State v. Mason, 238 P.3d 134

Defendant argued that one of his two convictions for aggravated assault with a deadly weapon or dangerous instrument violated double jeopardy. Although the assault had been carried out by two principals with two different weapons, it was nonetheless a single attack. The involvement of multiple accomplices could not by itself transform the commission of a single statutory offense into multiple crimes. Because defendant's second aggravated assault with a deadly weapon or dangerous instrument conviction, even if it resulted in no greater sentence, was an impermissible punishment, it had be vacated. In addition, the imposition of consecutive sentences for defendant's armed robbery and aggravated assault convictions did not violate Ariz. Rev. Stat. § 13-116 because defendant could have committed the aggravated assaults without committing the armed robbery and the risk of harm to the victim was increased by the accomplices' possession of dangerous weapons during the robbery. Finally, based on the sentencing transcript stating that the trial court was proceeding under former Ariz. Rev. Stat. § 13-604(C) and (D), the imposition of an aggravated sentence of 20 years was proper.

The appellate court reversed the trial court's judgment regarding defendant's two convictions for aggravated assault with a deadly weapon or dangerous instrument, remanded the case to the trial court with instruction for the trial court to decide which of the two convictions to vacate, and affirmed the remainder of the trial court's judgment.

Bail

18 USC § 3142 (c) (2) (1994)
Court may set bail the defendant cannot meet, but financial conditions may not purposefully be drawn beyond the defendants' means.

18 USC § 3143 (b) (1994)
Pending appeal defendant must provide clear and convincing evidence to overcome presumption of flight and dangerousness to community. The District Court must act on release application.

Baker v. McCollan, 433 US 137, 144 n.3 (1979)
The Supreme Court has indicated that excessive bail clause "has been assumed" to apply to the states.

Benson v. California, 328 F.2d 159, 162 (9th Cir. 1964),cert. denied, 380 US 951 (1965)
Release on bail should be granted to a prisoner pending post-conviction habeas review only when the petitioner has raised substantial constitutional claim upon which he has a high probability of success on the merits or in extraordinary cases involving exceptional circumstances which make granting of bail necessary to the effectiveness of the habeas remedy.

Hensley v. Municipal Court, 411 US 345, 36 L.Ed.2d 294, 93 S.Ct. 1571 (1973)
Strait v. Laird, 406 US 341, 32 L.Ed.2d 141, 92 S.Ct. 1693 (1972)
Carlson v. Landon, 342 US 524, 96 L.Ed 547, 72 S.Ct. 525 (1952)
Extremely restrictive bail may be argued that it merely extends the prison walls, thus defendant is still in the custody of the United States government.

Land v. Deeds, 878 F.2d 159, 162 (9th Cir. 1989)
Something more than any meritorious claim is required before release on bail is justified.

Lee v. Lawson, (1979 Miss) 375 S.Ct..2d 1019
Bail system based on monetary bail alone will be unconstitutional, with regard to due process rights of indigent pre-trial detainee.

Pugh v. Rainwater, (1978 CA5 Fla) 572 F.2d 1053
Incarceration of those individuals who cannot pay established money bail, without meaningful consideration of other possible alternatives, infringes on due process requirements.

In Re Roe, 257 F.3d 1077, 1080 (9th Cir. 2001)
Assuming arguendo, that a District Court has the authority to release a state prisoner on bail pending resolution of habeas corpus proceedings in extraordinary cases, the petitioner must demonstrate that he is an extraordinary case involving special circumstances or a high probability of success.

Reno v. Koray, 515 US 132 L.Ed.2d 46, 115 S.Ct. (1995)
Federal prisoner ordered confined to community treatment center, or "halfway house," to await sentencing held not in "official detention" for purposes of receiving sentence credit under Sentencing Reform Act of 1984. (adverse law).

Schilb v. Kuebel, 404 US 357, 365 (1973)
Three circuits have expressly held that the excessive bail clause applies to the states.

Sistrunk v. Lyons, 646 F.2d 64, 71 (3rd Cir. 1981)
Excessive bail clause integral to order, liberty and binding on states through fourteenth amendment.

US v. Delker, 757 F.2d 1390, 1394 (3rd Cir. 1985)
Rule line of the federal rules of appellate procedure requires District Court to provide written reasons for ordering, refusing or imposing conditions of release.

US v. DuBose, 146 F.3d 1141, 1145 (9th Cir. 1998)
When a court enters an order for pre-trial release containing a financial condition that the defendant in good faith cannot fulfill, the court must explain why the particular requirement is an indispensable component of the conditions for release. See also: Mantecon-Zayas, 949 F.2d at 556.

US v. Figuerola, 58 F3d 502 (9th Cir. 1995)
Bail bond is contract between government, defendant, and his sureties, and is governed by general contract principles.

US v. Fisher, 55 F.3d 481 (10th Cir. 1995)
Trial judge refusing release of defendant pending appeal must state in writing reasons for action taken.

US v. Frazier, 772 F.2d 1451, 1452-53 (9th Cir. 1985) (per curiam) Condition that property securing bond be unencumbered in order to protect government's ability to collect on security was improper basis for denying release because not reasonably necessary to assure defendants appearance.

US v. Gebro, 948 F2d 1118 (9th Cir. 1991)
US v. Orta, 760 F2d 887 (8th Cir. 1985)
Bail Reform Act requires release of person facing trial under least restrictive condition or combination of conditions that will reasonably assure appearance of person as required and safety of community; only in rare circumstances should release be denied, and doubts regarding propriety of release should be resolved in defendant's favor.

US v. Giraldi, 86 F.3d 1368, 1379 (5th Cir. 1996)
Defendant's application for release pending appeal improperly denied because defendants appeal presented issues raised in substantial likelihood of reduced sentence on new trial.

US v. Hart, 779 F.2d 575,5 76-77 (10th Cir. 1985) (per curiam)
District Court has duty pursuant to § 3145 (c) and federal rules of appellate procedure P. 9 (b) to act on application for release pending appeal and cannot decline to hear or rule on ground that it is a matter for appeals court to decide.

US v. Himler, 797 F.2d 156 (3rd Cir. 1986)
There is no per se presumption of flight by reason of charged crime involving production of fraudulent identification, for purposes of determining whether defendant should be subjected to pre-trial detention.

US v. Infelise, 934 F.2d 103 (7th Cir. 1991)
Government cannot be permitted to defeat Bill of Rights by indefinite delay in bringing defendants to trial.

US v. Leisure, 710 F.2d 422 (8th Cir. 1983)
Conditions which are impossible to meet are not to be permitted to serve as devices to thwart plain purpose of Bail Reform Act, nor are they to serve as thinly veiled cloak for preventive detention, and amount of bail should not be used as indirect, but effective, method of ensuring continued custody.

US v. Mett, 41 F3d 1281 (9th Cir. 1994)
Special circumstances justifying bail for habeas petitioners include serious deterioration of health while incarcerated and unusual delay in appeal process.

US v. Montalvo-Murillo, 495 US 711, 721 (1990)
Court must find in favor of defendants rights. The 9th circuit has announced that it has "not weighed in" on the issue of a District Court's power, to grant bail pending a decision on a habeas corpus petition.

US v. Nelson, 6 F.3d 1049 (4th Cir. 1993)
Evidence of international flight by defendant immediately after commission of crime may be considered along with other evidence in determining guilt.

US v. Notamedi, 767 F.2d 1403 (9th Cir. 1985)
Tradition of federal law is that one arrested for a noncapital offense shall be admitted to bail and only in rare circumstances should release be denied.

US v. O'brien, 895 F.2d 810 (1st Cir. 1990)
Government was not entitled, as matter of right, to hearing after narcotics defendant met conditions set by court for pre-trial release.

US v. Romano, 799 F.2d 17 (2nd Cir. 1986)
US v. Salerno, 794 F.2d 64 (2nd Cir. 1986)
Substantive due process prohibits pre-trial detention on the ground of danger to the community, regardless of the duration of the detention.

US v. Rose, 791 F.2d 1477 (11th Cir. 1986)
Addition of any condition to appearance bond to effect that it shall be retained by clerk to pay any fine that may subsequently be levied against defendant after criminal trial is over is "excessive" in violation of Eighth Amendment.

US v. Rubenstein, 971 F.2d 288 (9th Cir. 1992)
Courts should not presume that money posted as bail is defendants.

US v. Snyder, 946 F.2d 1125 (5th Cir. 1991)
All levels in the Federal Judicial System have jurisdiction to determine bail application while plaintiff's petition for certiorari is pending before the Supreme Court.

US v. Toro, 981 F.2d 1045 (9th Cir. 1992)
United States forfeiture action accrued and six year statute of limitations began to run, upon breach of bail bond agreement.

US v. Townsend, 897 F.2d 989, 993-94 (9th Cir. 1990)
Government has burden of proving risk of defendant's flight by preponderance of evidence. Release denied only in rare cases when person arrested for non-capital offenses; doubts regarding propriety of release resolved in favor of defendant.

Brady Violations

Anderson v. US, 788 F.2d 517 (8th Cir. 1986)
Definition of materiality for purposes of Brady vs. Maryland applies to all cases of prosecutorial failure to disclose favorable evidence, whether there was "no request," "general request," or "specific request."

Bartholomew v. Wood, 34 F.3d 870 (9th Cir. 1994)
Prosecution's failure to disclose material and favorable evidence to defendant will violate due process under BRADY, even when defendant makes no request for such evidence.

Brady v. Maryland, 373 US 83, 10 L.Ed.2d 215, 83 S.Ct. 1194 (1963)
Suppression of favorable evidence violates due process (GRANDADDY CASE)

Canion v. Cole, 208 Ariz. 133, 91 P.3d 355
It is true that, by its words, Rule 15.1 does not apply to PCR proceedings, but to agree with the State that this is conclusive would allow the prosecution that unlawfully failed to disclose exculpatory information in a timely manner to continue to evade that duty and thwart the due process of law to which an accused is entitled. The Arizona Supreme Court held in State v. Schreiber, 115 Ariz. 555, 556, 566 P.2d 1031, 1032 (1977), that a Rule 32 petition should be granted when the prosecution's non-disclosure of evidence denied the petitioner's right to due process, citing the United States and Arizona Constitutions. Remand was required after defendant showed good cause and made colorable allegations of newly discovered materials.

Edmond v. Collins, 8 F.3d 290 (5th Cir. 1993)
US v. Brumel - Alverez, 976 F.2d 1235 (9th Cir. 1992)
Brady doctrine requires prosecution to produce exculpatory evidence and evidence useful for impeachment when requested to do so by defendant.

Kyles v. Whitley, 514 US 131 L.Ed.2d 490, 115 S.Ct. (1995)
On Writ habeas corpus review, accused who had been convicted of murder and sentenced to death in Louisiana trial held entitled to new trial because of prosecution's failure to disclose material evidence favorable to accused.

Lawrence v. Lansing, 42 F.3d 255 (5th Cir. 1994)
Under BRADY, prosecution must disclose to defense both exculpatory evidence and evidence that would be useful for impeachment.

Martin-Costa v. Kiger, 235 P.3d 1040
While the parent of a minor crime victim had limited standing to enforce any right guaranteed to the victim, neither the Victims' Bill of Rights under Ariz. Const. art. 2, § 2.1, Ariz. Rev. Stat. § 13-4401 et seq., nor Ariz. R. Crim. P. 39 granted a crime victim the right to seek disqualification of the trial judge or defense counsel.

Myatt v. US, 875 F.2d 8 (1st Cir. 1989)
Evidence can be exculpatory, for purposes of compelling disclosure under BRADY, although the evidence is not directly about defendant; there will be many cases in which impeachment evidence concerning witness or codefendants will lead to reasonable doubt about defendant's guilt or innocence.

State v. Talmadge, 196 Ariz. 436
In criminal child abuse case, trial court's ruling preventing Scottish expert on temporary brittle bone disease from testifying as defense expert witness was an abuse of discretion, and the error was reversible.

US v. Aichele, 941 F.2d 761 (9th Cir. 1991)
To escape BRADY sanction, disclosure must be made at time when disclosure would be of value to accused.

US v. Clark, 988 F.2d 1459 (6th Cir. 1993)

US v. Carson, 9 F.3d 576 (7th Cir. 1993)

Smith v. Black, 904 F.2d 950 (5th Cir. 1990)

Brady violation occurs where prosecution suppresses evidence that is favorable to defendant and material to issue at trial.

US v. Farley, 2 F.3d 645 (6th Cir. 1993)

Evidence which may be used to impeach prosecution witness falls within scope of Brady Rule and therefore, must be disclosed upon defense counsel's request.

US v. Griggs, 713 F.2d 672 (11th Cir. 1983)

Exculpatory evidence could have existed in the prosecutors files which would have indicated the "TIP OF THE ICEBERG" (case remanded for further hearings).

US v. Hanna, 55 F.3d 1456 (9th Cir. 1995) 15.

"Brady material" is any evidence material either to guilt or punishment which is favorable to accused, irrespective of good faith or bad faith of prosecution. 16. Prosecutor's duty to reveal BRADY materials does not depend on request by defense.

US v. Oxman, 740 F.2d 1298 (3rd Cir. 1984)

When prosecutor receives a specific and relevant request for BRADY material failure to make any response is seldom, if ever, excusable.

US v. Rossy, 953 F.2d 321 (7th Cir. 1992)

Evidence is "material" under BRADY if there is reasonable probability that, had evidence been disclosed to defense, result of proceeding would have been different.

US v. Severson, 3 F.3d 1005 (7th Cir. 1993)

Brady requirements that government disclose exculpatory evidence also applies at sentencing.

US v. Zuno - Arce, 44 F.3d 1420 (9th Cir. 1995)

Under Brady, exculpatory evidence cannot be kept out of hands of defense just because prosecutor does not have it, where investigating agency does.

Williams v. Whitley, 940 F.2d 132 (5th Cir. 1991)

Prosecution is deemed to have knowledge of information readily available to it, and failure to provide that information, when exculpatory and when requested by defendant, is violation of Brady rule.

Burden Of Proof

Note:The burden of persuasion requires convincing the fact finder that any fact in issue should be decided in a certain way. The due process clause places on the prosecution the burden of persuasion on every element of the crime charged; only rarely does the burden shift to the defendant. Any shifting of the burden of persuasion must withstand constitutional scrutiny.

<u>Patterson v. Gomez</u>, 223 F.3d 959, 967 (9th Cir2000)
Instruction creating mandatory presumption for burden of persuasion on element of intent did not comport with due process because rest of charge does not explain or cure the error.

<u>Patterson v. New York</u>, 432 US 197, 210-11 (1997)
Requirement that defendant proved affirmative defense of "heat of passion" by preponderance of the evidence did not unconstitutionally shift burden of persuasion.

<u>State v. Abdi</u>, 602 Ariz. Adv. Rep. 4
Trial court erred in instructing the jury, under Ariz. Rev. Stat. § 13-419, to presume the victim had acted reasonably in defense of his residence. A mandatory presumption which shifted the burden of persuasion by requiring defendant to establish affirmatively the negative of an element of the offense was unconstitutional.

<u>State v. Karr</u>, 221 Ariz. 319 Even though the trial court erred by failing to instruct the jury that defendant bore the burden of proving self-defense, defendant was not prejudiced because he benefited from the omission, as the instructions agreed to by the trial court and counsel and given to the jury shifted the burden of disproving the defense to the State.

State v. Rios, 237 P.3d 1052

Murder conviction was reversed because the trial court erred in instructing the jury that defendant had the burden of proof on his justification defense; Ariz. Rev. Stat. § 13-205, which retroactively shifted the burden of proof to the State, did not violate the separation of powers clause under Ariz. Const. art. III.

State v. Valverde, 220 Ariz. 171

In a criminal trial for aggravated assault where defendant claimed that he was acting in self-defense, the trial court committed reversible error by failing to instruct the jury that self-defense was an affirmative defense requiring proof by a preponderance of the evidence under Ariz. Rev. Stat. § 13-205.

Civil Rights

Auguley v. General Motors, 52 F.3d 1364 (6th Cir. 1995)
"Disparate treatment" occurs when employer treats some employees less favorably than others because of race, religion, sex, or the like.

Bangerter v. Orem City Corp., 46 F.3d 1491 (10th Cir. 1995)
Under Fair Housing Act, the handicapped are "protected class" for purposes of statutory claim, as they are direct object of statutory protection, even if the handicapped are not protected class for constitutional purposes.

Bator v. State Of Hawaii, 39 F.3d 1021 (9th Cir. 1994)
Edwards v. Wallace Community College, 49 F.3d 1517 (11th Cir. 1995)
Employer will be held liable for employment discrimination based on hostile environment if it fails to discover the hostile atmosphere and take appropriate remedial steps.

Burgess v. Moore, 39 F.3d 216 (8th Cir. 1994)
Inmate's affidavit and civil rights complaint against corrections officers were signed under penalty of perjury and, thus, documents were sufficiently verified for purposes of refuting affidavits filed by corrections officers.

Bushanell v. Rossetti, 750 F.2d 298 (4th Cir. 1984)
Governments prosecutorial power may not be used either to exact releases of related civil rights claims or to retaliate for civil prosecution of such claims.

Danforth v. Minnesota, 128 S.Ct. 1029
Defendant was convicted in state court of criminal sexual conduct with a minor, but sought state post-conviction relief on the ground that admission of the victim's videotaped testimony violated a new rule of law announced by the U.S. Supreme Court. Upon the grant of a writ of certiorari, defendant appealed the judgment of the Minnesota Supreme Court which held that federal law precluded retroactive application of the new rule.

Dibiase v. Smithkline Beecham Corp., 48 F.3d 719 (3rd Cir. 1995) ADEA (Age Discrimination in Employment Act) broadly prohibits arbitrary discrimination in workplace based on age.

Faaita v. Liang, 2009 US Dist. LEXIS 2441
Relying on Heck and subsequent Ninth Circuit case law, this court ruled in 2001 that the statute of limitations applicable to a false arrest claim accrues: On a person's arrest if that person had been mistakenly arrested by an officer who only had probable cause to arrest someone else who resembled the person arrested. If the person arrested happened to have been involved in the same crime and was subsequently indicted and arrested based on evidence unrelated to the wrongful arrest, that person could bring a false arrest claim during the pendency of the criminal case. In that event, the court's determination of whether the officers lacked probable cause for the initial arrest would not necessarily imply the invalidity of the criminal case against that person. See: Pascual v. Matsumura, 165 F. Supp. 2d 1149, 1153 (D. Haw. 2001).

Gates v. Deukmejian, 977 F.2d 1300 (9th Cir. 1992)
Litigant need not prevail on every claim in order to receive full fee under federal civil rights statute.

Golino v. City Of New Haven, 950 F.2d 864 (2nd Cir. 1991)
Sanders v. English, 950 F.2d 1152 (5th Cir. 1992)
Right not to be arrested or prosecuted without probable cause is clearly established constitutional right for purposes of §1983 civil rights action. False arrest, illegal detention (false imprisonment), and malicious prosecution are recognized as causes of action under §1983.

Hafer v. Melo, 502 US 116 L.Ed.2d 301, 112 S.Ct. (1991)
State officials held subject to personal liability for damages under 42 USCS §1983 based on official acts, where §1983 actions were brought against officials in their individual capacities.

Hale v. Townley, 45 F.3d 914 (5th Cir. 1995)

US v. Koon, 34 F.3d 1416 (9th Cir. 1994)

Police officer who is present at scene and who does not take reasonable measures to protect suspect from another officer's use of excessive force may be liable for civil rights violations.

Harper v. Harris County, Tx., 21 F.3d 597 (5th Cir. 1994)

Plaintiff is not required to prove significant injury to assert §1983 Fourth Amendment excessive force claim against law enforcement officer.

Heck v. Humphrey, 114 S.Ct. 2364 (1994)

A civil complaint cannot be filed in regard to matters that may have a tendency to overturn the plaintiff's conviction in a criminal matter.

Hutsell v. Sayer, 5 F.3d 996 (6th Cir. 1993)

If police officer obtains warrant through material false statements made either knowingly or with reckless disregard for the truth, he may be sued under §1983 for Fourth Amendment violation.

Johnson v. Moore, 958 F.2d 92 (5th Cir. 1992)

Martinez v. City Of Opa Locka, Fla., 971 F.2d 708 (11th Cir. 1992)

Although local governments cannot be held liable merely on theory of respondent superior, single decision by official policy maker can establish the existence of an unconstitutional municipal policy.

Jones v. US, 16 F.3d 979 (8th Cir. 1994)

Sykes v. James, 13 F.3d 515 (2nd Cir. 1993)

In order to recover in federal court through § 1983, plaintiff must show that a federal constitutional right was violated and that the individual violating that constitutional right did so under color of law.

Leary v. Dalton, 58 F.3d 748 (1st Cir. 1995)

Alcoholism is a disability within meaning of Rehabilitation Act.

LeMaire v. Mauss, 12 F.3d 1444 (9th Cir. 1993)

While inmate challenging conditions of his confinement failed on most of his claims, his success on a few claims altered his legal relationship to prison superintendent and thus he was "prevailing party" under §1988.

Mendocino Environmental Center v. Mendocino Co., 14 F.3d 457 (9th Cir. 1994)

If plaintiff alleges discrete acts of police surveillance and intimidations directed solely at silencing him, civil rights claim will lie.

Mertik v. Blalock, 983 F.2d 1353 (6th Cir. 1993)

Section §1983 provides individuals with private course of action when constitutional deprivations occur under color of state law. Local governments can be subject to suit under §1983.

McDowell v. Jones, 990 F.2d 433 (8th Cir. 1993)

Verbal threats and name calling usually are not actionable under §1983.

McKinney v. Dekalb County, Ga., 997 F.2d 1440 (11th Cir. 1993)

Failure to properly train municipal police officers is "policy or custom" that gives rise to §1983 liability when such failure reflects deliberate indifference to constitutional rights of municipal inhabitants.

Moore v. McDonald, 30 F.3d 616 (5th Cir. 1994)

Buckley v. County Of Los Angeles, 957 F.2d 652 (9th Cir. 1992)

Civil rights complaints are to be liberally construed.

Morgan v. Woessner, 997 F.2d 1244 (9th Cir. 1993)

Jury may award punitive damages in a civil rights action under §1983, either when defendant's conduct was driven by evil motive or intent, or when it involved reckless or callous indifference to constitutional rights of others.

Palmer v. Bd. Of Educ. Comm. Unit School Dist., 46 F.3d 682 (7th Cir. 1995)

Complaints need not plead facts.

Pelfrey v. Chambers, 43 F.3d 1034 (6th Cir. 1995)
Inmates seeking damages under §1983 are required to set forth clearly in their pleadings that they are suing state officials in their individual capacities and not in capacities as state officials.

Spain v. Gallegos, 26 F.3d 439 (3rd Cir. 1994)
Employee may demonstrate that there is sexually hostile work environment without proving blatant sexual misconduct.

State v. Bartlett, 164 Ariz. 229, 792 P.2d 692
Defendant was convicted in the Superior Court, Cochise County, No. CR-87-00020, Richard A. Winkler, J., of two counts of sexual conduct with a minor under 15 years of age and sentenced to mandatory minimum consecutive sentences totaling 40 years without possibility of early release. The Court of Appeals affirmed, and the defendant petitioned for further review. The Supreme Court, Corcoran, J., held that defendant's sentences under dangerous crimes against children act of 15 years for first offense and 25 years for second offense were disproportionate to his crimes involving participation in nonviolent, non-incestuous, heterosexual, and consensual sexual intercourse with two 14-year-old girls and therefore violated Eighth Amendment proscription against cruel and unusual punishment. Remanded for resentencing.

State v. Davis, 206 Ariz. 377, 79 P.3d 64
Defendant was convicted, after a jury trial in the Superior Court, Maricopa County, No. CR 99-90084(B), Dennis W. Dairman, J., of four counts of sexual misconduct with a minor, as dangerous crimes against children, and defendant received mandatory minimum sentence of 52 years without possibility of parole under dangerous crimes against children sentencing enhancement.

Defendant appealed. The Court of Appeals affirmed. The Supreme Court, Berch, J., held that: (1) if the sentence imposed is so severe that it appears grossly disproportionate to the offense, the court must carefully examine the facts of the case and the circumstances of the offender, to determine if the sentence constitutes cruel and unusual punishment, overruling State v. DePiano, 187 Ariz. 27, 926 P.2d 494; (2) defendant's sentence constituted cruel and unusual punishment; (3) real

possibility of non-unanimous jury verdict on first count required reversal on that count; and (4) "on or about" instruction regarding date of offense charged in fourth count did not deprive defendant of ability to present alibi defense as to that count. Affirmed in part, vacated in part, and remanded.

State v. Fernane, 185 Ariz. 222

Appellant and her co-defendant, Joseph Stern, were convicted following a joint jury trial of two counts of child abuse and one count of first degree felony murder in connection with the death of appellant's two-year-old daughter, Katherine Rose Fernane. Appellant was sentenced to mitigated terms of twelve years and twenty-three years on the child abuse counts, and to life imprisonment without possibility of release for thirty-five [***2] years on the murder count, the sentences to run concurrently. She appeals from her convictions and sentences, contending that the trial court erred in (1) failing to sever her trial from Stern's; (2) failing to exclude or limit evidence of appellant's prior bad acts; and (3) denying her motion for judgment of acquittal based on insufficient evidence to support the verdict. We reject the third but agree with the first two contentions, and therefore reverse and remand for a new trial.

Ultimate Creations v. McMahon, 515 F.Supp.2d 1060

Well-known professional wrestler, who was a former employee of defendants, and co-plaintiffs brought action asserting claims of defamation and false light arising from statements made on video produced by defendants which chronicled his professional wrestling career. Defendants moved to dismiss. Holdings: The District Court, Roslyn O. Silver, J., held that:

(1) co-plaintiffs were not defamed by video;

(2) statements in video were reasonably capable of a defamatory meaning;

(3) complaint adequately pled actual malice;

(4) statements about wrestler's public life were not actionable under false light law; but

(5) statements about wrestler's private personal life were actionable under false light law; and

(6) wrestler was not required to plead pecuniary damages.

Motion granted in part and denied in part.

US v.Brooks, 145 F.3d 446

Motion in limine to preclude government from introducing certain evidence in criminal trial was granted by the United States District Court for the District of Massachusetts, Edward F. Harrington, J., and the government appealed. The Court of Appeals, Selya, Circuit Judge, held that:

(1) government had right to interlocutory appeal of the order, which extirpated evidence that the government considered to be substantial proof of specified elements of the charged offenses, even though ruling was on motion in limine rather than a suppression order;

(2) appeal was timely though jury was sworn before Court of Appeals stayed proceedings;

(3) district court abused its discretion in granting motion;

(4) appeal divested the district court of its authority to swear a jury and start the trial, and it actions in doing so were nullities; and

(5) district judge would be removed from further participation in the case and case would be assigned, on remand, to a different district judge. Vacated and remanded with directions.

Walton v. City Of Southfield, 995 F.2d 1331 (6th Cir. 1993)
Right to be free from excessive force is clearly established.

White v. Olig, 56 F.3d 817 (7th Cir. 1995) Section 1983 imposes liability only for violations of right protected by the Constitution and laws of the United States.

Valentine v. Konteh, 395 F.3d 626
Decades of existing case law have established the precedent that, when it comes to child victims, indictments might of necessity be vague as to the details of time and place. This does not mean, however, that they are constitutionally deficient. To the extent that this is a case of first impression, there is no authority to support the finding that the Ohio Court of Appeals unreasonably applied existing Supreme Court precedent.

Closing Arguments

Bell v. Evatt, 72 F.3d 421 (4th Cir. 1995)
Prosecutors closing argument may be grounds for reversing conviction.

Boyd v. French, 147 F.3d 319 (4th Cir. 1998)
A prosecutor should refrain from stating his personal opinions during argument and misleading the jury about the law.

Dubria v. Smith, 197 F.3d 390 (9th Cir. 1999)
Aus v. Garcia - Guizar, 160 F.3d 511 (9th Cir. 1998)
Prosecutors are not allowed to state their belief or opinion regarding the guilt of the defendant.

US v. Beckman, 222 F.3d 512 (8th Cir. 2000)
Prosecutorial misconduct during closing argument may be grounds for reversal of conviction.

US v. Iglestas, 915 F.2d 1524 (11 Cir. 1990)
It is improper for prosecutor to inject personal beliefs about the evidence into closing arguments or to call the defendant a liar.

US v. Loayaza, 107 F.3d 257 (4th Cir. 1997)
It is improper for the prosecutor to directly express his opinion as to veracity of witness.

US v. Tomblin, 42 F.3d 263 (5th Cir. 1994)
Statement in closing arguments that presupposes defendant's guilt can be the sort of foul blows long held improper.

State v. Lee, 142 Ariz. 227
In a criminal case, a new trial was warranted where the trial counsel's failure to present a closing argument deprived defendant of his sixth amendment right to effective assistance of counsel, resulting in a denial of due process and a fair trial.

<u>State v. Martinez</u>, 175 Ariz. 114

Trial court improperly permitted prosecutor to use appellate court opinion in its closing argument that a convicted felon could be expected to be untruthful, which effectively created a presumption against the credibility of a convicted felon.

Collateral Estoppel

Albert v. Montgomery, 732 F.2d 865

Appellant challenged a judgment of the United States District Court for the Middle District of Georgia, which dismissed his petition for a writ of habeas corpus as to his state convictions for aggravated assault, attempted armed robbery, attempted rape, kidnapping, kidnapping with bodily injury, and possession of a firearm during the commission of a crime. Appellant was identified as the assailant of two teenagers when the victims were driven by his house and saw him on his porch talking to police officers. Appellant was arrested and later identified in a lineup. At trial, the prosecution presented the testimony of the victim of a prior armed robbery, an offense of which appellant had been tried and acquitted by a jury. Appellant was convicted of aggravated assault, attempted armed robbery, attempted rape, kidnapping, kidnapping with bodily injury, and possession of a firearm during the commission of a crime. Appellant contends that the introduction [**11] of evidence at trial concerning the prior alleged attempted robbery of Miss Hatcher, for which appellant had been acquitted, contravenes the constitutional principle of collateral estoppel. Appellant further contends that the introduction of such evidence cannot be considered harmless error. We agree and therefore reverse the district court's denial of appellant's habeas petition.

Ash v. Swenson, 397 US 436, 444-45 (1970)

Collateral estoppel means simply that when an issue of ultimate fact has once been determined by a valid and final judgment, that issue cannot begin the litigated between same parties in any future lawsuit. The doctrine may bar the introduction in a subsequent trial of evidence that was used against the defendant in previous trial if the government attempts to use this evidence to prove a fact previously found against it.

Buck v. Maschner, (1989, CA10 Kan) 878 F.2d 344

Collateral estoppel forbids mention of evidence when acquitted at previous trial. (Licking or touching with mouth). Collateral estoppel doctrine for criminal cases barred admission of evidence in state prosecution for taking indecent liberties with child if testimony from previous child was sanctioned prosecution in which defendant was acquitted.

Note: The government and the defendant may take advantage of the collateral estoppel doctrine. Two conditions must be established for the doctrine to apply. First, the second prosecution must involve the same parties as the first trial. Second, the issue sought to be foreclosed must have been previously determined by a valid and final judgment.

Note: If there is no re-litigation of factual issues resolved in earlier trial, a court will not go beyond the Blockburger test to consider collateral estoppel.

State v. Hill, (App. Div1 1976) 26 Ariz. App. 37, 545 P.2d 999
In order for principal of double jeopardy to apply, the two alleged crimes must have identical components; test to be applied it is whether facts charged in later information would if found true, have justified conviction under earlier information.

State v. Jimenez, 130 Ariz. 138, 634 P.2d 950 (1991)
Dismissal of habeas corpus affirmed 45 F.3d 436, cert. denied 115 S.Ct. 2257, 515 US 1107, 132 L.ED.2d 264. Elements of collateral estoppel in criminal cases are: issue sought to be really gated must be precisely the same as the issue in previous litigation, final decision or issue must have been necessary for judgment in prior litigation and there must be mutuality of parties.

State v. Nunez, 167 Ariz. 272
Defendant's right to be free from double jeopardy was not violated because he was not subjected to a second prosecution after being acquitted or convicted of the same offense and he was not subjected to multiple punishments for the same offense.

State v. Stauffer, 112 Ariz. 26, 536 P.2d 1044 (1975)
Collateral estoppel is incorporated in the guarantee of the US Constitution, amendment five against double jeopardy which is binding on the states through the due process clause of the US Constitution, amendment 14.

Stone v. Murashige, 389 F.3d 880 (9th Cir. 2004)
Defendant only needed to show that retrial would have violated his right against double jeopardy to obtain habeas relief.

State v. Williams, 131 Ariz. 218
Collateral estoppel barred the state from trying defendant for sexual assault where the state had failed to prove that charge by a preponderance of the evidence in defendant's previous probation revocation proceeding.

US v. Johnson, 697 F.2d 735,7 39-40 (6th Cir. 1983)
Government estopped from introducing evidence of acts from acquittal of earlier counterfeiting charges in subsequent counterfeiting prosecution because jury must have necessarily decided defendant did not commit acts.

US v. Seley, 957 F.2d 717,7 22-23 (9th Cir. 1992)
Although double jeopardy analysis under Blockburger did not preclude retrial, evidence relating to charges for which defendant acquitted barred by collateral estoppel and thus government could not retry defendant.

Conduct of Trial

A.R.S. 1-211 special statutes.

Evans v. Young, 135 Ariz. 447, 661 P.2d 1148 (Ct. App. 1983)

When the provision of a general statute conflicts with those of a special statute, the special statute prevails.

A.R.S. 1-214 (1998 version)

State v. Wilhite, 160 Ariz. 228, 772 P.2d 582 (Ct. App. 1989)

Where the legislature leaves words undefined, the words are construed according to their common usage unless they have acquired some peculiar or appropriate meaning in the law.

28 USC § 455 (a) (2000)

Any Justice, Judge, or Magistrate shall disqualify him or herself in any proceeding is impartiality might reasonably be questioned.

28 USC § 455 (e) (2000)

Recusal for the appearance of impropriety under section 455 (a) may be waived by the parties, but recusal for actual bias or conflict under 455 (b) may not.

Ariz. Const. Art. 6 § 21 Speedy Decisions.

Every matter submitted to a judge of the Superior Court for his decision shall be decided within 60 days from the date of submission thereof. The Supreme Court shall by rule provided for the speedy disposition of all matters not decided within such.

Ariz. Const. Art. 6, § 26

Each justice, judge and justice of the peace shall, before entering upon the duties of his office, take an oath that he will support the Constitution of the United States and the Constitution of the state of Arizona, and then he will faithfully and impartially discharge the duties of his office to the best of his ability.

Abdullah v. Groose, 44 F.3d 692 (8th Cir. 1995)

Holbrook v. Flynn, 475 US 560, 56869, 89 L.Ed.2d 525, 106 S.Ct. 1340 (1986)

Illinois v. Allen, 397 US 337, 344, 25 L.Ed.2d 352, 90 S.Ct. 1057 (1970)

Forcing defendant to undergo trial in chains is inherently prejudicial and should only be tolerated in cases of dire necessity.

Arizona v. Fulminante, 499 U. S. at 310-11

Right to impartial judge not subject to harmless error review. See also: Chapman v. California, 386 US at 23 n.8

Baleman v. US Postal Service, 213F.3d 1220 (9th Cir 2000)

Parties failure to cite relevant authority, or discuss relevant legal principle, does not relieve the court of duty to apply correct legal standard.

Bannister v. Delo, 100 F.3d 610, 614 (8th Cir 1996) Whether judge's impartiality might reasonably be questioned by average person on the street who knows all relevant facts.

Blakely v. Washington, 124 S.Ct. 2531; 159 L.Ed.2d 403; 2004 US Lexis 4573; 72 US L.W. 4546; Fla. L. Weekly Fed. S. 430

Judge may not consider aggravating factors upon sentencing. Aggravating factors must be presented to the jury.

Bliss v. Treece, 134 Ariz. 516, 658 P.2d 169 (1983)

Where the record is incomplete a reviewing court must assume any evidence not available on appeal is supported by the trial court's action.

Boag v. McDougall, 454 US 364, 70 L.Ed.2d 551, 102 S.Ct. 700 (1982)

Pleadings filed by individuals representing themselves are held to a less stringent standard than those prepared by attorneys.

Bracy v. Schomig, 286 F.3d 406,414 (7th Cir 2002)
Harmless error analysis not relevant to issue of judicial bias. Where a judge is in "grave doubt", meaning "that in the judge's mind, the matter is so easily balanced that he feels himself in virtual equipoise, as to whether the error had any substantial and injurious in fact, the judge must find in favor of the petitioner.

Brasy v. Gramley, 520 US 899, 138 L.Ed.2d 97, 117 S.Ct 1793 (1997)
Petitioner for federal habeas corpus relief held to have made sufficient factual showing, under rule 6(a) of rules governing § 2254 cases, to establish good cause for discovery on claim of judicial bias with respect to state trial judge.

Broad v. Sealaska Corp., 85 F.3d 422 (9th Cir 1996)
Under supremacy clause, federal law preempts law either by express provision, by implication or by conflict between federal and state law.

Castro-Cortez v. INS, 239 F.3d 1037 (9th Cir 2001)
Neutral judge is one of the most basic due process protections.

Childress v. Johnson, 103 F.3d 1221, 1227 (5th Cir. 1997)
Solid meritorious arguments based on directly controlling precedent should be discovered and brought to the court's attention.

City of Auburn v. Qwest Corp., 260 F.3d 1160 (9th Cir 2001)
Under supremacy clause, state courts are obligated to apply and adjudicate federal claims fairly presented to them. See also: Boomer v. AT&T Corp., 309 F.3d 404 (7th Cir 2002); Ale Autobody & Towing Ltd. v. City of New York, 171 F.3d 765 (2nd Cir 1999)

Conley v. Gibson, 355 US 41, 45-46, 78 S.Ct. 99, 102 (1957)
As unartfully pleaded this section must be held to less stringent standards than formal pleadings drafted by lawyers and can only be dismissed. It appears beyond doubt that the plaintiff can prove no set of facts in support of his claim which would entitle him to relief.

Dale v. Weller, 956 F.2d 813 (8th Cir. 1992)
Leave to amend pleadings should be liberally granted unless other parties to suit would be prejudiced.

Ewing v. Williams, 596 F.2d 391, 395 (9th Cir. 1979)
Prejudice may result from the cumulative impact of multiple deficiencies.

Fernandez v. US, 941 F.2d 1488 (11th Cir. 1991)
Federal courts are to liberally construe the pleadings of pro se litigants.

Free Speech Coalition v. Reno, No. 97-16536, UNITED STATES COURT OF APPEALS FOR THE NINTH CIRCUIT, 198 F.3d 1083; 1999 US App. LEXIS 32704; 28 Media L. Rep. 1225; 99 Cal. Daily Op. Service 9839; 99 Daily Journal DAR 12675, March 10, 1998, Argued and Submitted, San Francisco, California , December 17, 1999, Filed , Rehearing and Rehearing En Banc Denied July 24, 2000, Reported at: 2000 US App. LEXIS 17718. Certiorari Granted January 22, 2001, Reported at: 2001 US LEXIS 944.
Judgment reversed upon holding the First Amendment prohibited Congress from enacting a statute that made criminal the generation of images of fictitious children engaged in imaginary but explicit sexual conduct.

Gasho v. US, 39 F.3d 1420 (9th Cir 1994)
Person is not criminally responsible unless criminal intent accompanies wrongful act. Penal statute must be strictly construed.

Griffith v. Kentucky, 479 US 314,328 (1987)
A new rule for the conduct of criminal prosecution is to be applied retroactively to all cases, state or federal pending on direct review or not yet final.

Grant v. Arizona Public Service Co., 133 Ariz. 434, 456, 652 P.2d 507, 529 (1982)
To abuse its discretion, a trial court must make an error of law, failed to consider the evidence, make some other substantial error of law, or have no substantial evidence to support its conclusion.

Haines v. Kerner, 404 US 519, 30 L.Ed.2d 652, 92 S.Ct. 595 (1972)

Darr v. Burford, 399 US 200,203-204, 70 S.Ct. 587, 590 (1950)

Pro se litigants pleadings are to be construed liberally and held to less stringent standard than formal pleadings drafted by lawyers; if court can reasonably read pleadings to state valid claim of which litigants could prevail, it should do so despite failure to cite proper legal authority, confusion of legal cites, poor syntax and sentence construction, or litigants unfamiliarity with pleading requirements.

Haupt v. Dillard, 17 F.3d 285 (9th Cir. 1994)

Right to fair trial is basic requirement to due process and includes right to unbiased judge.

Hellum v. Warden, US Penitentiary, 28 F.3d 903 (8th Cir. 1994)

Measures which single out defendant as particularly dangerous or guilty person threaten defendant's constitutional right to a fair trial.

Hughes v. Rowe, 449 US 9-10, n.7,100 S.Ct. 173,176, n.7 (1980) (decided in context of 1983 claims by prisoners)

Even though these cases were primarily dealing with civil matters in the form of prisoners civil rights litigations, it should even more so apply to a pro se or pro per prisoners' pleadings dealing with their criminal case. The US Supreme Court has stated that there is basically no difference between a civil and criminal court, as they are political subdivisions.

Jenkins v. Lane, 977 F.2d 266 (7th Cir 1992)

Judge must be fair to all parties and may not say anything that might prejudice either litigant's in the eyes of the jury. Due process requires that trial judge's actions never reach a point where it appears clear to the jury that court believes that accused is guilty.

Johnson v. Mississippi, 403 U. S. 212, 29L.Ed.2d 423, 91 S.Ct 1778

Trial before and unbiased judge is essential to due process.

K-S Pharmacies v. American Home Products, 962 F.2d 728 (7th Cir 1992)
Federal court may interpret state law. (Authors note: in other words federal law takes precedence over state law)

Leach v. Kolb, 911 F.2d 1249 (CA 7 Wis. 1990)
Defendant was not deprived of his right to fair trial by improper joinder of several criminal charges arising from separate incidents where evidence of defendants killed on each charged offenses was overwhelming and trial court gave explicit instructions to jury to deal with each count separately.

Liljerberg v. Health Serv. Corp., 486, US 847, 100 L.Ed.2d 855, 108 S.Ct 2194 (1988)
Right to a fair trial is a basic requirement of due process includes right to unbiased judge.

Marsin v. Udall, 78 Ariz. 309, 279 P.2d 721 (1995)
The government filed an information charging petitioner with the crime of kidnapping for ransom, a felony. The local rules of the superior court provided for the selection of the trial judge from nine judges available to be made by an assignment judge. Petitioner sought a writ of prohibition to prevent respondent from trying the case, arguing that to do so would have violated his right to a fair trial. The court issued an alternative writ. The court was committed to the rule that if a judge was allowed to receive evidence which of necessity was to be used and weighed in deciding the ultimate issues, it was too late to disqualify him on the ground of bias and prejudice. Respondent refused to recognize petitioner's affidavit upon the ground that he had theretofore heard and passed upon the foregoing motions and that the affidavit was, therefore, not timely made. The court determined that petitioner's affidavit complied with the law and was timely filed. Therefore, the alternative writ of prohibition was made permanent. There was a distinction between a judge being in fact disqualified and being disqualified by reason of the filing of affidavit of bias and prejudice and in the latter instance it was the affidavit that disqualifies, irrespective of whether the judge in fact was biased.

Matterson v. Lynch, 174 F.3d 549, 571 (5th Cir 1999)
Whether reasonable person with full knowledge of all circumstances would harbor doubts about judge's impartiality judge should recuse himself.

Note: Mad at a judge that has done you wrong? Do not file a judicial complaint to the Judicial Qualification Commission in your state. If you do, these complaints are seldom successful and will only invite retaliation from the judges who will hear your appeal. If you think the brotherhood of the bar is tight, the brotherhood of the bench is even more so. Save battles like this for another time, when you have gotten your freedom back and have been made whole again. Never start a battle from a position of weakness. Being a prisoner is a positon of weakness.

Parker v. Dugger, 498 US 308, 320, 111 S.Ct. 731, 739, 112 L.Ed.2d 812 (1991)
A state appellate court's factual findings are presumed correct unless they are not fairly supported in the record.

Parker v. Hill, 277 F.3d 1092, 1105 (9th Cir) Judges coercive action which affected verdict and substantial and injurious effect. Amended by 291 F.3d 569 (9th Cir 2002)

People of The Territory Of Guam v. Marquez, 963 F2d 1311 (9th Cir 1992)
It was not harmless error where the trial court sent a set of written instructions [i.e. the letter] to the jury, but did not read those instructions aloud. It is impossible to know whether any of the jury members read the instructions on the elements of the charged offenses.

Pontarelli v. Stone, 978 F.2d 773,775 (1st Cir 1992)
When trial judge wrongfully fails to disqualify self, remedy is for appellate court to reverse on the merits and order trial before new judge.

Rice v. Wood, 44 F.3d 1396 (9th Cir. 1995)
Criminal defendant charged with felony has right to be present at every stage of his trial.

Russell v. Cunningham, 279 F.2d 797, 804 (9th Cir. 1960)
Public policy favors disposition of an appeal on the merits over procedural terminations, when possible.

Scheehle v. Justices of the Supreme Court of the state of Arizona, 211 Ariz. 282,290 ¶ ¶ 28-29, 32, 120 P.3d 1092, 110 (2005)
Because attorneys are officers of the court, art. 6 §3 of the Arizona Constitution, which gives the Arizona Supreme Court "administrative supervision" over the courts, also gives it power to regulate attorneys. Id at 1130.

Schering Corp. v. Shalala, 995 F.2d 1103 (D.C. Cir. 1993)
No matter what agency has said in the past, or what it did not say, after agency issues regulations it must abide by them.

Silveira v. Lockyer, 312 F.2d 1052 (9th Cir. 2002)
Court is required, whenever possible, to give force to each word in every statute or constitutional provision.

Smith v. Lockhart, 923 F.2d 1314, 1321 (8th Cir 1991)
Right to counsel violated when court refused to appoint substitution of counsel after the defendant cited conflict of interest with appointed counsel and explained inability to communicate with counsel.

Soffar v. Johnson, 237 F.3d 411, 460 (5th Cir. 2000)
Certificate of appealability granted because court in doubt whether jury would have convicted without legally-obtained confessions.

State v. Amarillas, 141 Ariz. 620, 622, 685 P.2d 628, 630 (1984)
The granting of a motion for continuance is not a matter of right, but is left to the sound discretion of the trial judge, and such a decision will not be disturbed unless there is a clear abuse of discretion and prejudice results.

State v. Baker, 217 Ariz. 118

Because the record failed to show that defendant knowingly and voluntarily waived his right to a jury trial under U.S. Const. amend. VI, and Ariz. Const. art. II, §§ 23, 24, the court remanded for a new trial; there was no showing that the trial court personally addressed defendant on this issue under Ariz. R. Crim. P. 18.1(b)(1).

State v. Benak, 346 Ariz. Adv. Rep. 14, 18 P.3d 147 (2001)

The term "shall" is recognized by the Arizona courts as being mandatory.

State v. Brown, 124 Ariz. 97, 602 P.2d 478 (1979)

Right to a fair trial is a foundation stone upon which the judicial system rests; there is an indispensable right to trial presided over by a judge who is impartial and free of bias and prejudice.

State v. Bush, 148 Ariz. 325

Defendant was denied right to a fair trial because lack of courtroom security and decorum allowed assault victim's friends and relatives to create an atmosphere of fear and intimidation.

State v. Crane, 166 Ariz. 3, 799 P.2d 1380 (Ct. App. 1990)

The trial court did not err in admitting the testimony of previous victim molested by defendant in trial for molestation of another minor, as the offenses were sufficiently similar.

State v. Dann, 205 Ariz. 557, 568 ¶ 30, 74 P.3d 231, 242 (2003)

An appellate court reviews the trial court's refusal to allow evidence of a third-party defense for an abuse of discretion.

State v. Fisher, 176 Ariz. 69

A plea agreement containing a provision that required a witness to testify consistently with prior statements to authorities was unenforceable when the provision bound the witness to one version of the facts regardless of its truthfulness.

State v. Gendron, 168 Ariz. 153, 812 P.2d 626 (1991)
Error is fundamental when it goes to the foundation of the case or use of such dimension that the defendant cannot be said to have had a fair trial.

State v. Randy Lee Green, 200 Ariz. 496 , 29 P.3d 271 , 2001 Ariz. LEXIS 119 , 354 Ariz. Adv. Rep. 5. Aug. 17, 2001 filed.
Little v. Little, 193 Ariz. 518, 520, 975 P.2d 108, 110 (1999)
An abuse of discretion exists when record viewed in the light most favorable to upholding the trial court's decision is devoid of competent evidence to support the decision. See also: Fought v. Fought, 94 Ariz. 187, 188, 382 P.2d 667,668 (1963)

State v. Hanson, 138 Ariz. 296, 671 P.2d 850 (App. 1983)
Minute entry must be modified to reflect the oral pronouncement.

State v. Lichon, 163 Ariz. 186, 786 P.2d 1037 (App. 1984)
Absent objection, issue will be waived on appeal, unless it involves fundamental error.

State v. Lukezic, 143 Ariz. 60
Prosecutorial nondisclosure of state aid given two key witnesses that was discovered after murder trial provided sufficient grounds for order granting a new trial, which was not an abuse of discretion, and there was no speedy trial right deprivation.

State v. Miranda, 200 Ariz. 67, 68 n.1, 22 P.3d 506, 507 (2001)
Ran Berger v. S. Pac. Transp. Co., 157 Ariz. 547, 550, 760 P.2d 547, 550 (App. 1986) vacated on other grounds, 157 Ariz. 551, 760 P.2d 551 (1988)
A defendant does not waive error that could not have been recognized until the defendant's case was pending on appeal due to a change in the law.

State v. Neil, 102 Ariz. 110
After defendant's first conviction was reversed on appeal, defendant did not have the right to preemptory disqualify the trial judge and could only disqualify the trial judge upon proof that the trial judge was in fact biased and prejudiced.

State v. Ortega, 220 Ariz. 320

Defendant argued that the charges in counts four and five, molestation of a child and sexual conduct with a minor under the age of 15, arose from a single act, and his convictions on both charges constituted a double jeopardy violation. It was necessary for the court to compare the elements of sexual conduct with a minor under 15 with the elements of molestation. Defendant could not commit sexual conduct with a minor under 15 without also committing molestation of a child. Because molestation was a lesser included offense of sexual conduct with a minor under 15, the court concluded that defendant's conviction of both the greater and the lesser offenses violated double jeopardy. Therefore, defendant's conviction on count four, molestation of a child, had to be vacated. Regarding defendant's contention the prosecutor exerted improper influence over a victim's testimony, rendering it unreliable, the court concluded that the prosecutor was entitled to introduce the victim's prior statements to refresh the victim's memory or for impeachment purposes. Therefore, there was no error or misconduct in the prosecutor's detailed questions concerning the victim's previous statements. Defendant's conviction and sentence for count four, molestation of a child, was vacated, but the judgment was affirmed in all other respects.

State v. Radjenovich, 138 Ariz. 270

A defendant received ineffective assistance of counsel in a sexual assault case because counsel failed to interview a single prosecution witness, and was surprised when a defense expert, after learning the prosecution's theory, refused to testify.

State v. Superior Court (Gretzler), 128 Ariz. 583, 627 P.2d 1081 (1981)

A ruling on a motion in limine will not be disturbed on appeal absent a clear abuse of discretion by the trial court.

State v. Tarango,_Ariz._, 914 P.2d 1300, 1302 (Ariz. 1996)

When a statute is susceptible to more than one interpretation, the rule of lenity dictates that any doubt should be resolved in favor of the defendant. See also: Callanan v. US, 364 US 587, 596, 81 S.Ct. 321, 326-27, 5 L.Ed.2d 312 (1961)

State v. Washington, (1980) 182 Conn. 419, 438 A.2d 1144, 21 ALR 4th 435.

It is improper for jurors to discuss case among themselves until all evidence has been presented, all counsels have made their final arguments, and case has been submitted with final instructions; best where trial court expressly instructs jurors they are permitted to discuss evidence in jury room prior to termination of case there is denial of due process and unless state can show that such error is harmless beyond reasonable doubt, defendant is entitled to new trial.

Tarpley v. Dugger, 841 F.2d 359 (11Ith Cir. 1988)

Estelle v. Williams, 425 US 501, 48 L.Ed.2d 126, 96 S.Ct. 1691 (1976)

It is beyond peradventure that a state cannot compel a defendant to stand trial before a jury in identifiable prison attire.

Thomas v. Brewer, 923 F.2d 1361 (9th Cir. 1991)

As general rule, first sovereign to arrest defendant has priority of jurisdiction for trial, sentencing and incarceration.

Trent v. Dial Medical Of Florida, Inc., 33 F.3d 217 (3rd Cir. 1994)

Generally, pendency of case in state court will not bar federal litigation of case concerning same issues if federal court has jurisdiction over case before it.

Tuitt v. Fair, 822 F.2d 166, 177 (1st Cir 1987)

State court entitled to require express and unequivocal waiver before allowing defendant to proceed Pro Se.

US v. Brooks, 145 F.3d 466 (1st Cir 1988)

Judges must not only be scrupulously fair in the administration of justice but also must foster an aura of fairness.

US v. Cowan, 819 F.2d 89 (5th Cir 1987)

Error stemming from judge's ex parte meeting with deliberating jurors was not harmless error where it could not be clearly stated that jurors were not intimidated into deciding the case one way or the other.

US v. Cretacci, 62 F.3d 307 (9th Cir. 1995)
Defendant's claim of ownership at pretrial suppression hearing of property that he contends was unlawfully seized may not be used to prove defendant's guilt.

US v. Critton, 43 F.3d 1089 (6th Cir. 1995)
US v. Neal, 27 F.3d 1035 (5th Cir. 1994)
Severance is permissible if it appears that defendant or government is prejudiced by joinder of offenses or of defendants.

US v. Denny - Shaffer, 2 F.3d 999 (10th Cir. 1993)
Criminal justice system holds accountable only those who are morally culpable for their conduct.

US v. Detemple, 162F.3d 279, 286 (4th Cir 1998)
Whether a person who does not know if judge is actually impartial might reasonably question judge's impartiality on basis of all circumstances judge should recuse himself.

US v. Garrett, 179 F.3d 1143 (9th Cir 1999) (en Banc)
This court reviews for an abuse of discretion a district court's denial of a request for substitution of counsel. See also: US v. Gonzales, 113 F.3d 1026, 1028 (9th Cir 1997)

US v. Geyler, 932 F.2d 1390 (9th Cir 1991) US v. Pinto, 1 F.3d 1069 (10th Cir 1993)
Federal courts have the power to order expungement of government records where necessary to vindicate rights secured by Constitution or by statute. Purpose of expungement, a setting aside of a conviction, and a pardon is to nullify conviction relief.

US v. Gonzalez-Lopez,-US-, 126 S.Ct. 2557, 165 L.Ed.2d 409 (2006)
Mr. Gonzalez-Lopez wished to employ out of state attorney to defend him at his drug conspiracy trial. The district court denied admission of the attorney pro hoc vice because he had allegedly violated court rules. The 8th circuit concluded that the out of state attorney had not violated the rules and the petition to appear pro

hoc vice was therefore improperly denied, violating Mr. Gonzalez-Lopez's sixth amendment right to employ a counsel of his choice. 126 S.Ct. at 2561.

The issue before the Supreme Court was whether the denial of counsel of Mr. Gonzalez-Lopez's choice required reversal of his conviction. The court noted that "[t]he right to select a counsel of one's choice.., has never been derived from the sixth amendment's purpose of ensuring a fair trial. It has been regarded as the root meaning of the constitutional guarantee." Id at 2563. The court first addressed the government's contention that the sixth amendment violation is not "complete unless the defendant can show that substitute counsel was ineffective..." Id. It rejected this, concluding that, "whether right to be assisted by counsel of one's choice wrongly denied.., it is necessary to conduct and ineffectiveness or prejudice inquiry to establish a sixth amendment violation. Deprivation of the right is "complete" when the defendant is erroneously prevented from being represented by the lawyer he wants, regardless of the quality of the representation he received." Id at 2563. The court next concluded that deprivation of counsel of one's choice is structural error. Id at 2564.

US v. Gutierrez, 931 F.2d 1482 (11th Cir. 1991)
US v. Sazenski, 833 F.2d 741 (8th Cir. 1987)
Severance is compelled if joint defendants' defenses are antagonistic and mutually exclusive.

US Ex Rel Hagood v. Sonoma Co. Water Agency, 929 F.2d 1416 (9th Cir. 1991)
US v. Cheek, 882 F.2d 1263 (7th Cir. 1989)
Innocent mistake is a defense to both a criminal and civil complaint - so is mere negligence.

US v. Hernandez, 109 F.3d 1450, 1453 (9th Cir 1997)
Whether reasonable person with knowledge of all facts would conclude that judges impartiality might reasonably be questioned.

US v. Hill, 48 F.3d 228 (7th Cir. 1995)
The more recent a precedent, the more authoritative it is.

US v. Innamorati, 996 F.2d 456 (1st Cir. 1993)

Chapman v. California, 386 US 18, 2324, 17 L.Ed.2d 705, 87 S.Ct. 824 (1967)

"HARMLESS BEYOND REASONABLE DOUBT" standard presumes prejudice and places burden on beneficiary of errors to prove beyond reasonable doubt that errors did not contribute to verdict. Harmless plain error does not exist, all plain errors are harmful. Harmless constitutional error test is stringently applied, resolving all reasonable doubts against government.

US v. Jones, 10 F.3d 901 (1st Cir. 1993)

Bifulco v. US, 447 US 381, 65 L.Ed.2d 205, 100 S.Ct. 2247 (1980)

US v. Bass, 404 US 336, 92 S.Ct. 515 (1971)

Rule that, where there is ambiguity in criminal statute doubts are resolved in favor of defendant, applies to criminal prohibitions as well as penalties.

US v. King, 257 F.3d 1013,1029 (9th Cir 2001)

Failure to argue that case should be assigned to a different judge because of impartiality concerns resulted in forfeiture of issue.

US v. Lai, 944 F.2d 1434 (9th Cir. 1991)

Admission of evidence of defendants' prior crimes or wrongful acts, to show bad character or propensity to commit crimes, is prohibited.

US v. Lanier, 73F.3d 1380 (6th Cir. 1996)

Rule that, where there is ambiguity in criminal statute doubts are resolved in favor of defendant, applies to criminal prohibitions as well as penalties.

Note: Criminal statutes should normally be construed strictly. See also: Bifulco v. US, 447 US 381, 65 L.Ed.2d 205,100 S.Ct 2247 (1980)

US v. Bass, 404 U. S. 336, 92 S.Ct 551 (1971)

US v. Little, 52 F.3d 405 (4th Cir. 1995)

In adjudicating nonfederal questions, federal court must apply state law.

US v. Lussier, 929 F.2d 25 (1st Cir. 1991)

Frisbie v. Collins, 342 US 519, 96 F.2d 541, 72 S.Ct. 509 (1952)

Ker v. Illinois, 119 US 436, 30 L.Ed.2d 21, 7 S.Ct. 225 (1886)

Cases that established doctrine that a defendant may not challenge the courts jurisdiction over his person on the grounds that his presence before the court was unlawfully secured. (The "KER - FRISBIE DOCTRINE" taken from 744 at 1530, US v. DARBY)

US v. McKinney, 954 F.2d 471 (7th Cir. 1992)

Government must demonstrate that alleged constitutional error was harmless while defendant need not show harm.

US v. Olano, 62 F.3d 1180, 1205 (9th Cir. 1995)

State v. Bartlett, 164 Ariz. 229, 792 P.2d 692 (1990)

State v. Davis, 79P.2d 64, 2003 Ariz. LEXIS 132

In addition to raising specific objections at the proper time, a defendant generally must continue to assert the objection throughout the trial.

US v. Olvera - Cervantes, 960 F.2d 101 (9th Cir. 1992)

Under federal law, all offenses that carry a maximum penalty in excess of one year are felonies.

US v. Pendraza, 27 F.3d 1515 (10th Cir. 1994)

Guilt of conspirator may not be used to establish guilt of defendant.

US v. Phillips, 843 F.2d 438 (11th Cir. 1988)

Statutes of limitations [criminal/civil] are to be liberally interpreted in favor of accused.

US v. Polk, 56 F.3d 613 (5th Cir. 1995)

Government must prove that defendant was guilty beyond reasonable doubt, not merely that he could have been guilty.

US v. Price, 13 F.3d 711 (3rd Cir. 1994)

Jenkins v. Lane, 977 F.2d 266 (7th Cir 1992)

Judge must be fair to all parties and may not do or say anything that might prejudice either litigant in eyes of jury. 101. Due process requires that trial judge's actions never reach a point where it appears clear to jury that court believes that accused is guilty.

US v. Rivela - Rivera, 279 F.3d 1174, 1178 (9th Cir. 2002)

A court may permit review, however, when an objection at trial would have been futile. Defendant not required to objection when defendant has timely objected to admission of evidence and trial court has left no possibility of different ruling.

US v. Rogers, 150 F.3d 851,855 (8th Cir. 1998)

The Eighth Circuit has adopted a two-part test to determine when a denied pretrial motion has been preserved for appeal absent a renewal of the motion at trial based on:

The appellate courts practical ability to determine whether the appellate knew of the error and consented to it; and the lack of fairness of reversing the trial court on an issue it did not have the opportunity to consider.

US v. Tyler, 943 F.2d 420 (4th Cir. 1991)

State must provide indigent defendant with transcript of prior proceedings when that transcript is needed for effective defense or appeal.

US v. Walker, 234 F.3d 780 (1st Cir 2000)

District courts have an independent duty to ensure fairness of criminal trials.

US v. Walker, 92 F.3d 714, 716 (8th Cir 1996)

Impairment of defense most important type of prejudice.

US Dist. Ct. For Ed. Of Washington v. Sandlin, 12 F.3d 861 (9th Cir. 1993)

US v. McCusker, 936 F.2d 781 (5th Cir. 1991)

Requirements of Court Reporter Act are mandatory, and exceptions to requirements should be few and narrowly construed. Any editing of official court transcript, in any form, without parties' consent is prohibited.

US v. White, 222 F.3d 363 (9th Cir. 2000)

The government has a special responsibility to ensure the integrity of the criminal judicial process by living up to professional ethics and fair play at all times.

US v. Williams, 47 F.3d 658 (4th Cir. 1995)

When criminal defendant exercised his procedural right and successfully attacks criminal conviction, state cannot retaliate against defendant by seeking harsher punishment upon retrial.

US v. Wilson, 77 F.3d 105, 110-11 (5th Cir 1996)

Due process not violated when judge previously presided over severed trial of codefendant because no evidence that judge formed personal bias. If actual or apparent judicial prejudice exists either against or in favor of a party 28 USC § 144 and 455 provide mechanisms for judge's recusal.

US v. Wilkerson, 208 F.3d 794,797 (9th Cir 2000)

Whether reasonable person with knowledge of all facts would conclude that if judge's impartiality might reasonably be questioned judge should recuse himself.

US v. Yazzie, 188 F.3d 1178 (10th Cir 1999)

Four criteria for determining entitlement to instruction on lesser-included offense are 1) a proper request, 2) the lesser included offense contains some but not all of the elements of the offense charged, 3) the elements differentiating the two offenses are in dispute and 4) a jury could rationally connect the defendant of the lesser offense and acquit on the greater offense.

US v. Zimmerman, 943 F.2d 1204 (10th Cir. 1991)

Person who sees a crime being committed has no legal duty to either stop it or report it.

Willis v. Collins, 989 F.2d 187 (5th Cir. 1993)

Party may amend pleading at any time before responsive pleading is served.

Zugsmith v. Mullins, 81 Ariz. 185

Where a trial court granted defendant's motion for judgment notwithstanding a verdict, but did not rule on his motion for new trial, the motion for new trial was not denied by operation of law and was still pending.

Confession

USCA amendment 5

State v. Walton, 159 Ariz. 571, 769 P.2d 1017 (1989)

Even without express promise, police who imply a benefit to suspect in exchange for his information will not be remitted to introduce resulting confession at trial.

USCA amendment 5 &14

State v. Jimenez, 799 P.2d 785, 165, 444 (Ariz. 1990)

Confession resulting from custodial interrogations are presumed to be involuntary.

Arizona v. Fulminante, 499 US 279, 296, 306 - 12 (1991)

The standard used to determine when an error is harmless may be very high because "an in voluntary confession may have a more dramatic effect on the course of the trial than do other errors... but this simply means that any reviewing court will conclude in such a case and its admission was not harmless error." Id at 312.

Beecher v. Alabama, 480 US 234, 33 L.Ed.2d 317, 92 S.Ct. 1282 (1972)

Under due process clause of the fourteenth amendment, no conviction tainted by confession obtained by coercion can stand.

Boykin v. Alabama, 395 US 238, 89 S.Ct. 1709

The defendant was convicted in the Circuit Court, Mobile County, of robbery and he was sentenced to death by electrocution. The defendant appealed. The Alabama Supreme Court, 281 Ala. 659, 207 So.2d 412, affirmed. Certiorari was granted. The Supreme Court, Mr. Justice Douglas, held that there was reversible error where record did not disclose that defendant voluntarily and understandingly entered his pleas of guilty. Reversed.

Brown v. Mississippi, 278, 286 - 87 (1936)

Confession extracted through coercion and brutality violate due process clause of the fourteenth amendment.

Colorado v. Connelly, 479 US 157, 163 (1986) (dictum)
Involuntary confession violates due process of fifth and fourteenth amendment's. To prove a valid waiver, the government must show (1) the waiver was voluntary - that is, it represented an un-coerced choice, and (2) the defendant understood both the nature of the right being waved and the consequences of waiver. See: Moran v. Burbine, 475 US 412, 421 (1986)

Colorado v. Connelly, 479 US 168 (1986)
Lego v. Twomey, 404 US 477, 489 (1972)
The accuracy of the confession should not be considered at a voluntariness hearing.

Colorado v. Connelly, 479 US 157, 163 (1986) (dictum)
The Supreme Court emphasized that coercion by any state actor is a necessary element in satisfying his test. Among the factors court's commonly considered in assessing the totality of the circumstances surrounding testimonial evidence supplied by a defendant are:

1.The location of the questioning;
2. Whether Miranda warnings were given; and
3. Whether the accused initiated contact with law-enforcement officials.
4. An accused personal characteristics, such as youth, drug problem, psychological problems, physical condition, and inexperience with the justice system are also factors in the totality test, but have not been held individually sufficient to render a confession in voluntary. Courts generally have held the following practices insufficiently coercive to constitute a Fifth Amendment violation:

5. Promise of leniency or psychiatric treatment;
6. Confrontation of the accused with other evidence of guilt;
7. An interrogation that appeals to the defendant's emotions and an interrogators false or misleading statements.
8. Obtaining testimonial evidence from a defendant by means of torture or other physical coercion, however, violates the Constitution and the evidence of this obtained cannot be used to trial.

Crane v. Kentucky, 476 US 683 (1986)

Exclusion of testimony as to circumstances of a confession can deprive a defendant of a fair trial when circumstances bear on the credibility as well as the voluntariness of the confession.

Crane v. Kentucky, 476 US 683 , 90 L.Ed.2d 636, 106 S.Ct. 2142, 20 Fed. rules evid. serv. 801, on remand, (KY) 726 Sw2d 302, cert. denied, (US) 98 L.Ed.2d 70, 108 S.Ct. 111

State trial court's exclusion of testimony proffered by accused relating to physical and psychological environment in which is confession was obtained violated accused's fundamental constitutional right to fair opportunity to present complete defense, where although accused's pre-trial motion to suppress confession on ground of involuntariness had been denied and prosecution had moved to have proffered testimony excluded because voluntariness issue had already been resolved, (1) accused's entire defense was that there was no physical evidence to link him to crime and that his earlier admission of guilt was not to be believed, (2) accused sought to introduce testimony in order to show that confession was unworthy of belief, (3) introduction of proffered evidence was all but indispensable to success of defense, and (4) no rational justification had been advanced for exclusion of this evidence.

Culombe v. Connecticut, 367 US 568,602 (1961) Will overborne if statement not product of an essentially free and unconstrained choice by its maker.

Dody v. South Carolina DOC, 741 F.2d 76, 78 (4th Cir. 1984)

Trial court erred in considering truthfulness of confession in determining voluntariness.

Greenwald v. Wisconsin, 390 US 519, 88 S.Ct. 1152 L.Ed.2d 77 (1968)

The Supreme Court found a confession to be involuntary based on the fact that the defendant was questioned by the police for four straight hours during 13 hours of detention, was not provided counsel upon request, and was not given food or his medication.

Haynes v. Washington, 373 US 503, 513 – 14 (1963)

Townsend v. Sain, 372 US 293, 307 (1963)

Test for involuntariness is whether suspects will was overborn or whether confession was product of rational intellect and free will. Overruled on other grounds by Keeney v. Tamayo - Reyes, 504 US 1 (1992)

Hutto v. Ross, 429 US 28, 30, 97 S.Ct. 202, 203, 50 L.Ed 194, 197 (1976)

United States Supreme Court reaffirmed its prior holdings that a confession "obtained by any direct or implied promises, however slight" is involuntary.

In re Appeal in Pima County Juvenile Delinquency Action, No. 2 CA-Jv. 89-0039, Court of Appeals of Arizona, Division Two, Department B, 164 Ariz. 306; 792 P.2d 769; 1990 Ariz. App. LEXIS 43; 54 Ariz. Adv. Rep. 56, February 22, 1990, Review Denied June 19, 1990

Defendant was improperly adjudicated delinquent on one count of child molestation and sexual conduct with a minor under 15. Police officers' misrepresentations and promises in an interview made defendant's incriminating statements involuntary.

In re Timothy C., 1 CA-Jv. 97-0232, COURT OF APPEALS OF Arizona, DIVISION ONE, DEPARTMENT D, 194 Ariz. 159; 978 P.2d 644; 1998 Ariz. App. LEXIS 141; 275 Ariz. Adv. Rep. 43, August 13, 1998, Filed , Petition for Review DENIED on May 26, 1999 by Arizona Supreme Court Cv. -98-0419-PR. REVERSED AND REMANDED

A defendant's confession of child molestation to a child protective services worker was inadmissible because the statement had been given based on the worker's misrepresented promises.

Jackson v. US, 404 A.2d 911 (Dist. Col. App. 1979)

When defendant objects to use of his confession claiming it was product of coercion, he has constitutional right to have fair hearing and reliable determination on issue of voluntariness, this hearing shall be conducted by trial judge outside presence of jury and judge shall determine issue of voluntariness or influenced by veracity of statements.

Kern v. State, 426 N.E.2d 385 (Ind. 1981)
There is but one important factor that should be considered by trial court when examining totality of circumstances to determine whether state has met its burden of proof.

Lego v. Tomey, 404 US 477, 30 L.Ed.2d 618, 925 S.Ct. 619 (1972)
When confession challenged as involuntary is sought to be used against criminal defendant and his trial, prosecution must prove at least by preponderance of evidence that confession was voluntary; but although states are free to adopt higher standard, Constitution does not require proof of voluntariness beyond reasonable doubt.

Miller v. Fenton, 106 S.Ct. 445, 474 US 104, 88 L.Ed.2d 405, on remand, 796 F.2d 598, cert. denied 107 S.Ct. 585, 479 US 989, 93 L.Ed.2d 587 US N.J. 1985
Ultimate issue of voluntariness of the confession is any legal question requiring independent federal determination not only one claim is that police conduct was inherently coercive, but when interrogation techniques were improper only because, in the particular circumstances of the case, the confession is unlikely to have been the product of a free and rational will. Voluntariness of a confession is not an issue of fact presumed correct at federal habeas corpus proceeding under 28 USCA § 2254 (d), but is a legal question meriting independent consideration.

Milton v. Wainwright, 407 US 371 (1972)
Hoffa v. US, 385 US 263 (1966)
Spano v. New York, 360 US 315 (1959)
Under hostility of circumstances a confession obtained in any post-indictment interrogation lies involuntary.

Miranda v. Arizona, 384 US 436, 475 (1966)
The government must prove by a preponderance of evidence that the suspect waved his or her Miranda rights.

Moran v. Blackburn, 781 F.2d 444 D.C. Ark. 1983 Woodard v. Sergeant, 567 F.Supp. 1548, reversed, 753 F.2d 694, cert. granted and vacated, 106 S.Ct. 1694, 476 US 1112, 90 L.Ed.2d 650, on remand 806 F.2d 153 C.A. 5 (LA) 1986.
Evidence supported finding that testimony of government psychiatrist was more credible than that of petitioner's psychiatrist regarding petitioner's capacity to make a voluntary confession at the time he did confess.

New York v. Quarels, 467 US 649, 654 (1984)
Police interrogation of a suspect in custody threatens the exercise of the Fifth Amendment privilege because officers might actively compel confession through overtly coercive interrogation or passively compel them by exposing suspect to the inherent coercive environment created by custodial interrogation.

Note: To determine if testimonial evidence supplied by a defendant was voluntary, a court must ask whether, in the totality of the circumstances, law-enforcement officials obtained the evidence by overbearing of the will of the accused. The factual inquiry centers upon:

1. The conduct of law-enforcement officials in creating pressure and
2. The suspect's capacity to resist that pressure.

Note: Due process requires that jury not hear confession unless and until trial judge, or some other independent decision maker, has determined that it was freely and voluntarily given. Requirement that court makes pre-trial determination of voluntariness of accused's confession does not undercut accused his traditional prerogative to challenge confessions reliability during course of trial, since questions of credibility, whether of witness or of confession are for jury.

Note: The exclusionary rule requires the evidence obtained through direct or indirect violation of the fourth, fifth or six amendments may not be introduced by the prosecution at trial for the purpose of proving to defendant skills. Win a court improperly admits evidence in violation of the exclusionary rule, reversal is required unless the error was harmless beyond a reasonable doubt. The exclusionary rule is not a personal constitutional right, but rather any judicially created remedy to deter constitutional violations. Because the goal of deterrence

will not always be advanced by excluding relevant evidence that has been illegally obtained, the Supreme Court has identified several exceptions to the exclusionary rule discussed hereinafter:

1. Standing: challenge his own constitutional rights. Reasonable exception of privacy.

2. Good-faith exception: US v. Leon, 468 US 897, 920 (1984). Warrant search later found warrant was illegal.

3. Attenuation exception: Wong Son v. US, 371 US 471, 488 (1963). Evidence that would not have been discovered that for official misconduct.

4. Independent source exception: Murry v. US, 487 US 533, 537 (1988); Nix v. Williams, 467 US 431, 443 (1984)

5. Inevitable discovery exception: Murry v. US, 487 US at 539. 34.

6. Collateral uses: US v. Janis, 428 US 433, 454 (1976) Exclusionary rule not intended to tax proceedings.

7. Collateral uses: Civil tax proceeding, habeas, grand jury, deportation, parole revocation and sentencing hearing and for impeachment at trial when contradictory testimony.

Note: There are numerous Ariz. cases that held that a defendant may not be convicted solely on his own uncorroborated confession. See: State v. Loyd, 118 Ariz. 106, 574 P.2d 1325 (App. 1978); State v. Thompson, 146 Ariz. 552, 537, 707 P.2d 956, 961 (App. 1985); State v. Villalobos - Alverez, 155 Ariz. 244, 745 P.2d 991 (1987)

Schmerber v. California, 34 US 757, 761 (1966)

Mallory v. Hogan, 378 US 1, 8 (1964)

The United States Constitution amendment 5. The privilege against self-incrimination applies to state through the fourteenth amendment. This protection applies only to acts that are communicative and testimonial.

Smith v. US, 348 US 147 (1954)

The court in State v. Gillies, 135 Ariz. 500, 662 P.2d 1007 (1983), rule that the failure of a defendant to object to trial to the introduction of his statement does not waive his rights to question the advisability of the statement for the purpose of providing corpus delecti. "Before such confessions are admissible as evidence of a crime, the statement must establish the corpus delecti by proving that a certain result has been produced and that someone is criminally responsible for the result." State v. Gillies, Supra 135 Ariz. at 506 if the state fails to do so, a trial court must grant a motion for a directed verdict of acquittal.

State v. Adamson, 136 Ariz. 250, 665 P.2d 972 (1983) cert. denied, 464 US 865, 104 S.Ct. 204, 78 L.Ed.2d 178
State v. McVay, supra
Error does not require reversal if an appellate court can say beyond a reasonable doubt that it had no influence on the verdict.

State v. Cruz - Mata, 138 Ariz. 370, 674 P.2d 1368 (1983)
Three objective indica of custody must be considered, the site of the questioning, whether objective indica of arrest are present, and the length and form of the interrogation. State v. Cruz - Mata, supra. The Cruz - Mata court rejected the focus of the inquiry factor.

State v. Gerlaugh, 134 Ariz. 164, 654 P.2d 800 (1982)
The purpose of this rule is to prevent convictions based upon untrue confessions alone.

State v. Hatton, 161 Ariz. 142, 568 P.2d 1040 (1977)
The circumstances of each case determine whether individual in custody for purpose of administering Miranda warnings.

State v. May, 137 Ariz. 183, 669 P.2d 616 (Ct. App. 1963)
Quoting State v. Janice, 116 Ariz. 557, 570 P.2d 499 (1977) before a confession can be admitted into evidence, the state must produce independent evidence, apart from the confession, sufficient to warrant a reasonable inference that the crime was actually committed by some person.

State v. Mendacino, (1979) 288 OR. 231, 603 P.2d 1376
Appellate review of voluntariness of confession requires determination of whether historical facts found by trial court are sufficient to meet constitutional standards of due process.

State v. Montes, 136 Ariz. 1983 State v. Rivera, 152 Ariz. 507, 733 P.2d 1090; 1987 Ariz. Lexis 147
Voluntariness of confession and Miranda violations are two separate inquiries.

State v. Ross, 180 Ariz. 598, 886 P.2d 1354 (1994), cert den. 516 US 878, 116 S.Ct. 210, 133 L.Ed.2d 142 (1995)
A confession resulting from a promise is involuntary if 1) police make an express or implied promise and 2) the defendant relies on the promise in confessing.

State v. Thomas, No. 6576-PR, Supreme Court of Arizona, 148 Ariz. 225; 714 P.2d 395; 1986 Ariz. LEXIS 170, January 16, 1986. REVERSED AND REMANDED.
A confession should not have been admitted into evidence where defendant claimed he was coerced into admitting to the crime in order to receive a more lenient sentence, and the officer couldn't remember if he told defendant there might be leniency.

State v. Thompson, 146 Ariz. 552, 557, 707 P.2d 956, 961 (App. 1985)
Miranda warnings become a requirement only when a defendant is in custody or in fact is not free to leave the place of interrogation.

US v. Authement, 607 F.2d 1129, 5 Fed. rule evid. serv. 387 (CA 5 LA,1979)
Three elements that must exist simultaneously before Fifth Amendment is violated are: (1) compulsion of (2) testimonial communication that is (3) incriminating, and if any of these conditions is not satisfied, compelled to self-incrimination within the meaning of the Fifth Amendment is not at stake.

US v. Covington, 783 F.2d 1052

Defendant was charged with carnal knowledge of his 13-year-old daughter within the special maritime and territorial jurisdiction of the United States. The United States District Court for the District of Hawaii, Samuel P. King, J., suppressed the defendant's statements. Government appealed. The Court of Appeals, Hug, Circuit Judge, held that the exclusionary rule of Miranda and Edwards does not apply to statements obtained by foreign law enforcement officers in violation of foreign law and, therefore, if an investigator was acting as a law enforcement officer of the Marshall Islands, rather than as a law enforcement officer of the United States, the exclusionary rule would not apply, but a determination was required as to whether the trustworthiness of the confession satisfied due process standards. Reversed and remanded.

US v. Doe, 819 F.2d 206 (CA 9 Ariz. 1985)

Issue of whether defendant in fact knowingly and voluntarily waived his Fifth Amendment Miranda right is mixed question of law and fact in which applicable legal standard provides for strictly factual test and application of law to fact and consequently involves essentially factual inquiry reversible under clearly erroneous standard, since issue requires court to inquiry into totality of circumstances and defendants state of mind to ascertain whether he in fact knowingly and voluntarily waived his rights rather than to consider abstract legal doctrines, weigh underlying policy considerations and balance competing legal interest.

US v. Garibay, 143 F.3d 534, 539 (9th Cir. 1998)

Admission of statement obtained in violation of Miranda not harmless error because statements were thrust of prosecutors case and without statements there was insufficient evidence to support conclusion.

US v. Haywood, 350 F.3d 1029 (9th Cir. 2003)

A confession is involuntary if coerced by physical intimidation or psychological pressure.

US v. Nash, 910 F.2d 749 (Call Fla. 1990)

Instruction concerning voluntariness of defendants confession and the late it was to be given did not violate due process although it did not state that jury should disregard confession if jury found it to have been made involuntarily where statute provided that jury shall be instructed to give such weight to confession and is jury feels it deserves after jury heard all relevant evidence on the issue of voluntariness.

US v. Perdue, 8 F.3d 1455, 1469 (10th Cir. 1993)

Admission of confession obtained in violation of Miranda not harmless error because confession only direct evidence linking defendant and crime.

US v. Rico, 51 F.3d 495 (CA5 Tex. 1995)

Government has burden of proving by preponderance of evidence to defendant voluntarily waived constitutional rights against self-incrimination and the statements made our voluntary.

US v. Syzmaniak, 914 F.2d 434, 440 (2nd Cir. 1991)

Admission of confession obtained in violation of Miranda not harmless error because other evidence circumstantial.

US v. Tingle, 658 F.2d 1332 (CA 9 Cal 1981)

Confession that must not be extracted by any sort of threats or violence, nor obtained by any direct nor implied promises, however slight, nor by exertion of any improper influence; confession is involuntary whether coerced by physical intimidation or psychological pressure.

US v. Washington, 431 US 181, 52 L.Ed.2d 238, 97 S.Ct. 1814 (1977)

Fifth Amendment privilege against self-incrimination: Does not automatically preclude self-incrimination, whether spontaneous or in response to questions put by government officials; Does not preclude witness from testifying voluntarily in matters which may incriminate him, for the competent and free will to do so may give evidence against whole world, themselves included; Does not prohibit admissions of guilt by wrongdoers; Guarantees right to remain silent unless immunity is granted; Prescribes only self-incrimination obtained by genuine

compulsion of testimony; Absent some officially coerced self-accusation, is not violated by even the most damning admission.

Confrontation Clause

Barber v. Page, 390 US 719, 725 (1968) Unjustified limitations of defendant's right to cross-examine witnesses presented against him at trial may constitute a confrontation clause violation.

Delaware v. Van Arsdall, 475 US 673, 678 (1986)
Smith v. Illinois, 390 US 129 (1968)
Quoting Davis v. Alaska, 415 US 308, at 315 (1974) The right of confrontation includes as its main essential purpose the ability to effectively cross examine witnesses. In particular a defendant has the sixth amendment right to cross-examine a witness concerning her bias, motive and prejudice. Davis, 415 US at 316-18.

Don v. Nix, 886 F.2d 203, 206 (8th Cir. 1989)
Confrontation clause violated because defendant excluded from deposition intended for use at trial.

Fowler v. Sacramento County Sheriff's Dep't., No. 04-15885 , UNITED STATES COURT OF APPEALS FOR THE NINTH CIRCUIT, 421 F.3d 1027; 2005 US App. LEXIS 18840, June 14, 2005, Argued and Submitted, San Francisco, California , August 31, 2005, Filed.
Where petitioner was convicted of molesting his girlfriend's 14-year-old child but was precluded from cross-examining the girl as to her prior allegations of her mother's prior boyfriends' inappropriate conduct, and the state's case was one of credibility, a Confrontation Clause violation resulted in reversing the denial of the habeas petition.

Henry v. Speckard, 22 F.3d 1209, 12 14 - 15 (2nd Cir. 1994)
Confrontation clause violated because court refused to allow cross-examination of child witness regarding possible biases.

Mach v. Stewart, 137 F.3d 630, 633 (9th Cir. 1997)

Confrontation clause violated because defendant charged with sexual offense involving a minor was denied opportunity to cross-examine potential juror who lied to a social worker and who made expert-like statement during voir dire indicating that child sexual abuse victims did not lie.

Maryland v. Craig, 497 US 836, 845 (1990)
Kentucky v. Stincer, 482 US 730, 737 (1987)

Confrontation right designed to promote truth finding function of trial. Confrontation right does not turn on whether the stage is critical to the outcome of the trial. Id at 744 n.17. Confrontation right designed to promote truth-finding function at trial.

Kentucky v. Stincer, 482 U.S. 730

Exclusion of criminal defendant from Kentucky hearing on competency of two child witnesses to testify held not to violate either defendant's confrontation right or his due process right to be present.

Nelson v. O'Neill, 402 US 622 (1971)

The confrontation clause includes no guarantees that every witness called by the prosecution will refrain from giving testimony that is marred by forgetfulness, confusion, or evasion. To the contrary, a confrontation clause is generally satisfied when the defense is given a full and fair opportunity to probe and expose these infirmities through cross-examination.

Note: By guaranteeing these rights, the confrontation clause serves to ensure the reliability of the evidence against a criminal defendant by subjecting it to rigorous testing in adversarial proceedings.

Note: The necessity of limiting the right to confront witnesses must be determined on a case-by-case basis.

Note: When cross-examining a witness, the defendant must be permitted to test the witnesses credibility.

O'Brian v. Dubois, 145 F.3d 16, 26 - 27 (1st Cir. 1998)

If a prosecutor introduces a new matter on redirect examination, the defendant has a sixth amendment right to re-cross examination. If the witness claims a lack of memory while testifying, the defendant must receive a full and fair opportunity to probe and expose the witnesses' infirmities through cross-examination.

Olden v. Kentucky, 488 US 227, 231 (1998) (per curiam)

Confrontation clause violated because defendant accused of kidnapping and rape not permitted to cross-examine complainant regarding cohabitation with boyfriend.

People v. Vigil, 127 P.3d 916

The police officer was inextricably involved in the doctor's examination of the child and the circumstances surrounding the examination show that its primary purpose was to help the police gather evidence to prosecute Mr. Vigil. The lead investigating officer drove the child to the hospital and assisted the mother in signing the child in and filling out the hospital paperwork. Before [*936] the doctor conducted the forensic exam, this officer spoke with him about the background of her sexual assault investigation. At this time, the police had identified Mr. Vigil as a suspect and were working to build a sexual assault case against him. After providing the doctor with the background of the case, this officer gave him a Colorado Sexual Assault Evidence Collection Kit and asked the doctor to examine the child. Upon completion of this forensic exam, the doctor immediately sealed the exam and handed it to the officer who immediately took it to the police station and entered it into evidence. Hence, the circumstances surrounding the forensic examination imply direct police [**68] involvement and demonstrate that the purpose of the exam was to secure evidence for the prosecution of Mr. Vigil. I would apply the standard announced in Crawford to hold that an objective witness would reasonably believe that the statements he made to the doctor obtained under these circumstances would be used to prosecute Mr. Vigil, and that therefore, these statements were testimonial and could not be admitted unless the accused, Vigil, had the opportunity to cross-examine this witness.

Pointer v. Texas, 380 US 400, 403 (1965)

The sixth amendment provides in pertinent part: "in all criminal prosecutions, the accused shall enjoy the right… To be confronted with the witness against him. "US Constitutional Amendment 6. The right extends to state prosecution through the due process clause of the 14th amendment.

Redman v. Kingston, 240 F.3d 590, 591 - 92 (7th Cir. 2001)

Confrontation clause violated when defendant was prevented from cross-examining alleged rape victim about prior false claim of rape because testimony would have shown motive for lying. Confrontation clause violated when court precluded cross-examination of adolescent rape victim concerning prior false rape allegations because victims testimony constituted prosecutions only evidence against defendant.

State v. Fleming, 117 Ariz. 122, 571 P.2d 268 (1977)

The test for the denial of the right to cross-examination is whether the defendant has been denied the opportunity of presenting to the trier of fact information which varies either on the issue in the case or on the credibility of witness. (Note: deals with prior convictions)

State v. Gertz, 186 Ariz. 38, 41-43, 918 P.2d 1056, 1059-61 (App. 1995)

Cross examination for the purpose is especially important where the credibility of a key government witness is the central factor to be weighed by the prior of fact. Davis, 415 US at 317.

US v. Adamson, 291 F.3d 606,613 (9th Cir. 2002)

Confrontation clause violated when defendant is prevented from attacking witness's credibility, biases and motivations on cross-examination.

US v. Beckman, 222 F.3d 512, 525 (8th Cir. 2000)

Confrontation clause violated when defendant was precluded from questioning witness regarding sexual relationship with defendant's wife, which related to witnesses motivations and bias.

US v. Cronic, 466 US 648,658 (1984)
Denial of basic right to effective cross-examination.

US v. McHorge, 179 F.3d 889, 900 (10th Cir. 1999)
Witnesses loss of memory not basis for confrontation clause violation because defendant had opportunity to attack witnesses' credibility.

US v. Platero, 72 F.3d 806,816 (10th Cir. 1995)
Confrontation clause violated because court refused to allow defendant to ask alleged sexual assault victim questions about victim's sexual relationship with third person, which may have been the basis for fabricating allegations against defendant.

US v. Rhodes, 32 F.3d 867, 872 - 74 (4th Cir. 1994)
Confrontation clause violated because court, without presence of defendant, conducted in Chambers discussion with prosecution about substantive question sent out by jury in regard to instructions.

US v. Stewart, 93 F.3d 189, 193 (5th Cir. 1996)
Confrontation clause violated because judge restricted cross-examination of only government witness, thus preventing defense counsel from clarifying earlier testimony.

Conspiracy

<u>Bifulco v. US</u>, 447 US 381, 65 L.Ed.2d 205, 100 S.Ct. 2247 (1980)
Imposition of special parole term under 21 USC. § for individuals convicted of conspiracy to commit federal drug offenses, held not authorized.

<u>Hobson v. Wilson</u>, 737 F.2d 1 (D.C. Cir. 1984)
A "Civil Conspiracy" is an agreement between two or more people to participate in an unlawful act or a lawful act in an unlawful manner.

Note: Conspiracy laws in some states have been declared unconstitutional because they are vague and do not adequately inform its citizens as to what conduct is illegal. Moreover, conspiracy laws do not prohibit criminal activity they prohibit thinking about it.

<u>Pinkerton v. US</u>, 328 US 640, 90 L.Ed 1489, 66 S.Ct. 1180 (1946)
Each member of a conspiracy is criminally liable for all reasonably foreseeable crimes committed during the course and in furtherance of the conspiracy (Granddaddy case).

<u>TK7 Corp v. Estates Of Barboti</u>, 993 F.2d 722 (10th Cir. 1993)
Under Oklahoma law, showing that plaintiff suffered actual damages as result of conspiracy is essential element of civil conspiracy claim.

<u>US v. Blanding</u>, 53 F.3d 773 (7th Cir. 1995)
Kinship to members of conspiracy is insufficient to establish participation in conspiracy.

<u>US v. Chambers</u>, 944 F.2d 1253 (6th Cir. 1991)
<u>US v. Greenfield</u>, 44 F.3d 1141 (2nd Cir. 1995) US v. M.M.R. Corp., 907 F.2d 489 (5th Cir. 1990)
Law generally requires taking of some affirmative action in order to withdraw from conspiracy.

US v. Curley, 55 F.3d 254 (7th Cir. 1995)
Statute of limitations for narcotics conspiracy runs from last overt act in furtherance of that conspiracy. Confidential informants and government agents cannot serve as second party to conspiracy.

US v. Dimeck, 24 F.3d 1239 (10th Cir. 1994)
US v. Schmidt, 947 F.2d 362 (9th Cir. 1991)
There is neither true agreement nor meeting of the minds when individual "conspires" to violate the law with only one other person and that person is a government agent; individual must conspire with at least one bona fide coconspirator to meet formal requirements of a conspiracy.

US v. Flores - Rivera, 56 F.3d 319 (1st Cir. 1995)
Government must prove that conspiracy defendant possessed both intent to agree and intent to commit substantive offense.

US v. Gornto, 792 F.2d 1028 (11th Cir. 1986)
Statute of limitations for conspiracy is five years and begins to run when a defendant withdraws.

US v. Issaghollian, 42 F.3d 1175 (8th Cir. 1994)
For purposes of conviction of narcotics conspiracy, there must be some understanding beyond mere sales agreement with respect to contraband.

US v. Jones, 44 F.3d 860 (10th Cir. 1995)
One does not become participant in conspiracy merely by associating with conspirators known to be involved in crime; one must agree to participate in order to be conviction for conspiracy.

US v. Marks, 38 F.3d 1009 (8th Cir. 1994)
To prove conspiracy to distribute, some degree of knowing involvement and cooperation beyond mere knowledge must be established.

US v. McGowan, 58 F3d 8 (2nd Cir. 1995) Statute governing conspiracy to commit offense against or to defraud the United States Government requires that an over act be committed.

US v. Mergerson, 995 F.2d 1285 (5th Cir. 1993)
US v. Lorenzo, 995 F.2d 1448 (9th Cir. 1993)
Where two defendant's act in concert to achieve different goal, government has not shown meeting of minds as to common scheme or plan.

US v. Moss, 9 F.3d 543 (6th Cir. 1993)
Conspiracy has ended when its objectives have been achieved or have been rendered impossible.

US v. Powell, 982 F.2d 1422 (10th Cir. 1992)
Direct Sales Co. v. US, 319 US 703, 63 S.Ct. 758 (1943)
Separate transactions are not separate conspiracies as long as activities were aimed at common, illicit goal. Court of appeals will not sustain conspiracy conviction if evidence does no more than create suspicion of guilt if conviction results from piling inference on top of inference.

US v. Plescia, 48 F.3d 1452 (7th Cir. 1995)
US v. Zarnes, 33 F.3d 1454 (7th Cir. 1994)
Buyer - seller relationship, standing alone, does not establish existence of conspiracy.

US v. Ramirez, 45 F.3d 1096 (7th Cir. 1995)
To convict defendant of conspiracy, there must be substantial evidence that a particular defendant knew about conspiracy's illegal objective and that he agreed to participate in the conspiracy.

US v. Rivera, 6 F.3d 431 (7th Cir. 1993)
To convict defendant of conspiracy, prosecution must prove that conspiracy existed and that defendant knowingly joined it.

US v. Ross, 58 F.3d 154 (5th Cir. 1995)
US v. Jones, 30 F.3d 276 (2nd Cir. 1994)
US v. Sanchez - Galvez, 33 F.3d 829 (7th Cir. 1994)
Even actual presence at scene of crime is not sufficient proof of membership and participation in conspiracy.

US v. Williamson, 53 F.3d 1500 (10th Cir. 1995)
Lapses of time do not necessarily convert single conspiracy into multiple conspiracies. Mere associations with conspirators, even with knowledge of their involvement in crime, is insufficient to prove participation.

Constitutional Rights

Abramson v. Gonzalez, 949 F.2d 1567 (11th Cir. 1992)
If statement may not be censored by the federal government it is also protected from censorship by the states.

Acorn v. City Of Tulsa, 835 F2d 735 (10th Cir. 1987)
Conduct that is intended and reasonably perceived to convey a message falls within free speech guarantee of First Amendment.

Action For Children's Television v. F.C.C., 58 F.3d 654 (D.C. Cir. 1995)
Sexual expression which is indecent but not obscene is protected.

Ashcroft v. Free Speech Coalition, No. 00-795 , SUPREME COURT OF THE UNITED STATES, 535 US 234; 122 S. Ct. 1389; 152 L. Ed. 2d 403; 2002 US LEXIS 2789; 70 USL.W. 4237; 30 Media L. Rep. 1673; 2002 Cal. Daily Op. Service 3211; 2002 Daily Journal DAR 4033; 15 Fla. L. Weekly Fed. S 187, October 30, 2001, Argued , April 16, 2002, Decided , Costs and fees proceeding at Gonzales v. Free Speech Coalition, 2005 US App. LEXIS 9350 (9th Cir. Cal., May 23, 2005)
Ban on virtual child pornography was unconstitutionally overbroad since it proscribed speech which was neither child pornography nor obscene and thus abridged freedom to engage in substantial amount of lawful speech.

Bell v. Wolfish, 441 US 520, 60 L.Ed.2d 447, 99 S.Ct. 1800 (1979)
Procunier v. Martinez, 416 US 396, 40 L.Ed.2d 224, 94 S.Ct. 1800 (1974)
A prisoner is not stripped of constitutional rights (protections) at the prison gate, but, rather he retains all the rights of an ordinary citizen except those expressly, or by necessary implication taken from him by the law.

Bradbury v. Wainwright, 718 F.2d 1538, 1543 (11th Cir. 1983)
Prison administrator's bald assertions of security interests will not justify loss of prisoner's fundamental rights.

Bristor v. Cheatham, 75 Ariz. 227, 234, 255 P.2d 173, 177 (1953)

Von Moltke v. Gillies, 332 US 708,722 (1948)

It is a solemn duty of a federal judge before whom a defendant appears without counsel to make a thorough inquiry and to take all steps necessary to ensure the fullest protection of this constitutional right at every stage of the proceedings.

Brockett v. Spokane Arcades Inc., 472 US 491, 86 L.Ed.2d 394, 105 S.Ct. 2794 (1985)

American Booksellers Assn. Inc. v. Hudnut, 771 F.2d 323, 324 (7th Cir. 1985)

Miller v. California, 413 US 15, 37 L.Ed.2d 419, 93 S.Ct. 2607 (1973)

To be "obscene" under MILLER, "a publication must, taken as a whole, appeal to the prurient interest, must contain patently offensive depictions or description of specified sexual conduct. and on the whole have no serious literary, artistic, political, or scientific value Brockett, 105 S.Ct. @2799.

Brown v. Nix, 33 F.3d 951 (8th Cir. 1994)

US v. Migliaccio, 34 F.3d 1517 (10th Cir. 1994)

Courts indulge every reasonable presumption against loss of constitutional rights because of potentially grave consequences of their waiver.

Brown v. Texas, 443 US 47, 61 L.Ed.2d 357, 99 S.Ct. 2637 (1979)

Moya v. US, 761 F.2d 322 (7th Cir. 1985)

People are entitled to refuse to provide information to police. Moya went to the Supreme Court and back.

Buhl v. Cookey, 233 F.3d 783 (3rd Cir. 2000)

Defendant's waiver of constitutional right must be voluntary, knowing and intelligent. It is the court's duty to protect the defendant's constitutional rights.

Campbell v. US, 962 F.2d 1579 (11th Cir. 1992)

Harris v. McRae, 448 US 297, 65 L.Ed.2d 784, 100 S.Ct. 2671 (1980)

Roe v. Wade, 410 US 113, 35 L.Ed.2d 147, 93 S.Ct. 705 (1973)

A woman has a protected liberty interest in deciding whether to terminate a pregnancy.

Dept. Of Air Force v. Rose, 425 US 352, 48 L.Ed.2d 11, 96 S.Ct. 1592 (1976)
"Disclosure, not secrecy, is the dominant objective of the Act." Leading case on Exemption #6.

David v. Heckler, 591 F.Supp. 1033 (E.D. N.Y. 1984)
US district court judge Weinstein, one of the federal judiciaries more distinguished judges and better writers, ruled that bad writing in government documents violates the due process clause of the 14th amendment of the Constitution. Judge Weinstein took the highly laudable step of ordering the Department of Health and Human Services to rewrite its review letters to Medicare claimants because they were incomprehendable and contained insufficient and misleading information.

Department Of State v. Ray, 502 US, 116 L.Ed.2d 526, 112 S.Ct. (1991)
Exemption 6 of Freedom of Information Act held to authorize deletion of names and other identifying information from reports of interviews with Haitian Nationals returning to Haiti after attempting illegal immigration.

E.P.A. v. Mink, 410 US 73, 35 L.Ed.2d 119, 93 S.Ct. 827 (1973)
Requires the release of segregable portions of a file which was partially exempt.

F.E.R. v. Valdez, 58 F3d 1530 (10th Cir. 1995)
There is constitutional right to privacy in preventing disclosure by government of personal matters.

Foundation v. Massachusetts Bar Foundation, 993 F.2d 962 (1st Cir. 1993)
First Amendment protects right not to speak or associate, as well as right to speak and associate.

Freeman v. Lane, 962 F.2d 1252 (7th Cir. 1992)
Mr. Freeman had a meritorious Fifth Amendment argument under our precedent. Before Freeman took his appeal, this Court decided a number of cases including US v. Fearns, 501 F.2d 486 (7th Cir. 1974), and US v.Buge, 578F.2d 187 (7th Cir.) cert den. 439 US 871, 99 S.Ct. 203, 58 L.Ed.2d 183 (1978) which established that the prosecutor's comments violated the Constitution. No reasonable strategic

explanation has been given or exists for why counsel would forgo this issue on appeal.

General Electric Co. v. E.P.A., 53 F.3d 1324 (D.C. Cir. 1995)
Absent notice, such as where regulation is not sufficiently clear to warn party of what is expected of it, agency may not deprive party of property by imposing civil or criminal liability.

Gomillion v. Lightfoot, 364 US 339, 5 L.Ed.2d 110, 81 S.Ct. 125 (1960)
Lane v. Wilson, 307 US 368, 95 L.Ed. 110, 59 SC 872 (1951)
One must be ever aware that the Constitution forbids sophisticated as well as simple minded modes of discrimination.

Hinton v. Dept. Of Justice, 844 F.2d 126 (3rd Cir. 1988)
The government tried to appeal a judge's order for preparation of a Vaughn index and they lost.

Hovater v. Robinson, 1 F.3d 1063 (10th Cir. 1993)
Inmate has constitutional right to be secure in bodily integrity and free from attack by prison guards.

IDK, Inc. v. Clark County, 836 F.2d 1185 (9th Cir. 1988)
Official attack against law's constitutionality may proceed along four axes: law may impermissibly burden plaintiff's rights; it may impermissibly burden rights of third parties; it may fail to provide adequate notice of what conduct is prohibited, or it may lack sufficient guidelines to prevent arbitrary and discriminatory enforcement.

In Re Grand Jury Proceedings, 5 F.3d 397 (9th Cir. 1993)
News gatherers will be protected from grand jury inquiries where grand jury investigation is instituted or conducted in bad faith.

In Re Grand Jury Matter, 755 F.2d 1044 (3rd Cir. 1985)
First Amendment protects author of book from being forced to produce documentation for purpose of proving truth of statements contained in book.

Joe v. US, 510 F.2d 1038 (CA 10 N.M. 1974)
Defendant is denied due process protection where evidence warrants instructions on a lesser included offense and requested instruction to that effect is denied.

Julian v. Dept. Of Justice, 806 F.2d 1411 (9th Cir. 1986)
Crooker v. US Parole Commission, 760 F.2d 1 (D.C. Cir. 1985)
Presentence investigation reports are "agency records" when they are in the possession of the parole commission and thus must be disclosed by Commission upon request of prisoners who are subjects of reports.

Kolander v. Lawson, 461 US 352, 75 L.Ed.2d 903, 103 S.Ct. 1855 (1983)
California loitering statute requiring "credible and reliable" identification at police request held unconstitutionally vague.

Londrigan v. F.B.I., 670 F.2d 1164 (D.C. Cir. 1981)
Careful review of each document should be undertaken to determine nature of source and whether a promise of confidentiality was made which would bring it under protections of the Privacy Act.

Mackey v. United States, 401 US at 689, 91 S.Ct. at 1178, 28 L.Ed.2d 404 (1971)
It has been the law, presumably for at least as long as anyone currently in jail has been incarcerated. Justice Harlen wrote, in Mackey, "that procedures utilized to convict them must have been fundamentally fair, that is, in accordance with the command of the 14th amendment. That "no state shall... deprive any person of life, liberty or property without due process of law."

Massey v. FBI, 3 F.3d 620 (2nd Cir. 1993)
Court construes statutory exemption provided in the FOIA narrowly with doubts resolved in favor of disclosure.

Maynard v. CIA, 986 F.2d 547 (1st Cir. 1993)
Under the FOIA Government retains at all times burden of proving exempt status of withheld documents (Authors note: also a good case on Vaughn index's).

McFarland v. Cassidy, 779 F.2d 1428 (9th Cir. 1986)
The use of mandatory language, i.e. "shall" removes the matter from one of state law to constitutional.

Morgan v. Ford, 6 F.3d 750 (11th Cir. 1993)
State may not demote or discharge public employee in retaliation for protected speech.

Multimedia Pub. Co. v. Greenville Spartanburg Airport Dist., 991 F.2d 154 (4th Cir. 1993)
First amendment protects distribution as well as publication of protected material.

Norwood v. FAA, 993 F.2d 570 (6th Cir. (1993)
Exemptions to Freedom of Information Act are to be narrowly construed.

Note: Chief Justice Marshall's decision in Marbury v. Madison (1803). He asserted that since the Constitution is the supreme law, the courts must invalidate any law or action they considered in conflict with the Constitution.

Note: Prison labor is voluntary. The Constitution prohibits involuntary servitude except as a punishment for a crime. Which means that judges must sentence you accordingly, that is, either to a term of labor or a term of imprisonment. However, the Government, courts and the establishment do not recognize such distinctions in the law.

Note: Under the Freedom of Information Act (FOIA) and Privacy Act you may file for virtually anything the government has in its files that reference you. You may demand copies of anything the government has in any file, department, agency or databank that is indexed under your name, social security number or other identifier. The above laws may be used to supplement criminal discovery. You may also file a Vaughn request which will allow you to find out which files the government has on you that you're not aware of. See Vaughn, 484 F2d 820.1

Pell v. Procunier, 417 US 817, 41 L.Ed.2d 495, 94 S.Ct. 2800 (1974)
Prisoner retains First Amendment rights.

Ponchik v. Bogan, 929 F.2d 419 (8th Cir. 1991)
Prisoners may not be transferred for exercising their constitutional rights.

Procunier v. Martinez, 416 US 396, 40 L.Ed.2d 224, 94 S.Ct. 1800 (1974)
Case in which the Supreme Court established the two part test for determining if prison censorship policies are valid: FIRST, they must further an interest unrelated to the suppression of expression (security, order, and rehabilitation); SECOND, the limitation of First Amendment freedoms must be no greater than necessary, thus it will be invalid if it's sweep is unnecessarily broad.

Procunier v. Martinez, 416 US 396, 40 L.Ed.2d 224, 94 S.Ct. 1800 (1974)
Federal courts will discharge their duty to protect constitutional rights.

Sanjour v. E.P.A., 56 F.3d 85 (D.C. Cir. 1995)
Government may not regulate speech on the ground that it expresses a dissenting viewpoint.

Sellers v. Bureau Of Prisons, 959 F.2d 307 (DC Cir. 1992)
As long as information contained in agency's files is capable of being verified, then, under Privacy Act, agency must take reasonable steps to maintain accuracy of information to assure fairness to individual and, if agency willfully or intentionally fails to maintain its records in that way, and consequently makes determination adverse to individual, it will be liable to that person for money damages.

Simon & Schuster v. NY. Crime Victims Bd., 503 US116 L.Ed.2d 476, 112 S.Ct. (1991)
New York statute, requiring that criminal's income from books or other works describing crime be escrowed and made available to victims of crime, was held inconsistent with the federal Constitutions First Amendment.

State v. Alba, 13 Neb. App. 519

Defendant appeals the sentencing order of the Douglas County District Court after his plea of nolo contendere to two counts of sexual assault of a child, first offense, for which he was sentenced to 5 to 10 years' imprisonment on count 1 and 10 to 15 years' imprisonment on count 2, the sentences to run consecutively. The appeal centers on the fact that the State, defense counsel, and the judge treated the crimes in the plea bargain as Class 2 felonies when they in fact were lesser crimes, Class 4 felonies. Alba asks that he be resentenced under the lesser penalties for Class 4 felonies. Under § 28-320.01, first-offense sexual assault of a child at the time of the crime was a Class 4 felony, but the statute was later amended to change first-offense sexual assault of a child to a Class 3A felony. See 1997 Neb. Laws, L.B. 364 (operative date July 1, 1998). Alba contends that because the crimes set forth in the information were alleged to have occurred on or about January 1, 1997, the version of § 28-320.01 classifying first-offense sexual assault as a Class 4 felony controls here. We agree that the penalty provisions of § 28-320.01 in effect at the time of the alleged crimes set forth in the amended information, which provisions made first-offense sexual assault of a child a Class 4 felony, are controlling, rather than the legislative amendment operative July 1, 1998, which made the crimes Class 3A felonies. See State v. Gray, 259 Neb. 897, 612 N.W.2d 507 (2000) [***5] (law which creates or enhances penalties that did not exist when offense was committed is unenforceable ex post facto law).

State v. Boggs, 218 Ariz. 325, 332 ¶ 25, 185 P.3d 111, 118 (2008)
An appellate court reviews constitutional issues de novo.

State Of North Dakota Ex Rel - Olson v. Andrus, 581 F.2d 177 (8th Cir. 1978)
Once the government has voluntarily surrendered documents it can no longer claim that they are exempt from disclosure. (Excellent case on confidential informants.)

Stewart v. Smith, 202 Ariz. 446, ¶ 9, 46 P.2d 1067 (2002)
Defendants have two types of constitutional rights. Those counsel may waive, and of those only the defendant himself may waive. The Arizona Supreme Court cautioned in State v. McCrimmon, 187 Ariz. 169, 171, 927 P.2d 1298 (1996) that proceedings in criminal cases held outside the defendants presence are fraught with

danger and should be conducted, if at all... Only where the record clearly shows the defendant has waived his right to be present.

<u>Tennessee v. Garner</u>, 471 US 1, 85 L.Ed.2d 1, 105 S.Ct. 1694 (1985)
Police use of deadly force to prevent the escape of an apparently unarmed suspect felon held to violate the Fourth Amendment.

<u>Texas v. Johnson</u>, 491 US 397, 105 L.Ed.2d 342. 109 S.Ct. 2533 (1989)
Prosecution under Flag Protection Act for burning American Flag held to violate federal Constitution's First Amendment.

<u>Thornburgh v. Abbott</u>, 490 US 401, 104 L.Ed.2d 459, 109 1874 (1989)
Prison officials have the authority to reject publications and can reject the entire publication even if there is only a minimal section of offending material.

<u>US v. Dent</u>, 984 F.2d 1453 (7th Cir. 1993)
Doctrine of unconstitutional conditions prohibits government from forcing a defendant to choose between two constitutionally protected rights.

<u>US Ex Rel Anderson v. Northern Telecom, Inc.</u>, 52 F.3d 810 (9th Cir. 1995)
"Retroactive application" of law means that it changes legal consequences of conduct that took place before law went into effect.

<u>US v. Fapia</u>, 981 F.2d 1194 (11th Cir. 1993)
<u>US v. Erichman</u>, 496 US 3 10, 110 L.Ed.2d 287. 110 S.Ct. 2404 (1990)
New law may only be applied to conduct occurring after date of its enactment.

<u>US v. Frandsen</u>, 212 F.3d 1231 (11th Cir. 2000)
Criminal defendant who is convicted of violating a law may appeal his conviction by challenging constitutionality of the law on its face, and this is true even if defendant pleaded guilty to violating the law.

<u>US v. Garcia</u>, 23 F.3d 1331 (8th Cir. 1994)
Court is not empowered to suspend constitutional guarantees so that government can fight war on drugs more effectively.

US v. Johnson, 40 F.3d 436 (D.C. Cir. 1994)
"Strict scrutiny " is applied to determine constitutionality of statute which burdens exercise of fundamental right.

US v. Marshank, 777 F. Supp. 1507
Defendant charged with narcotics offenses filed motion to dismiss indictment against him. The District Court, Patel, J., held that Government's collaboration with defendant's attorney during investigation and prosecution of defendant violated defendant's Fifth and Sixth Amendment rights, requiring dismissal of indictment. Motion granted.

US v. Mills, 925 F.2d 455 (D.C. Cir. 1991)
US v. Nichols, 937 F.2d 1257 (7th Cir. 1991)
Blackledge v. Perry, 417 US 21, 40 L.Ed.2d 628, 94 S.Ct. 2098 (1974)
Due process protects criminal defendants against prosecutorial or judicial action intended as penalty for defendant's exercise of constitutional rights.

US v. O'Neal, 17 F.3d 239 (8th Cir. 1994)
Police officers are always free to approach citizens and question them, if they are willing to stay and listen.

US v. Pina, 844 F.2d 1 (1st Cir. 1988) Defendant has constitutional right not to appear in court in identifiable prison garb.

US v. Tubwell, 37 F.3d 175 (5th Cir. 1994)
Regulation may create protected liberty interest if it uses mandatory language to lace substantive limit on official discretion.

US v. Ullyses - Salazar, 28 F.3d 932 (9th Cir. 1994)
Criminal laws that are not sufficiently clear are voided by due process because of their vagueness.

US v. Zapata - Tamallo, 833 F.2d 25 (CA 2 N.Y. 1987)
Due process requires that a lesser included offense instruction beginning if evidence would permit jury rationale to find defendant guilty of lesser offense and acquit him of greater.

US Dept. Of Def. v. Fed. Labor Relations Authority, 510 US 127 L.Ed.2d 325, 114 S.Ct. (1994)
Privacy Act held to forbid disclosure of federal employees' addresses to labor unions pursuant to requests made under Federal Service Labor - Management Relations Statute.

US Dept. Of Justice v. Landano, 508 US 124 L.Ed.2d 84, 113 S.Ct. (1993)
Government held not entitled to presumption that all sources supplying info are exempt.

US Dept. Of Justice v. Tax Analysts, 492 US 136, 106 L.Ed.2d 112, 109 S.Ct. 2841 (1989)
The Supreme Court favorably broadened their interpretation of what constitutes "Agency Records" under the FOIA Act.

Weisberg v. Dept. Of Justice, 705 F.2d 1344 (D.C. Cir. 1983)
To meet its burden an agency must demonstrate that it has conducted a "Search reasonably calculated to uncover all relevant documents."

Woodward v. City Of Worland, 977 F.2d 1392 (10th Cir. 1992)
Moore v. City Of Kilgore, Texas, 877 F.2d 364 (5th Cir. 1989)
Public employer may not condition employment upon employee's relinquishment of his or her First Amendment rights.

Wells v. Franzen, 777 F.2d 1258 (7th Cir. 1985)
Youngberg v. Romeo, 457 US 307, 73 L.Ed.2d 28, 102 S.Ct. 2452 (1982)
Greenholtz v. Neb. Penal Inmates, 442 US 1, 18, 60 L.Ed.2d 668, 99 S.Ct. 2100 (1979)
The due process clause of the United States Constitution guarantees to every person freedom of bodily movement. This right survives criminal conviction.

Whalen v. Roe, 429 US 589, 51 L.Ed.2d 64, 97 S.Ct. 869 (1977)
The right to privacy includes an "individual interest in avoiding disclosure of personal matters."

White v. White, 925 F.2d 287 (9th Cir. 1991)
Waiver of constitutional right must be knowing and voluntary.

Williams v. Armontrout, 891 F.2d 656 (CA 8 MO 1989), vacated, reh gr. en banc (CA 8) 1990 US App. Lexis 1590
Due process considerations entitled to defendant charged with capital offense to have jury instructed on all lesser included offense is supported by evidence.

Wisconsin Action Coalition v. City Of Kenosha, 767 F.2d 1249 (7th Cir. 1985)
When statute infringes on exercise of First Amendment rights, burden of establishing its constitutionality is on its proponent.

Vaughn v. Rosen, 484 F.2d 820 (D.C. Cir. 1973)
Vaughn requires a detailed indexing of requested documents and the rational for applying exemptions.

Volunteer Medical Clinic, Inc. v. Operation Rescue, 948 F.2d 218 (6th Cir. 1991)
Zobel v. Williams, 457 US 55, 60 n. 6, 72 L.Ed.2d 672, 102 S.Ct. 2309 (1981)
The right to travel is protected by the Equal Protection Clause of the 14th Amendment. Right to travel is constitutionally protected against private as well as public encroachment.

Counsel

E.R. 1.2 Scope of Representation

In Re Davis, Ariz. Adv. Rep ., - P.2d -, 2000 LEXIS 20 (March 15, 2000)
Attorney, who had been disciplined numerous times in the past, was disbarred and ordered to pay restitution where she fails to consult with clients and abide by their decisions, fails to act with a reasonable diligence and promptness in representing clients, fails to keep clients are reasonably informed about the status of their case and fails to properly withdraw from representation and take steps a reasonably practicable to protect the client's interests.

E.R. 1.3 Diligence In Re Wolfram, 174 Ariz. 49, 897 P.2d 94 (1993)
A lawyer must not agree to representation if a lawyer's workload prohibits handling a matter in compliance with Arizona's professional rules.

E.R. 1.4 Communication In Re Curtis, 184 Ariz. 256, 908 P.2d 472 (1995)
The evidence supports a finding that the defendants counsel repeatedly failed to comply with reasonable requests for information in violation of this rule.

E.R. 1.4 Communication In Re Shannon, 179 Ariz. 52, 876 P.2d 548 (1994)
The intentionality or unintentionality of the attorney's conduct is irrelevant in determining a violation of this rule; the question is simply whether or not the attorney provided the client with sufficient information to enable the client to make an informed decision regarding the representation.

E.R. 1.4 Communication In Re Struthers, 179 Ariz. 216, 877 P.2d 789 (1994)
Attorney violated this rule where some clients requests for information are neglected.

Alen v. Lefkoff, Duncan, Grimes and Dermer, P.C., 453 S.E.2d 719 (GA. 1995)
To address specific harm client suffered, and lawyer disciplinary rules may be quoted to some extent as statutes and ordinances in negligence case.

Aparicio v. Artuz, 269 F.3d 78,100 (2d Cir. 2001)
Appellate counsel's failure to argue that trial counsel was ineffective for failing to object to jury instructions and failing to raise double jeopardy claim was not ineffective assistance because claim was meritless.

Attorney Grievance Commission v. Bailey, 480 A.2d 1330 (Md. 1997)
The requisite familiarity with well-settled legal principles extends to matters of procedure.

Baird v. Pace, 752 P.2d 507 (Ariz. 1987)
A lawyer must also discover those additional rules of law which although not commonly known may be readily found by standard research techniques.

Barry v. Brower, 864 F.2d 294 (3rd Cir. 1988)
An individual does not have to be totally indigent to be appointed counsel.

Beathard v. Johnson, 177 F.3d 340, 347 (6th Cir. 1999)
No adverse effect on performance against defendant did not demonstrate any plausible alternative defense strategies counsel could have pursued.

Bland v. California Department Of Corrections, 20 F.3d 1469 (9th Cir. 1994)
Denial of right to counsel of choice is reversible error regardless of whether prejudice is shown.

Boyd v. French, 147 F.3d 319, 327 (4th Cir. 1998)
Due process not violated by allegedly false testimony of police officers because testimony would not have affected verdict.

Ching v. Lewis, 895 F.2d 608 (9th Cir. 1990)
Prisoner's right of access to courts includes contact visitation with his counsel.

Clark v. US, 59 F.3d 296, 303 - 04 (2nd Cir. 1995)
It is a rare attorney who can be expected to contend on appeal that his representation was so poor that he deprived his client of a fair trial. Investigation of claim of ineffective assistance of counsel requires that new counsel have the

opportunity to conduct an investigation beyond the court record to uncover and present the case.

Corpus Juris Secundum attorney-client, p. 707
First duty not to client, counsel must remember that they are officers of the court, administrators of justice, oath bound servants of society; that their client's success is wholly subordinate.

Cronic, 466 US at 657
Griffin v. US, 109 F.3d 1217, 1219 (7th Cir. 1997)
Counsel's failure to file brief or jurisdictional statement and respond to courts inquiry constitutes denial of counsel because prejudice presumed from abandonment.

Cruz v. Warden, 907 F.2d 665, 670 (7th Cir. 1990)
An ineffective assistance claim alleging that counsel fails to prepare involves facts outside the trial record interest is a situation in which the Illinois courts will not invoke the res judicata or waiver doctrines.

Cuyler v. Sullivan, 446 US 335 (1980)
The 7th circuit has ruled that an attorney need not consult with his client before exercising a preemptory strike. See also US v. Boyd, 86 F.3d 719, 721 (7th Cir. 1996) cert denied, 117 S.Ct. 1825 (1997) Decision on selection of a jury are among the many things entrusted to counsel rather than to the defendant personally. Id at 721. Criminal law § 46.4-counsels duties. Representation of a criminal defendant entails certain basic duties. Counsels functioned is to assist the defendant, and hence counsel those the client a duty of loyalty, a duty to avoid conflicts of interest.

Dawan v. Lockhart, 31 F.3d 718 (8th Cir. 1994)
Garcua v. Bunnell, 33 F.3d 1193 (9th Cir. 1994)
Right to conflict free representation derives from Sixth Amendment as applied to states by due process clause of the Fourteenth Amendment.

Delgado v. Lewis, 223 F.3d 976, 980 - 82 (9th Cir. 2000)
Counsels failure to raise any arguable issues in appellate brief was ineffective assistance.

Deutscher v. Whitley, 884 F.2d 1152, 1156 (9th Cir. 1989)
Because actual prejudice is an aspect of ineffective assistance of counsel a defendant who proves ineffective assistance of counsel need not make any additional showing of prejudice to overcome procedural default. Vacated on other grounds, 500 US 901, 111 S.Ct. 1678, 114 L.Ed.2d 73 (1991)

Dixon v. Snyder, 266 F.3d 693, 703 (7th Cir. 2001)
Ineffective assistance because counsel was ignorant of applicable statute and failed to cross-examine.

Dixon v. Snyder, 266 F.3d 693, 704 (7th Cir. 2001)
Counsels failure to cross-examine prosecution witness amounted to prejudice because witnesses on a page statements were only evidence connecting defendant to crime.

Driscoll v. Delco, 71 F.3d 701 (8th Cir. 1995) Trial counsels failure to properly utilize witnesses prior inconsistent statements for impeachment purposes constitutes ineffective assistance of counsel.

Edwards v. Arizona, 451 US 477, 68 L.Ed.2d 378, 101 S.Ct. 1880 (1981)
Counsel must be present at custodial interrogation.

Everett v. Beard, 290 F.3d 500, 515 - 16 (3rd Cir. 2002)
Counsels failure to object to erroneous jury instructions prejudice to defendant because there was more than reasonable probability defendant would not have been convicted of first-degree murder.

Fields v. Calderon, 125 F.3d 757, 759-60 (9th Cir. 1997)
The right to the ineffective assistance of counsel is fundamental and a central part to fair trial.

Fisher v. Gibson, 282 F.3d 1283, 1309 (10th Cir. 2002)

Where defense counsels cross-examination merely bolstered credibility of witness defendant was prejudiced because evidence of guilt was not overwhelming. Counsels failure to investigate, to act as a professional advocate, and advanced any defense fairy, as well as his apparent sympathy for an assistant to state's case were objectively unreasonable.

Fishman v. Brooks, 487 N.E.2d 1377, 1381 - 82 (Mass. 1996)

Failure to comply with rules of professional conduct is not evidence of negligence per se, but is circumstances to be considered in determining whether lawyer exercise reasonable care in fulfilling his or her legal duties to client.

Florida Bar v. Sandstrom, 609 So.2d 583 (Fla. 1992)

Although reversal of appellants conviction on grounds of ineffective assistance will not always result in determination of ethical misconduct. See also: In Re Agrillo, 604 N.Y.S.2d 171 (App. Div. 1993)

Foretta v. California, 422 U. S. at 835

Stano v. Dugger, 921 F.2d 1125, 1148 (11th Cir. 1991) (en Banc)

Because the right to counsel is so precious to our jurisprudence, the waiver of this right must be asserted.

Frieman v. Lane, 962 F.2d 1252 (1992)

US ex rel, Simmons v. Gramely, 915 F.2d 1128, 1136 - 37 (7th Cir. 1990)

US ex rel, Bernard v. Lane, 819 F.2d 798, 805 (7th Cir. 1987)

Appellant defense counsel abandoned a vial federal defense on direct appeal in a situation that can hardly be turned as "tactical", the petitioner was deprived of ineffective assistance of counsel and has established "cause" for the failure to assert that right on direct appeal.

Glock v. Singletary, 84 F.3d 3 85,386 (11Th Cir. 1996) cert. denied, 117 S.Ct. 616 (1996)

Petitioner's claim that attorney was ineffective for failing to discover and present mitigating evidence was not meritless on its face, and that's why an evidentiary hearing was necessary.

Glover v. US, 531 US 198, 202 - 04 (2000)

The court explained that the outcome based prejudice inquiry set forth in Strickland should be applied in most cases, Id. at 203. The court reversed the 7th Cir.'s determination that any 6 to 21 months increase in petitioners sentence allegedly caused by the defective performance of defendant's counsel could not be considered prejudicial because the increase was not sufficiently significant to render the defendant's trial fundamentally unfair. The court stated: "authority does not suggest that a minimal amount of additional time in prison cannot constitute prejudice. Like to the contrary, our jurisprudence suggests that any amount of actual jail time has sixth amendment significance. In arriving at this conclusion to court made clear that Lockhart is only applicable in limited circumstances. Id. at 202. See also: Lockhart v. Fretwell, 506 US 364 (1993).

Goldberg v. Gordon, 607 P.2d 995 (Colo 1980)

A lawyer is expected to be familiar with well-settled principles of law applicable to clients' needs.

Green v. Johnson, 160 F.3d 1029, 1043 (5th Cir. 1998)

We judge counsels appellate performance under the same to prong test of Strickland v. Washington, 466 US 668, 104 S.Ct. 2052, 80 L.Ed.2d 674 (1984); Green, 160 F.3d at 1043. Nonetheless a reasonable attorney has an obligation to research relevant facts and law, or make an informed decision that certain avenues will not prove fruitful.

Groseclose v. Bell, 130 F.3d 453, 463 (6th Cir. 2001)

Counsels failure to interview witnesses, conduct any legal research or obtain and review any records was ineffective assistance.

Guinan v. US, 6 F.3d 468, 471 - 73 (7th Cir. 1993)

Holding the ineffective assistance of counsel claim is not raised on direct appeal were not waived if defendant continued to be represented by trial counsel or if the ineffectiveness claims required investigation outside of the trial record.

Haines v. Liggett Group Inc., 975 F.2d 81 (3rd Cir. 1992)
Attorney/client privileges extends to verbal statements, documents and tangible objects conveyed by both individual and corporate clients to attorney in confidence for purpose of any legal advice.

Harris v. Day, 226 F.3d 361 (5th Cir 2000)
Evitts v. Lucey, 469 US 387, 83 L.Ed.2d 821, 105 S. Ct. 830 (1985)
Defendant's right to effective assistance of counsel applies not just at trial but also on direct appeal.

Hart v. Gomez, 194 F.3d 106,1073 (9th Cir 1999)
Counsel's failure to introduce exculpatory records into evidence was ineffective assistance because objectively reasonable performance by counsel would have created reasonable probability of different verdict.

Hernandez v. US, 202 F.3d 486, 489 (2d Cir. 2000)
Prejudice presumed where alleged ineffective assistance of counsel based on unexcused failure to bring a direct appeal from a criminal conviction upon defendant's direction to do so.

Hirsch v. Burke, 40 F.3d 900 (7th Cir. 1994)
Battle v. Delo, 19 F.3d 1547 (8th Cir. 1994)
Counsel is obligated to meticulously review record in any case in which he challenges district court's disposition.

Holloway v. Arkansas, 435 US 475, 484-85 (1978)
Failure of courts to inquire into conflict of interest after defense counsel's pretrial warning of conflict violated right to ineffective assistance of counsel because Ct. has duty to avoid potential conflicts. When the trial court has notice of a potential conflict that fails to make such an inquiry, the reviewing court will presume a violation of the sixth amendment right to counsel. Violation of right to effective assistance of counsel when trial court knew of conflict of interest that fails to obtain either waiver or protect right to conflict free representation; the right to conflict free assistance of counsel may be waived by the defendant if the waiver is knowing and intelligent.

Holsomback v. White, 133 F.3d 1382, 1385-89 (11th Cir 1998)
Counsel's failure to investigate lack of medical evidence to support sexual abuse allegations was ineffective assistance.

Home v. Peckham, 1158 Cal. Rptr. 714 (Ct. App.)
Incompetence lay in failure to do basic research inadequate even for a general practitioner.

Hook v. Ward, 184 F.3d, 1206 (10th Cir 1999)
Ineffective assistance of appellate counsel claims are governed by the standards set forth in Strickland v. Washington, 80 L.Ed.2d 674 (1984)

Hudson v. Hunt, 235 F.3d 892 (4th Cir 2000)
The sixth amendment entitles any criminal defendant to effective assistance of counsel on direct appeal.

Hughes v. US, 258 F.3d 453, 463 (6th Cir. 2001)
Counsel's failure to strike juror who stated that she could not be fair to defendant given her links to police was ineffective assistance.

In Re Ames, 171 Ariz. 125, 829 P.2d 315 (1992)
When a lawyer is negligent and does not act with a reasonable diligence in representing a client, and causes injury or potential injury to a client censure is the appropriate disciplinary action.

In Re Augenstine, 177 Ariz. 581, 870 P.2d 399 (1994)
A member of the state bar of Ariz. was censured for inattention to his clients and their cases in violation of his duties and obligations as a lawyer.

In Re Black, 941 P.2d 1380 (Kan. 1997)
The analysis of President and evaluation of evidence are skills needed for competent representation. Lawyer improperly applied child support guidelines, using formula for two children rather than 5; his failure to properly learn, observe and apply rules for calculating child support demonstrates a lack of competency.

In Re Brown, 175 Ariz. 134, 854 P.2d 768 (1993)
Attorney failed to act with a reasonable diligence and promptness in his representation of clients.

In Re Deardorff, 426 N.E.2d 689 (Md. 1991) A lawyer's lack of experience in a particular area of law is no defense to a charge of incompetent representation.

In Re Evans, 175 Ariz. 404, 857 P.2d 1258 (1993)
Where attorney accepted representation, took initial action, then ignored the client until forced to address the matter began, the attorney's conduct exhibited lack of competence, lack of diligence, failure to adequately communicate with clients, failure to safe keep clients property, failure to respond to inquiries from the State Bar.

In Re Feeley, 176 Ariz. 196, 859 P.2d 1329 (1993)
Disbarment was appropriate for a lawyer who knowingly failed to perform services for client and engaged in a pattern of neglect with respect to clients matters, and caused serious or potentially serious injury to client.

In Re Evans, 175 Ariz. 404, 857 P.2d 1258 (1993)
Attorney censured for failure to act with diligence, failure to expedite litigation, and failure to maintain adequate communication.

In Re Galowski, 177 Ariz. 311, 868 P.2d 324 (1994)
In Re Dempsey, 632 F.Supp. 908 (N.D. Cal. 1986)
A lawyer is expected to know the rules of the court before which the lawyer practices.

In Re Mecker, 76 N.M. 354, 357, 414 P.2d 862, 864 (1996) appeal dismissed 383 US, 449 (1997)
Ethics rules are evidence of the scope of justice that a lawyer knows his or her client or former client.

In Re Miranda, 176 Ariz. 202, 859 P.2d 1335 (1993)

Seven month suspension was appropriate where attorney failed to act with diligence and promptness in representing his client, and failed to make a reasonable efforts to expedite litigation consistent with the interest of his client in violation of the rule.

In Re O'Brien-Reyes, 177 Ariz. 362, 868 P.2d 945 (1994)

Attorney was censured and placed on probation where she had failed to provide competent representation; fails to act with reasonable diligence and promptness in her representation, fails to keep clients appraised as to case status, and failed to cooperate with the bars investigation into her conduct.

In Re Offenhartz, 173 Ariz. 382, 843 P.2d 1274 (1992)

Attorney was censured, Where attorneys defense of the client against child molestation charges was so ineffective, that a different result may well have been achieved if the client had not been represented by ineffective counsel.

In Re Pappas, 159 Ariz. 516, 768 P.2d 1161 (1988)

Neglect cannot be limited to total abandonment of the legal matter, but must also include the failure to act with minimal efficiency.

In Re Talmadge, 171 Ariz. 548, 832 P.2d 201 (1992)

In failing to actively pursue his client's case and failing to respond to letters from his client, despite his statements to the contrary, and attorney was clearly negligent, and censure was the appropriate sanction.

In Re Tarletz, 163 Ariz. 548, 789 P.2d 1049 (1990)

Standard 4.4, when a lawyer is negligent and does not act with reasonable diligence in representing a client, and causes injury or potential injury to a client. Criminal law key 641.12 (1) forms a two-part test in ineffective assistance of counsel claim requires defendant to show bad but for his counsel's errors and omissions, outcome of trial would probably have been different.

In Re Willis, 505 A.2d 50 (D.C. 1985)

The skills required of a lawyer included the ability to draft pleadings and documents.

In Re Wolfram, 174 Ariz. 49, 897 P.2d 94 (1993)

Where attorneys' client faced a mandatory prison sentence ranging from 12 to 22 years, not reading the grand jury transcript, not examining physical evidence, and not discussing the possibility of lesser included offenses could not be reconciled with any sensible defense strategy, and the attorneys' preparation was clearly deficient. A lawyer has an obligation to explain the problem, layout the significant choices, and help the client make an informed, rational decision.

In Re Wolfram, 847 P.2d 94 (Ariz. 1993)

Ineffective assistance may serve as the predicate for disciplinary action.

Joseph Massaro v. US, 123 S.Ct. 1690, 155 L.Ed.2d 714; 2003 US Lexis 3243; 71 USL.W. 4310; 2003 Cal. Daily Op. Service 3369; 2003 Daily Journal DAR 4285; 16 Fla. L. Weekly Fed. S 238

The government contended that since the prisoner was represented by new counsel on appeal and the prisoner's claim of ineffective assistance of counsel was based solely on the trial record, the prisoner's failure to assert the claim on direct appeal barred the claim from consideration on collateral review. The US Supreme Court held, however, that the prisoner's failure to raise an ineffective assistance of counsel claim on direct appeal did not bar the claim from being brought in a subsequent proceeding for collateral review, regardless of whether the prisoner could have raised the claim on direct appeal. The trial record was developed for the purpose of determining whether the prisoner was guilty of the charged offenses, rather than whether the prisoner was adequately represented, and collateral review in the trial court was the proper forum for assessing the performance of counsel, the reasons underlying counsel's actions or any prejudice the prisoner might have suffered due to the alleged errors.

Keller v. Larkins, 251 F.3d 480, 419 (3rd Cir. 2001)

Counsel's failure to object to admission of expert testimony was not ineffective assistance because under state law, testimony was admissible.

Kitchen v. US, 227 F.3d 1014 (7th Cir 2000)
When appellate counsel omits a significant and obvious issue without legitimate strategic purpose his performance will be deemed deficient.

Lambright v. Stewart, 241 F.3d 1201 (9th Cir. 2001)
Rule 32.2 did not clearly require the defendant to raise claim of ineffective assistance of counsel on appeal; therefore the procedural default is inadequate to bar federal review.

Lindstadt v. Keane, 239 F.3d 191, 202 (2nd Cir 2001) Ineffective assistance because counsel failed to consult expert, conduct research, and request copies of studies relied on by expert witness.

Lockhart v. TerHune, 250 F.3d 1223 (9th Cir 2001)
Defendant's sixth amendment right to counsel includes the right to be represented by an attorney with undivided loyalty.

Mason v. Hanks, 97 F.3d 887, 894 (7th Cir 1996) Counsel's failure to raise obvious and significant issues was ineffective assistance because it was without a legitimate strategic purpose.

Matire v. Wainwright, 811 F.2d 1430 (11th Cir. 1987)
Standard of ineffective assistance of counsel is the same for trial and appellate counsel. Ineffective assistance of counsel on appeal when potentially meritorious issue not raised.

Matthews v. Rakiey, 54 F.3d 908, 916-17 (1st Cir. 1995)
Counsel strategy emphasizing that the victim misidentified defendant as her attacker, rather than highlighting alleged inconsistencies in victim's testimony, not ineffective assistance, but rather reasonable trial tactic.

Matter Of Prudhomme, 43 F.3d 1000 (5th Cir. 1995)
Under Louisiana law, unearned portion of retainer fees are client funds and must be held by lawyer in trust for client.

Mayol v. Summer, Watson & Kimpel, 585 N.E.2d 1176 (Ill. App. Ct.) appeal denied, 596 N.E.2d 630 (Ill. 1992)
Court found it stated a claim for relief based upon breach of common law fiduciary duty using bar rules merely to provide some evidence of standard of care.

McMahon v. Fulcomer, 821 F.2d 934, 944 (3rd Cir. 1987)
Court must conduct inquiry to determine if defendant waived right to counsel with awareness of dangers inherent in self representation.

McMann v. Richardson, 397 US 759, 771 n.14 (1970)
Effective assistance of counsel---the right to counsel is the right to the effective assistance of counsel. (1)Sixth amendment right to counsel is right to effective assistance of counsel. Second prong of Strickland: (2) that counsels performance prejudiced the defendant resulting in unreliable or fundamentally unfair outcome of the proceedings.

McNair v. Rainsford, 499 S.E.2d (S.C. Ct. App. 1998)
Glasser v. US, 315 US 60 (1942)
Makes it clear that ineffective assistance of counsel is guaranteed by the sixth amendment to the Constitution, which constitute in the pertinent part provides: "In all criminal prosecutions, each accused shall enjoy the right to have the assistance of counsel for his defense." This says that the accused shall have which is mandatory, the right which may be waived, declined or refused, to have the assistance of, which is not the same thing as representation by counsel (counsel does not mean the same thing as bar licensed attorney). No provision of the Constitution mandates compulsory representation by any bar licensed attorney. Representation by any bar licensed attorney requires the fully informed consent by both the client and the attorney and creates a specific performance contract between the attorney and the client. American Bar Association and rules of professional conduct, rule 1.8 (f) and Arizona Bar Association ethics rule ER-4 provides: (f) a lawyer shall not accept compensation for representing a client from anyone other than the client unless: (1) the client consents after consultation, (2) there is no interference with a lawyer's independence of professional judgment or with the client-lawyer relationship. ER-4 paragraph (f) requires disclosure of the

fact that the lawyer services are being paid for by a third party. Such an arrangement must also conform to Rule 1.7 concerning conflict of interest.

Rule 1.7 (a) (1) and (ER-3) provides: 1. A lawyer shall not represent a client if the representation will be directly at first to another client, unless; 2. Each client consents after consultation. ER-3) as a general proposition, loyalty to a client prohibits considering representation directly at first to that client without the client's consent.

Michigan v. Jackson, 475 US 625, 89 L.Ed.2d 631, 106 S.Ct. 1404 (1986)
State has burden of establishing valid waiver of defendants Sixth Amendment right to counsel.

Mirabiti v. Liccardo, 5 Cal. Rptr.2d 571 (Ct. App. 1992)
Ethics rules may be incorporated to show that lawyer breaches his or her fiduciary duty to client.

Murray v. Carrier, 477 US 478, 496 (1986)
The right to effective assistance of counsel… may in a particular case be violated by even an isolated error of counsel if the error is sufficiently egregious and prejudicial.

Murray v. Carrier, 477 US 478, 488, 106 S.Ct. 2639, 2645, 91 L.Ed.2d 397 (1986)
The court held that ineffective assistance of counsel violates the sixth amendment is cause for ignoring any procedural default.

Newton v. Armontrout, 118 Ariz. 46 0, 577 P.2d 1079 (1978)
The petitioner must show that the alleged improprieties were so egregious that they totally infected the proceedings and rendered his entire trial fundamentally unfair.

Nolan v. French, 134 F.3d 208 (4th Cir 1998)
Counsel has duty to keep their client informed of important developments in trial and to consult with defendant on important issues.

Note: Where there are various kinds of state interference with counsels assistance, prejudice may be presumed. Strickland 466 US at 692.

Note: In some cases, the court will inquire further to determine whether counsel's ineffective assistance deprived the defendant of a substantive or procedural right to which the law entitled him or her.

Note: Your attorney may not charge you an unrealistic fee even if you agree to it. Moreover, your entitled to a refund of any unearned fees and your attorney must document and prove his billing If you can prove fraud your entitled to collect those funds through the state bar association which maintains a mutual fund to cover defrauded clients.

Note: Most bar associations require an attorney to provide their clients with a "Statement of Clients Rights." This warrant" is usually a standard type that is provided to any customer which purchases the lawyers services. Write the state bar for a copy if your attorney didn't give you one.

Note: The sixth amendment guarantees the right to effective assistance of counsel in criminal prosecutions. In Strickland v. Washington, the Supreme Court established a two-pronged test to evaluate ineffective assistance of counsel claims. To obtain reversal of a conviction to defendant must prove: That counsel's performance fell below an objective standard of reasonableness and. That counsel's deficient performance prejudiced the defendant resulting in an unreliable or fundamentally unfair outcome of the proceedings. A defendant's failure to satisfy one prong of the Strickland test negates a court's need to consider the other.

Note: If counsel entirely fails to subject to prosecution's case to meaningful adversarial testing, the adversarial process itself becomes presumptively unreliable.

Note: In federal cases the defendant's exercise of preemptory challenges is not denied or impaired when the defendant chooses to use a preemptory challenge to remove a juror who should have been excused for cause.

Northrop v. Trippett, 265F.3d 372, 373 - 84 (6th Cir. 2001)
Counsels failure to seek suppression of only evidence against defendant was unreasonable because evidence was obtained in violation of fourth amendment.

Odle v. Calderon, 919 F.2d 1430, 1438 (N.D. Cal. 1996)
Defense counsels tactical choices based on proper understanding of law and facts are virtually unintelligible.

Osborn v. Schillinger, 861 F.2d 612, 623 (10th Cir. 1988)
Ineffectiveness claims are ordinarily inappropriate to raise on direct appeal because they... Cannot be made on the basis of the record.

Pavel v. Hollins, 261 F.3d 210, 228 (2d Cir. 2001)
Counsels failure to prepare and call witnesses prejudice defendant, especially in light of weakness of prosecution's case. Counsels failure to, prepare, calling important witnesses, and call medical expert amounted to deficient performance, because testimony of those witnesses or to have rebounded prosecutors already weak case.

People v. Boyle, 442 P.2d 1199 (Colo. 1997)
The interrelated obligations of thoroughness and preparation required a lawyer to investigate the facts of the matter and research the applicable law.

People v. Primavera, 942 P.2d 496 (Colo. 1997)
The duty of diligence is closely related to competence, as one often accompanies the other.

People v. Yoakum, 552 P.2d 291 (Colo. 1976)
Lawyer handling closing sale of business lease that on its face was assignable only with lessors consent and made no inquiries concerning assets and debts of business being purchased.

Poe v. Armontrout, 42 .F3d 1173 (8th Cir. 1994)
In order for ineffective assistance of counsel claim to succeed, convict must show prejudice stemming from lawyer's error.

Powell v. Alabama, 287 US 45, 77 L.Ed 158, 53 S.Ct. 55 (1932)

An accused has a fundamental right to be represented by counsel of his own choice.

Powell v. Alabama, 287 US at 68-69, 77 L.Ed 158, 53 S.Ct. 55, 84 ALR 527

From counsel's function as assistant to defendant derives the overreaching duty and the more particular duties to consult with the defendant on important developments in the course of the prosecution. Counsel also has a duty to bring to bear such skill and knowledge as will render the trial a reliable adversarial testing process.

Reese v. Delo, 94 F.3d 1177, 1185 (8th Cir. 1996)

Holding that counsel has discretion to abandon losing issues on appeal.

Riggs v. US, 209 F.3d 828, 831 - 34 (6th Cir. 2000)

No adverse effect on performance during alleged "lax" cross examination because Transcript indicates counsel effectively crossed and re-crossed the witness.

Roe v. Flores - Ortega, 528 US 470, 483 - 84 (2000)

Prejudice presumed where defendant demonstrates a reasonable probability that but for counsels deficient failure to consult defendant about appeal, counsel would have timely appealed.

Ross, 478 US at 89

Ross v. Oklahoma, 487 US 81, 85-86 (1968)

In Ross the Supreme Court held that the defendant sixth amendment right to an impartial jury was not violated when he was required to use a preemptory challenge to excuse a juror whom the state trial court erroneously declined to excused for cause because the defendant failed to shows that juror who ultimately convicted him was partial.

Sanders v. Ratelle, 21 F.3d 1446, 1460 (9th Cir. 1994)

Coleman v. Caldron, 150 F.3d 1105 (9th Cir. 1985)

The cannons of professional ethics must be enforced by the courts and must be respected by members of the bar if we are to maintain public confidence in the integrity and impartiality of the administration of justice.

Sargent. v. Buckley, 697 A.2d 1272 (Me 1997)

If plaintiff can demonstrate the disciplinary rule intended to protect one in his position, violation may be some evidence of lawyer's negligence; expert properly could base his opinion on attorney's failure to conform to the disciplinary rule; rules are admissible evidence on par with liquor laws, workers compensation and building codes.

Smith v. Louis, 530 P.2d 589 (Cal. 1975)

A lawyer must undertake reasonable research to ascertain relevant legal principles.

Smith v. Robbins, 528 US 259, 287 (2000)

Listing three categories of cases were prejudice is presumed is (1) denial of counsel, (2) various kinds of state interference, and (3) were counsel is hindered by an actual conflict of interest.

Standing Committee v. Yagman, 55 F.3d 1430 (9th Cir. 1995)

Attorneys may be sanctioned for impugning integrity of judge or of court only if their statements are false; truth is absolute defense.

Stanford v. Parker, 266 F.3d 442, 445 (6th Cir 2001)

Strickland specifically holds that the two prongs of the test need not be applied in order or in totality.

State v. Barto, 232 N.W. 553,202 Wis. 329.

The sixth amendment right to effective assistance of counsel implicitly recognizes that criminal defense counsel must be competent.

State v. Carver, 160 Ariz. 167, 175, 771 P.2d 1382, 1390 (1998)
We do not review an ineffective assistance of counsel claim on direct appeal unless we may clearly determine from the record that the ineffective assistance claim is meritless.

State v. Geotis, 187 Ariz. 521, 930 P.2d 1324 (App. Div. 1 1996) review denied 189 Ariz. 109, 938 P.2d 1110
Generally ineffective assistance of counsel claims should be raised on post-conviction relief proceedings.

State v. Hall, 118 Ariz. 460, 577 P.2d 1079 (1978)
To determine whether relief may be granted on grounds of ineffective assistance of counsel, is whether counsel was so ineffective that proceedings were reduced to a mere farce, sham, or mockery of justice.

State v. Lee, 142 Ariz. 210, 220, 689 P.2d 153, 163 (1984)
Quoting Strickland "the right counsel is the right to ineffective assistance of counsel".

State v. Moody, 192 Ariz. 505, 507 ¶ 11, 968 P.2d 578, 580 (1998)
A criminal defendant has 86 in the right to representation by competent counsel.

State v. Robbins, 166 Ariz. 531, 533, 803 P.2d 942,944 (Ariz. App. 1991)
Ineffective assistance of counsel that prejudices the defendant is a ground for relief under rule 32.1 (a) of the Arizona rules of criminal procedure as the conviction or sentence would be one that violates the Constitution of the United States or state of Arizona. The petitioner must only show such violation by a preponderance of the evidence. See rule 32.8 (c) Arizona rules of criminal procedure. With ineffective counsel, the petitioner must only show such violation by a preponderance of evidence. See rule 32.8 (c) Arizona rules of criminal procedure.

State v. Shrock, 149 Ariz. 433, 917 P.2d 1049 (1986)
Allegation that defense counsel was deficient in failing to assert defendant's speedy trial rights, to renew or preserve pretrial motions in subsequent trials, and to make a record regarding denial of confrontation of a state witness was sufficient to state

a colorable claim sufficient to warrant and evidentiary hearing on the post-conviction petition for ineffective assistance of counsel.

State v. Tapia, 151 Ariz. 62, 725 P.2d 1096 (1986)
After reviewing the circumstances surrounding the representation defendant received, the Supreme Court concluded that it fell below the required standard and that there was a reasonable probability that defendant's trial would have had a different result if the defendant had been given a competent defense.

State v. Ysca, 191 Ariz. 372, 377 956 P.2d 499, 504 (1998)
To find ineffective assistance of counsel the court must find that counsel 1) performs efficiently under prevailing professional norms and 2) counsels deficiency prejudice the defendant.

Stouffe v. Reynolds, 168 F.3d 1155, 1162-68 (10th Cir 1999)
Defendant entitled to evidentiary hearing because alleged cumulative instances of prior performance of trial counsel, if proved, would constitute ineffective assistance.

Strickland v. Washington, 466 US 668, 687 (1984)
The court in Strickland stated that "the purpose of the effective assistance guarantee of the sixth amendment is… To ensure that criminal defendant's received a fair trial." Id. at 689. Strickland states that a court; Judge the reasonableness of counsel's challenged conduct on the facts of the particular case, viewed as of the time of counsel's conduct. A convicted defendant making a claim of ineffective assistance must identify the acts or omissions of counsel that are alleged not to have been the result of reasonable professional judgment. The court must then determine whether, in light of the circumstances, the identified acts or omissions were outside the wide range of professionally competent assistance. In making that determination and court shall keep in mind that counsel's function, as elaborated in professional norms, is to make the adversarial testing process work in the particular case. At the same time, the court should recognize that counsel is strongly presumed to have rendered adequate assistance and make all significant decisions in the exercise of a reasonable professional judgment. Id at 690. Claim of ineffective assistance of counsel must show that counsels performance and

counsels errors prejudiced defense to the extent that petitioner was deprived of fair trial. Right to effective assistance of counsel impaired when defense counsel operates under a conflict of interest, because "counsel preach is the duty of loyalty perhaps the most basic of counsel's duties.

Strickland v. Washington, 466 US 688, 80 L.Ed.2d 674, 104 S.Ct. 2052 (1984)
Two part test of effective assistance of defense counsel held (1) reasonably effective assistance and (2) reasonable probability of different result with effective assistance. LANDMARK CASE.

Strickland, 466 US at 690
A single error may in some circumstances render counsels performance ineffective.

Tabron v. Grace, 6 F.3d 147 (3rd Cir. 1993)
Mallard v. US Dist. Court For S. Dist. Of Iowa, 490 US 296, 104 L.Ed.2d 318,109 S.Ct. 1814 (1989)
Attorney cannot be compelled to represent an indigent defendant in a civil case.

Trass v. Maggio, 731 F.2d 288, to 93 (5th Cir. 1984)
Holding that ignorance of a relevant law constitutes an identifiable lapse in constitutionally adequate representation.

Tuitt v. Fair, 822 F.2d 166, 177 (1st Cir. 1987)
State court entitled to require express and unequivocal waiver before allowing defendant to proceed Pro Se.

US v. Andrews, 75 F.3d 552, 557 (9th Cir. 1996)
US v. Gordon, 4 F.3d 1567, 1570 (10th Cir. 1993)
State v. Robbins, 166 Ariz. 531, 533, 803 P.2d 942, 944 (Ariz. App. 1991)
Ineffective counsel, the petitioner must only show such violation by a preponderance of evidence (see rule 32.8 (c) Arizona rules of criminal procedure.

US v. Beasley, 48 F.3d 262, 268 n5 (7th Cir. 1995)

Erroneous refusal to strike juror for cause arguably deprives defendant of statutory right to preemptory challenges under federal rules of criminal procedure, rule 24 (b).

US v. Collins, 60 F.3d 4, 7n.1 (1st Cir 1995)

Court may review ineffective assistance claim on direct appeal "if record is sufficiently developed to allow analysis".

US v. Cruz, 785 F.2d 399, 404 (2nd Cir. 1986)
Aulet, 618 F.2d at 186

The court may decide a case of ineffective assistance of counsel even when raised for the first time on appeal, when its resolution is beyond any doubt or to do so would be in the interest of justice.

US v. DeCoster, 487 F.2d 1197 (D.C. Cir. 1983)
Mc Mann v. Richardson, 397 US 759 (1970)

Courts have declined to adopt a per se rule that successful post-conviction relief based on ineffective assistance will constitute an ethics violation, or conversely, that denial of post-conviction relief will insulate a lawyer from discipline.

US v. DeCoster, 487 F.2d 1197 (D.C. Cir. 1973)

An accused is entitled to reasonably competent assistance of a lawyer acting as the accused's diligent and conscientious advocate. Defense counsel should be guided by the American Bar Association standards, should inter alia, can fire with client without delay and as often as necessary to elicit matters of defense, ascertained potential defense is, discussed potential strategies and tactical choices with the client, promptly advise client of right and take prompt action to preserve clients right. Conduct investigations determined matters of defense that can be developed, interview available prosecution witnesses secure information in possession of the prosecution and do adequate research.

US v. Finley, 245 F.3d 199, 204 (2nd Cir 2001)

Court may hear ineffective assistance claim on direct appeal because defendant was represented by new counsel on appeal and did not argue any ground not supported by the record.

US v. Frank, 53 F.2d 128, 129 reversed on other grounds

US v. Laughlin, 57 F.2d 1080, reversed on other grounds

Pearce v. US, 59 F.2d 518 In Re Kelly, 243 F. 696, 705

In case of conflict between attorney's duty to client and that to court, his duty to the court must prevail.

US v. Fry, 51 F.3d 543, 545 (5th Cir 1995)

Court may review ineffective assistance claim on direct appeal only in rare cases where the record allows the court to evaluate fairly the merits of the claim.

US v. Gallegos, 108 F.3d 1272, 1282 (10th Cir. 1997) Violation of right to ineffective assistance of counsel when trial court knew of conflict of interest that fails to conduct further inquiry.

US v. Gambino, 788 F.2d 938, 950 (3rd Cir. 1986)

There is a narrow exception to this rule when the defendant raises an objection at trial or win the trial record clearly reflects counsels actual conflict of interest. Claims of ineffective assistance of counsel are generally limited to collateral review and ordinarily will not be considered on direct appeal. When the court denies a direct appeal, appellants remain free to initiate a habeas corpus proceeding to resolve their ineffective assistance claim.

US v. Greig, 967 F.2d 1018, 1022 (5th Cir. 1992)

Violation of right to effective assistance of counsel when trial judge failed to investigate claim of possible conflict of interest on part of defendant's attorney.

US v. Gonzalez-Airmont, 268 F.3d 8,13 (1st Cir 2001)

Court may hear ineffective assistance claim on direct appeal because the critical facts are not generally in dispute and the record is sufficiently developed to allow reasoned consideration of an ineffective assistance claim.

US v. Gwiazdzinski, 141 F.3d 784, 789 (7th Cir 1998)

Court may review ineffective assistance claim on direct appeal because appellant had new counsel and trial record was sufficiently developed.

US v. Harrison, 213 F.3d 1206,1209 (9th Cir. 2000)

Kirby v. Illinois, 406 US 682, 689 (1972)

The sixth amendment right to counsel attaches at or after the initiation of adversarial judicial criminal proceedings whether by way of formal charge, preliminary hearing, indictment, information or arrangement.

US v. Jiminez Recio, 258 F.3d 1069, 1074 (9th Cir. 2001)

Government's concession that defendant would have been granted new trial but for counsels failure to move for acquittal on charge provided adequate record to allow review of ineffective assistance claim on direct appeal. Cert. granted, 122 S.Ct. 2288 (2002)

US v. Johnson, 954 F.2d 1015 (5th Cir. 1992)

Maine v. Moulton, 474 US 159, 88 L.Ed.2d 481, 106 S.Ct. 477 (1985)

Massiah v. US, 377 US 201, 12 L.Ed.2d 246, 84 S.Ct. 1199 (1964)

Sixth Amendment limits governments' investigative methods after defendant has been indicted and counsel has been retained.

US v. Lagrone, 43 F.3d 332 (7th Cir. 1994)

Hanson v. Passer, 13 F.3d 275 (8th Cir. 1994)

Once government initiates formal charges against defendant, he has right to counsel at all future critical stages.

US v. Mannino, 212 F.3d 835 (3rd Cir 2000)

The Strickland test of ineffective assistance of counsel applies with equal force to analysis of the performance of appellate counsel.

US v. Martinez - Salazar, 528 US 304, 307 (2000)

In state criminal proceeding, impairment of a statutory right to preemptory challenges violates due process "only if the defendant does not receive debt which state law provides."

US v. Morrison, 449 US 361,365 (1981)

The court has held that even deliberate government intrusion into the attorney - client relationship did not warrant dismissal of the indictment in the absence of any demonstrable prejudice, or substantial threat thereof. Morrison court suggested that the defendant could seek a remedy for the violation of his rights in any collateral proceeding. Id. at 367.

US v. Morrison, 449 US 361, 66 L.Ed.2d 564, 101 S.Ct. 665 (1981)

Reversal mandated if prejudice is proven on attorney client relationship.

US v. Padilla - Martinez, 762 F.2d 942 (11th Cir. 1985)

The Sixth Amendment provides that, "in all criminal prosecutions, the accused shall enjoy the right to have the assistance of counsel for his defense." This broad guarantee of counsel has been interpreted to include four rights:

The right of counsel, Powell v. Alabama, 287 US 45 (1932)

The right of effective assistance of counsel, Glasser v. US, 315 US 60 (1942) 159.

The right to a preparation period sufficient to insure a minimal level of quality of counsel.

The right to be represented by counsel of one's choice. Id at 70, 62 S.Ct. 464.

US v. Russell, 221 F.3d 615 (4th Cir 2000)

Attorney has duty to adequately examine the law and facts relevant to representation of his client.

US v. Stevens, 149 F.3d 747, 748 (8th Cir. 1998)

Court may review ineffective assistance claim on a direct appeal because District Court's hearing on a new trial motion created adequate record for appellate court to consider claim.

US v. Stites, 56 F.3d 1020 (9th Cir. 1995)
Lawyers may change their position on the law from case to case without disgrace.

US v. Toms, 136 F.3d 176, 182 (D.C. Cir. 1998)
Court may review ineffectiveness of counsel if trial court record alone shows that defendant is either conclusively entitled to relieve or to no relief.

US v. Tucker, 716 F.2d 576 (9th Cir. 1983)
Trial counsels failure to impeach prosecution witnesses with prior inconsistent statement was ineffective assistance.

US v. Verderame, 51 F.3d 249 (11th Cir. 1995)
Implicit in right to counsel is notion of adequate time for counsel to prepare defense.

US v. Williams, 183 F.3d 458 (1999)
US v. Wallace, 32 F.3d 921, 931 (5th Cir. 1994)
The cases equally addressed an issue exactly on point for Williams's appeal. Regardless of the standard of review we would have employed, Williams is counsel by failing to cite directly controlling precedent, rendered deficient assistance. Note: such directly controlling precedent is rare. Actual factual differences will make authority easily distinguishable whether pervasively or not in such cases, it is not necessarily providing ineffective assistance of counsel to fail to construct an argument that may or may not succeed. But failure to raise discreet, purely legal issue, where the president could not been more pellucid and applicable denies adequate representation.

US v. Williamson, 183 F.3d 458, 463-64 (5th Cir 1999)
Counsel's failure to cite directly controlling president was ineffective assistance because it was objectively unreasonable and resulted in prejudice to defendant.

US v. Wilson, 922 F.2d 1336 (7th Cir. 1991) Defense attorney should neither withdraw nor threaten to withdraw from representation of criminal defendant because defendant refused to enter plea that attorney has recommended.

Walderman v. Levine, 544 A.2d 693 (D.C. 1998)

Ethics rules are used for determining what standard of care is appropriate.

White v. McAninch, 238 F.3d 988, 997- 98 (6th Cir. 2000)

Counsels failure to request limited instruction with respect to evidence he improperly elicited was ineffective assistance because wholly unreasonable.

Williams v. Taylor, 529 US 362, 391-93 (2000)

In Williams, the Supreme Court clarified that the earlier exceptions explained in Nixs v. Whiteside, 475 US 157 (1986) and Lockhart v. Fretwell, 506 US 364 (1993), or to be narrowly applied and do not justify a departure from a straightforward application of Strickland when the ineffectiveness of counsel does not deprive the defendant of any substantial or procedural right to which the law entitled him. Williams US at 393, except in the narrow category defined by Nix and Lockhart, courts need not dealt into a separate inquiry concerning fundamental fairness were both prongs of Strickland have been satisfied.

Williams v. Turpin, 87 F.3d 1204,1211 (11th Cir. 1996)

Petitioner entitled to evidentiary hearing and the opportunity to establish "cause and prejudice" for failing to develop facts in state proceedings supporting claims of ineffective assistance. If petitioner succeeds in demonstrating ineffective assistance of appellate counsel, thereby establishing cause and prejudice, and the evidence may be considered in connection with the underlying claim of ineffective assistance of trial counsel.

Williams v. Washington, 59 F.3d 673 (7th Cir. 1995)

Attorney clearly has duty to familiarize himself with the discovery materials provided by the state.

Wolfolk v. Rivera, 729 F.2d It 14 (7th Cir. 1984)

Sixth Amendment guarantee of assistance of counsel does not apply in civil cases.

<u>Young v. Duckworth</u>, 733 F.2d 482 (7th Cir. 1984)

Although criminal defendants sometimes switch counsel, responsible lawyer will not resign and court will not let him resign, until new counsel if appointed. Assistance of counsel, to be fully effective, must be continuous from time when prosecution began.

<u>Zarabia v. Bradshaw</u>, 185 Ariz. 1, 4, 912 P.2d 5, 8 (1996)

The Superior Court's assertion that it lacked authority to rule on the motion (substitution of counsel) cannot rest upon the motion and a judge may not apply to particular lawyer as defense counsel. A court has the inherent authority to achieve justice by appointing a particular lawyer to represent a defendant or client in a particular case, even if the appointment is pro bono or causes financial hardship to the appointed lawyer. Holding that county's practice of appointing private attorneys to represent criminal defendant's constitutional rights to adequate representation. See also Arizona rules of criminal procedure 6.5 (b) public defender shall represent all persons entitled to appointed counsel whenever he or she is authorized by law and able in fact it is so. Arizona rules of criminal procedure 6.5 (c) if the public defender is not appointed, a private attorney shall be appointed to the case. All criminal appointment shall be made in any manner fair and equitable to the members of the bar, taking into account skill likely to be required in handling a particular case. Thus, although a court may prefer to appoint an office such as the office of court-appointed counsel, is not required to do so and is not forbidden from naming a lawyer. On the other hand, an indigent defendant has no right to choose a particular lawyer: although indigent criminal defendant has a sixth amendment right to competent counsel, is right does not include counsel of choice. See <u>State v. LaGrand</u>, 152 Ariz. 483, 486, 733 P.2d 1066, 1069 (1987) does this right guarantee a meaningful relationship between an accused and his counsel. See <u>Morris v. Slappy</u>, 461 US 1 (1983)

Cumulative Harmless Errors

Cargle v. Mullin, 317 F. 3d 1196 (10th Cir. 2003)
McDowell v. Calderon, 107 F. 3d 1351 (9th Cir. 1997)
US v. Wallace, 848 F. 2d 1464 (9th Cir. 1988)
The cumulative effect of two or more individual harmless errors has the potential to prejudice the defendant to the same extent as a single reversible error. The purpose of the "cumulative error" analysis is to address that possibility.

Chapman v. California, 386 US 18 (1967)
Analysis and as a two-part test: (1) the court must ask what evidence to jury actually considered in reaching a verdict, and (2) the court must weigh the probative of force of the evidence against the probative force of the presumption standing alone.

Hill v. Lockhart, 28 F.3d 832,839 (8th Cir. 1994), cert. denied, 115 S.Ct. 778 (1995)
If petitioner demonstrates prejudice pursuant to Strickland, court does not conduct Brecht harmless error analysis. Prejudice inquiry is at least as stringent as any harmless error test and thus harmless error analysis would be superfluous.

Offer v. Scott, 72 F.3d 30, 33 (5th Cir. 1995)
Violation of right to confrontation was not harmless under Brecht; a court cannot find an error harmless simply because it thinks the petitioner would have been convicted even if the constitutional error had not taken place.

Orndorff v. Lockhart, 998 F.2d 1426, 1430 (8th Cir. 1993)
The record is reviewed de novo, and the issue is whether there is a reasonable possibility the error contributed to the conviction.

Seiler v. Thalacker, 101 F.3d 536, 539 (8th Cir. 1996)
When a state court has not reviewed on direct appeal whether a constitutional error was harmless, this court examines the error to determine whether it was harmless beyond a reasonable doubt.

State v. Hughes, 193 Ariz. 72, 969 P. 2d 1184 (1998)

At the outset, we need to clarify Arizona's position regarding the cumulative error doctrine in criminal cases. Our general rule has been stated several times over the years and was recently stated in State v. Dickens, 187 Ariz. 1, 21 P. 2d 468, 488 (1996) as follows: "this court does not recognize the so-called cumulative error doctrine." See also: State v. Roscoe, 184 Ariz. 484, 494, 910 P. 2d 635, 648 (1996); State v. White,168 Ariz. 500, 508, 815 P. 2d 869, 877 (1991). This lack of recognition is based on the theory that "something that is not prejudicial error in and of itself does not become such error when coupled with something else that is not prejudicial error." Roscoe, 184 Ariz. At 497, 910 P. 2d at 648. In Roscoe, for example, each error was either "no error at all or no prejudice to Roscoe." We restate the general rule that when several non-errors and harmless errors cannot add up to one reversible error. We also clarify the fact that this general rule does not apply when the court is evaluating a claim that prosecutorial misconduct deprives defendants of a fair trial.

US v. Cunningham, 145 F.3d 1385, 1388 (D.C. Cir. 1998)

Error not harmless beyond a reasonable doubt because redacted 911 tape violated the sixth amendment submitted to jury.

US v. Fredrick, 78 F.3d 1370 (9th Cir. 1996)

Cumulative effect of multiple errors may require reversal were case is a close one and evidence is not overwhelming.

US v. Hands, 184 F.3d 1322, 1334 (11th Cir. 1999)

Combined impact of prosecutor's inappropriate statements and evidentiary errors by trial judge works to deprive defendant of fair trial and thus not harmless error.

US v. Fulmer, 108 F.3d 1486 (1st Cir. 1997)

Individually harmless errors may be harmful when considered cumulatively. Cumulative effect of improperly admitted hard evidence and testimony required new trial.

US v. Innamorati, 996 F.2d 456 (1st Cir. 1993)

Chapman v. California, 386 US 18, 23-24, 17 L.Ed.2d 705, 87 S.Ct. 824 (1967)

2.1. Harmless beyond reasonable doubt standard presumes prejudice in places burden on beneficiary of error to prove beyond reasonable doubt that error did not contributed to verdict.

2.2. Harmless plain error does not exist, all plain errors are harmful.

2.3. Harmless constitutional error test is stringently applied, resolving all reasonable doubts against government.

US v. McKinney, 954 F.2d 471 (7th Cir. 1992)

Government must demonstrate that alleged constitutional error was harmless while defendant need not show harm.

US v. Tarwater, 308 F.3d 494, 521 (6th Cir. 2002)

Errors in jury instructions shifting the government's burden of proof to the defendant not harmless beyond a reasonable doubt.

Williams v. Clark, 40 F.3d 1529, 1541 (8th Cir. 1994)

Rhoden in v. Roland, 172 F.3d 633,637 (9th Cir. 1999)

The Ninth Circuit held that shackling of petitioner was not harmless because at least some of the jurors saw the shackles and because the shackles is centrally branded petitioner as having a violent nature in a case where in his propensity for violence was a crucial issue.

Damages

State v. Strayhand, 184 Ariz. 571, 911 P.2d 577 (1995) rev. den. (1996)
Promises that offer will ensure that the defendant goes to prison if he fails to cooperate are impermissible as means of obtaining confession.[8] threatening to inform prosecutor of suspects refusal to cooperate with violates her Fifth Amendment right to remain silent.

Bivens v. Six Unknown Agents, 403 US 388, 29 L.Ed.2d 619, 91 S.Ct. 1999 (1970)
When a government agent acts in an unconstitutional manner he becomes liable for money damages.

Blackburn v. Snow, 771 F.2d 556 (1st Cir. 1985)
Joan v. City Of Chicago, 771 F.2d 1020 (7th Cir. 1985)
Two women were strip searched and both collected large monetary damages.

Debiasio v. Illinois Cent. R.R., 52 F.3d 678 (7th Cir. 1995)
Verdict of $4,201,000 awarded to injured railroad worker whose arm was amputated was not monstrously excessive, particularly as $1.2 million of damages represented lost earnings.

Bounian v. Block, 940 F.2d 1211 (9th Cir. 1991)
Olympia Equip. Co. v. Western Union Telegraph Co., 797 F.2d 370 (7th Cir. 1986)
Speculation has its place in estimating damages, and doubts should be resolved against the wrongdoer. Reviewing court must uphold award of damages whenever possible and all presumptions are in favor of judgment.

Brunnemann v. Terr Intern, Inc., 975 F.2d 175 (5th Cir. 1992)
Johnson v. Hugo's Skateway, 949 F.2d 1338 (4th Cir. 1991)
Verdict is excessive as matter of law if shown to exceed any rational appraisal or estimate of damages that could be based upon evidence before jury.

Deisler v. McCormack Aggregates, Co., 54 F.3d 1074 (3rd Cir. 1995)
Compensatory damages serve to compensate for harm sustained by party.

Dunn v. Denk, 54 F.3d 248 (5th Cir. 1995)
Award of $17,500 in attorney fees to civil rights defendant who had recovered only $10,000 in damages was not abuse of discretion.

Dunn v. Hovic, 1 F.3d 1371 (3rd Cir. 1993)
Punitive damages were to be assessed with respect to harm defendant caused plaintiff and not other persons. Ability to pay is relevant factor in assessing award of punitive damages.

Graham v. Satkoski, 51 F.3d 710 (7th Cir. 1995)
Punitive damages are appropriate in §1983 case only if judge finds conduct motivated by evil intent or callous indifference to plaintiff's federally protected rights. Trier of fact has considerable discretion in calculating damages under §1983, and damage award will not be reversed unless it is clearly erroneous.

Griffith v. State Of Colo., Div. Of Youth Services, 17 F.3d 1323 (10th Cir. 1994)
Word "damages" is commonly understood to connote payment in money for defendant's losses caused by defendant's breach of duty.

Hafer v. Nielo, 502 US, 116 L.Ed.2d 301, 112 S.Ct. (1991)
State officials held subject to personal liability for damages under 42 USCS §1983 based on official acts, where §1983 actions were brought against officials in their individual capacities.

Lester v. Resolution Trust Corp., 994 F.2d 1247 (7th Cir. 1993)
Illinois law does not require lost profits to be proven with absolute certainty, but they must be established with reasonable degree of certainty.

Memphis Community School Dist. v. Stachura, 477 US 299, 91 L.Ed.2d 249, 106 S.Ct. 2537 (1986)
Purpose of punitive damages is to punish the defendant for his willful or malicious conduct and to deter others from similar behavior.

Smith v. Wade, 461 US 30, 75 L.Ed.2d 632, 103 S.Ct. 1625 (1983)
The Supreme Court held that a prison guard may be liable for "PUNITIVE" damages.

Tingley Systems, Inc. v. Norse Systems, Inc., 49 F.3d 93 (2nd Cir. 1995)
Punitive damages may not be so high as to shock judicial conscience.

US v. Balistrieri, 981 F.2d 916 (7th Cir. 1992)
Punitive damages are appropriate in cases of reckless or callous disregard for plaintiff's rights or intentional violations of federal law.

Vasbinder v. Scott, 976 F.2d 118 (2nd Cir. 1992)
Punitive damage award should not be so high as to result in financial ruin of defendant.

Defense to a Charge

State v. Davis, 206 Ariz. 377
Defendant's 52-year sentence for four counts of sexual misconduct with a minor was grossly disproportionate to his crimes, because the post-pubescent victims were willing participants. They sought out defendant by voluntarily going to his home.

State v. Gordon, 161 Ariz. 308, 778 P.2d 1204 (1998)
Under the Gordon analysis, when two felonies are of the same class of felony and neither crime is clearly more serious than the other, court must look at the ultimate crime. Sexual conduct of a minor is a more serious of child molestation. When charged with sexual conduct the molestation is the lesser included offense and the jury should be instructed on that issue. In applying Gordon's second factor, must consider whether, given the entire transaction, it was factually impossible to commit the ultimate crime without also committing the secondary crime. If so then the likelihood will increase that the defendant committed a single act.

State v. Hunter, 142 Ariz. 88, 668 P.2d 980 (1984)
It is a defense to a charge of molestation of a child that the defendant was not motivated by sexual interest.

State v. Klokic, 219 Ariz. 241
In trial for aggravated assault, trial court erred in denying defendant's request to require the State to elect which particular act it was charging because defendant allegedly pointed a handgun on two separate occasions, which were not part of the same transaction.

State v. Machado, 138 P.3d 742
Defendant was not entitled to spousal defense to sexual assault under Ariz. Rev. Stat. § 13-1401(4) because evidence did not support contention that defendant and wife were cohabitating. Renunciation of solicitation to murder was not admissible under Ariz. R. Evid. 803(3) because statement was not relevant as to state of mind.

<u>State v. Sepahi</u>, 204 Ariz. 185 (App. 2003)

To constitute a dangerous crime against children within meaning of statute requiring penalties for certain enumerated offenses, the defendant's conduct must be focused on, directed against, aimed at, or targeted at a victim under the age of 15.

<u>US v. Davis</u>, 183 F.3d 231 (3rd Cir. 1999)

Intoxication can negate specific intent.

Discovery

Banco De Credito Indus., Sa v. Tesoreria General, 990 F.2d 827 (5th Cir. 1993)
Rules of Civil Procedure contemplate that parties will be afforded adequate time to conduct necessary discovery.

Charash v. Oberlin College, 14 F.3d 291 (6th Cir. 1994)
Purpose of discovery after motion for summary judgment is to test truth of allegations of the pleadings.

Church Of Scientology Of San Francisco v. IRS, 991 F.2d 560 (9th Cir. 1993)
Party may need to use discovery to establish whether adequate Freedom of Information (FOIA) search has occurred.

Doe v. Roe, 187 Ariz. 605
Where an adult victim of child abuse suffered from a repressed memory of such abuse, the applicable statute of limitations began to run when the victim first remembered the alleged abuse.

Farnsworth v. Procter & Gamble Co., 758 F.2d 1545 (11th Cir. 1985)
Federal Rules of Civil Procedure strongly favor full discovery whenever possible.

Katz v. Batavia Marine & Sporting Supplies, Inc., 984 F.2d 422 (Fed. Cir. 1993)
Federal Rules of Civil Procedure contemplate liberal discovery in interest of just and complete resolution of disputes.

Murray v. Carrier, 477 US 478, 106 S.Ct. 2639
Petitioner filed petition for writ of habeas corpus. The United States District Court for the Eastern District of Virginia dismissed case, and petitioner appealed. The Court of Appeals for the Fourth Circuit, 724 F.2d 396, reversed and remanded. On rehearing en banc, the Court of Appeals, 754 F.2d 520, adopted panel majority's decision, and certiorari was granted. The Supreme Court, Justice O'Connor, held that petition for habeas review of procedurally defaulted discovery claim was subject to dismissal for failure to establish cause for default. Reversed and remanded.

State v. Armstrong, 208 Ariz. 345

In a murder case, the prosecutor did not act in bad faith or engage in willful misconduct by entering into a last-minute plea agreement with defendant's girlfriend to obtain her testimony; the prosecutor's change of strategy was reasonable.

State v. Killean, 185 Ariz. 270

The trial court did not abuse its discretion in precluding admission of corroborative documentary evidence as a sanction for defendant's violation of discovery rules by failing to reveal the existence of the evidence until trial.

State v. Krone, 182 Ariz. 319

Defendant's murder conviction was reversed because the proper sanction for the state's last-minute disclosure of crucial videotape evidence against defendant should have been a continuance or preclusion of the evidence.

State v. Riggs, 186 Ariz. 573

In a forgery case, court held that defendant's inquiry into victim's exercise of right to decline a pre-trial interview was improper because victim had a constitutional right to decline a pretrial interview; thus, forgery conviction was affirmed.

State v. Tucker, 157 Ariz. 433

An undisclosed witness was permitted to testify at defendant's murder trial. Because defendant knew of the existence of the witness prior to trial, he was not prejudiced thereby, and the testimony was properly allowed.

State v. Wilson, 152 Ariz. 127

The federal crime of misprision of felony was not the equivalent to the state crime of hindering prosecution therefore the federal crime could not be used as a prior offense to enhance defendant's punishment.

US v. Drogoul, 1 F.3d 1546 (11th Cir. 1993)

Depositions are disfavored in criminal cases.

US v. Grier, 866 F.2d 908 (7th Cir. 1989)

Weatherford v. Bursey, 429 US 545, 51 L.Ed.2d 30, 97 S.Ct. 837 (1977)

There is no general constitutional right to discovery in a criminal case.

US v. Kalter, 5 F.3d 1166 (8th Cir. 1993)

Subpoena duces tecum must be reasonable and specific, and documents sought must be relevant.

US v. Nixon, 418 US 683, 41 L.Ed.2d 1039, 94 S.Ct. 3090 (1974)

The Supreme Court expounded on the rules of discovery.

Williamson v. US Dept. Of Agriculture, 815 F.2d 368 (5th Cir. 1987)

If discovery could uncover one or more substantial issues, plaintiff was entitled to reasonable discovery prior to district courts granting of motion for summary judgment.

Division of Power

<u>Allcarn v. Bailey</u>, 104 Ariz. 250, 451 P.2d 30 (1969)
It is essential that sharp separation of power be carefully preserved by courts so that one branch of government not be permitted unconstitutionally to encroach upon the functions properly belonging to another.

<u>State ex rel. Corbin v. Superior Court</u>, 138 Ariz. 500
The presiding judge of a superior court was required to reassign several inmates' post-conviction relief petitions to the sentencing judges because the local rules, which provided otherwise, conflicted with the Rules of Criminal Procedure.

<u>State v. Berger</u>, 164 Ariz. 426
Defendant's sentence for a conviction for a dangerous crime against children in second degree was modified to delete all reference to lifetime parole. Lifetime parole provision, as it related to second-degree offenders, violated separation of powers.

<u>State v. Montes</u>, 245 P.3d 879
The Supreme Court of Arizona held that SB 1449, which made amendments to Arizona's self-defense statute, Ariz. Rev. Stat. § 13-205(A), retroactive, was a valid exercise of legislative authority and did not violate the separation of powers doctrine in Ariz. Const. art. 3.

<u>Martin v. Moore</u>, 61 Ariz. 92, 95, 143 P.2d 334, 335 (1943)
By declaring the meaning of an "existing law", the legislature violates separation of powers.

<u>State v. Buonafede</u>, 168 Ariz. 444
No legal authority existed for the trial court to issue a "Certificate of Rehabilitation" for a defendant who had been convicted of a felony, completed probation, and was granted an order restoring his civil rights.

State v. Jones, 142 Ariz. 302 (App. 1984)

The concept of separation of power is fundamental to constitutional government as we know it.

State v. Murray, 194 Ariz. 373

Pursuant to the separation of powers doctrine the legislature did not have the authority to retrospectively change a court ruling to deny defendant eligibility for parole on defendant's conviction for sexual assault.

Double Jeopardy / Forfeiture

Arizona Constitution Article 2 § 10 Due Process.

Hernandez v. Superior Court ex rel. Co. of Maricopa, 179 Ariz. 515, 880 P.2d7 35 (1994)

The mere fact that petitioner could be subject to more than one sanction for the same conduct does not raise the double jeopardy bar to the present prosecution; the federal and state Constitution do not bar multiple prosecutions or multiple punishments for the same conduct as long as each charged offense requires proof of at least one element not required for the other offenses.

Abney v. US, 431 U.S. 651, 660-62 (1977)

Double jeopardy challenges immediately appealable because double jeopardy clause protects against even at risk of conviction including personal strain, public embarrassment, and expense of a trial more than once for same offense.

Ashford v. Edwards, (1985, CA4 NC) 780 F.2d 405

First inquiry in considering claim that multiple punishments were imposed for single offense must be directed to question of legislative intention as to whether continuing criminal episode should be treated as a single offense for which only one punishment may be imposed or as two or more units of prosecution based upon particular factors of time or other circumstances dividing hole into discrete parts.

Austin v. US, 509 U.S. 1125 L.Ed.2d 488, 113 S.Ct. (1993)

Eighth Amendment excess fines clause held to apply to drug related forfeitures of property to United States under 21 U.S.CS §§881(a)(4) and 881(a)(7). Certain civil forfeiture actions constitute "punishment" under HALPER.

Baker v. Metcalf, CA5 (Tex) 1981, 633 F.2d 1180, reh denied, 638 F.2d 1234, cert. denied, 101 S.Ct. 2055, 451 U.S. 974, 68 L.Ed.2d 354

Right not to be put twice in jeopardy of life and limb was a fundamental right applicable to the states through USCA 14 and therefore habeas corpus petition was proper to review state court adjudication of petitioners constitutional plea of double jeopardy.

Booker v. Phillips, (1969, CA10 Kan) 418 F.2d 424,cert. denied, (1970) 399 U.S. 910, 26 L.Ed. 564, 90 S.Ct. 2194

If defendant is charged with first-degree murder and convicted of first-degree manslaughter, and conviction is later reversed and remanded for new trial, he cannot be prosecuted for first-degree murder in 2nd trial, since this would violate constitutional guarantee against double jeopardy.

Brown v. Alabama, (1980, CA5 Ala) 619 F.2d 376

Double jeopardy test as to what constitutes same offense is satisfied if each offense requires proof of fact that the other does not, even though there may be substantial overlap in proof offered to establish crimes.

Brown v. Ohio, 432 U.S. at 166, 97 S.Ct. at 2225, 53 L.Ed.2d 187, 194 (1977)

If each provision requires proof of an additional fact that the other does not, they're not the same offense.

Brown v. State, (1986, Fla App. D5) 483 S.Ct..2d 743, 11 FLW to 71, 11 FLW 536

If two statutory offenses have exact same essential constituent elements, or when one statutory offense includes all elements of other, those two offenses are constitutionally the same offense, and person cannot be put in jeopardy as to both such offenses unless two offenses are based on two separate and distinct factual events.

Burks v. US, 437 U.S. 1 (1978)

For the purpose of determining whether the double jeopardy clause precludes a second trial after the reversal of a conviction, a reversal based on insufficiency of evidence is to be distinguished from a reversal for trial error. In holding the evidence insufficient to sustain [437 U.S. 1, 2] guilt, an appellate court determines that the prosecution has failed to prove guilt beyond a reasonable doubt. Given the requirements for entry of a judgment of acquittal, to permit a second trial would negate the purpose of the double jeopardy clause to forbid a second trial in which the prosecution would be afforded another opportunity to supply evidence that it failed to muster in the first trial.

Crist v. Bretz, 437 U.S. 28, 37-38 (1978)
The double jeopardy limitations now apply to both federal and state governments and state rules on double jeopardy, with regard to such matters as when double jeopardy attaches, must be considered in light of federal standards.

Curry v. Superior Court of San Francisco, (1970) 2 Cal 3d 707, 87 Cal Rptr 361, 470 P.2d 345
Decision of United States Supreme Court applying double jeopardy provision of the Fifth Amendment two states does not forbid state from according to greater degree of protection to defendants.

Dixon v. Dupnik, (1982, CA9 Ariz.) 688 F.2d 682
State statute which prohibits commission of felony while released on bail or recognizance violates double jeopardy clause of the Fifth Amendment. Since elements of conviction required for proof under statute subsumes elements of underlying felony.

Durrough v. State, (1981, Tex Crim) 620 SW.2d 134
Defendant may be tried to second time for offense when prior conviction for that same offense is set aside on appeal; where reversal grants appellant new trial he may be tried on original indictment or are the new indictments charging same offense.

Grabowski v. Jackson County Public Defenders Office, 47 F.3d 1386 (5th Cir. 1995)
Test for double jeopardy is whether each offense requires proof of additional fact which the other does not.

Greyson v. Kellam, 937 F.2d 1409 (9th Cir. 1991)
Wade v. Hunter, 336 U.S. 684, 93 L.Ed.2d 974, 69 S.Ct. 934 (1949)
Ordinarily, when conviction is overturned because of trial error, state is free to retry defendant until he is convicted in error free trial, though once he is acquitted, whether or not in error free proceeding, that is the end and the bar of double jeopardy descends.

Green v. US, 355 U.S. 184, 2 L.Ed.2d 199, 87 S.Ct. 221 (1961)
The Constitutional right not to be placed in double jeopardy, being a vital safeguard in American society, should not be given a narrow, grudging application.

Hernandez v. Superior Court, 179 Ariz. 515, 522, 880 P.2d 735, 742 (App. 1994)
Arizona's courts generally interpret this clause in conformity to the interpretation given by the U.S. Supreme Court to the federal double jeopardy clause.

Illinois v. Vitale, 447 US 410, 415,100 S.Ct. 2260, 65 L.Ed.2d 228 (1980)
North Carolina v. Pearce, 395 U.S. 711,717, 89 S.Ct. 2072, 23 L.Ed.2d 656 (1969)
The Supreme Court has held that the double jeopardy clause contains three separate guarantees. First it protects against a second prosecution for the same offense after acquittal. Second, it protects against a second prosecution for the same offense after conviction. Third it protects against multiple punishments for the same offense.

Lemke v. Rayes, 213 Ariz. 232, ¶ 10, 141 P.3d 407, 411 (App. 2006)
U.S. Constitution, amendment five, Arizona Constitution, Article 2 §10 multiplictious charges alone do not violate double jeopardy; only resulting multiple convictions or punishments are prohibited. The mere commencement of retrial can violate double jeopardy. The Double Jeopardy Clause also incorporates the additional protection of collateral estoppel. In criminal cases, collateral estoppel is not favored and therefore sparingly applied. See also: State v. Rodriguez, 198 Ariz. 139, 141, ¶ 6, 7 P.3d 148, 150 (App. 2000)

Lutes v. State, (1980) 272 Ind. 699, 401 NE.2d 671
Defendant can waive constitutional rights against double jeopardy if he fails to raise it by objection in timely manner.

McLaughlin v. Fahringer, 150 Ariz. 274, 277, 723 P.2d 92, 95 (1989)
Benton v. Maryland, 395 U.S. 784, 794, 89 S.Ct. 2056, 206 to, 23 L.Ed.2d 707 (1969)
Article 2 § 10 of the Ariz. Constitution affords similar protection. The double jeopardy clause provides three distinct guarantees to a criminal defendant, (1) freedom from re-prosecution following acquittal (2) freedom from re-prosecution

following conviction, and (3) freedom from multiple punishments for the same offense. The Fifth Amendment double jeopardy provision is applicable to state through fourteenth amendment. Defendant cannot be forced to waive valid double jeopardy plea.

Montana Dept. Of Rev. v. Kurth Ranch, 511 U.S. 1 128 L.Ed.2d 767, 114 S.Ct. (1994)
Montana's assessment of tax on possession and storage of dangerous drugs, in proceeding separate from state criminal prosecution on drug charges, held to violate Fifth Amendment's double jeopardy clause.

Morgan v. Devine, (1915) 237 U.S. 632, 59 L.Ed. 1153, 35 S.Ct. 712
Defendant has been in jeopardy if on the first charge he could have been convicted of offense charged in 2nd proceeding.

Note: In other words the prosecutor cannot reprove or use a crime you've already been prosecuted or convicted of to prove his current case.

Note: The double jeopardy clause of the Fifth Amendment protects the defendant against multiple prosecution for the same offense, and applies to the state through the fourteenth amendment.

Ohio v. Johnson, (1984) 467 U.S. 493, 81L.Ed.2d 425,104 S.Ct. 2536, reh. denied, (1984) 468 U.S. 1224, 82 L.Ed.2d 915, 105 S.Ct. 20
Double jeopardy clause (1) protects against 2nd prosecution for same offense after acquittal, (2) protects against 2nd prosecution for same offense after conviction and (3) protects against multiple punishments for same offense. Double jeopardy clause protects against multiple punishments following retrial, defendant receives credit for time already served.

Price v. Georgia, (1970) 398 US 323, 26 L.ed.2d 300, 90 S.Ct. 1757
Fifth Amendment's double jeopardy prohibition is not being twice punished, but against being twice put in jeopardy; "twice put in jeopardy" language relates to potential risk that accused for second time will be convicted of "same offense" for which he was initially tried.

<u>Reimintz v. State's Attorney of Cook County</u>, 761 F.2d 405, C.A. 7 (Ill.) 1985
State criminal defendant who has colorable double jeopardy claim is entitled to seek federal habeas corpus relief prior to retrial; burden of 2nd trial is one of the harms that double jeopardy clause is intended to prevent, and they harm that, unlike the harm of conviction, is irreparable once the 2nd trial has been conducted.

<u>Schiro v. Farley</u>, 510 US 222, 223, 114 S.Ct. 783, 127 L.Ed.2d 47 (1994)
The defendant carries the burden of demonstrating that the issue whose re-litigation he seeks to foreclose was actually decided in the first proceeding.

<u>State v. Brown</u>, 217 Ariz. 617, ¶ 7, 177 P.3d 878, 881 (App. 2008)
The double jeopardy clause of the US and Arizona constitutions protect criminal defendants from multiple convictions and punishments for the same offense. ¶ 13 at 882.

<u>State v. Cook</u>, 185 Ariz. 358, 365, 916 P.2d 1074, 1081 (App. 1995)
There is no indication that there is a different double jeopardy analysis under the Ariz. Constitution.

<u>State v. Eagle</u>, 196 Ariz. 188 ¶ 5, 994 P.2d 395, ¶ 5 (2000)
We review de novo whether double jeopardy applies.

<u>State v. Fero</u>, (1987) 105 NM 339, 732 P.2d 866
Double jeopardy does not barred consecutive sentencing where different elements are required to provide in order to sustain that multiple convictions and different evidence is admitted to prove different elements.

<u>State v. Halper</u>, 490 U.S. 435, 109 S.Ct. 1892, 104 L.Ed.2d 489 (1989)
To require remand, not dismissal on double jeopardy issue.

<u>State v. Hill</u>, (App. Div. 1, 1999) 26 Ariz. App. 37, 545 P.2d 999
In order for principal of double jeopardy to apply, the two alleged crimes must have identical components, test to be applied in whether facts charged in later information would if found true, have justified conviction under earlier information.

State v. Leyva, (Ariz. App. Div. 1, 1995) 909 P.2d 506, C.A. 2 (Conn) 1995
US v. Morgan, 51 F.3d 1105
Double jeopardy clause safeguards individuals against three distinct abuses: (1) 2nd prosecution for same offense after acquittal; (2) 2nd prosecution for same offense after conviction; and (3) multiple punishments for same offense.

State v. McGill, 213 Ariz. 147 ¶ 21, 140 P.3d 930, 936 (2006)
A double jeopardy violation constitutes fundamental, prejudicial error.

State v. Moody, 208 Ariz. 424, 437 P.18, 94 P.3d 1119, 1132 (2004)
State v. Powers, 200 Ariz. 123, P.5, 23 P.3d 668, P.5 (App.2001) approved 200 Ariz. 936, 26 P.3d 1134 (2001)
The court determines de novo whether the state violated a defendant's right against double jeopardy.

State v. Ortega, 2008 WL 4571814 (Ariz.App. Div. 2)
Both offenses, sexual conduct with a minor under fifteen and molestation of a child require the same mens rea, and both may only be committed against a victim who is under the age of fifteen. Furthermore, by penetrating the penis, vulva, or anus with a body part or object or by engaging in masturbatory contact with the penis or vulva, one has necessarily also touched, fondled, or manipulated the genitals or anus of that person. Therefore, one cannot commit sexual conduct with a minor under fifteen without also committing molestation of a child. Molestation is a lesser included offense of sexual conduct with a minor under the age of fifteen. Accordingly, Ortega's conviction of both the greater and the lesser offenses violates the Double Jeopardy Clause, Lemke, 213 Ariz. 232, ¶¶ 16-18, 141 P.3d at 413-14, and we must vacate his conviction for molestation of a child. See also State v. McGill, 213 Ariz. 147, ¶ 21, 140 P.3d 930, 936 (2006).

State v. Powers, 200 Ariz. 123, ¶ 5, 23 P.3d 668 ¶ 5 (App. 2001) approved, 200 Ariz. 363, 26 P.3d 1134 (2001)
State v. Millanes, 180 Ariz. 41/8, 421, 885 P.2d can 106,109 (App. 1994)
FN2 Prohibition against double jeopardy is fundamental right that is not waived by the failure to raise it in the trial court. ¶10 district statutory provisions constitutes the same offense if they are comprised of the same elements. Judicial expansion of

statutory language can violate defendant's due process rights to a fair warning of proscribed conduct. See generally ARS 13-101

State v. Price, 218 Ariz. 311, ¶ 5, 183 P.3d 1279, 1281 (2008)
In determining whether offenses are the "same" for the purpose of double jeopardy analysis, we look to the elements of the offenses and not to the particular facts that will be used to prove them.

State v. Salazar, (App. Div. 1, 1975) 24 Ariz. App. 472, 537 P.2d 946
In determining whether facts are so intertwined as to preclude more than one charge, test is to eliminate elements in one charge in determining whether facts left with support other charge.

State v. Siddle, 202 Ariz. 512, 47 P.3d 1150 (Ariz. App. Div2, 2002)
The state and federal double jeopardy clause is generally provide the same protection to criminal defendants.

State v. Soloman, (1980) 125 Ariz. 18, 607 P.2d 1
Jeopardy attaches as soon as jury is impaneled.

Simpson v. US, (1978) 435 U.S. 6, 55 L.Ed.2d 70, 98 S.Ct. 909
Double jeopardy clause of the Fifth Amendment protects and prohibits against multiple punishments for same offense and prohibits multiple prosecution for same offense.

Swisher v. Brady, (1978) 438 U.S. 204, 57 L.Ed.2d 705, 98 S.Ct. 2699, 25 FR Ser 2d 1463
Ariz. v. Washington, (1978) 43 U.S. 497, 54 L.Ed.2d 717, 98 S.Ct. 824
Constitutional protection against double jeopardy unequivocally prohibits second trial following acquittal, and so strong is public interest in finality of criminal judgments that acquitted defendant may not be tried even though acquittal was based upon egregiously erroneous foundation; if innocence of accused has been confirmed by final judgment, Constitution conclusively presumes that second trial would be unfair.

Swisher v. Brady, (1978) 438 U.S. 204, 57 L.Ed.2d 705, 98 S.Ct. 2699, 25 FR Ser 2d 1463

Central purpose of double jeopardy clause is prohibition against successive trials is to bar prosecution from another opportunity to supply evidence which it failed to muster in the first proceeding.

Thomas v. Kerby, 44 F.3d 884 (10th Cir. 1995)

Two checks forged and deposited on the same day gave rise to only one offense under New Mexico's single larceny doctrine and thus, separate convictions violated double jeopardy clause.

US v. $405,089.23 In US Currency, 33 F.3d 1210 (9th Cir. 1994)

The Ninth Circuit held that the seizure and forfeiture of narcotics proceeds DOES constitute punishment, such that the Double Jeopardy Clause is implicated.

US v. Easley, 942 F.2d 405 (6th Cir. 1991)
Grady v. Corbin, 495 U.S. 508, 109 L.Ed.2d 548, 110 S.Ct. 2084 (1990)

The double jeopardy clause bars subsequent prosecution where to establish essential element of offense, prosecutor will prove conduct constitution previously prosecuted offense.

US v. Ball, (1896) 163 US 662, 41 Ed. 300,16 S.Ct. 1192

Prohibition is not against being twice punished, but against being twice put in jeopardy , and accused whether convicted or acquitted is equally put in jeopardy at first trial.

US v. Blockburger, 284 U.S. 299, 304 (1982)

On post-trial double jeopardy review, the defendant alone carries the burden of proving double jeopardy. The Blockburger test determines whether multiple prosecutions for single act constitutes prosecution for the same offense. Under Blockburger, double jeopardy has subsequent prosecutions for a single act unless the act can be prosecuted and punished under different statutory provisions that require proof of different elements.

US v. Boney, 977 F.2d 624 (1992)

Neither due process nor the double jeopardy clause requires that a defendant convicted on multiple counts under the same statute received a different sentence from a defendant convicted of only one count.

US v. Bradford, (1975, D.C. App.) 344 A.2d 208

Charging of different offenses in single count of indictment may infringe right to protection against double jeopardy because, if count is to pleasures and it is unclear of which crimes accused has been convicted, he may thereby be vulnerable to subsequent prosecution for offense for which he has once been tried.

US v. Chick, 61 F.3d 682 (9th Cir. 1995)

Double jeopardy clause precludes government from bringing separate civil forfeiture action based on same offense for which claimant/defendant has already been criminally prosecuted; correspondingly, where claimant/defendant has been subjected to civil forfeiture that amounts to punishment and judgment has already been entered, double jeopardy clause precludes government from bringing separate criminal action for same offense.

US v. Christiansen, (1994, CA9 Cal.) 18 F.3d 822, CDOS 2360, 94 daily journal DAR 4446

District Court committed reversible error by failing to conduct in-depth colloquy as to whether defendant's written waiver of jury trial was voluntary, knowing and intelligent where there was reason to suggest that defendant suffered from mental and emotional instability.

US v. Dortch, 5 F.3d 1056, 1060 (7th Cir. 1993)

Defendant has burden because lower standard in pretrial jeopardy based on concern with defendants limited access to information, which is not a problem in post-trial review.

US v. Fiallo - Jacome, 784 F.2d 1064 (CA11 Fla 1986)

Double jeopardy clause barred imposing eight consecutive sentences on defendant for two counts of possession of cocaine where one count charging defendant with possession on specific date in Florida town was included with another count

charging possession over four-month period in Miami and elsewhere in Southern district of Florida, in light of conclusion that defendant had continuous possession.

US v. Garner, 32 F.3d 1305 (8th Cir. 1994)
Double jeopardy clause does not bar federal prosecution of defendant who had been prosecuted for same acts in state court.

US v. Halper, 490 U.S. 435, 109 S.Ct. 1892 (1989)
Civil proceedings designed to impose "punishment" may implicate double jeopardy concerns.

US v. Keller, (1980, CA3 PA) 624 F.2d 1154
Doctrine of collateral estoppel as applied in criminal case bar is not only re-prosecution but also evidence of crime which defendant has been acquitted in prior prosecution.

US v. McCaslin, 863 F.Supp. 1299 (W.D. Wash. 1994)
1. Double jeopardy clause is not limited to "life or limb" sanctions, and applies to imprisonment and monetary penalties as well. 2. Label "civil" attached to penalty makes no difference in determining whether penalty is punishment for double jeopardy purposes. A Seattle court granted habeas corpus relief to a man convicted of narcotics trafficking on the grounds that a civil judgment of forfeiture which served to "punish" him under AUSTIN was entered prior to his conviction and the conviction was barred under the Double Jeopardy Clause and vacated. Mr. McCaslin was the first man to walk out the front door of a correctional facility on HALPER - AUSTIN grounds.

US v. McCormick, 992 F.2d 437 (CA2 VT 1993)
Double jeopardy clauses protection against multiple punishment was violated by defendants prosecution for fraud related conduct that had already been used to determine his guideline offense level in prior prosecution, since defendants prosecution for conduct that was already incorporated into prior sentence would be second punishment within meaning of clause.

US v. Mintz, 16 F.3d 1101 (10th Cir. 1994)

North Carolina v. Pearce, 395 U.S. 711, 23 L.Fd.2d 656, 89 S.Ct. 2072 (1969)

Double jeopardy clause protects against second prosecution for same offense after acquittal, second prosecution for same offense after conviction, and against multiple punishments for same offense. Government violates double jeopardy clause if it divides single conspiracy into multiple prosecutions.

US v. Moos, (1981, CA9 Alaska) 660 F.2d 748

Jeopardy attaches in double punishment context when defendant begins serving sentence; if defendant has not begun serving sentence pursuant to challenge to order, jeopardy has not attached and if Ct. reverses and remands for sentencing, sentence on remand would not constitute jeopardy.

US v. Nash, (1971, CA4 VA) 447 F.2d 1382

Defendant is twice put in jeopardy when verdict at second trial depends upon resolution of any matter previously tested and found in favor of defendant when acquitted at first trial.

US v. Rivera, (1989, CA1 Mass) 872 F.2d 507, cert. denied, (1989) 493 U.S. 818, 107 L.Ed.2d 38,110 S.Ct. 71

Defendant's failure to plead defense of double jeopardy did not constitute knowing and intelligent waiver of right, absent evidence of knowing and plain error was applicable since it would be absolute defense.

US v. Rodriguez, (1980, CA5 Fla,) 612 F.2d 906,reh denied, (1980, CA5 Fla) 617 F.2d 1214 and aff'd (1981) 450 U.S. 333, 67 L.Ed.2d 275, 101 S.Ct. 1137

Test to determine whether there are two offenses or only one is whether each provision requires proof of fact which other does not and focus is on elements of offense charged, not on evidence adduced at trial.

US v. Salamone, (1989, CA3 PA) 869 F.2d 221, cert. denied, (1989) 493 US 895, 107 L.Ed.2d 196,110 S.Ct. 246 and motion gr., vacated on other grounds, remanded (1990) 493 US 1038,107 L.Ed.2d 826, 110 S.Ct. 830

Where jury's acquittal of defendant in the first prosecution necessarily was grounded upon its resolution of particular issue, re-prosecution is constitutionally

barred under principle of collateral estoppel where redetermination of issue would be essential to defendant's conviction.

US v. Seley, 957 F.2d 717, 7 22-23 (9th Cir. 1992)
Although double jeopardy analysis under Blockburger did not preclude retrial of defendant, evidence relating to charges for which defendant was acquitted barred by collateral estoppel and thus government could not retry defendant. If there is no re-litigation of factual issues resolved at an earlier trial, a court will not go beyond the Blockburger test to consider collateral estoppel.

US v. Sutton, (1983, CA6 Ohio) 700 F.2d 1078
Under double jeopardy clause, where same act or transaction constitutes violation of two distinct statutory provisions, test to be applied to determine whether there are two offenses or only one is whether each provision requires proof of additional fact which the other does not.

US v. Trammell, 133 F.3d 1343, 1349 (10th Cir. 1998)
Defendant bears burden of proving double jeopardy on post-trial review.

Walker v. Lockhart, (1980, CA8 Ark.) 620 F.2d 683, cert denied, (1981) 449 U.S. 1085, 66 L.Ed.2d 811,101 S.Ct. 874
Defense counsel in criminal case cannot validly waive constitutionally protected right of defendant to be free from double jeopardy in absence of intelligent and involuntary consent by defendant to action that counsel proposes to take; however this rule does not apply in an unusual case in which exceptional circumstances exist which make it mandatory in interest of justice to permit waiver of constitutional claim over objection of defendant.

Willhauck v. Halpin, 953 F.2d 689 (1st Cir. 1991)
US v. Butler, 41 F.3d 1435 (11th Cir. 1995)
Jeopardy attaches in a jury trial after the jury is empaneled and sworn, or in the case of a bench trial, when the court begins to hear the evidence.

Drugs

<u>Gray v. Irwin</u>, 195 Ariz. 273, 987 P.2d 759

Defendant sought special action relief from prison sentence imposed by the Superior Court, La Paz County, No. CR 98-000244, Michael Irwin, J., for second conviction of possession of dangerous drugs. The Court of Appeals, Berch, J., held that: (1) for a second drug possession conviction, defendant who had prior felony conviction for non-violent, non-drug-related offense could only be placed on probation, subject to terms including treatment and up to a year in jail, and (2) sentencing court erred when it treated prior non-violent felony as prior drug possession conviction to boot-strap defendant into provision requiring prison sentence for defendants with three convictions for personal drug possession or use. Jurisdiction accepted; relief granted.

<u>In Re Kurth Ranch</u>, 986 F.2d 1308 (9th Cir. 1993)

Montana's marijuana tax was unconstitutional on its face and, as applied, violated taxpayer's double jeopardy rights.

<u>Smith v. US</u>, 508 US 124 L.Ed.2d 138, 113 S.Ct. (1993)

Exchange of gun for narcotics held to constitute use of firearm during and in relation to drug trafficking crime.

<u>State v. Farley</u>, 106 Ariz. 119, 471 P.2d 731

State brought original proceeding request for special action following order by Superior Court that justice court lacked jurisdiction to enter judgment that defendant was guilty of driving while under influence of intoxicating liquor. The Supreme Court, McFarland, J., held that enactment of statute providing for imposition of additional 10% Of amount of fine for violation of statute prohibiting driving while under influence of alcoholic beverages or drugs was not intended to change maximum fine of $300 or thereby deprive justice court of jurisdiction, but was only intended to provide means of raising money, and maximum fine under each of the statutes, including additional 10% Of fine, could not exceed $300 limit. Order of Superior Court vacated.

State v. Vargas-Burgos, 162 Ariz. 325, 783 P.2d 264

Defendant pled no contest in the Superior Court, Pima County, Cause No. CR-24337, Thomas Meehan, J., to charge of unlawful possession of marijuana. State appealed from sentence imposed by trial court. The Court of Appeals, Howard, J., held that: (1) trial court's failure to impose mandatory fine raised question of subject matter jurisdiction which was not waived by State's failure to object below, and (2) sentence not in compliance with mandatory provisions of sentencing statute was illegal and appealable. Sentence vacated and matter remanded.

US v. $31,990 In US Currency, 982 F.2d 851 (2nd Cir. 1993)

Possession of large amount of cash is not per se evidence of drug related illegal activity for forfeiture purposes.

US v. $53,082.00, 985 F.2d 245 (6th Cir. 1993)

Evidence did not establish probable cause to justify forfeiture of cash; narcotics detection dog's reaction could not be used to establish probable cause, as it was illegally obtained and no other evidence showed substantial connection between cash and illegal drug activity.

US v. Crain, 33 F.3d 480 (5th Cir. 1994)

Mere occupancy of place in which drugs are found is insufficient to establish constructive possession of the drugs.

US v. Crespo, 982 F.2d 483 (11th Cir. 1993)

Negotiations between defendant and agents for five or three kilograms of cocaine which was never delivered, were insufficient in themselves to prove capability of defendant to actually produce either five or three kilos and thus, sentence for conspiracy to distribute cocaine and conspiracy to possess it with intent to distribute could not be based on five or three kilos.

US v. Delaney, 52 F.3d 182 (8th Cir. 1995)

Ration of 100 - to - 1 between crack cocaine penalties did not violate equal protection rights of black defendant sentenced for crack cocaine offense.

Note: The Constitution only authorized 2 federal crimes; 1) treason; and 2) counterfeiting. All other crimes are matters of state jurisdiction which means that all federal drug crimes are unconstitutional. Congress got around this roadblock by simply writing the drug laws under CIVIL not CRIMINAL authority. All federal drug laws come under Title 21 USC. and are not part of the criminal code which is Title 18. In sum the Government is applying criminal sanctions to a civil law.

US v. Dunlap, 28 F.3d 823 (8th Cir. 1994)
US v. Thorne, 997 F.2d 1504 (DC Cir. 1993)
Mere presence is not sufficient to support conviction for narcotics possession.

US v. Estrada, 42 F.3d 228 (4th Cir. 1994)
When amount of drugs for which defendant should be held accountable at sentencing is disputed, district court must resolve factual question.

US v. Johnson, 26 F.3d 669 (7th Cir. 1994)
US v. Hanif, 1 F.3d 998 (10th Cir. 1993)
To establish constructive possession of a controlled substance, government must show ownership, dominion or control over drugs or premises or vehicle in which they were concealed. "Constructive possession" means that the defendant has some appreciable ability to guide destiny of drugs.

US v. Johnson, 46 F.3d 1166 (D.C. Cir. 1995)
To prove crime of use of a firearm during crime of drug trafficking, government must show: (1) that defendant used or carried firearm, and (2) that use or carrying of firearm was during and in relation to predicate offense.

US v. Lindsey, 47 F.3d 440 (D.C. Cir. 1995)
Mere proximity to drugs or guns is not sufficient to establish possession; constructive possession requires that defendant knew of, and was in a position to exercise dominion and control over, the contraband.

US v. Martinez, 44 F.3d 148 (2nd Cir. 1995)

Simple possession of cocaine is not a "felony" under federal law and thus will not provide basis for conviction of use of a firearm during a drug trafficking crime.

US v. McOuagge, 787 F.Supp 637 (E.D. Texas 1992)

Reasonable suspicion that defendant is involved in illegal drugs cannot, standing alone, justify protective search of auto.

US v. McMurray, 34 F.3d 1405 (8th Cir. 1994)

To enhance defendant's sentence for possession of firearm in connection with drug offense, government must prove preponderance of evidence connection between gun and criminal activity; mere possession of firearm is not sufficient of trigger enhancement.

US v. Morrison, 991 F.2d 112 (4th Cir. 1993)

Mere joint tenancy of residence in which narcotics are found is insufficient to prescribe possession to all occupants.

US v. Premises Known As R.R. No. 1, 14 F.3d 864 (3rd Cir. 1994)

Mere possession of cocaine on property for property owner's own personal use was insufficient, standing alone, to support civil forfeiture of the property.

US v. Robinson, 35 F.3d 442 (9th Cir. 1994)

Until marijuana cutting develops roots of its own, it is not a plant itself but a mere piece of some other plant and therefore. marijuana cuttings are not "plants" for sentencing purposes unless there is readily observable evidence of root formation.

US v. Teffera, 985 F.2d 1082 (D.C. Cir. 1993)

It is not a crime simply to travel, even knowingly, with someone who is carrying drugs.

US v. Vaandering, 50 F.3d 696 (9th Cir. 1995)
US v. Butler, 41 F3d 1435 (11th Cir. 1995)

Finding as to quantity of drugs for which defendant was responsible, for purposes of computing sentence, must be supported by preponderance of the evidence.

Due Process

5 USC § 556(d), 557, 706

Once due process is denied all jurisdiction ceases. The above US code is made applicable in the state by instrumentality rule with: 28 USC § 3001/3002 (15)(A)(C) Wherefore any alleged jurisdiction has already been voided by the denial of due process.

Arizona Constitution, article 2 § 4

In deciding whether a person has been deprived of a protected liberty or property interest without due process of law, a three tier analysis is used. 1) Does the states action implicate a protected liberty interest; 2) if so does the states interest justify the degree of infringement on the liberty interest; and 3) if so, is appropriate process provided to assure that liberty is not arbitrarily deprived?

A.R.S. 21-412 Evidence on behalf of person under investigation.

The person under investigation shall have the right to advice of counsel during the giving of any testimony by him before the grand jury, provided that such counsel may not communicate with anyone other than his client. Without notification of the date, time and place of the grand jury proceedings, it is impossible to exercise this right. Therefore due process has been denied.

Owen v. City of Independence, 100 S. Ct. 1398
Maine v. Thiboutot, 100 S. Ct. 2502
Hafer v. Melon, 502 US 21
42 USC § 1983
18 USC § 241/242 28
USC § 1746
Judges have no immunity.

Blaylock v. Schwinden, 856 F.2d 107 (9th Cir. 1988)

Rochin v. California, 342 US 165, 96 L.Ed 183, 72 S.Ct. 205 (1952)

Substantive due process refers to certain actions that the government may not engage in, no matter how many procedural safeguards it employs.

Broyles v. Lewis, 66 F.3d 334

The federal district court denied the inmate's petition for habeas corpus relief from his child molestation conviction. On appeal, the inmate argued that relief was warranted because numerous errors had deprived him of a fair trial in violation of the due process clause and his trial and appellate attorneys' errors had deprived him of effective assistance of counsel. The court reversed the denial and directed a writ of habeas corpus be issued unless the inmate was given a new trial or allowed to appeal his conviction. The court concluded that the inmate had been denied effective assistance of appellate counsel during his direct appeal to the state appellate court. The court found that appellate counsel's various errors and omissions, his failure to investigate key portions of the trial record, and his misunderstanding of the judicial appellate process constituted deficient performance. The inmate had been prejudiced because there was a reasonable probability that the outcome of the appeal would have been different absent the errors and omissions.

Buttons v. Nevin, 44 Ariz. 247, 257

Public officials may not violate the plain terms of a statute because in their opinion, better results will be obtained by doing so. They have a duty, and that is to enforce the law as it is written, and, if the effect of their action is disastrous, the responsibility is upon the Legislature, and not upon them. But if they knowingly, even with the best intentions in the world, violate the law, they and their bondsmen must take the consequences.

Caldwell v. Miller, 790 F.2d 589 (7th Cir. 1986)

Liberty interest protected under due process clause may be either interest protected by due process clause itself or interest created by state or federal law.

Carroll v. Robinson, 1 CA-Cv. 91-0593, COURT OF APPEALS OF Ariz.ONA, DIVISION ONE, DEPARTMENT D, 178 Ariz. 453; 874 P.2d 1010; 1994 Ariz. App. LEXIS 98; 164 Ariz. Adv. Rep. 76, May 12, 1994, Filed. AFFIRMED IN PART; REVERSED IN PART; REMANDED

Accusations of child molestation leading to former school director's termination implicated his Fourteenth Amendment liberty interest, which required that he be afforded procedural due process from State of Arizona, state agencies, and employees.

Chambers v. Mississippi, 410 US 284 (1973)

A defendant has a due process right under the federal and state constitutions to present a defense. There is a fundamental concern of due process which is that a defendant be allowed to present any defense that needs a minimal standard of reliability. For example it is established by federal law that when a hearsay statement bears persuasive assurance of trustworthiness and is critical to a defense, preclusion of the statement may rise to the level of a due process violation. See also: Chia v. Cambra, 360 F.3d 997 (9th Cir.2004)

Chiah v. Cambra, 360 F.3d 997 (9th Cir.2004)

Trial court erred in excluding the hearsay statements by alleged co-conspirator exonerating defendant and inculpated co-conspirator because the evidence was sufficiently reliable and due process required admissibility of evidence.

Curry v. Secretary of Army, (1979) 194 US App. D.C. 66, 595 F.2d 873

Showing of actual prejudice is not prerequisite to finding conviction constitutionally invalid on due process grounds.

DeWeese v. Town Of Palm Beach, 812 F.2d 1365 (11th Cir. 1987)

Citizen's liberty interest in personal dress is protected by due process.

Fowler v. Sacramento CO Sheriffs, 421 F.3d 1027

Defendant-Appellant Jeff Fowler was convicted of annoying or molesting Charla Lara in violation of California Penal Code § 647.6 following a jury trial in which he was precluded from cross-examining Lara regarding two prior incidents in which she alleged that other men had molested her. We conclude that the proffered

cross-examination sufficiently bore upon Lara's reliability or credibility such that the jury might reasonably have questioned it and, thus, that the cross-examination implicated Fowler's Sixth Amendment [**2] right to confrontation. We further conclude that the trial court's implicit determination -- that precluding the proffered cross-examination, rather than limiting it, was not unreasonable, arbitrary or disproportionate given the trial court's concerns about waste of time, confusion of the issues, and prejudice -- was itself objectively unreasonable. Finally, because Lara's testimony was crucial to the State's case, which, in any event, was not strong, we conclude that this error had substantial and injurious effect or influence in determining the jury's verdict. We therefore reverse the district court's order denying Fowler's petition for a writ of habeas corpus, and remand for issuance of a conditional writ.

Fushek v. State, 215 Ariz. 274
The State charged defendant with the misdemeanors of assault and contributing to the delinquency of a minor. A justice court ruled that these offenses were not jury eligible. Defendant brought a special action in Maricopa County Superior Court (Arizona) challenging the denial of a jury trial, and the superior court granted relief. The State appealed. The appellate court reversed the superior court's ruling and remanded the case to the justice court for further proceedings.

Harmon v. Marshall, (1995 CA9 Cal) 57 F.3d 763, 95 CDOS 4296, 95 daily journal DAR 7442
Defendant's due process rights were violated by courts failure to instruct jury on any of elements constituting two counts out of 12 on which prisoner was convicted and era required automatic reversal even though evidence establishing defendant's guilt on charges was overwhelming.

In re Appeal in Maricopa County Juvenile Action etc., No. 15389-PR, Supreme Court of Arizona, 131 Ariz. 25; 638 P.2d 692; 1981 Ariz. LEXIS 266, December 7, 1981. Reversed and remanded.
A father was denied due process when he was not given the opportunity to challenge his daughter's testimony in chambers because the testimony was to establish parental misconduct, giving him the right under an adversary process to cross-examine her.

Kelm v. Hyatt, 44 F.3d 415 (6th Cir. 1995)

Matthews v. Eldridge, 424 US 319, 333, 47 L.Ed.2d 18, 96 S.Ct. 892 (1976)

Arnstrong v. Monzo, 380 US 545, 552, 14 L.Ed.2d 62, 85 S.Ct. 1187 (1965)

Due process requires as general matter opportunity to be heard at meaningful time and in a meaningful manner. Citizens must be afforded due process before deprivation of life, liberty or property.

Lambright v. Lewis, 932 F.SUPP. 1547 (Ariz. 1996)

State trial courts violation of state law constitutes violation of Federal constitutional right to due process.

Large v. Superior Court ex rel. County of Maricopa, 148 Ariz. 229, 714 P.2d 399 (1986)

State v. Flower, 159 Ariz. 469, 768 P.2d 201 (1989)

Where a defendant has been denied an essential component of due process, such denial constitutes fundamental error.

Main v. Gibson, 287 F.3d 1224 (10th Cir. 2002)

Conviction upon charges not made in charging instrument constitutes denial of due process.

Marco v. Superior Court, 17 Ariz. App. 210, 496 P.2d 636 (1972)

Due process contemplates that no citizen shall be deprived of life, Liberty, or property without reasonable notice and a reasonable opportunity to be heard according to the regular and established rules of procedure.

Marquez v. Rapid Harvest Co., 1 Ariz. 562, 565, 405 P.2d 814 (1965)

Protection of the rights of individuals is the bedrock of our nation and we cannot judicially depart from the Constitution, all rights preserved therein. It is our absolute duty to protect constitutional rights.

Matter Of Special March 1981 Grand Jury, 753 F.2d 575, 580 (9th Cir. 1985)

Even temporary deprivation of property entitled property owner to due process which means, as a general rule, reasonable notice and opportunity for fair hearing.

McKinney v. Boles, N.D. W.VA. 1966, 254 F.Supp. 433

Court must be guided in federal habeas corpus cases by federal due process standards rather than by state criteria.

McSherry v. City of Long Beach, No. 06-55837, UNITED STATES COURT OF APPEALS FOR THE NINTH CIRCUIT, 560 F.3d 1125; 2009 US App. LEXIS 6911, February 14, 2008, Argued and Submitted, Pasadena, California, March 30, 2009, Filed. AFFIRMED in part, REVERSED in part, VACATED...

Officer was denied qualified immunity on § 1983 claim he fabricated evidence, as victim denied providing description of home where rape occurred that officer ascribed to victim. Fabricating evidence would violate plaintiff's due process right not to be subjected to criminal charges based on false evidence that government deliberately fabricated.

Miles v. Dorsey, 61 F.3d 1459 (10th Cir. 1995)

Conviction of accused who is legally incompetent violates due process.

Olson v. Walker, 162 Ariz. 174, 781 P.2d 1015 (Ct. App. 1989)

A person may be punished or deprived of property only after due process has been accorded.

Osborne v. Ohio, No. 88-5986 , SUPREME COURT OF THE UNITED STATES, 495 US 103; 110 S. Ct. 1691; 109 L. Ed. 2d 98; 1990 US LEXIS 2036; 58 USL.W. 4467, December 5, 1989, Argued , April 18, 1990, Decided

Although a statute prohibiting possession or viewing of child pornography was constitutional under the First Amendment, the Due Process Clause required the state to prove each element of the statute to sustain a conviction.

Pearson v. City Of Grand Blanc, 961 F.2d 1211 (6th Cir. 1992)

Fourteenth Amendment substantive due process requires that both state legislative and administrative actions that deprive citizens of life, liberty and property must have some rational basis.

Price v. Barry, 53 F.3d 369 (D.C. 1995)

Liberty interest may arise from either due process clause itself or from state law.

Porter v. Singletary, 49 F.3d 1483 (11th Cir. 1995)

Muse v. Sullivan, 925 F.2d 785 (5th Cir. 1991)

Due process requires that litigant claim be heard by fair and impartial fact finder applies to administrative as well as judicial proceedings.

Roviaro v. US, 353 US 53, 77 S.Ct. 623, 1 L.Ed.2d 639 (1957)

The problem of balancing competing interests, privilege versus a proper defense, is a difficult one, but the balance always weighs in favor of achieving a fair determination of the cause. A state's rules of evidence cannot deny and accused's right to present a proper defense.

State v. Brady, 122 Ariz. 228, 230, 594 P.2d 94, 96 (1979)

Exclusion of witness's testimony violated due process because it went to the heart of the defense and was material.

State v. Dann, 205 Ariz. 557, 568 ¶30, 74 P.3d 231, 242 (2003)

An appellate court reviews the trial court's refusal to allow evidence of a third-party defense for abuse of discretion.

State v. Espinosa, 200 Ariz. 503

Because Espinosa's Rule 32 claim was precluded, the trial court abused its discretion in granting post-conviction relief. We therefore grant review and grant relief. The trial court's order giving Espinosa an opportunity to accept the plea agreement is vacated.

State ex rel. Romley v. Superior Court (Roper), 172 Ariz. 232, 236, 836 P.2d 445, 449 (App.1992)

Subsumed within the right to present a defense is a defendant's ability to show that another person committed the crime for which he is charged.

State v. Garcia, 2009 Ariz. App. LEXIS 807

Defendant argued there was insufficient evidence to support ten of his convictions and that the trial court imposed illegal sentences for three of his convictions. The appellate court found that sufficient evidence supported the jury's conclusion defendant had taken steps that he had intended to culminate in touching his daughter sexually and the daughter touching his penis, thereby committing attempted child molestation and attempted sexual conduct with a minor. Given the evidence, the jury could have concluded defendant's touching of a victim's leg was a step planned to culminate in molesting the victim. A reasonable jury could have concluded defendant intentionally fondled his daughter's buttocks, planning to progress to fondling her vagina or anus. Ariz. Rev. Stat. § 13-1404(A) proscribed sexual contact with the female breast, regardless of its developmental stage, of a person under fifteen years of age. For count six, attempted sexual conduct with his daughter, the jury did not determine the victim's precise age, and the case had to be remanded for that determination and any necessary alteration to defendant's sentence. The judgment was affirmed except for defendant's sentence for attempted sexual conduct with a minor as alleged in count six; the case was remanded to the trial court for the state to establish the victim's age and for defendant to be resentenced on that count if necessary.

State v. Getz, Supreme Court No. CR-96-0595-PR, SUPREME COURT OF Ariz.ONA, 189 Ariz. 561; 944 P.2d 503; 1997 Ariz. LEXIS 93; 250 Ariz. Adv. Rep. 10, August 14, 1997, Filed , As Corrected November 25, 1997.. AFFIRMED IN PART REVERSED IN PART. Memorandum...

Giving a sexual abuse statute its plain meaning, one would clearly believe that a person between the ages of 14 and 17 could consent to a sexual touching and thus, the state should have been required to prove a victim's lack of consent.

State v. Gibson, 202 Ariz. 321, 323 ¶12, 44 P.3d 1001, 1003 (2002)

To be relevant, the evidence need only tend to create a reasonable doubt as to the defendant's guilt, Id at 324, ¶16, 44 P.3d at 1004. To be relevant the evidence need only tend to create a reasonable doubt as to the defendant's guilt.

State v. Johnson, No. 1 CA-CR 7517, Court of Appeals of Arizona, Division One, Department B, 145 Ariz. 482; 702 P.2d 711; 1985 Ariz. App. LEXIS 537, April 16, 1985 , Review Denied July 2, 1985. REVERSED AND REMANDED
Although it was an especially grave step to require a new trial when to do so, made it necessary for children to testify again, there was no valid conviction without due process of law.

State v. McCumber, 112 Ariz. 569, 573, 544 P.2d 1084, 1086 (1976) It is basic that an accused has the right to present a defense to a criminal charge and to accomplish this right the accused has the right to compel the attendance of witnesses and the right to present their testimony.

State v. Mejas, 163 Ariz. 531, 532, 789 P.2d 398, 399 (App.1990)
Error to exclude accomplices here say confession that exculpated defendant, but lacked corroborating evidence, "on the grounds that confession might be false."

State v. Noble, No. 1 CA-CR 88-1281, Court of Appeals of Arizona, Division One, Department C, 167 Ariz. 440; 808 P.2d 325; 1990 Ariz. App. LEXIS 399; 75 Ariz. Adv. Rep. 61, December 13, 1990 , Review Granted April 23, 1991. Affirmed in part; Reversed in part
Requirement that defendant register as sex offender after conviction and sentence for child molestation and sexual conduct with minor violated Ex Post Facto Clause of Arizona constitution where it was a criminal penalty applied retroactively.

State v. Tankersley, 191 Ariz. 359, 369 ¶38, 956 P.2d 486, 496 (1998)
State v. Oliver, 169 Ariz. 589, 590, 821 P.2d to 50, 251 (1991)
The appropriate evidentiary analysis to determine if a defendant is entitled to make a third-party defense is found in Rules of Evidence rule 401, 402 and 403.

State v. Tibbetts, 281 N.W.2d 499
We are of the opinion that the charge as given obscured and diluted the time-honored rule that in a criminal case the state must prove all facts beyond a reasonable doubt, and accordingly we hold that defendant was denied due process [**4] of law and is entitled to a new trial. By instructing the jury that "the touching could reasonably be construed as being for the purpose of satisfying the

defendant's sexual impulses" the degree of proof was shifted from acts which must be proved beyond a reasonable doubt to acts which could reasonably be construed or interpreted to be for an improper purpose. In ordinary parlance the use of the word "could" means something which is "possible," here suggesting to a jury that it had the right to convict if it found that an improper purpose was only one of several reasonable alternatives. It was tantamount to charging that if this purpose could reasonably be inferred; to reach a verdict of guilty the jury need not exclude other reasonable inferences which might lead to an opposite conclusion. In other words, by failing to charge that proof of guilt must be beyond a reasonable doubt and by charging instead that it could merely be a reasonable construction of the evidence the protection afforded an accused is emasculated and the jury is invited to select one of several possible conclusions if each of them can be logically supported.

State v. Von Reeden, 9 Ariz. 190, 450 P.2d 702 (1969)
Requires state to inform defendant of nature and cause of the charges against him.

US v. Augen Blick, (1969) 393 US 348, 21 L.Ed.2d 537, 89 S.Ct. 528
Apart from criminal trials conducted in violation of express constitutional mandates, constitutionally unfair trial takes place where barriers and safeguards are so relaxed or forgotten that proceeding is more spectacle or trial by ordeal than disciplined contest.

US v. Baker, 999 F.2d 412 (9th Cir. 1993)
Due process requires that defendant's be able to exercise their constitutional right to remain silent and not be penalized at trial for doing so.

US v. Barker Steel Co., Inc., 985 F.2d 1123 (1st Cir. 1993)
US v. Nevers, 7 F.3d 59 (5th Cir. 1993)
When a person of ordinary intelligence does not receive fair notice that his contemplated conduct is forbidden, prosecution for such conduct deprives him of due process. "Fair warning doctrine" invokes due process rights and requires that criminal statute at issue be sufficiently definite to notify persons of reasonable intelligence that their planned conduct is criminal.

US v. Bodiford, (1985, CA5 Tex) 753 F.2d 380

"No punishment without law to authorize it." Is requisite of due process; and defendant may be convicted only for offense defined by statute, not because his conduct is reprehensible.

US v. Boothe, 994 F.2d 63 (2nd Cir. 1993)

Due process bars prosecutor from making knowing use of false evidence and conviction may not stand if such evidence has any reasonable likelihood of affecting judgment of jury.

US v. Conkins, 987 F.2d 564 (9th Cir. 1993)

Due process of law is violated when government vindictively attempts to penalize a person for exercising protected statutory or constitutional rights.

US v. Deters, 143 F.3d 577 (10th CIR. 1998)

When government action deprives a person of life, liberty or property without fair procedures it violates procedural due process.

US v. Guthrie, 789 F.2d 356 (5th Cir. 1986)

For the government to punish a person because he had done what the law plainly allows him to do is a due process violation of the most basic sort.

US v. Henderson, 19 F.3d 917 (5th Cir. 1994)

When hearing is necessary to protect defendant's due process rights, then failure to hold hearing would be abuse of discretion.

US v. Ienco, 92 F.3d 564, 570 (7th Cir. 1996)

Failure to submit element of crime to jury not subject to harmless error analysis.

US v. Layne, 43 F.3d 127 (5th Cir. 1995)

Lambert v. California, 355 US 225, 2 L.Ed.2d 228, 78 S.Ct. 240 (1957)

Prosecution of citizen who is unaware of any wrongdoing for "wholly passive conduct" violates due process.

US v. Uchimura, 92 F.3d 564, 570 (9th Cir. 1997) (en Banc)
Removal of an element from the jury is a structural error that cannot be harmless.

US v. Williams, 998 F.2d 258 (5th Cir. 1993)
Prosecutor's suppression of evidence which would tend to exculpate defendant or reduce his sentence violates due process.

Washington v. Texas, 388 US 14, 87 S.Ct. 1920, 18 L. Ed. 2d 1019 (1967)
Even a claim of privilege may have to give way when faced with the necessity by the accused to present a defense.

Weimer v. Amen, 870 F.2d 1400 (8th Cir. 1989)
Cornerstone of due process is prevention of abusive governmental power.

Weaver v. Graham, 450 US 24, 101 S.Ct. 960
State prisoner sought writ of habeas corpus challenging application to him of change in state law with respect to good time or gain time credits. The Supreme Court of Florida, 376 So.2d 855, denied the application and certiorari was granted. The Supreme Court, Justice Marshall, held that: (1) for a criminal or penal law to be ex post facto, it must be retrospective and it must disadvantage the offender affected by it; (2) the effect, not the form, of the law, determines whether to ex post facto; (3) fact that statute reducing good time credits was enacted in conjunction with other statutes providing additional bases for credits against sentence did not save it from an ex post facto challenge; and (4) as applied to a prisoner whose crime was committed before its effective date, the statute reducing the amount of good time credit violated the ex post facto clause. Reversed and remanded.

Duress

State v. Herrera, 174 Ariz. 387

An 18-year old who shot a police deputy at his father's direction had his death sentence reduced to life imprisonment because the trial court failed to consider the mitigating circumstance of duress during the sentencing phase of defendant's trial.

State v. Kinslow, 165 Ariz. 503

Defendant, who was convicted for crimes committed during his escape from a penitentiary, was not entitled to assert his duress offense because he failed to show that he feared imminent physical injury from a governor's "shoot to kill" order.

State v. Sands, 145 Ariz. 269

A promise of immunity given by a sheriff to defendant was unenforceable because it was obtained by duress while defendant held the sheriff at gunpoint.

State v. Starks, 122 Ariz. 531

Defendant charged with armed robbery was not entitled to the admission of testimony regarding his subjective state of mind where his defense of duress required the application of the objective standard that his actions were reasonable.

State v. Strayhand, 184 Ariz. 571, 911 P.2d 577 (1995) rev. den. (1996)

Promises that offer will ensure that the defendant goes to prison if he fails to cooperate are impermissible as means of obtaining confession.[8] threatening to inform prosecutor of suspects refusal to cooperate with violates her Fifth Amendment right to remain silent.

US v. Sixty Acres In Itowah Co., 930 F.2d 857 (11th Cir. 1991)

General concern that conspirator might retaliate does not establish duress defense.

US v. Bailey, 444 US 394, 62 L.Ed.2d 575, 100 S.Ct. 624 (1980)

The availability of a duress and necessity defense held to depend on there being a bona fide effort to surrender or return.

US v. Bifielo, 702 F.2d 342 (2nd Cir. 1983)

Defendant appealed on the grounds that the court did not allow him a duress defense on an escape charge. (Authors Note: this case explains the criteria for a duress defense)

US v. Contento - Packon, 721 F.2d 691 (9th Cir. 1984)

The district court refused to allow a defense of duress. The appellate court reversed and said that the defendant presented a triable issue of the fact.

US v. Johnson, 956 F.2d 894 (9th Cir. 1992)

There are 3 elements of a duress defense; immediate threat of death or serious body injury, well-grounded fear that threat will be carried out, and no reasonable opportunity to escape threatened harm.

US v. LaFleur, 971 F.2d 200 (9th Cir. 1991)

When defendant commits a criminal act under the direct threat of another person, defendant commits crime under "duress."

US v. Mitchell, 725 F.2d 832 (2nd Cir. 1983)

In federal trials once a defendant introduces evidence sufficient to warrant jury instruction on duress defense, government must disprove at least one element of that defense beyond reasonable doubt.

US v. Rawlings, 982 F.2d 590 (D.C. Cir. 1993)

Defendant cannot claim defense of duress when he had, but passed up, opportunity to seek aid of law enforcement officials.

US v. Riffe, 28 F3d 565 (6th Cir. 1994)

Defendant has preliminary burden to introduce some evidence to trigger consideration of duress defense, although that burden is not a heavy one.

US v. Veilleux, 40 F.3d 9 (1st Cir. 1994)

Uncontrollable duress, to excuse defendant's failure to appear for sentencing must be sufficient to produce unavoidable fear of serious bodily injury or death.

US v. Webb, 747 F.2d 278 (5th Cir. 1984)

Necessity or duress may excuse conduct that is otherwise criminal.

Electronic Surveillance

Franks v. Delaware, 438 US 154, 57 L.Ed.2d 667, 98 S.Ct. 2674 (1978)
False and misleading information in government affidavits concerning the necessity of the wiretaps required suppression of the information derived from the wiretaps.

Little v. Armontrout, 835 F.2d 1240 (8th Cir. 1987)
Destruction of tapes violated due process if they had exculpatory value which was apparent before their destruction.

US v. Antoon, 933 F.2d 200 (3rd Cir. 1991)
The United States cannot use intercepted communications in a criminal prosecution unless party to communication first consents to interception. (Authors note: With the passing of the Patriot Act the above may no longer be true.)

US v. Barnes, 47 F.3d 963 (8th Cir. 1995)
Only statutory remedy for improper disclosure of wiretap evidence before grand jury is suit for civil damages, not suppression.

US v. Davanzo, 699 F.2d 1096 (11th Cir. 1983)
When paid informer gives his consent before recording conversation in which he was involved, the conversations were free from warrant requirements.

US v. Hanson, 41 F.3d 580 (10th Cir. 1994)
Two elements comprise statutory crime of wire fraud; scheme or artifice to defraud and use of interstate wire communication to facilitate that scheme.

US v. Herring, 933 F.2d 932 (11th Cir. 1991)
Wiretap law did not prohibit conspiring to sell descramblers to view satellite television.

<u>US v. Meling</u>, 47 F.3d 1546 (9th Cir. 1995)
District court must suppress evidence seized pursuant to wiretap if defendant can show wiretap application contained intentionally or recklessly false information that was material to finding of probable cause.

<u>US v. Ojeda Rios</u>, 495 US 257, 109 L.Ed.2d 224, 110 S.Ct. 1845 (1990)
Delay in sealing recordings derived from electronic surveillance held to require suppression, unless government gives "satisfactory explanation," at suppression hearing, why delay is excusable.

<u>US v. Tavarez</u>, 40 F.3d 1136 (10th Cir. 1994)
Federal wiretap statute requires federal courts to defer to state law on question of validity of wiretap order obtained in state court under state law. Because an order authorizing a wiretap must conform to all provisions of the Oklahoma Security of Communications Act, an improper application results in an invalid order.

<u>US v. Torres</u>, 908 F.2d 1417 (9th Cir. 1990)
Hits many areas on current wiretap law - some positive; some negative.

<u>US v. Tomblin</u>, 42 F.3d 263 (5th Cir. 1994)
Government has the burden of proving consent to tape recording of conversations.

<u>US v. Williams</u>, 774 F.2d 258 (8th Cir. 1985)
<u>US v. McCowan</u>, 706 F.2d 863, 865 (8th Cir. 1983)
These cases established the 7 factors to be used to determine the admissibility of a tape recording.

Entrapment

US v. Al - Talib, 55 F.3d 923 (4th Cir. 1995)

Purpose of entrapment doctrine is to ensure that government does not implant in mind of innocent person the disposition to commit alleged offense and induce its commission.

US v. Daniel, 3 F.3d 775 (4th Cir. 1993)

Hampton v. US, 425 US 484, 48 L.Ed.2d 113, 96 S.Ct. 1646 (1976)

Entrapment has 2 related elements; government inducement of crime and lack of predisposition on part of defendant to engage in criminal conduct. "Predisposed defendant" for purposes of defendants allegation of entrapment, is one who is ready and willing to commit the offense.

US v. Davis, 15 F.3d 902 (9th Cir. 1994)

Where informant was clearly acting on behalf of government before inducing defendant, informant is government agent, for purposes of entrapment defense.

US v. Eldeeb, 20 F.3d 841 (8th Cir. 1994)

When entrapment is an issue, government must prove absence of entrapment beyond a reasonable doubt.

US v. Garza - Juarez, 992 F.2d 896 (9th Cir. 1993)

Even though misconduct did not rise to level of entrapment or outrageous government conduct, it mitigated seriousness of defendant's participation in crimes and warranted a downward departure in the Sentencing Guidelines.

US v. Gleason, 980 F.2d 1183 (8th Cir. 1992)

Government conduct in promoting the commission of a crime may be so outrageous as to violate fundamental fairness regardless of defendant's predisposition.

US v. Hollingsworth, 9 F.3d 593 (7th Cir. 1993)
Doctrine of entrapment protects privacy of citizen rather than economy of law enforcement (Authors note: conviction was reversed on appeal).

US v. Hollingsworth, 27 F.3d 1196 (7th Cir. 1994)
Defense of "derivative entrapment" exists if private person, himself entrapped, acts as agent of conduit for government efforts at entrapment of others.

US v. Hudson, 985 F.2d 160 (5th Cir. 1993)
US v. Young, 954 F.2d 614 (10th Cir. 1992)
Once defendant makes prima fascia showing entrapment so as to be entitled to jury instruction thereon, burden shifts to government to prove beyond reasonable doubt that defendant was disposed to commit criminal act prior to first being approached by government agents.

US v. Ivey, 949 F.2d 759 (5th Cir. 1991)
Entrapment defense is available to defendant even if defendant denies committing acts upon which criminal charge is based.

US v. Lakich, 23 F.3d 1203 (7th Cir, 1994)
For purposes of entrapment defense, "predisposed" individual is one who is prepared and eager for opportunity to commit crime.

US v. Mitchell, 915 F.2d 521 (9th Cir. 1990) When undercover agents or informers engineer and direct criminal enterprise from start to finish, due process prevents conviction of even predisposed defendant.

US v. Price, 945 F.2d 331 (10th Cir. 1991) Court may find entrapment as a matter of law if evidence satisfying essential elements of entrapment is un-contradicted.

US v. Skarie, 971 F.2d 317 (9th Cir. 1992)

US v. Salmon, 948 F.2d 776 (D.C. Cir. 1991)

With respect to affirmative defense of entrapment, "inducement" is government behavior that would cause un-predisposed person to commit crime.

US v. Straach, 987 F2d 232 (5th Cir. 1993)

Defense of entrapment is not available if there is evidence that defendant was predisposed to commit the crime.

Equal Protection

Ariz. Constitution Article 2§ 13
Equal Privileges and Immunities. B.) No law shall be enacted granting to any citizen, class of citizens, or corporations other than municipal privileges or immunities which, upon the same terms shall not equally belong to all citizens.

Bills v. Dahm, 32 F.3d 333 (8th Cir. 1994) Equal protection clause keeps governmental decision makers from treating disparately persons who are in all relevant respect similarly situated.

Cleburne v. Cleburne Living Ctr. Inc., 473 US 432, 439 (1985)
Plyler v. Doe, 457 US 202, 216 (1982)
The equal protection clause of the fourteenth amendment is essentially a direction that all persons similarly situated should be treated alike.

Dyszel v. Marks, 6 F.3d 116 (3rd Cir. 1993)
Amount of deference shown to state created categories on equal protection review varies according to group discriminated against and infringed upon right or interest.

Eagleston v. Guido, 41 F.3d 865 (2nd Cir. 1994)
Threshold requirement of equal protection claim is a showing that government discriminated among groups.

Edmonson v. Leesville Concrete Co. Inc., 860 F.2d 1308 (5th Cir. 1988)
Principle of equal protection applies to governmental action in civil and criminal matters.

Hong v. Childrens Memorial Hospital, 993 F.2d 1257 (7th Cir. 1993)
To prevail on disparate treatment claim under Title VII, plaintiff must prove that she was victim of intentional discrimination.

Jacobs, Visonsi & Jacobs Co. v. City Of Lawrence, Ks, 927 F.2d 1111 (l0th Cir. 1991)

City Of Cleburne v. Cleburne Living Center, 473 US 432, 87 L.Ed.2d 313, 105 S.Ct. 3249 (1985)

The equal protection clause essentially requires that all persons similarly situated be treated alike. Equal protection violation occurs when government threats someone differently than another who is similarly situated.

Larson v. Larson v. Miller, 55 F.3d 1343 (8th Cir. 1995)

Women as class enjoy heightened scrutiny of state action under equal protection clause.

Mackenzie v. City Of Rockledge, 920 F.2d 1554 (11th Cir. 1991)

Unequal application of state law may violate equal protection clause.

Myers v. Ridge, 712 A.2d 791, 799 (PA. Comm. 1998)

Capital Cities Media Inc. v. Chester, 797 F.2d 1164 (3rd Cir. 1986)

In order to properly state and equal protection claim, a plaintiff must allege that he is receiving different treatment from that received by other similarly situated individuals.

O'Bar v. Pinion, 953 F2d 74 (4th Cir. 1991)

Class is suspect for equal protection purposes when it is defined from deep seated prejudice, rather than rational pursuit of some legislative objective. "Fundamental right," for equal protection purposes is one that is otherwise guaranteed in the constitution.

Powers v. Ohio, 499 US 400, 113 L.Ed.2d 411, 111 S.Ct. 1364 (1991)

White criminal defendant held to have standing to raise equal protection objection to prosecutors allegedly race based exercise of peremptory challenges to exclude black perspective jurors.

Saulpaugh v. Monroe Comm. Hospital, 4 F.3d 134 (2nd Cir. 1993)

Sexual harassment of women employees constitutes disparate treatment based on gender in violation of equal protection clause and is actionable under §1983.

US v. Cobb, 975 F.2d 152 (5th Cir. 1992)
Equal protection clause forbids prosecutor to exercise peremptory challenges against prospective jurors solely on account of their race.

US v. Gutierrez, 990 F.2d 472 (9th Cir. 1993)
Under equal protection standards, racial and ethnic classification should be reviewed under strict scrutiny.

US v. LaFleur, 952 F.2d 1537 (9th Cir. 1991)
Equal protection claims under the Fifth Amendment are treated the same as those under the Fourteenth Amendment.

US v. LaFleur, 971 F.2d 200 (9th Cir. 1991) 18.
Fifth Amendment includes equal protection component, which requires that the federal government accord every person within its jurisdiction equal protection of the laws. Equal protection claims under the Fifth Amendment are treated the same as those under the Fourteenth Amendment.

Evidence

Blacks Law Dictionary 976 (6th edition 1990)
Material evidence is the quantity of evidence which tends to influence the trier of fact because of its logical connection with the issue.

5th And 14th Amendment Burden Of Proof, burden of proof, presumption.
The due process clause of the 5th and 14th amendments protect the accused against conviction except upon proof beyond a reasonable doubt of every fact necessary to constitute the crime with which he is charged.

A.R.C.P. 19.3 Evidence
A. General Rule.
The law of evidence relating to civil actions shall apply to criminal proceedings except as otherwise provided.

a. Prior Inconsistent Statements.
No prior statement of the witness may be admitted for the purpose of impeachment unless it varies materially from the witness's testimony at trial.

b. Prior Recorded Testimony.

c. Admissibility.
Statements made by a party or a witness during a previous judicial proceeding or a deposition under rule 15.3 shall be admissible in evidence if:

> (i) the party against whom the former testimony is offered was a party to the action or proceeding during which a statement was given and had the right in opportunity to cross-examine the declaring within interest and motive similar to that which the party has now (no person for less on represented by counsel at the proceeding during which a statement was made shall be deemed to have had the right in opportunity to cross-examine the declaring, unless such representation was waived) and

(ii) the declaring is unavailable as a witness, or is present in subject to cross-examination.

d. Limitations and Objections.

The admissibility of former testimony under this section is subject to the same limitations and objections as though the declaring were testifying at the hearing except that the former testimony offered under this section is not subject to:

(iii) objections to the form of the question which were not made at the time the prior testimony was given.

(iv.) objections based on competency or privilege which did not exist at the time the former testimony was given.

A.R.Cr.P. 15.1 (b) Provision of evidence for expert examination.

Supplemental disclosure scope. Except as provided by rule 39 (b) the prosecutor shall make available to the defendant the following material and information within the prosecutor's possession or control:

(5) a list of all papers, photographs or tangible objects that the prosecutor intends to use at trial or which it were obtained from or purportedly belong to the defendant.

A.R.Cr.P. 15.1 (e) Additional disclosure upon request and specification.

Unless otherwise ordered by the court, the prosecutor shall within thirty days of a written request make available to the defendant for examination testing and reproduction of the following: (1) any item specified in the list submitted under rule 15.1 (b).

A.R.Cr.P. 15.7 Sanctions Failure to make disclosure.

If a party fails to make disclosure required by Rule 15, any other party may move to compel disclosure and for appropriate sanctions. The court shall order disclosure and shall impose sanction it finds appropriate, unless the court finds that the failure to comply was harmless or that the information could not have been disclosed earlier even with due diligence and the information was disclosed immediately

upon discovery. All orders imposing sanctions shall take into account the significance of the information not timely disclosed, the impact of the sanction on the party and the victim and the stage of the proceedings at which the disclosure is ultimately made. Available sanctions include, but are not limited to:

a. Precluding or limiting the calling of a witness, use of evidence or argument in support of or in opposition to a charge or defense, or

b. Dismissing the case with prejudice or without prejudice, or

c. Granting a continuance or declaring a mistrial when necessary in the interests of justice, or

d. Holding a witness, party, person acting under the direction or control of a party, or counsel in contempt, or

e. Imposing costs of continuing the proceedings, or

f. Any other appropriate sanction.

A.R.Cr.P. 26.10 (2006 Ed) Judicial Decisions/Set-Aside

A sentence must be set-aside where the defendant can demonstrate that false information formed part of the basis for the sentence; the defendant must show:

a. That the information before the sentencing court was false or misleading.

b. That the court relied upon the false information in passing sentence. See also: State v. Grier, 146 Ariz. 511, 701 P.2d 309 (1985)

A.R.Cr.P. 26.14 Resentencing

Where a judgment or sentence or both, have been set-aside on appeal, by collateral attack or on post-trial motion accord may now impose a sentence for the same offense, or a different offense based on the same conduct, which is more severe than the prior sentence unless:

(1) It concludes on the basis of evidence concerning conduct by the defendant occurring court was false or misleading.

(2) the original sentence was unlawful and on remand it is corrected in a lawful sentence imposed, or

(3) That the court relied upon the false information in passing sentence. See also: State v. Grier, 146 Ariz. 511, 701 P.2d 309 (1985)

A.R.E. Rule 401 & 403
State v. Oliver, 158 Ariz. 22, 760 P.2d 1071 (1988)
The right is not absolute and requires scrutiny of the proposed evidence for relevance under rule 401 and 403. ID at 158 Ariz. 27-28 and 30-32, 760 P.2d at 1076-77 and 1079-81.

A.R.E. Rule 402 Relevant Evidence.
Unfair prejudice-all relevant evidence is admissible except in those cases where its pro rata value is substantially outweighed by the danger of unfair prejudice.

A.R.E. Rule 403 Exclusion of Relevant Evidence.
There are five factors to be considered in assessing the danger of unfair prejudice; 1) the witness being impeached denies making the impeaching statement; 2) the witness presenting to be in teaching statement has an interest in the proceeding and there is no other corroboration that the statement was made; 3) there are other factors affecting the reliability of the impeaching witness, such as age or mental capacity; 4) the true purpose of the offer is substantive use of the statement rather than impeachment of the witness; 5) the impeachment testimony is the only evidence of guilt.

A.R.E. Rule 701 Opinion Testimony by Lay Witness.
Inadmissible testimony. Social worker improperly gave an opinion regarding the truthfulness of the victim.

A.R.E. Rule 702 Testimony by Experts.
Admissible testimony assists the trier of facts.

A.R.E. Rule 901 14. General provision
The requirement of authentication or identification is a condition precedent to add visibility, is satisfied by evidence sufficient to support a finding that the matter in question is what its proponent claims.

Illustrations.

By way of illustrations only, and not by way of limitation, the following are examples of authentication or identification conforming with the requirements of this rule:

Comparison by trier or expert witness.

Comparison by the trier of fact or by expert witnesses with specimens which have been authenticated.

A.R.E. Rule 1002 Requirement of Original.

To prove the content of a writing, recording, or photograph, the original writing, recording or photograph is required, except as otherwise provided in these rules or by applicable statute or rule. (Source: Federal Rules of Evidence, Rule 1002)

A.R.E. Rule 1003 Admissibility of Duplicates.

(1) A duplicate is admissible to the extent as an original unless:

(2) A genuine question is raised as to the authenticity of the original.

In the circumstances it would be unfair to admit the duplicate in lieu of the original. (Source: Federal Rules of Evidence, Rule 1003)

A.R.S. Rule 13-35.1

(J) except as provided below, nothing in this rule shall be construed to require the prosecutor to reproduce or lease for testing or examination any items listed in rule 15.1 (b) (5) if the production or possession of the items is otherwise prohibited by A. R. S. 13-35.1. Reproduction of or release for examination and testing shall be subject in addition to such other terms and conditions ordered by the court in any particular case, to the following restrictions: (1) the items shall not be further reproduce or distributed except as allowed in court order.

A.R.S. 13-2407 Tampering With A Public Record; Classification.

A person commits tampering with a public record if, with the intent to defraud or D.C., such person knowingly:

> 1. Makes or completes a written instrument knowing that it has been falsely made, which purports to be a public record or true copy there of or alters or makes a false entry in a written instrument which is a public record or a true copy of a public record; or

2. Presents or uses a written instrument which is or purports to be public record, knowingly that it has been falsely made, with intent that it be taken as genuine; or

3. Records, register or files in a governmental office or agency a written statement which has been falsely made, completed or altered or in which a false entry has been made or which contains a false statement or false information; or

4. Destroyers, mutilates, conceals, removes or otherwise in pairs the availability of any public record; or

5. Refuses to deliver a public record in such person's possession upon proper request of a public servant entitled to receive such record for examination or other purposes.

A. In this section (stress that "public records" means all official books, papers, written instruments or records created, issued, received or kept by others for the information of government.

B. Tampering with a public record is a class six felony.

A.R.S. 13-2409 Obstructing Criminal Investigations or Prosecutions; Classification.

A person who knowingly attempts by means of bribery, misrepresentation or force or threats of force to obstruct, delay or prevent the communication of information of testimony relating to a violation of any criminal statute to a peace officer, magistrate, prosecutor or grand jury or who knowingly injures another in his person or property on account of the giving by the latter or by another person of any such information or testimony to a peace officer magistrate, prosecutor or grand jury is guilty of a class 5 felony.

A.R.S. 13-2809 Tampering With Physical Evidence: Classification

A person commits tampering with physical evidence if, with intent that it be used, introduced, rejected or unavailable in any official proceeding which is pending or which such person knows is about to be instituted, such person:

1 Destroys, mutilates, alters, conceals our removes physical evidence with the intent to impair its veracity or availability; or

2. Knowingly makes, produces or offers any false physical evidence; or

3. Prevents the production of physical evidence by active force, intimidation or deception against any person.

A. Inadmissibility of the evidence in question is not a defense.

B. Tampering with physical evidence is a class six felony.

Berger v. New York, 388 US 41, 44n.2 (1967)
Other demonstrative evidence may be obtained through the warrant process or without a warrant where "special needs of government" are shown. See also: Zurcher v. Stanford Daily, 436 US 547, 553-60 (1978)

B.K.B. v. Maui Police Dep't, Nos. 99-17087, 99-17158, UNITED STATES COURT OF APPEALS FOR THE NINTH CIRCUIT, 276 F.3d 1091; 2002 US App. LEXIS 276; 87 Fair Empl. Prac. Cas. (BNA) 1306; 82 Empl. Prac. Dec. (CCH) P40,914; 58 Fed. R. Evid. Serv. (Callaghan) 1011; 2002 Cal. Daily Op. Service 185; 2002 Cal. Daily Op. Service 1594; 2002 Daily Journal DAR 283; 2002 Daily Journal DAR 1933, May 17, 2001, Argued and Submitted, Honolulu, Hawaii , January 9, 2002, Filed , As Amended February 20, 2002. ... in part and reversed in part.
A court properly imposed sanctions against an employer in an employee's sex discrimination action because counsel for the employer acted in bad faith when they introduced testimony regarding the employee's sexual behavior and predisposition.

Byers v. US, 227 US 28, 32, 47 S.Ct. 248 (1927)
Quoting Boyd. The state and federal courts have the same responsibility to protect the persons from violation of their constitutional rights.

Carpenter v. Superior Court, 176 Ariz. 486, 862 P.2d 246 (Ct. App. 1993)
If a Defendant has reason to believe that the prosecutor has not disclosed information within the possession or control of such agency, his proper recourse is

to seek relief pursuant to this rule rather than to circumvent the rules of criminal procedure. See also: State v. Gonzalez Perez-Ariz, 392 Ariz. Adv. Rep. 3, 62 P.3d 126, 2003 Ariz. App. Lexis 13 (Ct. App. 2003) State v. Tucker, 157 Ariz. 433, 759 P.2d 579 (1988) State v. Khoshbin, 166 Ariz. 570, 804 P.2d 103 (Ct. App. 1990) State v. Miller, 187 Ariz. 254, 928 P.2d 678 (Ct. App. 1996)

Caye v. Louisiana, 498 US 39 (1990) (Percuriam)
Jury instruction that explains a reasonable doubt as doubt that would give rise to a grave uncertainty, as equivalent to any substantial doubt and as requiring a moral certainty, suggests a higher degree of certainty that is required for acquittal and therefore violates the due process clause and it operates to ensure that the jury considers the case solely on the evidence.

Cervantes v. Cates, 1 CA-SA 03-0157 , COURT OF APPEALS OF ARIZONA, DIVISION ONE, DEPARTMENT A , 206 Ariz. 178; 76 P.3d 449; 2003 Ariz. App. LEXIS 154; 409 Ariz. Adv. Rep. 3, September 23, 2003, Filed , Review denied by Cervantes v. Cates, 2004 Ariz. LEXIS 32 (Ariz., Mar. 16, 2004)
Despite the fact that certain videotapes and pictures depicted child pornography; the State was required to copy the materials for defendant to aid in the preparation of his defense.

Coffin v. US, 156 US 432,453 (1895)
Justice Harlan's concurrence, Id at 365, proceeded on the basis that inasmuch as there is likelihood of error in any system of reconstructing past events, the error of convicting the innocent should be reduced to the greatest extent possible through the use of the reasonable doubt standard. In many past cases, the standard was assumed to be the required one. The court held that the presumption of innocence was evidence from which the jury could find a reasonable doubt.

Cook v. American S.S. Co., 53 F.3d 733 (6th Cir. 1995)
First and universal requirement for admissibility of expert opinion testimony is that evidence must be reliable and relevant.

Cooper v. Sielaff, 640 F. Supp. 345, E.D. VA. 1985
Petitioner failed to allege any circumstances impugning fundamental fairness or infringing specific constitutional protection to permit habeas corpus review of claim that trial court erred in going against its own ruling that Commonwealth of Virginia could not use certain evidence at trial.

DA v. Osbourne, 2009 US LEXIS 4536
Federal courts should not presume that state criminal procedures will be inadequate to deal with technological change. The criminal justice system has historically accommodated new types of evidence, and is a time-tested means of carrying out society's interest in convicting the guilty while respecting individual rights. That system, like any human endeavor, cannot be perfect. DNA evidence shows that it has not been. But there is no basis for Osborne's approach of assuming that because DNA has shown that these procedures are not flawless, DNA evidence must be treated as categorically outside the process, rather [***39] than within it. That is precisely what his § 1983 suit seeks to do, and that is the contention we reject. The judgment of the Court of Appeals is reversed, and the case is remanded for further proceedings consistent with this opinion.

Deutch v. US, 367 US 456, 471 (1961)
The presumption of innocence is invaluable in assuring defendants a fair trial.

Dick v. Kemp, 833 F.2d 1448, 1451 (11th Cir 1989)
Instruction in establishing presumption that defendant voluntarily under influence of alcohol intended legitimate consequences of on action unconstitutionally shifted burden of proof on element of intent.

ExLine v. Gunter, (1993, CA 10 Colo) 985 F.2d 487
Defendants due process rights in his prosecution for sexual assault of a 9-year-old child were violated by trial court's failure to review in accordance with defendants offer of proof alleged victims social service records in camera to determine whether records which contained facts relating to victims credibility and earlier sexual assault by other man or necessary for determination of defendant's guilt or innocence.

Flores v. Minnesota, 906 F.2d 1300, 1303 (8th Cir 1990)
Upholding instruction that defendant required to prove by preponderance of evidence that he was too intoxicated to form premeditation because it also provided that prosecution had burden of proving intent beyond a reasonable doubt.

Fortini v. Murphy, 257 F.3d 39 (1st Cir 2001)
Even highly prejudicial evidence can be excluded it is unduly prejudicial.

Franklin v. Henry, No. 96-16320, UNITED STATES COURT OF APPEALS FOR THE NINTH CIRCUIT, 122 F.3d 1270; 1997 US App. LEXIS 22793; 97 Cal. Daily Op. Service 7017; 97 Daily Journal DAR 11327, March 11, 1997, Argued, Submitted, San Francisco, California , August 29, 1997, Filed. REVERSED AND REMANDED.
The district court improperly denied the defendant's petition for habeas corpus because the exclusion of the proffered evidence was error was of constitutional magnitude and the excluded evidence might have tipped the verdict to acquittal.

G. L. J.
It is now settled that such evidentiary items as fingerprints,
Davis v. Mississippi, 394 US 721 (1969)

blood,
Schmerber v. California, 384 US 757 (1966)

urine,
Skinner v. Railway Labor Executives Assoc., 489 US 602 (1989)

fingernail and skin scrapings
Cupp v. Murphy, 412 US 291 (1973)

conversations, voice and handwriting exemplars,
US v. Dionisio, 410 US 1 (1973)

G. L. J.

An accused has the right to the assistance of counsel during a polygraph examination, since it is the functionally equivalent of interrogation. However, and accused may waive the right and agree to submit to a polygraph was out the assistance of counsel. Generally, polygraph results are not admissible without direct evidence at trial. However some prosecutors use the results to determine whether to prosecute an accused.

Guthrie v. Warden, 683 F.3d 820, 822-23 (4th Cir 1982)
Instruction that defendant required to persuade jury that defendant was too intoxicated to form specific intent to commit murder unconstitutionally shifted burden of proof on element of intent.

Hamling v. US, 418 US 87, 41 L.Ed.2d 590, 94 S.Ct. 2887 (1974)
Glasser v. US, 315 US 60, 86 L.Ed 680, 62 S.Ct. 457 (1942)
When reviewing the sufficiency of evidence to support a guilty verdict, the evidence, and all reasonable inferences therefrom, is viewed in the light most favorable to the government.

Henry v. Estelle, (1993, CA9 CAL) 993 F.2d 1423, 93 CDOS 3626, 93 Daily Journal DAR 6251, 37 F.R.E. Rule 267
Defendant's due process rights were violated by state courts admission of uncharged crime and subsequent jury instructions since both were highly prejudicial and rendered defendant's trial fundamentally unfair. Note: Twenty-year-old evidence is what is referred to here.

Holt v. US, 218 US 245, 253 (1910)
Agnew v. US, 165 US 36 (1897)
The above cases overturned.

Idaho v. Wright, 497 US 805,110 S.Ct. 3139 (1990)
Circumstances surrounding interview demonstrate danger of unreliability which, because interview was not audio/videotaped or otherwise recorded, can never be fully assessed.

Illinois v. Gates, 462 U. S. 213, 103 S.Ct. 2317, 76 L.Ed.2d 527 (1983)
Gates failed to establish "...A fair probability that contraband or evidence of a crime will be found in a particular place..."

In re Winship, 397 US 358, 364 (1970)
The reasonable doubt standard plays a vital role in the American scheme of criminal procedure. It is a prime instrument for reducing the risk of convictions resting on factual error. The standard provides concrete substance for the presumption of innocence--backed bedrock "axiomatic and elementary" principle boost enforcement lies at the foundation of the administration of our criminal law. Id at 363.

Ison v. Western Vegetable Distributors, 48 Ariz. 104,111, 59 P.2d 649 (1936)
"Preponderance of the evidence means such evidence as weighed with the opposed to it has more convincing force, and from which it results that a greater probability is in favor of the party upon whom the burden rests. It does not necessarily depend on the number of witnesses; it merely means that the testimony which points to one conclusion appears to the trier of facts to be more credible than the testimony which points to the opposite one. The capacity of the submitted testimony to enforce belief on the arbiter to whom it is submitted the touchstone of preponderance as applied to the testimony of witnesses."

Jackson v. Garrison, 495 F. Supp. 9, 11 (W.D.N.C. 1979)
There is no reason why, subject to proper (jury) instruction, the jury should be allowed to consider polygraph evidence.

Jeffers v. Ricketts, 627 F.Supp. 1334, affirmed in part, reversed in part 832 F.2d 476
Review by federal habeas corpus court of petitioner's 4th amendment claims is limited to determination of whether he received full and fair hearing on those claims by state courts. 28 USCA SS 2254.

Kennedy v. US, 330 F.2d 26
Proceeding to correct an illegal sentence. The United States District Court for the District of Oregon, Gus J. Solomon, Chief Judge, entered an order, and the accused

appealed. The Court of Appeals, Jertberg, Circuit Judge, held that ten year concurrent sentences for breaking and entering post office with intent to commit larceny were not absolutely void even though statute fixed maximum penalty at five years; the sentences were void only as to the excessive five years; after commencement of legal five year portions of sentences the excessive portions were correctable by appropriate amendment and not by discharge of prisoner; in making the correction the sentences could not be made to run consecutively. Remanded with instructions.

Larrison v. US, 24 F.2d 82 (7th Cir 1928)
A new trial should be granted when (a) the court is reasonably well satisfied that the testimony given by a material witness is false; (b) that without it to the jury might have reached a different conclusion; and (c) that the party seeking the new trial was taken by surprise when the false testimony was given and was unable to meet or did not know of its falsity until after the trial. (Note: as discussed this case was the basis for the Larrison standard followed by many circuits.) See also: US v. Natanel, 938 F.2d 302 (1st Cir 1991) US v. Nixon, 881 F.2d 1305 (5th Cir 1989) US v. Mass, 867 F.2d 174 (3rd Cir 1989) US v. Butler, 567 F.2d 885 (9th Cir 1978) US v. Anderson, 509 F.2d 312 (1975) US v. Johnson, 487 F.2d 1278 (4th Cir 1973)

Johnson v. Makowski, 823 F.2d 387 (10th Cir. 1987)
US v. Enzor, 820 F.2d 684 (5th Cir. 1987)
Jury's use of or exposure to extrinsic material requires new trial if there is slightest possibility that harm could have resulted.

Mapp v. Ohio, (1961) 367 US 643, 6 L.Ed.2d 1081, 81 S.Ct. 1684, 16 Ohio Ops 2d 384, 86 Ohio L.ABS. 513, 84 ALR 2d.reh. den.
US 871, 7L.Ed.2d 72, 82 S.Ct. 23
Rule which excludes unconstitutional evidence from being admitted in state criminal trial is essential part of both 4th and 14th amendments.

McMorris v. Israel, 643 F.2d 43 F.2d 458 (7th Cir 1981) (en Banc), cert denied, 445 US 967 (1982)
A polygraph test records changes in blood pressure, respiration, pulse and galvanic skin response.

Neil v. Biggers, 409 US 188 (1972)
Reliability of pretrial identification procedures.

Nix v. Williams, 467 US 431, 81 L.Ed.2d 377, 104 S.Ct. 2501 (1984)
Unlawfully obtained evidence held admissible if ultimately or inevitably it would have been discovered by lawful means.

Novak v. Navistar Intern Transp. Corp., 46 F.3d 844 (8th Cir. 1995)
If prior incidents are not substantially similar to one giving rise to case in issue, they are not admissible.

Offor v. Scott, 72 F.3d 33, 36 (5th Cir 1995)
Petitioner's confrontation clause rights were transgressed in child sexual abuse case as a result of the admission of videotaped interview between child and police at which no representative of the defense was present.

Old Chief v. US, 519 US 172, 181, 117 S. Ct. 644, 651, 136 L.Ed.2d (1997)
The defendant was charged with the prohibited possession of a firearm, although the defendant offered to stipulate to the fact of a prior conviction, the government declined to stipulation and the trial court allowed the government to prove the prior conviction was for assault causing serious bodily injury.

People v. Barney, 8 Cal. App. 4th 798, 10 Cal. Rpt.2d 731 (1992)
HN3 – Before DNA evidence is submitted to the jury an evidentiary hearing must be held.

People v. Cantrell, 9 Cal Rptr.2d 188 In a prosecution arising from a photographer's lewd conduct with three minors, a jury found defendant guilty of contributing to the delinquency of a minor (Pen. Code, ß 272), of annoying or molesting a child under 18 (Pen. Code, ß 647.6), of committing a lewd act on a

child under 14 (Pen. Code, ß 288, subd. (a)), of battery (Pen. Code, ß 242), of sexual filming of a minor (Pen. Code, ß 311.4, subd. (c)), of procuring a minor for an indecent purpose (Lab. Code, ß 1308), and of penetration by a foreign object (Pen. Code, ß 289, subd. (i)). (Superior Court of Napa County, Nos. 6780, 6785 and 7110, W. Scott Snowden, Judge.) We modify the judgment as follows: (1) that part of the judgment indicating that appellant has been found guilty on counts 1, 2 and 3, is ordered stricken as is that part of the judgment ordering that a six-month jail sentence be served on these counts concurrent to the sentence in count 16; (2) the following language is added: "Counts 1, 2 and 3 are dismissed." In all other respects the judgment is affirmed. The trial court is directed to send a copy of the amended abstract of judgment to the Department of Corrections.

People v. Gonyea, 421 Mich. 462, 365 N.W.2d 136 (1984)
Statement obtained in violation of the right to counsel are inadmissible for both substandard and impeachment purposes.

People v. Leonard, 421 Mich. 207, 210, 364 N.W.2d 625 (1984) Statements obtained after a polygraph examination are not admissible for impeachment purposes where the parties had an agreement that the polygraph examination and any opinions drawn therefrom would not be admissible in evidence.

People v. Regan, 395 Mich. 306, 235 N.W.2d 581 (1975)
Prosecutors are in agreement that if defendant passes a polygraph examination, the charges would be dropped is binding. Polygraph results also may be used for impeachment purposes if the defendant testifies at trial. A defendant, as part of an agreement with the prosecutor, may take a polygraph that if passed, would result in the charges being dismissed. But the failure to pass the examination could be used by the prosecutor to impeach the defendant if testifying at trial. See also: Harris v. New York, 401 US 222 91 S.Ct. 643, 28 L.Ed.2d 1 (1971)

People v. Strieter, 119 Mich. App. 332, 326 N.W.2d 502 (1982). Iv. Vacated, 418 Mich. 946 (1984)
Statements obtained during a polygraph examination in violation of an agreement between the parties are inadmissible for both substandard and impeachment purposes.

People v. Stricter, supra 58

Counsel had an agreement that only certain procedures would be followed and the police, with knowledge of the agreement exceeds these procedures; therefore the statements were suppressed.

Polygraph

Most people think that the polygraph, or the "lie detector", is a reliable method for determining the truth. However few courts have allowed the results of the polygraph to be introduced and a criminal trial as direct evidence on the issue of innocence or guilt. A major reason why the courts have excluded polygraph results are the unreliability of the evidence.

Every polygraph examination has three parts. The first part is the pretest, at which the defendant is interviewed to obtain the background information needed to formulate the questions to be asked. The second part is the actual examination. The third part is the post-test interview, at which the defendant is informed of the results and given an opportunity to explain any answer indicating deception. Before commencement of the polygraph examination defense counsel, the prosecutor, and the polygraph examiner should need to establish the guidelines for each stage of the polygraph examination. Defense counsel should be present for all pre and post examination questioning and should obtain an agreement that all stages of the polygraph questioning of the accused will be recorded. Some polygraph examiners will allow counsel to be present during the actual testing is counsel agrees not to say or do anything to interfere with the questioning after it begins, but other examiners will not allow counsel to be present. Before the examination, counsel should review the questions the accused will be asked during the testing an object to those that are improper. Counsel should also obtain an agreement and after the polygraph examination has been completed, the accused will not be told the results nor questioned about it even if he or she asks. After the polygraph examination, the examiner or will usually ask the accused to explain any unfavorable results. Without an agreement that the accused will not be questioned about the results of the polygraph, any statement made will be admissible unless contrary state law exists. In Wyrick v. Fields, the Supreme Court held that new

Miranda warnings to questions asked to explain the tests unfavorable results were admissible.

People v. Barney, 8 Cal. App. 4th 798, 10 Cal. Rpt.2d 731 (1992)
HN3 – Before DNA evidence is submitted to the jury an evidentiary hearing must be held.

People v. Wallach, 110 Mich. App. 37, 312 N.W.2d 387 (1981) remanded on other grounds, 417 Mich. 937, 331 N.W.2d 730(1983)
Warnings which omit advice about the right to have counsel present "during questioning" may be incomplete and a basis for suppression.

Rhue v. Dawson, 173 Ariz. 220, 841 P.2d 215 (Ct. App. 1992)
Where evidence of the parties' alcoholism would affect his credibility and memory loss, the trial court did not abuse its discretion by admitting the evidence as relevant, or as not being substantially outweighed by unfair prejudice to the party.

Sandstorm v. Montana, 422 US 510-24 (1979)
On the interrelated concept of the burden of the prosecution to prove guilt beyond a reasonable doubt and defendants entitlement to a presumption of innocence, see Taylor v. Kentucky, 436 US 478, 483-86 (1978) and Kentucky v. Whorton, 431 US 786 (1979)

Shows v. M/V Red Eagle, 695 F.2d 114 (5th Cir. 1983)
It was reversible error to admit into evidence, plaintiff's conviction that was over 10 years old.

Simmons v. US, 390 US 377, 383-84 S.Ct. 967, 70-71, 19 L.Ed.2d 1247 (1968)
No lineup was conducted. Under these circumstances, we cannot find the error harmless beyond a reasonable doubt. See also: Chatman v. California, 386 US 18, 24, 87 S.Ct. 824, 828 7 L.Ed.2d 705 (1967); Hanrahan v. Thieret, 933 F.2d 1328, 1336-37 (6th Cir) cert denied, 502 US 970, 112 S.Ct. 446, 116 L.Ed.2d 464 (1991);

Sneed v. State, Criminal No. 766., Supreme Court of Arizona, 40 Ariz. 441; 14 P.2d 248; 1932 Ariz. LEXIS 226, September 17, 1932, Filed. ... Fickett, Judge. Judgment reversed and cause remanded...

Conviction for rape alleged to have been committed on defendant's daughter was improper because trial court erred in admitting testimony from witness, another daughter, over defendant's objection, indicating that defendant previously raped witness.

Speiser v. Randall, 357 US 513, 525-26 (1958)

But because it was so widely accepted only recently has the court had the opportunity to pronounce it guaranteed by the due process. See also: Estelle v. Williams, 425 US 501, 503 (1976); Miles v. US, 103 US 304, 312 (1881); Davis v. US, 160 US 469, 488 (1895); Holt v. US, 218 US 245, 253 (1910); Henderson v. Kibbe, 431 US 145, 153 (1977); Ulcer County Court v. Allen, 442 US 140, 156 (1979)

State v. Aguilar, Arizona Supreme Court No. CR-03-0332-PR , SUPREME COURT OF ARIZONA, 209 Ariz. 40; 97 P.3d 865; 2004 Ariz. LEXIS 99; 442 Ariz. Adv. Rep. 14, September 16, 2004, Filed.

Convictions and sentences reversed; remanded to the ... Court of appeals erred in concluding that evidence of defendant's other sexual assaults was inadmissible because the aberrant sexual propensity exception to prohibition against character evidence included nonconsensual sexual assaults against adults.

State v. Alvardo, 178 Ariz. 539, 541, 875 P.2d 198, 200 (App. 1994)

In determining whether sufficient evidence supports the conviction we view the evidence in light most favorable to sustaining the verdict, and... Resolve all reasonable inference against the defendant. See also: State v. Atwood, 171 Ariz. 576, 596, 832 P.2d 593, 613 (1992) overruled on other grounds by State v. Nordstrom, 200 Ariz. 229, 25 P.3d 717 (2001)

State v. Anthony, Arizona Supreme Court No. CR-04-0098-AP, SUPREME COURT OF ARIZONA, 218 Ariz. 439; 189 P.3d 366; 2008 Ariz. LEXIS 123, July 28, 2008, Filed... in Maricopa County, REVERSED AND REMANDED.

Trial court's application of wrong legal standard, in deciding whether defendant's prior bad acts, allegedly consisting of molesting wife's daughter, should be admitted under Ariz. R. Evid. 404(b) in defendant's murder trial, was not harmless error; proper question was if there was clear and convincing evidence that defendant molested daughter.

State v. Atwood, 171 Ariz. 576, 638, 832 P.2d 593, 655 (1992) cert. Denied, 506 US 1084, 113 S.Ct. 1058, 122 L.Ed.2d 364 (1993)

Under A.R.E. Rule 404 (b), evidence of other crimes is admissible to prove person's bad character or the likelihood that he or she acted in conformity with it. However it may be introduced for other relevant purposes such as proving motive, opportunity, intent, preparation, plan, knowledge, identity, and absence of mistake or accident Id. The probative value of such evidence must not be substantially outweighed by the danger of unfair prejudice, and there should be a limiting instruction if requested.

State v. Arthur Leon Thompson, 198 Ariz. 142; 7P.3d 151; 2000 Ariz. App. LEXIS 112; 326 Ariz. Adv. Rep.5 July 25, 2000 Filed.

A prior conviction under 13-604 applies only when the defendant was sentenced on the prior offense before committing the present offense.

State v. Berceiga, 146 Ariz. 353, 705 P.2d 1384 (Ct. App. 1985) Defendant's prior conviction for theft was inadmissible to rebut the defense of entrapment in a case charging attempted trafficking in stolen property.

State v. Bojorquez, 151 Ariz. 611, 619, 729 P.2d 965 (Ct. App. 1986)

Evidence was not admissible as it did not complete the story of the offense, rather it was evidence of a completely separate criminal action whose only purpose could be to prejudice the jury; therefore, admission of the evidence was harmful error.

State v. Boles, 1 CA-CR 93-0333, COURT OF APPEALS OF ARIZONA, DIVISION ONE, DEPARTMENT B, 183 Ariz. 563; 905 P.2d 572; 1995 Ariz. App. LEXIS 170; 196 Ariz. Adv. Rep. 6, August 3, 1995, Filed. REVERSED AND REMANDED

Defendant's convictions based on expert testimony that a DNA autorad match positively identified defendant, was reversed because there was no generally accepted scientific method of calculating the frequency of a random match.

State v. Brady, 105 Ariz. 190, 196, 461 P.2d 488 494 (1969)

Evidence of later date inadmissible because of differences from crime at issue. For this error to require reversal however, they must be a reasonable probability that the verdict would have been different hand the evidence not been admitted.

State v. Carlisle, 198 Ariz. 203, ¶ 11, 8 P.3d 391, 394 (App. 2000)

¶ 8 conviction must be based on substantial evidence. "Substantial evidence is more than a mere scintilla and is such proof that a reasonable person could accept as adequate and sufficient to support a conclusion of a defendant's guilt beyond a reasonable doubt."

State v. Coghill, 216 Ariz. 578, 169, P.3d 942 (App. 2007)

Introduction into testimony of the presence of adult pornography for the purpose of proving capability of downloading contraband and for proving intent, is inadmissible when other downloaded files were available that could have served the same purpose without the potential of prejudicing the jury against defendant. Presence of adult pornography cannot be used as proof of intent.

State v. Crane, 166 Ariz. 3, 799P.2d 1380 (Ct. App 1990)

If certain types of opinion testimony are inherently unhelpful, and any danger or prejudice requires holding the evidence inadmissible.

State v. Davis, 205 Ariz. 174, 398 Ariz. Rep. 3, 68 P.3d 127, 2002 Ariz. App. Lexis 209 (Ct. App. 2002)

Willits instruction is appropriate when the state destroys or loses evidence potentially helpful to the defendant; however destruction or non-retention of evidence does not automatically entitled defendant to it Willits instruction. To

merit the instruction, a defendant must show: 1. That the state failed to preserve material and reasonably accessible evidence having a tendency to exonerate him; and 2. That this failure resulted in prejudice.

State v. Dickens, 187 Ariz. 1, 24, 926 P.2d 468,491 (1996)
A defendant has the burden of establishing mitigating circumstances by a preponderance of the evidence.

State v. Escalante, Nos. 1 CA-CR 8949, 1 CA-CR 8965, Court of Appeals of Arizona, Division One, Department A, 153 Ariz. 55; 734 P.2d 597; 1986 Ariz. App. LEXIS 726, July 17, 1986 , Review Denied March 31, 1987. REVERSED. Defendant's convictions for sexual assault, kidnapping, and aggravated assault arising out of two separate incidents with two victims were reversed because the police wrongfully permitted destruction of evidence by not freezing victims' underwear.

State v. Faller, 88 S.D. 685, 227 N.W.2d 433, 435 (1975)
The situation that the lie detector presents can best be described as a psychological rubber hose. A defendant when suddenly faced with the impersonal accuracy of a machine, may believe it is safer to confess and place himself at the mercy of the law rather than lie to the examiner and sacrifice any possibility of leniency.

State v. Ferguson, 149 Ariz. 200, 717 P.2d 879 (1986)
Rule 402. Searches seizure.
At police officers pursuit, stop, detention and request for defendants identification papers where impermissible under the fourth amendment without any founded suspicion of criminal activity. Evidence derived from an illegal search and seizure is "fruit of the poisonous tree" and should have been suppressed.

State v. Fernane, 2 CA-CR 94-0652, COURT OF APPEALS OF ARIZONA, DIVISION TWO, DEPARTMENT A, 185 Ariz. 222; 914 P.2d 1314; 1995 Ariz. App. LEXIS 242; 202 Ariz. Adv. Rep. 84, October 31, 1995, Filed.
A Petition for Review was filed and DENIED by Order of the Arizona Supreme Court May 20, 1996. REVERSED AND REMANDED The trial court erred in failing to narrow evidence of prior bad acts to avoid undue prejudice and in

refusing to sever defendant's trial from co-defendant's where his alternative defense was that defendant was guilty based on her prior bad acts.

State v. Garcia, 1 CA-CR 99-0852, COURT OF APPEALS OF ARIZONA, DIVISION ONE, DEPARTMENT B, 200 Ariz. 471; 28 P.3d 327; 2001 Ariz. App. LEXIS 104; 351 Ariz. Adv. Rep. 10, July 10, 2001, Filed ,
The State of Arizona's Petition for Review and Cross-Petition for Review DENIED January 10, 2002. Petition for Review DENIED on January 8, 2002, by Arizona Supreme Court CR 01-0309-PR. AFFIRMED IN PART; REVERSED IN PART. Two molestation convictions were affirmed but indecent exposure conviction was reversed where court did not fully consider the prejudicial effect of the testimony of several young victims, each testifying to multiple uncharged molestations.

State v. Gates, 182 Ariz. 459, 897 P.2d 1345
The Court of Appeals, Noyes, J., held that defendant's making of three videotapes of minors was insufficient to sustain conviction where minors were not engaged in sexual conduct.

State v. Getz, 189 Ariz. 561 The state acknowledges that, in this case, the undisputed evidence shows that the victim/participant consented to the touching of her breasts. Therefore, the trial court should have granted judgments of acquittal on counts six, seven, eight and nine, and it is now so ordered. The memorandum decision of the court of appeals is vacated insofar as it addresses the issue dealt with in this opinion and the balance of the memorandum decision is approved. We remand for resentencing This opinion does not affect the convictions on counts three and ten for sexual exploitation of a minor, class two felonies. The seventeen-year-sentence imposed on count three is affirmed, as is the twenty-eight-year sentence on count ten, which shall be served consecutively to the sentence on count three.

State v. Grannis, 183 Ariz. 52, 57, 900 P.2d 1, 6 (1995)
The US Supreme Court has held that in determining whether the probative value of a given piece of information outweighs the risk of unfair prejudice the court must consider alternative evidence that could prove the same thing but which is less prejudice.

State v. Green, 200 Ariz. 496, 29 P.3d 271 (2001)
Evidence of prior convictions admissible at court.

State v. Greene, 168 Ariz. 104
Jacqueline Greene appeals from her conviction on three counts of child abuse for which she was sentenced to three consecutive terms of 12 years, to be served in full. She raises a number of issues on appeal. We need address only one, however, finding that the evidence was insufficient to support the verdict. Affirmed as modified; remanded for resentencing.

State v. Gulbrandson, 184 Ariz. 46, 60, 906 P.2d 579, 593 (1995)
Admission of other act evidence is reviewed for abuse of discretion in line.

State v. Holsinger, 115 Ariz. 271, 564 P.2d 1238
The Supreme Court, Cameron, C.J., held that prosecutor's failure to disclose to defense counsel that immunity had been granted to the only state witness who tended to corroborate testimony of accomplice constituted prejudicial error requiring reversal of defendant's conviction, since fact of immunity was relevant, not only to test witness' credibility, but also to determine if witness was herself an accomplice.

State v. Jackson, 124 Ariz. 202, 204, 603 P.2d 94, 96 (1979)
Evidence of prior crimes not admissible under rule 404 (b) because the crimes were dissimilar.

State v. Joachim, 202 Ariz. 566, 48 P.3d 516
Defendant filed motion in limine to suppress data seized on defendant's computer equipment in prosecution for sexual exploitation of a minor. The Superior Court, Maricopa County, Cause No. CR 2001-001690, Louis A. Araneta, J., granted the motion, and State appealed. The Court of Appeals, Edward C. Voss, J., held that a magistrate's decision to return seized property pursuant to statute allowing motion to controvert grounds for issuance of a search warrant does not necessarily preclude the State from offering that evidence in a subsequent felony prosecution. Vacated.

State v. Lacy, 187 Ariz. 340, 929 P.2d 1288 (1996) The evidence of prior bad acts was not admissible under A. R. E. Rule 404 (b) because the crimes were dissimilar, however the erroneous admission was harmless.

State v. Lehr, Supreme Court No. CR-97-0317-AP, SUPREME COURT OF ARIZONA, 201 Ariz. 509; 38 P.3d 1172; 2002 Ariz. LEXIS 15; 378 Ariz. Adv. Rep. 6, January 30, 2002, Filed , Writ of certiorari denied: Lehr v. Arizona, 2002 US LEXIS 8359 (US Nov. 12, 2002). US Supreme Court certiorari denied by Lehr v. Arizona, 154 L. Ed. 2d 428, 123 S. Ct. 550, 2002 US LEXIS 8359 (US, 2002) Appeal after remand at, Remanded by State v. Lehr, 2003 Ariz. LEXIS 60 (Ariz., Apr. 30, 2003).AFFIRMED IN PART, REVERSED IN PART
Trial court abused its discretion when it found that the probative value of DNA evidence from a Frye hearing was outweighed by the risk of juror confusion regarding the protocol, validation studies, and match window of the DNA analysis.

State v. Lujan, Supreme Court No. CR-97-0375-PR, SUPREME COURT OF ARIZONA, 192 Ariz. 448; 967 P.2d 123; 1998 Ariz. LEXIS 636; 281 Ariz. Adv. Rep. 6, October 22, 1998, Filed in Pima County REVERSED AND REMANDED. Memorandum
Evidence of prior sexual abuse along with expert testimony as to behavior was admissible to bolster a defense theory that the child was predisposed to misinterpret touching as sexual in a molestation case.

State v. Mathers, 165 Ariz. 64, 796 P.2d 866
The Supreme Court, Moeller, J., held that defendant was entitled to acquittal on charges notwithstanding that evidence was ample to support convictions of two codefendants with whom defendant was seen leaving California to go to Arizona, place where incident occurred, and that defendant admitted being in Arizona on day of incident in light of complete absence of probative facts placing defendant at or near scene of crime. Quoting State v. Jones, 125 Ariz. 417, 419, 610 P.2d 51, 53 (1980)."We will not set aside a jury verdict for insufficient evidence unless it clearly appears that upon no hypothesis whatever is there sufficient evidence to support the conclusion reached by the jury." See also: State v. Arredondo, 155 Ariz. 314, 316, 746 P.2d 484, 486 (1987)

State v. Moran, 151 Ariz. 378, 728 P.2d 248 (1986)

Witnesses have a right to testify about their opinion concerning the mental condition of a party. Jurors most of whom are unfamiliar with the behavioral sciences, may benefit from expert testimony explaining behavior they might otherwise attribute to inaccuracy or prevarication. See also: Starkins v. Bateman, 150 Ariz. 537, 724 P.2d 1206 (Ct. App. 1986)

State v. Mills, 196 Ariz. 269, 275, 28, 995 P.2d 705, 711 (App 1999)

Evidence is unfairly prejudicial if it has an undue tendency to suggest decision on an improper basis, commonly, though not necessarily an emotional one.

State v. Mott, 187 Ariz. 536, 545 P.2d 1046, 1055 (1997)

Improper basis included in motion, sympathy or horror.

State v. Perez, 141 Ariz. 459, 687 P.2d 1214 (1984)

The state has a duty in the interest of justice, to act in a timely manner to ensure the preservation of evidence is aware of, where the evidence is obviously material and reasonable with its grasp.

State v. Plew, 155 Ariz. 44, 745 P.2d 102 (as 1987)

Expert testimony in the behavioral sciences is admitted to educate and assists the jury in understanding the evidence which will determine the facts in issue.

State v. Polan, 78 Ariz. 253, 278 P.2d 432 (1954)

A defendant who takes the stand may be impeached by prior felony convictions, in the same manner as any other witness. See also: State v. Sorrel, 85 Ariz. 173, 333 P.2d 1081 ARS 13-163

State v. Richcreek, 187 Ariz. 501, 903 P.2d 1304 (1997), cert. denied, 520 U. S. 1276, 117 S.Ct. 2458, 138 L.Ed.2d 215 (1997)

Relevant evidence can and should be excluded where the probative value of the item is substantially outweighed by its prejudicial effects. See also: State v. Merez, 152 Ariz. 588, 734 P.2d 73 (1987)

State v. Riggs, 189 Ariz. 327, 330, 942 P.2d 1159, 1162 (1997)
If a trial court excludes essential evidence, thereby precluding a defendant from presenting a theory of defense, the trial court's decision results in a denial of defendant's right to due process that is not harmless. See also: Oshrin v. Coulter, 142 Ariz. 109, 111, 688 P.2d 1001, 1003 (1984)

State v. Roberts, 139 Ariz. 117, 677 P.2d 280 (Ct. App. 1983)
In a child molestation case the jury would have been in a much better position to determine nine-year-old victims credibility if it had been aided by expert testimony. Thus, victim's credibility was a proper subject for expert testimony.

State v. Robinson, 165 Ariz. 51, 56, 796 P.2d 853, 858 (1990) cert. denied, 498 US 1127, 111 S.Ct. 1091 (1991)
As stated in State v. Lacy, 187 Ariz. 340, 929 P.2d 1288, 1996 Ariz. LEXIS 129; 233 Ariz. Adv. Rep. 3 appellate court will not reverse evidentiary rulings absent an abuse of discretion.

State ex rel Romley v. Superior Court (Roper), 172 Ariz. 232, 836 P.2d 445 (App. 1992)
But, any privilege that resents a barrier to the production of evidence relevant to cross examination is trumped by the defendant's constitutional due process right to present his defense and conduct effective cross examination.

State v. Salazar, 1 CA-CR 92-1586, COURT OF APPEALS OF ARIZONA, DIVISION ONE, DEPARTMENT E, 181 Ariz. 87; 887 P.2d 617; 1994 Ariz. App. LEXIS 194; 173 Ariz. Adv. Rep. 3, September 6, 1994, Filed , Petition for Review DENIED on January 25, 1995 by Arizona Supreme Court No. CR-94-0416-PR. REVERSED AND REMANDED
The trial court erred by allowing the admission of inflammatory details of defendant's prior sexual crimes without considering appropriate restraints to limit the overly prejudicial effect of the evidence.

State v. Sanchell, 191 NeB. 505, 508, 216 N.W.2d 504 (1974)
A polygraph examination agreement requires the court's approval to be binding. If the defendant does not agree before the examination to provide the polygraph

results to the government, the results will not be admissible at trial. Prior notice is required since a defendant would be under psychological pressure during the examination if he knew the government would not have access to the results of the polygraph examination for years at trial, even for impeachment purposes.

State v. Smith, 146 Ariz. 491, 707 P.2d 289 (1985)
It is for the trial court to determine whether evidence properly admissible should nevertheless, be excluded as unduly prejudicial that determination is to be made by balancing the probate value of the evidence against the prejudicial effect the evidence would have on those hearing it.

State v. Speers, 1 CA-CR 02-0578 , COURT OF APPEALS OF ARIZONA, DIVISION ONE, DEPARTMENT B, 209 Ariz. 125; 98 P.3d 560; 2004 Ariz. App. LEXIS 139; 435 Ariz. Adv. Rep. 3, September 28, 2004, Filed , Review denied by State v. Speers, 2005 Ariz. LEXIS 60 (Ariz., May 24, 2005)
State sought to introduce evidence of alleged child molestation as propensity evidence in defendant's trial for sexual exploitation of a minor. Trial court's ruling, which precluded expert testimony to rebut this evidence, was reversible error.

State v. Stolp, No. 5397, Supreme Court of Arizona, 133 Ariz. 213; 650 P.2d 1195; 1982 Ariz. LEXIS 233, June 2, 1982, Rehearing Denied September 14, 1982. ... in part and reversed and remanded in part.
Reversible error occurred in defendant's trial where victim's post-hypnotic testimony was admitted even though she could not identify defendant until after hypnotic session and no precautions were taken to safeguard against suggestibility in session.

State v. Taylor, 196 Ariz. 584, 589 ¶ 15, 2 P.3d 674, 679 (App. 1999)
Reversible error where "credibility was the primary issue-there was no corroborating physical evidence or eyewitness testimony, and the appellant's and victims stories were markedly different."

State v. Terrazas, 189 Ariz. 580, 944 P.2d 1194
Following bench trial in which evidence of prior thefts of pickup trucks was admitted, defendant was convicted in the Superior Court, Maricopa County, Cause No. CR 94-06193, Michael J. O'Melia, J., of theft of third truck, and he appealed. The Court of Appeals, 187 Ariz. 387, 930 P.2d 464, affirmed. Review was granted. The Supreme Court, en banc, Moeller, J., held that: (1) prior bad acts are not admissible in criminal case unless profferer can prove by clear and convincing evidence that prior bad acts were committed and that defendant committed acts, and (2) evidence that library books which had been located in stolen truck were found on defendant's property was not admissible as prior bad acts evidence. Conviction and sentence reversed and remanded. Opinion of Court of Appeals vacated.

State v. Thompson, 169 Ariz. 471,820 P.2d 335 (Ct. App. 1991)
The crucial question is whether declarant's out-of-court statements were reasonably pertinent to diagnosis or treatment; a two-part test is used to aid in deciding whether the proffered statements were reasonably pertinent to diagnosis or treatment. 1. Was the declarants' apparent motive consistent with receiving of medical care; 2. Was it reasonable for the physician to rely on information in diagnosis or treatment. In a prosecution involving alleged sexual molestation of a child, the Arizona Court of Appeals held that a child's statement during a videotaped interview with a social worker were not reasonably pertinent to diagnosis or treatment and what is inadmissible pursuant to this rule.

State v. Tucker, 165 Ariz. 340, 798 P.2d 1349 (Ct. App. 1990)
Scope of expert testimony. The expert may neither quantify nor express an opinion about the veracity of a particular witness or type of witness and may not explained that, based upon the characteristics and behavior he has described a person's conduct is consistent or inconsistent with the crime having occurred.

State v. Tucker, 759 P.2d 579, 157 Ariz. 433 (1988)

US Constitutional Amendments 5 and 14.

There is no general federal constitutional right to discovery in criminal case the Constitution does impose procedural due process obligation to disclose exculpatory evidence that is essential on issue of guilt or punishment.

State v. Valdez, 1 CA-CR 93-0094, COURT OF APPEALS OF ARIZONA, DIVISION ONE, DEPARTMENT B, 182 Ariz. 165; 894 P.2d 708; 1994 Ariz. App. LEXIS 266; 181 Ariz. Adv. Rep. 7, December 30, 1994, Filed

Defendant could be convicted on only one charge of sexual exploitation of minor, despite fact that roll of film he possessed produced five pornographic pictures, because roll constituted one "visual medium" under sexual exploitation statute.

State v. Weaver, 158 Ariz. 407, 762 P.2d 1361 (Ct. App. 1988)

Evidence that tends only to suggest that defendant has any prior criminal history must be excluded.

State v. Williams, 144 Ariz. 433, 698 P.2d 678, 1985 Ariz.. Lexis 194

In the words of classic admonition in Boyd v. US, 116 US 616, 635, 6 S.Ct. 524 (1886) it may be that it is the obvious thing in its mildest and least repulsive form, but illegitimate and unconstitutional practices get their first foot in that way, namely, by silent approaches and slight deviation from legal modes of procedure. This can only be obviated by adhering to the role that constitutional provisions for the security of person and property should be liberally construed. A close and literal construction deprives them of half their efficacy and lead to gradual depreciation of the right as if it consisted more in sound than in substance. It is the duty of courts to be watchful for the constitutional rights of the citizens and against any stealthy encroachment thereon.

State v. Youngblood, Nos. 2 CA-CR 3979, 2 CA-CR 4364-2, Court of Appeals of Arizona, Division Two, Department B, 153 Ariz. 50; 734 P.2d 592; 1986 Ariz. App. LEXIS 728, October 2, 1986 , Review Denied March 27, 1987. REVERSED.

Defendant's molestation of a child, sexual assault, and kidnapping convictions were reversed because the state failed to adequately preserve certain physical

evidence and disposed of other evidence in violation of defendant's due process rights.

Stovall v. Denno, 388 US 293
The conduct of identification procedures must not be so unnecessarily suggestive and conducive to irreparable mistaken identification as to be a denial of due process of law.

Ulibarri v. Gerstenberger, 1 CA-Cv. 91-0154, COURT OF APPEALS OF ARIZONA, DIVISION ONE, DEPARTMENT D, 178 Ariz. 151; 871 P.2d 698; 1993 Ariz. App. LEXIS 88; 139 Ariz. Adv. Rep. 14, May 20, 1993, Filed.
Patient who claimed that her psychiatrist engaged in improper sexual conduct while she was hypnotized survived summary judgment on statute of limitations grounds because there was an issue as to whether she was able to discover her injuries.

US v. A&S Counsel Oil Co., 947 F.2d 1128 (4th Cir. 1991)
US v. Barger, 931 F.2d 359 (6th Cir. 1991)
Polygraph results are generally inadmissible.

US v. Adams, 110 F.3d 31 (8th Cir 1997)
When Supreme Court's "Franks" decision, search warrant is invalid and affidavits knowingly and intentionally, or with reckless disregard for the truth, includes false statement in warrant affidavit.

US v. Agurs, 427 US 97 (1996)
The court summarized and somewhat expanded the petitioners obligation to disclose to the defendants expelled Atari evidence in his possession, even in the absence of a request, or upon a general request by the defendant. The obligation is expressed in a tripartite tests of materiality of expelled toward evidence in the context of the trial record. First if the prosecutor knew or should have known that testimony given to the trial was perjury, the conviction must be set-aside if there is any reasonable likelihood that the false testimony would have affected the outcome of the trial. Id at 103-04. This situation is the Mooney v. Holohan type of case. Second is the defense specifically requested certain evidence and the prosecution

withheld it, the conviction must be set-aside if the suppressed evidence might have affected the outcome of the trial. Id at 104-106. And this is a Brady situation. Third, (the new law created in Agurs) if the defendant did not make a request in all, or simply ask for "all Brady material" or for "anything exculpatory" a duty resides in the prosecution to reveal to the defendants obviously exculpatory evidence; if the prosecutor does not reveal it, reversal of the conviction may be required, but only if the undiscovered evidence creates a reasonable doubt as to the defendant's guilt. Id at 106-14.

US v. Aims Back, No. 77-2662, UNITED STATES COURT OF APPEALS, NINTH CIRCUIT, 588 F.2d 1283; 1979 US App. LEXIS 17861, January 4, 1979
Admission of testimony of co-defendant's victim in regard to sexual encounter with defendant was highly prejudicial because he was charged with raping a different woman and, therefore, the evidence should have been excluded.

US v. Aldrich, 169 F.3d 526 (8th Cir 1999)
Evidence of a prior crime is always prejudicial to a defendant because it diverts the attention of the jury from the question of the defendant's responsibility for the crime charged to the improper issue of his bad character.

US v. Alexander, 526 F.2d 116, 168 (8th Cir 1975)
The potential is that juries may improperly regard polygraph evidence as infallible.

US v. Anderson, 933 F.2d 1261 (5th Cir. 1991)
US v. Waechter, 771 F.2d 974 (6th Cir. 1985)
Government cannot convict defendant of being bad person, engaging in sharp practices, or discovering loopholes in government policies. Jury may not premise criminal verdict on defendant's character, jury from the question of the defendants responsibility for the crime charged to the improper issue of his bad character, but only on evidence relevant to charged crime.

US v. Binder, No. 84-1249, UNITED STATES COURT OF APPEALS FOR THE NINTH CIRCUIT, 769 F.2d 595; 1985 US App. LEXIS 21930, February 11, 1985, Argued and Submitted , August 22, 1985, Decided. Reversed.

Conviction for child molestation and sexual conduct with a minor was reversed because trial court erred in replaying children's videotaped testimony to jury because it unduly emphasized that portion of testimony.

US v. Boone, 62 F.3d 323 (10th Cir. 1995)

Evidence that is acquired because of prior illegal police activity generally must be excluded as fruit of that illegality.

US v. Bradley, 173 F.3d 225 (3rd Cir 1999)

In balancing the probate of value of evidence against its prejudicial effect, the district court must appraise the genuine need for the challenged evidence and balance that necessity against the risk of prejudice to the defendant.

US v. Casel, 995 F.2d 1299 (5th Cir. 1993)
US v. James, 590 F.2d 575 (5th Cir. 1978 - en banc)

"James Hearing" is held to determine whether out of court statement of alleged co-conspirator should be admitted into evidence.

US v. Chamberlin, 139 F.Supp.2d 637

Minors and their parents sued photographer who took nude pictures of minors for violation of Protection of Children Against Sexual Exploitation Act, infliction of emotional distress, invasion of privacy, and negligent supervision. On photographer's motion for summary judgment, the District Court, Caputo, J., held that: (1) some photographs did not contain exhibition of minors' genitals as required to establish violation of Act; (2) other photographs which did exhibit genitals were not lascivious; (3) affidavits describing photographs not in record did not establish lasciviousness; and (4) there was no affirmative reason to retain jurisdiction over state-law claims. Summary judgment granted in part, and claims dismissed in part.

US v. Clark, 598 F.2d 994 (5th Cir 1979) cert denied, 449 US 1128 (1981)
US v. Fife, 573 F.2d 369 (6th Cir 1976)
Results of polygraph test is not competent evidence.

US v. Davis, 183 F.3d 231 (3rd Cir 1999)
Intoxication can negate specific intent.

US v. DeCoito, 764 F.2d 690 (9th Cir. 1985)
Jurors are generally entitled to examine documents properly admitted in evidence.

US v. Doane, 975 F2d 8 (1st Cir. 1992)
1. "Exclusionary Rule" provides that illegally obtained evidence to which timely objection was made, cannot be admitted into evidence. 2. Exclusionary rule reflects not, the personal constitutional right of person aggrieved but, instead, judicially created remedy designed primarily to deter improper conduct by law enforcement officials.

US v. Donaghe, No. 93-30058, UNITED STATES COURT OF APPEALS FOR THE NINTH CIRCUIT, 50 F.3d 608; 1994 US App. LEXIS 38736; 94 Cal. Daily Op. Service 7471; 94 Daily Journal DAR 13741, December 15, 1993, Argued, Submitted, Seattle, Washington , September 30, 1994, Filed , As Amended on Denial of Rehearing January 31, 1995.
Defendant's child molestation convictions, investigation into sexual misconduct with nephew, and diagnosis of homosexual sexual deviation were improper factors upon which to upwardly depart from sentencing guidelines for false statement conviction.

US v. Dorgman, 532 F. Supp. 1118, 1135 (N.D. Ill. 1981)
The validity of polygraph results depends on many different factors related to the accused, the examiner and the test itself. These factors include: the physiological and mental abnormalities of the accused; the inadequate phrasing of questions; the appropriateness of the control questions; the expertise of the examiner; the methodology employed in reading the grass; the number of indices employed to generate data; and the use of auxiliary sources of data.

US v. Feldman, 711 F.2d 758 767 (7th Cir 1983)

US v. Tucker, supra note 51

The defendant's refusal to agree to use of the results regardless of the results prior to polygraph examination would make the results unreliable.

US v. Gay, 774 F.2d 368 (10th Cir. 1985)

Absent an abuse of discretion, deficiencies in a chain of custody go to weight of evidence and not its admissibility.

US v. Flyer, No. 08-10580, UNITED STATES COURT OF APPEALS FOR THE NINTH CIRCUIT, 633 F.3d 911; 2011 U.S. App. LEXIS 2362, April 15, 2010, Argued and Submitted, San Francisco, California, February 8, 2011, Filed

Where child pornography images were located in "unallocated space" containing deleted data defendant could not access or download, and no evidence showed he knew those images were on his computer's hard drive, an 18 U.S.C.S. § 2252(a)(4)(B) conviction was reversed; deletion of an image alone was insufficient to show possession on an alleged date. Note: In this case the only evidence presented was deleted files in unallocated space.

US v. Gourde, No. 03-30262 , UNITED STATES COURT OF APPEALS FOR THE NINTH CIRCUIT, 382 F.3d 1003; 2004 US App. LEXIS 18584, June 9, 2004, Argued and Submitted, Seattle, Washington , September 2, 2004, Filed , Rehearing, en banc, granted by United States v. Gourde, 416 F.3d 961, 2005 US App. LEXIS 14215 (9th Cir., 2005)Different results reached on rehearing at United States v. Gourde, 2006 US App. LEXIS 5890 (9th Cir. Wash., Mar. 9, 2006)

Affidavit for warrant establishing that it was possible to infer that defendant might possess child pornography was not enough to justify a warrant to search his home and seize his computer. Thus, trial court improperly denied his motion to suppress.

US v. Ghent, 279 F.3d 1121

Petitioner sought federal habeas corpus relief following affirmance, on direct appeal, 43 Cal.3d 739, 239 Cal.Rptr. 82, 739 P.2d 1250, of his conviction by original jury for first-degree murder, attempted rape, and assault with intent to commit rape, and of death penalty imposed pursuant to second jury's verdict in special circumstances retrial. The United States District Court for the Northern

District of California, William A. Ingram, Chief District Judge, denied petition. Petitioner appealed. The Court of Appeals, Reinhardt, Circuit Judge, held that: (1) admission of testimony in violation of Miranda violated petitioner's due process rights; (2) erroneous admission of psychiatrist's testimony did not have substantial or injurious effect on original jury's verdict; (3) erroneous admission of psychiatrist's testimony during special circumstances retrial warranted habeas relief; (4) jurors' brief glimpses of petitioner in restraints did not rise to level of due process violation; and (5) failure to give lesser-included instruction did not prejudice petitioner. Affirmed in part, reversed in part, and remanded with directions.

US v. Givens, 767 F.2d 574, 585 (9th Cir 1985)
Henry v. Dees, 658 F.2d 406 (5th Cir 1981)
Polygraph examination results used at sentencing

US v. Hitt, 981 F.2d 422 (9th Cir 1992)
Where evidence is of very slight if any probative value, it is abuse of discretion to admit it if there is even modest likelihood of unfair prejudice or small risk of misleading the jury.

US v. Little Bears, 583 F.2d 411, 414 (8th Cir 1978)
Citing State v. Henry, 652 So.2d 643 (LA. Sup. Ct. 1977) the court held that due to the coercive impact of the polygraph someone taking it should be advised of his right: (1) to refuse to take the test, (2) to discontinue it at any point, and (3) to decline to answer any individual questions.

US v. Lowery, 135 F.3d 957 (5th Cir 1998)
Court's exclusion of evidence in defendant's trial for obstruction of justice was an order requiring reversal when evidence was relevant and necessary to defendant affirmative defense.

US v. McCoy, No. 01-50495 , UNITED STATES COURT OF APPEALS FOR THE NINTH CIRCUIT, 323 F.3d 1114; 2003 US App. LEXIS 5378; 2003 Cal. Daily Op. Service 2483; 2003 Daily Journal DAR 3129, August 6, 2002, Argued and Submitted, Pasadena, California , March 20, 2003, Filed , Rehearing denied

by, Rehearing, en banc, denied by <u>United States v. McCoy</u>, 2003 US App. LEXIS 17573 (9th Cir. Cal., June 24, 2003)

Federal child pornography statute was unconstitutional as applied to a mother's simple intrastate possession of a pornographic photo of her daughter that had not been transported interstate and was not intended for any economic or commercial use.

<u>US v. Meadows</u>, 91 F.3d 851 (7th Cir 1996)

Conviction of defendant when the prosecution provided no evidence of essential element of offense was subject to appeal.

<u>US v. Moore</u>, 115 F.3d 1348 (7th Cir 1997)

Other crimes evidence may not be used to demonstrate individual's propensity to commit crime.

<u>US v. Moore</u>, 956 F.2d 843 (8th Cir. 1992)

If state officials seize evidence in violation of the Fourth Amendment and turn that evidence over to federal officials, the evidence must be excluded in the resulting federal prosecution.

<u>US v. Morrow</u>, 39 F.3d 1228 (1st Cir. 1994)

Normally, where evidence is wrongly admitted over objection, it is for government to show that evidence was harmless.

<u>US v. Murray</u>, 784 F.2d 188 (6th Cir 1986)
<u>US v. Falsia</u>, 724 F.2d 1339, 1341 (9th Cir 1983)

Introduction of polygraph evidence will inject a time-consuming potentially prejudicial and perhaps confusing collateral issue into the court.

<u>US v. Nabors</u>, 901 F.2d 1351 (6th Cir. 1990)

If evidence is procured in violation of knock and announce statute, evidence must be suppressed.

<u>US v. Oliver</u>, 525 F. Supp. 731 (8th Cir 1976)

Parties had stipulated to admit the results but; court denied the motion.

US v. Oloyede, 982 F.2d 133 (4th Cir. 1992)
Government may not seize legitimate files even when it has evidence of extensive fraud scheme in one particular area of business.

US v. Ridling, 350 F. Supp. 90 (E.D. Mich 1972)
In perjury trial, polygraph results are admissible under detailed guidelines.

US v. Saelee, 162 F.Supp. 2d 1097
Prior to trial defendant moved to exclude testimony by government forensic document analyst comparing hand printing found on packages in which drugs were shipped to hand printing exemplars obtained from defendant. The District Court, Holand, J., held that: (1) testimony was not admissible as opinion by lay witness, and (2) testimony was also inadmissible as expert opinion, since government had not established reliability of theories and methods used by document examiner. Motion granted.

US v. Schwimmer, 924 F2d 443 (2nd Cir. 1991)
Government must demonstrate that evidence it uses to prosecute was derived from legitimate, independent sources.

US v. Sebetich, 776 F.2d 412 (3rd Cir 1985)
At trial five years later, the trial court denied defendant's request for and in court identification lineup or placement in the audience. The appellate court held that the trial court should have followed the standard set forth in US v. Archibald, 756 F.2d 223 (2nd Cir 1984). During an in court identification the defendant can be required to speak.

US v. Tom Yu, D.C. Ariz., 1 F.Supp. 357 (1952)
"... a person should not be subject to search of premises on mere suspicion of fact..."

US v. Tucker, 773 F.2d 136, 141 (7th Cir 1985)

People v. Barbara, 400 Mich. 352, 255 N.W.2d 171 (1977)

Polygraph and admissibility left to discretion of trial court.

US v. Tucker, supra note 51

Courts have also stated that [t]he lie detector does not tear into the mind; it is a list of a relative anxiety and if the person taking the test has nothing to lose and everything to gain, [the accused] may not be anxious and... Passing the test may prove nothing.

US v. Vandyke, 14 F.3d 415 (8th Cir. 1994)

Evidence should not be excluded on the grounds that it is exculpatory.

US v. Wade, 388 US 218, 87 S.Ct. (1926)

The influence of improper suggestion upon witnesses accounts for more miscarriages of justice than any other factor.

US v. Weber, No. 89-10096, UNITED STATES COURT OF APPEALS FOR THE NINTH CIRCUIT, 923 F.2d 1338; 1990 US App. LEXIS 25891, April 17, 1990, Argued and Submitted , September 28, 1990, Filed , As Amended, January 15, 1991

Defendant was improperly convicted of receiving of visual depictions of minors engaged in sexually explicit conduct because evidence seized under warrant should have been suppressed after affidavit did not give substantial basis for probable cause.

US v. Wheeler, No. 23712, UNITED STATES COURT OF APPEALS FOR THE NINTH CIRCUIT, 434 F.2d 1195; 1970 US App. LEXIS 6164, December 2, 1970

Conviction was error where large portion of trial was focused on issue unnecessary for conviction and thus may have infringed defendant's due process rights and where conflicting testimony provided insufficient evidence to support conviction.

US v. Williams, 436 F.2d 1166, 1168 (9th Cir. 1970)

The courts have the discretion to determine what type of in court identification procedure to use. The court may require a lineup or it may seek the defendant in

the courtroom audience before and during the testimony of the identification witness. However when the defendant's appearance has been significantly altered by the passage of time and in court identification procedure may be inappropriate.

US v. Williams, 704 F.2d 315, 319-20 (6th Cir), cert denied, 464 US 991 (1983)
In, in court lineup defendant may be required to wear particular close, including a mask. See also: US v. Domina, 74 F.2d 1361, 1369 (9th Cir 1986)

US v. Wulferdinger, 782 F.2d 1473 (9th Cir 1986)
Franks v. Delaware, 438 US 154, 57 L.Ed.2d 667, 98 S.Ct. 2674 (as 1978)
A "Franks" hearing is used to determine whether the search warrant was invalid because the affidavit provided to the magistrate issuing the warrant was misleading or incorrect.

US v. Zeiger, 354 F.Supp. 685 (D.D.C. 1972)
Court must alert jurors to the value and limitations of the polygraph technique.

Valdez v. Ward, 219 F.3d 1222, 1245 (10th Cir 2000)
Defendant not entitled to voluntary intoxication instruction because he failed to Raise a reasonable doubt concerning ability to form criminal intent.

Watkins v. Sowders, 449 US 341, 101 S.Ct. 654 (1981)
It is the reliability of identification evidence that primarily determines it's admissibility.

Webb v. Lewis, 44 F.3d 1387 (9th Cir 1994) cert. denied 115 S.Ct. 2002 (1995)
After his conviction for child sexual abuse was affirmed and the Arizona Supreme Court denied his petition for review, defendant filed habeas corpus petition. The United States District Court for the District of Arizona, Stephen M. McNamee, J., denied petition, and appeal was taken. The Court of Appeals, Noonan, Circuit Judge, held that: (1) videotaped interview with victim, conducted by social worker, was not admissible under hearsay exception for medical diagnosis or treatment, and (2) videotape of interview, conducted by social worker, of alleged victim did not have sufficient guarantees of trustworthiness to be admissible absent firmly established hearsay exception. Reversed with instructions.

Weeks v. US, 232 US 383, 398 (1914)

Exclusionary rule applies in federal court to evidence obtained through 4th amendment violation. See also: Mapp v. Ohio, 367 US 643, 654 (1961)

Wyrick v. Fields, 459 U. S. 42, 103 S.Ct. 394, 74 L.Ed.2d 214 (1982)

The issue not raised on appeal, but which could be considered on remand, will at least determine six amendment right to counsel was violated. The court held that before the examination and request of counsel's presence... It would have been unreasonable for Fields and his attorney to assume that Fields would not be informed of the polygraph readings and asked to explain any unfavorable results. Id. at 47-48. Police and are required to give a technical explanation of the polygraph to someone who has consented to take it. See also: Monte v. Jenkins, 626 F.2d 584 (7th Cir 1980)

About The Author

My career began in the United States Coast Guard. My first unit was Coast Guard Station Saginaw River. There I was responsible for search and rescue in Saginaw Bay and Lake Huron, where I performed numerous rescues. Earned Coast Guard Good Conduct Award, Meritorious Unit Commendation with Operational Designator and Meritorious Unit Commendation I was also responsible for standing a radio watch, listening for distress calls on the VHF-FM marine radio. I was transferred to Coast Guard Cutter Bristol Bay WTGB 102 where I worked as a Fireman and Oiler. I advanced to the rank of Machinery Technician Third Class at Yorktown, Virginia and spent my last two years of enlisted service at Search and Rescue Station Panama City Florida. Honorably Discharged after 4 years active duty service.

I obtained my FAA Airframe and Powerplant mechanics license in 1988 and began working as a mechanic for the Midway Commuter, which was a wholly owned subsidiary of Midway Airlines. From there I worked for Midway Aircraft Engineering in Miami, Florida working as a mechanic on DC-9 and B-737 aircraft. I advanced to the Position of Senior Aircraft Maintenance Planner where I was responsible for scheduling both routine overnight maintenance and heavy maintenance for one third of Midway's fleet. After Midway went out of business I moved to California and began working as a mechanic on B-747 aircraft which was something that I had always wanted to do. Later I began working in Phoenix, Arizona at Sky Harbor Airport and various repair stations throughout the region.

I obtained a Bachelor of Science Degree in Legal Study's from Kaplan University in 2011 while on the President's List. In 2013, I studied Computer Numeric Control at Glendale Community College and earned a position on the Dean's List and a Certificate of Completion in that program. I was released in 2017 after fighting my case for 14 years and obtained my Certificate of Absolute Discharge from the Arizona Department of Corrections in 2018. My only remaining requirement is to register for life and abide by all local SO laws as well.

It's true. In life one wears many hats.